Praise for *The Ultimate CRM Handbook*

"Customers are, and will always be, at the heart of the Virgin brand. As illustrated in this important new book, our never-ending pursuit of excellence in customer treatment has paid big dividends."

—Sir Richard Branson
Chairman, The Virgin Group

"A smart and practical book about CRM that's good for any executive who wants to create stronger, more profitable customer relationships. *The Ultimate CRM Handbook* not only helps executives understand how customer relationships are changing—it shows them what to do about it."

—Beth Eisenfeld
Research Director, Gartner Inc.

"Concise, comprehensive, field-proven insights . . . *The Ultimate CRM Handbook* is the map and the compass required to navigate your customer relationship management initiatives through the treacherous waters of failure, towards your required goal of success."

—Jim Dickie
Author of *CRM2000: Reinventing the Way We Sell*

"Improving a company's relationships with its most important customers is a critical business imperative that no company can afford to ignore. *The Ultimate CRM Handbook* captures what it takes to manage the whole customer experience, including all the interactions. It is an excellent collection of ideas for any business person who is trying to understand CRM and shows how they can improve their bottom-line business performance, by understanding their customers and partners more closely."

—Charles Stevens
Corporate Vice President
Enterprise and Partner Group, Microsoft

THE ULTIMATE CRM HANDBOOK

Strategies and Concepts
for Building Enduring Customer Loyalty
and Profitability

John G. Freeland
Editor

McGraw-Hill

New York   Chicago   San Francisco
Lisbon   London   Madrid   Mexico City
Milan   New Delhi   San Juan   Seoul
Singapore   Sydney   Toronto

*The **McGraw·Hill** Companies*

Library of Congress Cataloging-in-Publication Data

The ultimate CRM handbook : strategies and concepts for
building enduring customer loyalty and profitability /
[edited] by John Freeland.
    p. cm.
  Includes bibliographical references.
   ISBN 0-07-140935-1 (hardcover : alk. paper)
   1. Customer relations—Management. 2. Brand name
products—Marketing—Management. 3. Customer loyalty.
I. Title: CRM handbook. II. Freeland, John.
  HF5415.5 .U48 2002
  658.8'12—dc21

                                    2002010873

2 3 4 5 6 7 8 9 0 DOC/DOC 0 9 8 7 6 5 4

ISBN 0-07-140935-1

McGraw-Hill books are available at special quantity discounts to use as premiums
and sales promotions, or for use in corporate training programs. For more information, please write to the Director of Special Sales, Professional Publishing, McGraw-
Hill, Two Penn Plaza, New York, NY 10121-2298. Or contact your local bookstore.

 This book is printed on recycled, acid-free paper containing a
minimum of 50% recycled, de-inked fiber.

Contents

Preface   vii

Acknowledgments   ix

Part 1   **The New CRM Imperative**   **1**

Chapter 1 The New CRM Imperative   3
John G. Freeland

Part 2   **Setting the Strategy**   **11**

Chapter 2 Introduction: Strategy First, Then CRM   13
Steven S. Ramsey

Chapter 3 Customer Strategy: Whom Do You Want to Reach?   18
Clive Whitehouse, Ruth E. Spencer, and Michael Payne

Chapter 4 Brand Strategy: Why Brand Is at the Forefront
of Next-Generation CRM   30
Stephen F. Dull

Chapter 5 Channel Strategy: Avoiding Channel Conflicts   44
Paul F. Nunes, Bruce W. Bendix, and John B. Goodman

Chapter 6 CRM Strategy: Capabilities for Creating
the Customer Experience   54
Brian K. Crockett

Part 3   **Gaining Customer Insights**   **65**

Chapter 7 Introduction: Gaining Customer Insights
in a World of Change and Uncertainty   67
J. Patrick O'Halloran

Chapter 8 The Critical Element: Using Data to Become
a Customer-Centric Organization   72
Shep Parke and Holly Porter

Chapter 9 The Foundation of Insight: Three Approaches
to Customer-Centric Understanding   78
Brian K. Crockett and Kenneth L. Reed

Chapter 10 Silence Is Golden: The Emerging
Opportunities of Silent Commerce   85
Timothy Stephens

Chapter 11 Beyond the Data: Making the Most
of Customer Knowledge   94
Jeanne G. Harris and Thomas H. Davenport

Chapter 12 More Than Data Warehousing:
An Integrated View of the Customer   102
Kevin N. Quiring and Nancy K. Mullen

Part 4   Reinventing Customer Contact   109

Chapter 13 Making Customer Interaction
More Profitable   111
Philip J. Tamminga

Chapter 14 Let's Talk: Applying the Art of Conversation
to Customer Contact   118
Brian A. Johnson and Paul F. Nunes

Chapter 15 Collaboration: Effective Personalization's
Missing Ingredient   126
Paul F. Nunes

Chapter 16 Untethered Relationships: How Wireless
Is Changing Customer Contact   135
John C. Beck, Patrick D. Lynch, and Mitchell E. Wade

Chapter 17 Aligned Goals: Transforming Customer
Interactions   145
Robert E. Wollan and Paul F. Nunes

Chapter 18 Partner Relationship Management:
The Next Generation of the Extended Enterprise   153
Marc F. Hayes and Ron Ref

Chapter 19 Mission-Critical Workforces: Developing
a Source of Value 165
Dorothy V. VonDette and Patrick Mosher

Chapter 20 The Message Must Go Through: Messaging
Technologies and Customer Care 174
Marc F. Hayes

Chapter 21 Customer-Centric Service Management:
Maximizing Life-Cycle Revenue for OEMs 181
Dean J. Teglia and Luis Vassal'lo

Part 5   Transforming Marketing 189

Chapter 22 Introduction: Bringing Rigor and Discipline
to Creative Pursuits 191
Brian A. Johnson and Steven S. Ramsey

Chapter 23 Market Madness: The State of Marketing
Campaign Management 198
*J. Patrick O'Halloran, Theodore Ansusinha, Shep Parke,
and Mark C. Giometti*

Chapter 24 The Next Frontier: Just-in-Time Marketing 212
J. Patrick O'Halloran and Todd R. Wagner

Chapter 25 The New Integrated Marketing 221
Paul F. Nunes

Chapter 26 Marketing by the Numbers: How to
Optimize Marketing ROI 231
Jeffrey Merrihue

Chapter 27 The Case for Marketing Resource
Management 242
Naveen K. Jain and Marianne Seiler

Part 6   CRM at Work 255

Chapter 28 Communications: Recovering from the Fall,
Repositioning for the Future 257
Julie F. Nelson

Chapter 29 Government: Giving the People
What They Want 269
Sean Shine and Craig B. Cornelius

Chapter 30 Manufacturing: Gradual Shift from Product
to Customer   280
Gregory J. Supron

Chapter 31 Resources: CRM Is a Competitive Necessity   292
James O. Etheredge

Chapter 32 Retail: Customer Demands Intensify
the Pressure for CRM   303
Brian Kalms and Dennis A. Mullahy

Notes   313
Glossary   320
Contributing Authors   329
Index   339

Preface

You may ask yourself if another book about customer relationship management (CRM) is really necessary. We believe it is if it has something new to say.

This book provides a perspective on CRM that we believe has been lacking for some time: that is, how to use CRM to dramatically improve a company's customer relationships and enhance brand value while mitigating risk and ensuring a satisfactory return on invested capital. It is a new approach to a topic that has had much written about it, and it is an approach that will be of value to any company seeking to build enduring customer loyalty.

The size of this book may seem imposing at first. Recognizing this, we have organized the material in a way that will help readers get the most out of the book while being sensitive to the time constraints that every businessperson faces today. The book is arranged in six parts, each of which focuses on a broad aspect of CRM. Within these parts are self-contained chapters that explore a specific CRM concept. You can opt to read the book from cover to cover—which we highly recommend— or skip around to those chapters that are particularly germane to your situation.

The book begins with Part 1, The New CRM Imperative, which provides a basis for understanding how customer relationships have changed during the past decade, how CRM has evolved to help companies deal with changes in customer needs and expectations, and what the next wave of CRM will involve.

Part 2, Setting the Strategy, reviews why and how companies must address strategy issues well before they purchase any CRM software package or define any business requirements. The chapters in this section offer practical advice on how to more effectively develop and align customer, channel, brand, and CRM strategies to ensure that CRM projects are aligned with a company's mission and result in capabilities that create customer experiences appropriate to a company's brand.

Part 3, Gaining Customer Insights, takes a closer look at how companies can develop deeper insights into their customers' needs, preferences, and behavior and use those insights to design better ways of interacting with individual customers or customer segments.

Part 4, Reinventing Customer Contact, explores in more detail how companies can leverage customer insights to create customer contact strategies and operations that not only better satisfy customer needs, but do so in a way that is sensitive to the financial community's desire for a more robust bottom line.

Part 5, Transforming Marketing, looks at the myriad challenges that marketing organizations face today in stimulating demand; reviews the need to integrate marketing into CRM initiatives that have primarily focused only on sales and service; and demonstrates how instilling more discipline and rigor in marketing practices will boost performance and reduce the waste associated with many of today's practices.

Finally, Part 6, CRM at Work, provides an in-depth look at CRM in five key industry segments: communications, government, manufacturing, resources, and retail. In addition to reviewing critical CRM activities in the industry to date, these chapters provide numerous case studies that illustrate how industry leaders are putting the preceding CRM concepts to use for serious competitive advantage.

One final note about this book: What you are about to read is not a theoretical treatise on CRM, nor is it an untested vision of futurists. To the contrary, every chapter is based on the authors' real-world observations and experiences with companies. The result is a book that is not only highly readable, but also eminently practical for companies that truly want to succeed in what is proving to be a very turbulent decade.

Acknowledgments

Writing a provocative yet practical book on the subject of customer relationship management is a significant challenge. And while my name appears on the cover, there are a number of individuals that I would like to recognize for their contributions to making this book a reality.

First and foremost I want to thank the executives at our clients from around the world who agreed to share their CRM experiences. Their willingness to contribute their time in support of this effort has greatly enriched the ideas presented in this book.

I also want to sincerely thank the talented professionals at Accenture who helped to shape the content of this book with their valuable insights gained during our work at hundreds of CRM client engagements. I particularly want to thank the authors of each of the individual chapters. Without the collective knowledge of these dedicated professionals, this book would not have been possible.

Finally, I want to extend a special note of gratitude to the individuals at Accenture who managed this project and kept it on track. I specifically would like to thank Heather Dyke, Scott Egler, Karim Klaus Emara, Edward Flood, Rowena Rees, and Bernie Thiel. I would also like to thank Ela Aktay, our editor at McGraw-Hill, and her team for their tireless efforts on our behalf. This book could not have been completed without their help.

—*John G. Freeland*

The New CRM Imperative

1

The New CRM Imperative

John G. Freeland

Few would question the importance of strengthening customer relationships in the CEO agenda. Regardless of a company's size or industry, customer issues consistently receive considerable attention in the executive suite—and for good reason. Enhancing customer value, delivering a higher level of service, and enriching the brand all play a critical role in a company's ability to grow profitably and consistently outpace its competition.

Consequently, thousands of companies embraced customer relationship management (CRM) concepts and technologies during the past decade, often creating significant benefits for their business. Most executives recognize that keeping customer relationships strong and profitable in the future will require the right mix of innovative information technology, more effective business processes, better data management, and new workforce initiatives.

Nevertheless, executives have also grown increasingly skeptical of CRM, suspecting that it may be destined to become yet another business fad on which organizations spend huge amounts of money and still fail to achieve their objectives. An executive survey conducted by the research and advisory firm Gartner, for instance, reported that 55 percent of all CRM projects have not produced significant benefits, and numerous articles have appeared in the business press citing the many pitfalls encountered by CRM projects.

We believe there are two principal reasons why CRM at times falls short of expectations:

1. *The disconnection of CRM vision and execution.* Too many CRM projects focus on the mechanics (specific tools and single channels) rather than the ultimate goal: increasing the value of the customer relationship. At times, decisions about technology are made well before achieving clarity on customer

strategy. In other cases, project execution is flawed, suffering from lack of senior management support, poor project management, or insufficient skills to complete the project, for example. A common thread in these cases is a lack of attention to financial structure: setting the appropriate level of capital investment, variablizing cost where possible, and otherwise mitigating financial risk.

2. *The rising standard for CRM excellence.* The past decade was one of intense change and explosive innovation. New technologies emerged more frequently, disrupting the stability of entire markets. Customers became more mobile, informed, and demanding, and competitors became more adept at quickly improving their operations. As a result, companies watched as processes and technologies that once provided competitive advantage became baseline capabilities. With the standard of excellence continually rising, companies have been forced to outdo themselves with each successive customer initiative.

In sum, companies are now challenged not only to deliver more sophisticated sales and service capability, but also to deliver and manage these capabilities more quickly and cost-effectively. Alone, either challenge would be daunting. Combined, they might seem insurmountable. What seems clear is that traditional approaches to managing customer relationships have run their course. In fact, we predict that companies that settle for making incremental improvements to current capabilities will find themselves losing more revenue and share with each passing year.

We believe that more dramatic changes are required, that transforming sales, service, and marketing capability is now essential for many organizations. But before focusing on how CRM should be approached differently in the future, it may be useful to provide some historical context.

THE EVOLVING FOCUS OF CRM

CRM has always encompassed the broad set of sales, marketing, and customer service activities associated with serving customers and attracting new ones. While the *scope* of CRM has remained constant, the *focus* has changed considerably.

The first CRM initiatives launched in the early 1990s focused primarily on improving a single service channel—namely, the call center. Companies adopted new technologies and performance measures designed to streamline the process of answering and handling customer inquiries, hoping to increase customer satisfaction and their own operating efficiency.

Later, companies widened this focus to include sales as well, implementing new automation tools to enhance sales force efficiency and productivity. In the mid- to late 1990s, the focus of CRM expanded yet again to include more service and sales channels (such as the Web, e-mail, and instant messaging) giving customers alternatives for interacting with a company. Complex channel integration programs characterized this phase of CRM, still underway today, with companies focused on standardizing customer treatment across channels and gathering more customer data at each contact point. Many companies also implemented data warehouses and customer analytics programs to help manage this data and mine it for deeper insights into customer preferences.

All of these previous efforts have produced important benefits. Contact center initiatives enabled companies to reduce service costs while making transactions more convenient for customers (for example, by providing more self-service options). Sales force automation software made salespeople more efficient and boosted their ability to help customers (for example, by giving salespeople immediate access to pricing information on any product). Better channel integration made it easier for customers to deal with providers and enabled companies to gather more information about customers. And Internet-based initiatives opened up a new avenue into customers' homes and offices for selling and serving.

THE NEW CRM AGENDA

Unfortunately, companies are now realizing that these investments, while necessary, are not enough to sustain a leadership position—soon, they will not be sufficient to enable companies to maintain parity within their industries. Even as they perfect their sales and service applications, add more channels, and expand their customer data management capabilities, companies are discovering that they must do more. Customers already expect more, and what they expect changes at an ever-increasing rate. As a result, the costs of acquiring and serving customers are also skyrocketing, considerably impacting margin per customer and customer lifetime value.

Consider just one change indicator: *brand loyalty.* While the shopping habits of consumers in the 1970s and 1980s were highly influenced by the brand of the product or the company that sold the item, consumers today are less likely to purchase a specific brand or patronize a particular company simply because the brands are well known. As Exhibit 1-1 illustrates, the percentage of consumers who claim that they tend to stick with well-known brands when purchasing products and services dropped dramatically for all age groups from 1975 to 2000. Even the percentage for individuals over 60 years old   typically among the most brand loyal consumers dropped 20 points over those 25 years.[1]

Many factors contribute to the erosion of brand loyalty. One is the explosion in choice: The number of companies selling to consumers has mushroomed in the past two decades. In the U.S. retail sector, for instance, the number of book retail outlets has more than tripled since 1975; the number of discount stores has nearly doubled since 1970; and the number of apparel outlets has increased by 50 percent since 1970.[2]

Concurrently, the variety of items available to consumers has expanded significantly. The typical U.S. supermarket now carries, on average, more than 30,000 products.[3] In the financial services sector, individual investors now have to select among 8200 mutual funds for their retirement portfolios.[4] Hungry consumers in the United States have almost 850,000 eatery outlets to choose from—nearly 220,000 of which are part of a regional or national chain.[5] Given all these new options, it is not surprising that buyers are spreading their purchases around—especially in the

EXHIBIT 1-1. Despite increased spending on marketing, the percentage of consumers who try to stick to well-known brand names continues to fall steadily. (*Data from* DDB Life Style Study 2000.)

Age	1975	2000
20–29	66%	59%
30–39	73%	59%
40–49	77%	60%
50–59	82%	59%
60–69	86%	65%
70–79	93%	73%

United States and Europe, where an essentially static population bases enjoys an ever-expanding array of choices.

Accompanying the increase in choice is a huge jump in the number of messages (marketing and advertising, e-mails, phone calls, etc.) to which consumers are exposed. In 1985, consumers experienced an average of 650 such messages a day;[6] today, that figure is 3000.[7] Direct mail certainly plays a role: The number of direct-mail pieces consumers receive each year has ballooned in the past two decades from 35 million in 1980 to 85.6 million in 1999.[8] Telemarketing is also on the rise, as the average consumer receives between 60 and 90 telemarketing phone calls every month.[9] The average Internet user is flooded with hundreds of e-mail messages a week—many of them unsolicited commercial pitches.

Finally, customers are increasingly sophisticated, and increasingly unwilling to settle for less than the best. The Web and cable television give consumers access to more information than ever before, enabling them to compare offers from competing companies more easily.

This combination of forces ensnares companies in a vicious circle of "Can you top this?" Today's customers know they don't have to accept shoddy service, high prices, or inferior products. Through their experiences with value and service leaders such as Virgin Atlantic, FedEx, Wal-Mart, and the BMW Group, consumers have been taught to expect more: What was once considered exceptional service provided by only a few is now viewed as "table stakes" for any company that wishes to enter the game.

Customer expectations now increase at a faster rate than most companies can match by relying on the traditional approaches to CRM. Consider the findings of a recent study, which revealed that 74 percent of online customers will shop elsewhere if their inquiries are not quickly answered, and that most expect these online responses within an hour.[10]

Consequently, many executives feel as though they are running in place. For companies to break free, the practice of CRM will need to evolve as dramatically as the business context has. Organizations will need to change the strategic focus behind their CRM programs once more, adopting the new methods and tools required to satisfy a new set of customer expectations and competitive demands. They will also need to find new, better ways to execute their vision, to deliver the outcomes they seek.

NEW GUIDING PRINCIPLES

In the next phase of CRM, what will companies need to get right?

First, they should base future investments on a holistic approach that ties together customer, channel, and brand strategies with supporting processes and technologies.

Companies should focus not only on generating customer insights, but also on realigning their customer treatment protocols with the highly individualized view of the customer that emerges from those insights.

Finally, they should broaden their CRM focus to include marketing as well as sales and service. As a business practice, marketing needs to be revitalized by reintroducing the rigor of marketing analytics to what has often been viewed as primarily a creative activity.

As companies reshape the focus of their CRM programs, they should bear in mind three guiding principles:

1. *Customer experience is essential to creating brand value.* Smart logos, catchy jingles, or memorable commercials can play a major role in generating awareness, but they are just part of the brand equation. Brand strength and brand value are the sum total of experiences that customers have with the company and all its products and services.

2. *Customer insight should inform and drive customer treatment.* Every contact customers have with a company contributes to their perception of the company, and either enhances or destroys economic value.

3. *CRM programs should be executed in a pragmatic way that mitigates financial and delivery risk.* CRM is not about building elegant capabilities (based on the latest software packages) or serving customers at any cost. Rather, companies must be pragmatic, learning how to acquire the new capabilities they need with reduced up-front investment, how to mitigate financial risk with innovative business structures, and how to improve their ability to predict and variablize operating costs.

ORGANIZING FOR CRM SUCCESS

Given these guiding principles, we recommend that companies organize their CRM initiatives around four components:

1. Setting the strategy
2. Gaining customer insights
3. Realizing greater value from customer contact activities
4. Transforming marketing

Setting the Strategy

To generate the greatest return, CRM must be viewed from a strategic perspective that encompasses *customer strategy,* identifying the customers that the company wants, based on its existing business model and corporate mission; *channel strategy,* selecting the most appropriate and effective channels for reaching desired customers; *brand strategy,* understanding how all interactions with customers (not just advertising or logos) contribute to the company's brand value; and *CRM strategy,* determining the most appropriate CRM capabilities for supporting the critical interaction points and channels needed to reach chosen customers and prospects.

Gaining Customer Insights

Many past CRM initiatives lacked the element of customer insight—the ability to understand customer needs and accurately predict customer behavior. This has become particularly critical as customers have become more mobile, more fickle, and more demanding. Companies must have all the capability required to capture and analyze critical customer data and analyze that data to create deep insights into how customers behave, how they would like to interact with the company, and what they truly want and need from the company. In turn, these insights should determine how the company interacts with customers in the future—what offers they make, what service options they provide, and so on.

Realizing Greater Value from Customer Contact Activities

One frequent criticism of CRM initiatives today is that they often fail to generate a satisfactory return on invested capital. One major cause is that many companies have built elegant but extremely expensive CRM infrastructures that are now difficult to justify. We believe organizations face a dual challenge: improving the quality of customer interactions while at the same time driving down the cost to serve. Accomplishing this task will involve reengineering the customer experience, adopting innovative sourcing strategies, and optimizing workforce performance in the contact center.

Transforming Marketing

The primary focus of past CRM efforts has been on enhancing aspects of sales and service; by contrast, marketing has been relatively neglected. This has prevented companies from generating deeper customer insights, because they have not been able to "close the loop" on customer information. In addition, by neglecting to apply CRM concepts and technologies to marketing, companies have missed an opportunity to bring more discipline to a function that has been left to operate largely on its own terms.

Effective marketing is not a matter of guesswork or gut instinct. It can and must be quantified and optimized in ways that most have not yet attempted—just as companies streamlined their manufacturing processes or made their logistics activities more effective and efficient. Given the challenges that all companies face today in being heard above the market noise, it is essential that they begin to take a more rigorous approach to marketing—one that not only makes their activities more effective, but also identifies where money is being wasted or misspent.

CONCLUSION

To be sure, companies face some significant challenges in making their CRM initiatives pay off. But this does not mean that CRM is fated to become nothing more than a fad. When properly conceived and executed, CRM programs can create exceptional economic value.

The next few years will give rise to a new generation of business leaders who will redefine the gold standard for managing customer relationships. These new leaders will make developing the customer franchise their core business strategy, and they will make achieving a new standard of CRM excellence their chief operating imperative.

This book is written for companies that aspire to be among those leaders.

In the chapters that follow, we explore in much more detail the aspects critical to success in CRM   from setting the strategy and developing deep customer insights to wringing greater value from customer contact activities and transforming the marketing organization. In addition, the last part of the book, "CRM at Work," presents a comprehensive look at CRM in five different industry segments—communications, government, manufacturing, resources, and retail—and describes how the leaders in each of those industries already are emerging because of their new approach to CRM.

Consider this book your guide to the next phase in the evolution of CRM. After reading it, you will have an in-depth understanding not only of what this next phase will entail but of how your company can take advantage of new CRM strategies, concepts, and technologies to develop stronger, more rewarding, and more profitable customer relationships in the dynamic present and in the uncertain years ahead.

Setting the Strategy

2

Introduction: Strategy First, Then CRM

Steven S. Ramsey

Since companies began their push into what is now known as CRM, such initiatives were rarely, if ever, launched with strategic goals in mind. Instead, as companies rushed to realize the benefits, their CRM efforts were characterized by an ad hoc, tactical approach lacking an overarching strategy. Worse yet, these fledgling efforts had few if any ties to the company's overall customer, channel, and brand strategies.

The reasons for this are many, but can be boiled down to three key factors. The first is *definition*. Since it began, CRM has been surrounded by confusion. Like any hot new concept, CRM has suffered from a lack of consensus on exactly what it is. To some it was the new data warehouse; to others it was laptops for sales representatives; to still others it meant a new call center or Web site. Without a clear definition, managers have had a difficult time understanding how CRM related to other aspects of their company's operations. Furthermore, because of its integral technology component, CRM has been both blessed and cursed by innovation. While CRM tools have been constantly evolving, incorporating ever-more-powerful features, companies have been unsure of where to place their bets and accommodate obsolescence that could be just around the corner.

The second major factor is *leadership*. Leaders of CRM efforts historically have been functional heads—marketing, sales, or customer service managers—who either didn't have a higher-level strategic perspective of CRM or were being tightly measured on improving specific activities within their functions (e.g., enhancing the efficiency of the call center or providing the sales force with remote access to corporate databases). Often, CRM efforts were driven by the head of information technology, in which case the project took on a decided technology emphasis that translated into a focus on technical requirements instead of business needs. Whether these initiatives were led by functional heads or IT, though, strategy was an after-thought—if it was a thought at all.

Finally, there are the CRM *vendors*. Providers of CRM tools, too, share some of the blame for CRM's lack of strategic perspective. Most vendors have highlighted only the slice of CRM that involves their products, addressing specific challenges within sales or customer service instead of acknowledging that CRM has broader implications for many areas of the business and, as such, requires much more than a software package. This technical focus was also in part responsible for senior exec-utives ignoring CRM until recently, when it became clear that CRM was a bigger issue than any of them had imagined.

Not surprisingly, many companies have become disillusioned with CRM. They are dissatisfied with the results of their CRM efforts, believing that they have failed to realize the hoped-for significant benefits or value. Although some tactical CRM solutions have delivered business benefits, these benefits are nowhere near what is possible if companies take a strategic, holistic view.

An interesting twist in the story is the fact that because companies' CRM efforts weren't tied more closely to corporate strategy, many companies found themselves chasing the illusion of pure customer-centricity—when in actuality few companies can build a profitable business on such a model (nor do they need to). They have been so narrowly focused on the notion of transforming their businesses into customer-centric one-to-one relationships that they've overlooked the significant cost and revenue impacts of simply improving the efficiency and effectiveness of their customer-facing operations.

STRATEGY FIRST, THEN CRM

For companies to realize the full potential of CRM—ensuring they get the best return on their CRM investments and aren't wasting precious resources building unnecessary capabilities—they must begin to incorporate a strategic perspective into all of their CRM efforts. In particular, they must address four critical strate-gies, and understand the key interplay between them, before investing in any CRM project.

1. *Customer.* Identifying the customers that the company wants, based on its existing business model and corporate mission.
2. *Channel.* Selecting the most appropriate and effective channels for reaching these customers.
3. *Brand.* Understanding how all interactions with customers, not just advertis-ing, contribute to the company's brand value.
4. *CRM.* Determining the most appropriate CRM capabilities for support-ing these critical interaction points and channels to reach the chosen customers.

Customer

If the most recent CRM initiatives have proved anything, it's the fact that few companies can operate a profitable business with a complete one-to-one focus on customers. It's simply impractical for most organizations to build themselves around serving segments of one. Therefore, before beginning any CRM project, a company must get a better handle on the types of customers it should be serving and, subsequently, identify the types of interactions with each segment that will generate the greatest loyalty among customers—and the most profit for the business. A very effective approach to this is customer segment management.

Customer segment management is the process of segmenting groups of customers based on like attributes and managing those segments in a way that maximizes both the benefits to customers and the long-term profit potential of the organization. In essence, customer segment management is a way toward the achievement of managing relationships with each customer on an individual basis for companies that want to reach that stage eventually, and it's a more realistic customer-centric approach to managing customer relationships for companies that still need some element of product focus in their approach to their markets.

In concept, customer segment management views a company's market as a *customer-centric continuum* with six stages, ranging from a pure product focus on the left and a total customer focus on the right. The approach recognizes that every company will have a different point on this continuum that is best for it—that is, offers the right mix of product and customer emphasis to boost customer loyalty without compromising the financial well-being of the organization. Of course, each point on the continuum has different requirements for people, processes, and technology. Determining what these requirements are will help ensure that future CRM capabilities contribute significantly to the company's efforts to attract and retain the customer segments that are important to it.

Channel

It used to be that channels were relatively constant and well defined. That's no longer the case. With new technologies—such as, but not limited to, the Web—arriving on the scene with amazing frequency, the lines between existing channels can become blurred and entire new channels can emerge in the relative blink of an eye. As a result, companies are increasingly challenged to ensure that their channel strategies are current and relevant and that movement to capitalize on new channels won't harm or destroy relationships with current channel partners.

In today's volatile world, companies must, on a regular basis, evaluate the potential channels available to them, which ones they should use, and how well they are using those they've chosen. In doing so, companies are better able to understand their channel dynamics and conceive of new ways of organizing and executing channel activities that add value to the companies and their brands.

Two critical tools that can help in this effort are the *channel map* and the *channel conflict strategy matrix*. The former offers a bird's-eye view of who's who and who does what in the various channels through which the company currently sells and markets and in those it could leverage. It helps the company ensure that it's not missing out on potential profit and growth while pointing out channel relationships that may no longer be producing sufficient value for the company. The channel conflict strategy matrix helps companies analyze the forces and opportunities for change in their industries by each existing channel and identify strategies that will enable them to effectively shed nonperforming channels or adopt new ones.

Certainly, companies' entering and exiting of channels will have a large impact on the types of CRM capabilities that are needed to help them maximize the value of each channel in which they choose to operate. That's why it's critical for channel strategy to be firmly set before the company initiates any CRM effort—particularly those with a cross-channel scope.

Brand

Many people are under the misconception that CRM has nothing to do with brand. To the contrary, CRM has *everything* to do with brand. Why? For many, brand is viewed as a company's name or logo, and the primary brand-building tool is advertising. To be sure, these elements are all important to crafting a strong brand. However, brand is much more than that. Brand is to equal the sum of everything a company says, everything it does, and how it says and does it. Put another way, brand is the sum total of a customer's experience of a company and, as such, encompasses the entire range of the company's products, services, behaviors, distribution channels, technologies, and processes.

Thus defined, it's easy to understand how CRM relates to brand. A company that prides itself on its great products and superior customer service yet makes customers wade through a long list of complex options when they call its service center is damaging its brand. Similarly, a company that continually fails to deliver goods when promised is undermining its advertising and marketing efforts to create a strong, positive brand.

The fact is that marketers, who often "own" the company's brand, can't ignore the impact that activities traditionally out of their control—such as call center and sales interactions—have on their brand-building efforts. By embracing a broader definition of brand, marketers can move past their preoccupation with advertising and consumer awareness–building activities and start seeing branding from a much more holistic perspective. They can begin to use a more complete set of metrics, above and beyond market share and consumer awareness, to measure brand value. And they can work with their colleagues in sales and customer service to ensure consistency in messaging and experience for critical channel partners and customers interacting with the call center.

An expanded definition of brand also makes it clear that CRM plays a critical role in the branding process and that activities formerly considered outside the scope of a company's brand actually are the principal contributors to the brand's strength or weakness. As a result, companies must fully understand their brand promise, and how they intend to execute that promise, before committing to building specific CRM capabilities.

CRM

As the cost of a typical CRM implementation continues to grow, organizations will have to become more vigilant in addressing the strategic elements of CRM instead of continuing to build ad hoc capabilities that may have limited benefit to the company. This entails adopting a new approach to CRM that enables a company to identify, prioritize, and build the right CRM capabilities for creating customer and company value.

This approach is distinctly different from those used in the past. It focuses on business outcomes, not capabilities alone. It is analytically rigorous, relying on an ROI focus instead of subjective considerations. It emphasizes both the revenue and cost aspects of CRM so that CRM investments can be tied directly to a company's income statement. And it provides a value-based, prioritized plan for CRM implementation to ensure that the most important areas are addressed first.

There are four key elements of this approach. The first is understanding how CRM fits into the context of a company's overall business strategy. This entails confirming the company's vision for the CRM project as well as the project's business imperative—taking into consideration the existing business environment and the company's corporate strategic priorities. The second is conducting a comprehensive assessment of existing CRM capabilities to help a company understand how well it uses these capabilities relative to competitors and the industry at large, determining which capabilities are most germane to the company's particular situation, and identifying which contribute the most to the company's ability to create customer value. The third element is developing a solid business case for the CRM project that demonstrates a positive return on investment, then prioritizing the adoption of specific capabilities. The fourth is creating a road map that defines the technical, process, and organizational elements that must be addressed to complete the CRM initiative.

This more strategic approach ensures that the capabilities built in a CRM project are consistent with a company's mission and support the activities that enable the company to realize its business goals—and thus have the greatest potential to provide the highest return in the form of reduced costs and enhanced revenue.

CONCLUSION

Given the bad press that CRM has received recently, it's clear that something must be done to improve CRM's return on investment. That something is attending to strategy before any CRM package is purchased or any business requirements are defined. In the following four chapters, we delve deeper into this issue and offer practical advice on how companies can effectively develop and align customer, channel, brand, and CRM strategies to ensure that they generate more value for the business.

Customer Strategy: Whom Do You Want to Reach?

Clive Whitehouse, Ruth E. Spencer, and Michael Payne

A growing number of companies have come to accept that their fate hinges on applying a more customer-centric approach to serving customers. This approach represents an evolutionary shift from focusing merely on product sales and delivery to focusing more explicitly on satisfying the needs and wants of today's customers. The quest for customer-centricity is driven primarily by three key factors:

1. The wearisome struggle to reach customers engulfed each day in a flood of competing messages
2. Ever-rising expectations of how companies interact with customers
3. Mounting financial pressures to optimize the return on investments in customer relationships

Ignoring these factors leads to a painfully familiar series of problems: poor customer acquisition and cross-sell rates, customer dissatisfaction and disloyalty, and dwindling profit margins. Customer segment management is one model of customer-centricity that offers companies new hope for surmounting these problems to ultimately achieve a more effective and profitable state of customer interaction.

CUSTOMER SEGMENT MANAGEMENT DEFINED

Customer segment management is the process of segmenting groups of customers based on like attributes and managing those segments in a way that maximizes both

The content of this chapter originally appeared in the book *Defying the Limits: Setting a Course for CRM Success*, published by Montgomery Research.

the benefits to customers and the long-term profit potential of the organization. For example, this may include segmenting customers according to product and service needs, buying behaviors, and actual and potential profitability.

In essence, customer segment management can be viewed as a stage on the way to achieving "true nirvana"—managing relationships with each customer on an individual basis. Traditionally, companies have exploited a mass, or one-to-many, approach to targeting customers, but with diminishing results in satisfying the needs and wants of customers. On the other hand, targeting and managing customers on a one-to-one basis is currently not practical for most companies. For the time being, customer segment management offers a more realistic customer-centric approach to managing customer relationships.

Although many companies intuitively feel that becoming more customer-centric will provide the answer to their problems, the concept is often poorly defined and not well understood. In this chapter, we offer a pragmatic approach to becoming a customer-centric organization through the application of a model for customer segment management. The model is based on actual observation and real-life experience in successfully implementing customer-centric initiatives across different industries. We examine how the model may be applied across different industries, and we have chosen to highlight the retail financial services industry to provide more in-depth examples of how the model can be applied effectively.

THE MODEL IN CONCEPT

In concept, the typical model for customer segment management depicts the supply, demand, and distribution functions of a company as being separate from each other (Exhibit 3-1). These core functions are supported by a shared group of services, such

EXHIBIT 3-1.   Typical customer segment management model.

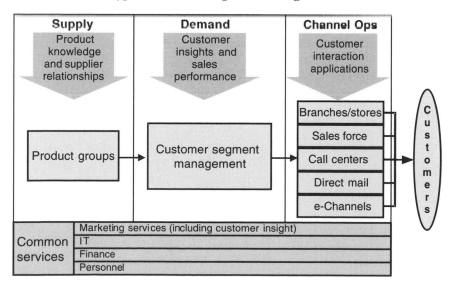

as information technology, accounting and finance, and marketing services, which may also include a customer analysis or insight function.

Based on this concept, customer segment managers within the demand function are viewed as entrepreneurs charged with the goal of maximizing market penetration and profitability within their segment. They depend largely on customer insight analysis to identify customer buying behaviors and needs. They also work collaboratively with product groups in the organization to spot new customer product and service propositions, which then are developed by the product groups. These propositions most likely will differ by customer segment.

The customer segment managers are responsible for determining which product offers their customers or prospects will receive and through which channels they will be delivered. Where possible, segment managers also define the rules for interacting with customers across the different contact points, which may range from in-store checkout to Web-based or phone-based interaction. These rules are applied consistently across channels.

Segment managers receive frequent reports on their performance and are expected to continually refine and improve on their management tactics.

Exhibit 3-1 is primarily useful for demonstrating only what an organization may aspire to achieve in concept. However, this simplified illustration of the model does not show the many different stages of customer segment management that may apply in helping an organization become more customer-centric.

A MORE PRAGMATIC VIEW OF THE MODEL

Based on our experience with many organizations, Exhibit 3-2 depicts a more realistic view of the several degrees of customer segmentation management.

Stage 0: Product-Centric Analysis

At the far left of the continuum, in the product-centric analysis stage, analysis of customers is focused on product lines. The dominant element is the product or product

EXHIBIT 3-2.   Customer-centric continuum.

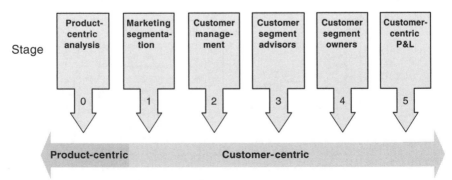

line, and customer analysis tends to be based on purchase behavior. Information collected is used primarily for tactical promotions and targeting. Product profit and loss is used as the primary measure for gauging an organization's performance.

Stage 1: Marketing Segmentation

In the marketing segmentation stage, the organization begins consolidating information across product lines and using the insight gained for high-level market analysis, strategy development, and customer communication planning. The nature of the segmentation tends to be offline, periodic, and not well integrated into the operational environment, except where it influences more tactical direct-marketing operations.

Stage 2: Customer Management

A qualitative change takes place when an organization enters the customer management stage. Rather than being used primarily as a planning tool, customer segments are treated as a management dimension. Typically, it is at this stage that a customer management function is formed. The function assumes responsibility for developing business strategies and measuring performance along customer segments. The customer manager also assumes a coordination role to ensure that the customer element is considered in operations, and this often includes responsibility for setting customer contact rules within a product-led communication plan.

Stage 3: Customer Segment Advisors

In the customer segment advisors stage, the customer management function is further solidified by the introduction of segment managers, who each may assume responsibility for one or more segments. The role of the segment managers becomes clearly focused on specific segments, and they serve as key advisors to product and channel management. However, their challenge at this stage is operating with minimal budget and exerting influence over a strong channel manager or product development function.

Stage 4: Customer Segment Owners

Authority is no longer such an issue in the customer segment owners stage, as segment managers assume an overtly operational role with responsibility for setting the rules that govern nearly all forms of customer contact in their segment—regardless of the product, channel, or nature of the interaction. In this advanced role, segment managers are more powerful: They own the proactive marketing budget, thus controlling which product offers are made available to their customers and how they are delivered. They will be responsible for setting the rules for customer interaction, whether in a marketing, sales, or service context—tailoring the rules to suit the customer's segment.

Stage 5: Customer-Centric Profit and Loss

At the far right of the continuum in the customer-centric profit and loss stage, the role of segment managers is taken to the ultimate managerial level. Segment managers become responsible for measuring profit and loss along customer segments, which subsequently poses a more challenging reporting task. Products and distribution channels assume a subordinate position relative to customers. The sum of the profit and loss measures for the segments, in turn, becomes representative of the organization's overall profit and loss performance. However, measuring profit and loss along customer segments will never completely replace the need for measuring profit and loss by product units and channels. Product profit and loss typically is still reported as a secondary measure of performance and may in some cases be required for public accounting reports.

IS THERE A RIGHT PLACE TO BE ON THE CONTINUUM?

There is no single right answer for where an organization should be on this continuum. Depending on the industry, strategic intent, and current situation of the organization, any stage along the continuum may be applicable.

For example, a credit card company focused on being a single-line producer is more likely to be at the far left of the continuum. On the other hand, a company that strives to be a full-service financial provider is more likely to be at the far right of the continuum.

Whatever the case, the primary objective is to create an organization with a strong focus on improving profitability by more effectively anticipating and understanding customer needs and wants, which subsequently means developing products and services that are manageable in execution, innovative, and, to the extent possible, profitable in their own right. The key is to choose the right balance for your organization and then determine how to achieve that balance.

ACHIEVING THE RIGHT BALANCE

Intense debate naturally arises over the issue of whether all product lines should be profitable in their own right or whether individual product profitability can be sacrificed in carefully selected cases as a means to encourage overall customer loyalty. The answer, however, clearly depends on the overall management strategy of the organization, the nature of the product, and often the individual personalities of the managing executives involved.

The nature of an organization's industry also factors into determining the right position along the continuum. For example, industries such as retail, where the customer often is not known on an individual level and the product is standardized, tend to be better positioned along the far left of the continuum. This positioning particularly applies to industries driven by product innovation, such as electronics or mobile phone companies.

At the far right of the continuum are industries with a very strong need to interact with customers on an individual level and with tailored products that tend to be primarily organized around customers or customer segments. For example, many service-based organizations, including marketing and other types of business-to-business professional services firms (e.g., merchant banks), are generally organized around customer segment groups, often referred to as *industry segments,* or *portfolios.*

On the other hand, some organizations, such as those in retail financial services, can effectively assume a position virtually anywhere along the continuum. This is where other factors (e.g., a company's overall business strategy, culture, and individual management personalities) come into play. As a general rule, retail financial services companies are moving steadily toward the right end of the continuum. However, those we've tracked that have attempted to move all the way to stage 5 have encountered difficulties.

Let's take a look at a couple of specific examples:

- In one case, a South African bank attempted to jump all the way from stage 1 to stage 5 in one push and met with failure, primarily because fundamental issues of ownership and profitability had not been resolved. With management unable to reach agreement on key decisions such as product pricing, the company reverted to a position between stages 1 and 2 on the continuum.

- In another example, a U.K.-based bank also attempted to jump to stage 5 and encountered operational difficulties in the pricing and delivery of services. It has since settled on a position between stages 4 and 5, where the segment managers are responsible for planning and delivering most of the customer contact, but are not responsible for profit and loss.

These two examples suggest that in industries such as retail financial services, where overall profitability is primarily driven by fundamental product characteristics, stage 5 is difficult to sustain.

Frequently, lack of a suitable infrastructure will inhibit a move toward achieving a more customer-centric organization. For instance, one financial services company realized that because its systems and processes could not support rapid product development, its ability to reach stage 5 was compromised. With only a limited product set, very little product customization possible, and no ability to bundle products, the segment managers could in effect influence only communications to customers. Segment management likely will drive the need for a more sophisticated and elaborate infrastructure.

ALIGNING PEOPLE AND PROCESSES

Most organizations respond to these challenges by adopting fixed and very rigid segment structures. However, this ignores the fact that customer segments should be dynamic, reflecting the fact that consumer behaviors change and evolve over time. Building an infrastructure to sustain customer segmentation requires flexibility in aligning an organization's processes and people to continually anticipate and respond to changing customer behaviors. This in turn poses an ongoing challenge for organizations in building critical mass around key skills to implement customer-driven segment management teams.

A larger, multiline organization, such as a retail banking services company, will find customer segmentation particularly challenging because different lines within the organization may be positioned along several different points of the continuum. Rather than adopting fixed segment structures, organizations managing positions at the right end of the continuum need to consider building virtual customer segment management teams to cost-effectively deploy the greater number of required resources.

Let's take a look at how an organization's people and processes might be aligned effectively at a more tactical level to support segment management:

- Operationally, an organization would comprise cross-functional teams with skills and processes centrally coordinated.

- Segment management teams would be supported by specialists deployed from specialist teams.

- The primary role of the specialists is to ensure that their areas of competency support the development and implementation of their assigned segment's strategy.

- The cross-functional segment teams assume responsibility for the development of their customer base through a segment strategy, embracing communication activities, product development, and channel management to meet goals set by the strategy development teams.

- Central coordination of processes promotes optimization of timing, ensuring that activities are structured in the best interests of the whole organization and at the same time avoiding intergroup rivalry and duplication.

- The primary structure is bound together by core processes.

Exhibit 3-3 illustrates typical roles, responsibilities, and key performance indicators.

SUPPORTING INFORMATION TECHNOLOGY SYSTEMS

So far, we have described the stages along the continuum in terms of process and organizational characteristics. As the organization moves toward a more customer-centric approach, however, there is an increasing need for information technology systems to support four main areas:

1. Data
   - Richer customer data supplemented with external sources
   - Integration of customer data across products and channels
   - Integration of primary market research with internal data
   - Availability of customer information at all points of need, including customer contact points organized into a data warehouse, data marts for marketing and analysis, and an operational customer database that links to core information management systems

2. Analytics
   - Sophisticated data-mining tools for segmentation and profiling
   - Advanced tools for predictive modeling
   - Advanced self-learning and pattern-detection software in industries with significant transaction volumes

EXHIBIT 3-3.   Roles, responsibilities, and key performance indicators.

Role	Responsibility	Key performance indicators
Customer segment management:	*Maximize segment profitability and customer lifetime value:* Create customer value propositions, ensure consistency across channels, coordinate efforts with product and channel management, develop strategies and business cases, and monitor activities of competitors for each segment	• Profit/lifetime value • Market share/share of wallet over time • Customer acquisition-to-retention ratios
Specialist Teams Deployed to Support Customer Segment Management Teams		
Customer insight	*Gather, collate, and transform data into actionable knowledge:* Use research, statistical analysis, and data-mining techniques to provide understanding of customers and prospects, and their actual or potential relationships with the enterprise	• Quality and timeliness of strategic research plan • Speed of response to requests • Timeliness and usefulness of insights • Accuracy of predictive models • Speed and effectiveness of insight communication
Channel management	*Optimize channel mix for customer segments:* Balance distribution channel capacity with segment demands and explore new channel opportunities	• Cost-effective routes to market • Customers have access to services when it is required
Marketing services management	*Optimize marketing campaign effectiveness:* Maximize economies of scale by interacting with third-party agencies that support marketing efforts and provide tactical marketing capability to segment management	• Speed of response • Cost-effectiveness of campaigns
Product management	*Deliver quality products and configurations in a timely manner:* Act as content experts on emerging product development and existing product offerings, develop and manage product-level brands, and investigate opportunities for product enhancements and diversification	• Product profitability • Time to market • Product development costs
Brand management	*Define brand values and communicate consistently and effectively:* Understand customer perception of the brand, identify key brand attributes, create new attributes, and develop plans to promote attributes to customers and prospects	• Brand awareness • Brand consistency

3. Marketing automation
   - Systems that can apply the insight gained about the customers to support sophisticated marketing and sales and differentiated service—in a transparent and easy-to-use manner—consistently across channels
   - In some industries, automated detection systems that identify sales opportunities and generate leads automatically

4. Monitoring and reporting
- Systems that can track activity and report key metrics so that the effectiveness of segment strategies is understood and can be modified when necessary

There is nothing to stop an organization from developing very sophisticated systems support for CRM activities while still operating with a relatively product-focused approach. In fact, quite sophisticated predictive modeling techniques may be used to help target offers on a per-product basis. However, in practice, the development of more powerful integrated systems tends to go hand in hand with the development of the customer-centric organization model, with each driving the other.

For example, an organization that wants to more effectively manage the lifetime value of its customers across all products may create the supporting data warehouse, analytics, and marketing tools. However, the sponsors will find quickly that it is difficult to maximize the value of this infrastructure without clarifying ownership and responsibility for achieving the goal by customer segment group.

INNOVATIVE TOOLS

In other cases, new tools make possible a more centralized approach across organizations. For example, the new generation of real-time, cross-channel marketing systems enables a central group to define the rules for sales prompts consistently across all of an organization's channels and then move those rules into the production environment with just a few clicks of a mouse. This is a powerful tool for ensuring that segment-specific strategies are translated into appropriate action at the point of customer interaction, enabling a much more centralized and consistent approach.

Similarly, as more data becomes available, there is a need for very high capacity, including high-speed data processing platforms and databases to support data analysis. For example, a major U.S. retailer is building a database that will capture all transactions from its stores, by customer, so that these can be used to generate real-time, personalized offers for customers at the checkout. Only a few specialized technologies can currently meet the huge demand for data capacity and retrieval in these situations. Where these systems are implemented, they provide another tool for the segment manager to put his or her strategies into action.

SUCCESS FACTORS

Based on our observation of customer segment management initiatives in several industries during the past three years, we have established a set of factors that we believe are essential to ensuring success:

1. *Get the segmentation right from the start.* The criteria used to define the segmentation must be very carefully thought out. Developing effective customer segmentation is a voluminous subject in itself, but bear in mind the following points:
- For an operational segmentation, the membership criteria should be explicit and mutually exclusive; that is, it should be clear to which seg-

ment an individual customer belongs. For this reason, for operational segmentations, behavioral and geodemographic segmentations are more effective than attitude segmentations based on market research alone.

- Our model builds in flexibility to respond to changing segmentation definitions; however, time and effort (not to mention morale) will be saved if
the segmentation is thoroughly tested and relatively stable before the
organization structure around it is implemented.

- The number of segments should not exceed an organization's ability to service them in terms of providing both resources and differentiated offerings.

- It is a good principle to include customer value models and algorithms as a
dimension in all segmentations, regardless of other criteria used, to focus
the organization on retaining its most valuable customers and driving up
the value of the other customers.

2. *Keep the end in mind.* It is important to understand the implications of advancing through the stages along the right side of the continuum. Experience has
shown, for instance, that retail banks find it difficult and impractical to operate
in stage 5. Again, the ultimate stage on the continuum for your organization
depends on the nature of your business and industry, and it must be realistic in
terms of investment, with buy-in from key management personnel in your
organization.

3. *Plan the journey.* The more stages you attempt to move your organization
through at a given time, the bigger the implementation challenge. Moving from
product-centric to customer-centric requires a change of culture and outlook,
and it seems to work more predictably if done gradually, in stages. A clear road
map that lays out the steps toward achieving the end goal also will help to gain
buy in from the business and technology stakeholders.

3. *Define responsibilities and performance metrics.* Possibly the most common
issue encountered with these programs is disagreement over responsibilities.
Classic issues such as "Who owns the customer?" will be raised and—unless
dealt with proactively—waste valuable time and effort. It is essential that the
responsibilities and metrics be socialized and agreed to up front so that turf
wars are avoided. This means aligning resources with the value gained from
customer relationships.

4. *Select segment managers with the right skills and attitude.* The segment management role is a challenging one. In many ways, segment managers are entrepreneurs, always looking for ways to better understand and improve the
profitability of their segment. Yet, in organizations, negotiation skills are also
critical. Segment managers will need to negotiate with both their product supplier and distributor counterparts, who have historically played more significant roles.

They also need to be good team players with the ability to recognize when
applying collaborative approaches, rather than developing unique solutions,
would be more appropriate. They must be able to think strategically and opera-

tionally. For instance, it might be more profitable to develop a new product with moderate appeal across several customer segments rather than strong appeal exclusively to one segment.

Finally, the segment manager must be analytical and have an appreciation of data and technology. Consequently, effective segment managers are hard to find, and care should be taken in their selection.

6. *Continually evolve skill sets to meet changing needs.* As you organize your segments around specific skill sets, realize that you will need to continually evolve those skill sets based on the changing needs of the organization. For example, if you decide to move your organization from segmenting along product lines to segmenting by customer groups, the product managers with whom your customers exhibit the greatest propensity to buy in the future likely will evolve into segment manager roles.

7. *Build the right supporting infrastructure.* The key requirement here is to have in place tools that enable the segment manager to understand his or her segment, develop strategies, establish and implement contact rules, and monitor performance. Without the right tools and data, segment managers will be unable to maximize the potential of their segment. For instance, it is critical to develop a single, integrated view of the customer that gives the segment managers a rich and more complete understanding of what segments need and how they interact with the company.

8. *Create a customer-centric culture.* Moving along the customer-centric continuum is not the single answer to fix all problems in the culture and working practices of an organization. Organizations must be able to manage cross-functional teams, establish accountability, and be passionately interested in understanding and meeting customer needs and wants.

IS IT ALL WORTH IT? YOU CAN BET IT WILL BE

The changes required to implement segment management are fundamental and, depending on where you are aiming and how you plan to get there, can require significant effort and expenditure. Is it worth all the effort? The answer is a resounding *yes,* for two reasons:

- Segment management enables organizations to realize the benefits from other CRM capabilities. Recent Accenture research revealed that a typical $1 billion business unit could boost pretax profits by $120 million to $150 million by moving from average to high performance in the top 21 capabilities identified in the study. Not surprisingly, segmentation is one of the top capabilities, and its impact on the performance of other capabilities is clear. For example, one U.K.-based financial services provider that implemented segment management similar to stage 4 in our model achieved a 6 percent increase in its bottom-line profits.

- Just as important in the long term, the move to higher degrees of customer-centricity is a strategic response to a clear change in the business environment: Consumer attitudes have changed, permanently. Customers know what is possible, and they expect nothing less. At the same time, the competition for their attention is growing ever more fierce. A customer-centric organization is best aligned (with the caveat of achieving the right balance) to meet these challenges now and in the future.

AS GOOD AS IT GETS FOR NOW

When carefully applied, customer segment management can help effectively position organizations to grow and to protect their share of customers in the twenty-first century. But again, customer segment management is just one step in the journey toward managing customers on a one-to-one level with individually tailored products and messages. As we get closer to achieving that nirvana, customer segment management will naturally fade away.

For the foreseeable future, however, we believe customer segment management offers the most practical approach for achieving customer-centricity, supported by ever-increasing levels of individual targeting and personalization.

4

Brand Strategy: Why Brand Is at the Forefront of Next-Generation CRM

Stephen F. Dull

Visa, Coca-Cola, Virgin, Sony, Nokia . . . everybody recognizes the value of a strong brand. But few companies manage their brand value as well as they should, and even fewer think of their brand as having much, if anything, to do with their creation and management of customer relationships, or CRM. It is becoming increasingly clear, however, that CRM is indispensable in creating a successful brand, one that can bring tangible benefits to the company and its stakeholders. To capture those benefits, brand managers first must expand their definition of *brand* and move beyond seeing it as merely a sign or logo that identifies a particular product or service.

Rather than playing the guessing game about what will grab the customer's imagination, brand managers must use more statistical measurement and analysis to direct their decisions. Instead of leaving channel management to the sales force, marketers must actively target the business-to-business (B2B) relationships that increasingly influence consumer brand choice. And rather than dismissing the call center as the purview of customer service, brand managers must do a better job of understanding how brand value can be strengthened or destroyed with every customer call.

MORE THAN A NAME

Many people instinctively associate brand with a name. To be sure, a company's name is an important element of its brand. However, a brand is far more than a name, icon, or slogan. It encapsulates *all* the customer's interactions with the company, its products, and its services. Marketers who ignore or minimize the important contribution these elements make to branding will fail to generate significant value from their branding efforts. For example, a company that prides itself on great products and prompt, courteous customer service, yet makes those customers slog through an inordinate list of complex options when they call its service center, is damaging its brand. Similarly, a company that continually fails to deliver goods when promised is undermining its advertising and marketing efforts to create a strong, positive brand.

It is quite evident that customer's broad conceptions about a company go a long way in determining how they receive and embrace that company's brand. The most successful companies in branding are those that create and deliver what we call the "customer delight experience." In this context, we can understand brand to equal the sum of everything a company says, everything it does, and how it says and does it. Put another way, brand encompasses the entire range of the company's products, services, behaviors, distribution channels, technologies, and processes.

All strong brands share three characteristics. First, they offer something better and different on a dimension that customers care about; in other words, the promise they make is differentiated from the competition's. Second, this promise is executed very consistently. And third, the brand promise is communicated consistently and persistently. A lesson in building a strong global brand, Wal-Mart has established its reputation on its promise to deliver the products that customers want at consistently low prices in a family-oriented shopping space where shoppers always feel welcome and are rarely disappointed. Most Wal-Mart shoppers would agree, the store lives up to its promise.

These three characteristics—the promise of something different or better, the consistent execution on that promise, and its effective communication to customers—call into question several other traditionally held beliefs about brand. Weeding them out is very difficult, but that's the only way that a strong brand can grow and flourish. We hereby pull each one up by its roots:

1. *Brand must be top-of-mind.* Probably no other assumption has cost as much money as the notion that to be successful, a brand must be top-of-mind. The bursting of the Internet bubble is only the most recent evidence that this singular focus on brand awareness can lead to disaster. Hundreds of millions in investments were eagerly poured into attempts to make customers aware of new brands. Marketers for emerging dot-coms were convinced that by capturing top-of-mind status, their companies could unseat incumbent competitors and flourish. As we know now, these efforts were misguided. The public's mere awareness of a brand is not sufficient to guarantee business success.

   Given that brand is *experience,* it has to show more than top-of-mind awareness to be successful. It has to be relevant to a target market willing to pay the price. It has to attract people to try it out at least once and then must be available for reuse or repeat purchase because it did bring such a good experience. In short, the brand has to build a base of loyal customers, emotionally and financially committed to repeat purchasing.

It is one thing for a brand to capture everyone's attention, quite another for a company to create the behavioral patterns and loyalty that make a brand a consistent success. If managers define brand as merely the name or product logo, they are likely to associate rising awareness with big-time success. Many will derive a false sense of brand strength from reports that the product has garnered a lot of attention. The broader definition of brand as the sum of the customer's experiences with the company will encourage that company to measure more of the experience than just the awareness factor. In the process, the company is much more likely to find opportunities to improve how customers experience its products and services.

Now-defunct Internet retailer eToys is one of the best examples of a company that pinned its hopes on generating widespread awareness, only to be undone by shoddy service and delivery that undermined customers' trust and loyalty. The company certainly did a phenomenal job of creating and reinforcing a unique position in consumers' minds through innovative advertising. However, its failure to meet critical customer needs—summed up most famously by its inability to deliver toys in time for Christmas 2000—contributed to increasingly negative customer experiences. The management at eToys realized the problem, but by then it was too late. Burned once, customers abandoned eToys, as did Wall Street shortly thereafter.

Wireless company Cingular would do well to learn from eToys' mistakes. The wireless phone service provider has enjoyed stunning success in building customer awareness of its brand in an extremely short period of time through a widespread and ambitious multimedia campaign to promote the brand's distinctive imagery. However, the company understands that this success can be undone quickly if it doesn't mind the rest of the house—that is, if customers receive uneven phone reception (which the company has little control over because all wireless companies use the same network) or are treated by customer service representatives in ways that contradict the friendly tone of Cingular's ads. Despite its initial success—of which Cingular can be proud—the company's hard work in brand building has only just begun.

2. *Advertising is the key to successful brand building.* Managers who hold firmly to the belief that top-of-mind awareness is the essence of brand will readily accept this proposition, again largely to their detriment. True, thanks to good advertising, a handful of companies have built strong brands: Absolut Vodka, for instance, has bought its way into the public awareness through a 20-year campaign of distinctive images. For those companies that spend huge sums on advertising while skimping on the quality of the customer's experience, however, the life of the brand will be brutally short.

Advertising is just one element of the brand experience—and a very small one at that. It is just one of many tools that innovative and broad-thinking companies use to build their brands. Starbucks uses almost no advertising, yet the company has established dominance in its industry, and it seems there is hardly a street corner or airport concourse in any major American city where the distinctive green and black logo is not in full view. Building on its strength in its home country, the company is expanding its reach to the rest of the world as well, and now has a significant presence in many countries in Europe, Asia, and the Middle East.

The Coca-Cola Company and PepsiCo spend similar amounts on advertising in North America, but Coca-Cola maintains its superior brand strength primarily by dominating the vending and fountain outlets. To a lesser extent, Coca-Cola shows superior execution in the grocery stores. This market reach is extended by the distinctive promise that the company has devised—namely, to put a Coca-Cola "within an arm's reach of the consumer" practically anywhere in the world. This promise has spearheaded Coca-Cola's focus on distribution, which is far superior to Pepsi's.

As these examples suggest, advertising is doubtlessly important, but it is only part of the company's overall effort in playing the brand value game. In the cases of Starbucks and Coca-Cola, advertising occupies a much smaller portion of the marketing budget and focus than many people realize. Similarly, New York–based TIAA-CREF is perhaps the largest financial services provider that nobody has heard of. The 80-year-old company manages more than $280 billion in assets and has a large base of extremely loyal customers. This loyalty has been built on a long history of reputable products, investment management expertise, excellent service, and stability—characteristics critical for companies that individuals and institutions trust to manage their money. The company only recently began to advertise to increase awareness of its strong brand among potential customers who are unfamiliar with the company.

3. *Brand must be consumer-driven.* The importance of listening to the consumer has, of late, been much in the news, to the point of becoming something of a marketer's mantra. Although that advice may work in some industries or with some products, the fact is that more and more consumer decisions are being made by channel customers or partners rather than by consumers themselves. For example, McDonald's serves Coca-Cola, not Pepsi, in its restaurants. Similarly, Wal-Mart customers looking for Whirlpool appliances will be disappointed; the retailer no longer carries that brand.

McDonald's and Wal-Mart are major brands themselves, each with an enormous marketing effort directed at consumers. But those consumers are increasingly restricted to making decisions in effect already made by others. As the marketing world grows more complex, the relationships between manufacturers and their channel partners have in many ways eclipsed the relationships between manufacturers and consumers. In other words, today's brand experiences (from the consumer's point of view) encompass myriad B2B relationships further back on the production and distribution side. Those B2B relationships are thus critical in building and sustaining brand value in the business-to-customer (B2C) arena. Ignoring or downplaying those B2B relationships can jeopardize even the best-laid plans and strategies devised by marketers.

4. *Marketing owns the customer.* This used to be the rule when marketers were the only ones talking to customers through traditional advertising channels. Now, however, that is no longer the case. All too often the marketing message hardly gets through to the customer. Instead, it's the customer service representative who owns the customer, and often that ownership amounts to something closer to taking the customer prisoner. Today's innovations in automated service technology—those infuriating telephone answering services that instruct the caller which number to press for this or that service—are symptomatic of the loss of marketing's control over communications with customers. As customers' experiences are increasingly determined by interactions with call centers and customer care representatives or through Web sites, it does not take many bad experiences to erode a customer's confidence in a brand and to chip away at the brand's value. Simply put, CRM is rapidly becoming the pivotal point for determining whether a brand is strong, weak, or something in between.

Consider, for example, the cable television service providers. If asked about their cable provider, rarely will customers express pleasure with the company's range of channels, digital services, or reception—the company's core offerings. Instead, customers will rail about the dreadful service they get from call center representatives. Remarkably, the same company's service may be loved in one city and hated in another—a result of the company's failure to upgrade its facilities consistently as it enters new markets (generally through acquisition of another company). Despite having good products, the company's brand is defined by the negative experiences its customers encounter when dealing with its call center—which demonstrates how powerfully CRM is linked to brand.

Most B2B companies, however, say they recognize the importance of maintaining a high-quality relationship with long-term customers. Building and enhancing those relationships, they know, has become the province of the sales force and the customer care representatives, not the marketers. Moreover, they recognize that CRM technology helps make people more efficient and effective at enhancing the customer's overall experience with the brand.

Strong Brands Pay Real Dividends

Ultimately, the primary reason to care about strong branding is that it increases shareholder returns. Several studies point to the validity of this assertion. Most recently, a study of the consumer goods industry by the Marketing Science Institute found that brand value is strongly tied to shareholder returns. Furthermore, best-practice companies are including these statistics in their ongoing measures of brand health.

Brand competition within a category provides supporting evidence as well. Although PepsiCo and Coca-Cola had almost equal sales in 2000 (approximately

$20.5 billion each), Coca-Cola—with its greater global brand strength—enjoyed a market capitalization almost twice that of PepsiCo in the same year: $112 billion versus $66 billion.[1] The reasons for this differential are complex; in general, however, they boil down to the fact that a strong brand not only increases a company's revenue, it also contributes to greater capital efficiency.

Increased Revenues

It's a fact that companies with strong brands typically command higher prices. Although Toyota and General Motors use the same California assembly line to make identical vehicles—the Corolla and the Prizm, respectively—Toyota can charge more for the Corolla. Same parts, same assembly, same cars, but the difference is the value of Toyota's brand. Over time, consumer experience has been much more consistently positive with Toyota than with GM, and the strength of that experience gives Toyota tremendous pricing leverage. Given that a 1 percent increase in price can translate into as much as a 10 percent increase in profit, Toyota's brand strength easily contributes to greater shareholder value.

Likewise, Sony leads its competitors in the electronics business, not only because consumers want Sony products, but also because they are more willing to pay premium prices for those products. Sony's products carry a price premium of 10 to 50 percent over those from other manufacturers, despite sharing many common internal components. The difference is that Sony's brand conveys higher levels of quality and reliability than competing brands today. In cases where the products of two competitors are identical or nearly so, it is clear that the customer's experience has to include the sense of increased status and self-assurance for having purchased the higher-priced item.

Even with commodities, where one might expect less pricing differential, the power of a good brand—that is, the sum of all the customer's experiences with that brand—can be seen in the bottom-line results. The best-performing brands in paper, steel, cement, and chemicals, for instance, extract price premiums—sometimes in market share, sometimes in providing less discounting than the competition or discounting less frequently. DuPont's products dominate in their categories, even though substitutes are offered at cheaper prices. Some customers are always willing to pay a higher price for the brand they want, no matter what price incentives are proffered by lower-priced competitors. That behavior translates into increased revenues and ultimately into greater benefits for shareholders.

Higher prices are not the only factor in increased revenues. Customers typically purchase strong brands more frequently and in greater quantities. Although the raw numbers vary by industry—obviously customers buy soap products more frequently than they purchase automobiles—the *pattern* does not vary from industry to industry: Strong brands benefit from both the quality and quantity of transactions with customers. It may be blindingly obvious, but Coca-Cola is so far ahead of PepsiCo because *more* consumers drink Coca-Cola *more frequently.* With its dominance of the fountain market, Coca-Cola ensures that a greater number of consumers have more opportunities to select Coca-Cola than any other brand.

Companies with strong brands also can attract better partners and cobrands. When a strong partner such as McDonald's chooses to serve Coca-Cola over Pepsi (or any other soft-drink manufacturer), the sales results are clearly reflected in both companies' sales revenues, much to the shareholders' delight. As consumer research in several categories demonstrates, cobranded offerings generate higher consumer propensity to purchase and a higher willingness to pay top dollar. Thus, strong brands do a much better job of attracting strong partners. Home Depot, to take another example, has a history of choosing only the best brands to put on its shelves. Those brands in turn benefit tremendously from Home Depot's scale and visibility. Likewise, Microsoft has the luxury of deciding which software companies it wishes to partner with to create new products and, eventually, greater shareholder value.

Similarly, companies with strong brands attract better employees, capable of generating more and better ideas with potentially higher revenues. A 1999 Accenture study to determine how CRM capabilities affect performance revealed that companies with the strongest brands tended to have more high-performing employees and that the strongest brand within a given company also was supported by the most capable people. Microsoft, for example, looks at approximately 25,000 U.S. graduates in computer science each year, identifies the top 8000, and after additional screening, invites about 2600 of them for an on-campus interview. From this pool, the company selects, on average, 800 graduates to visit its headquarters in Redmond, Washington, and offers jobs to about 500 of them. Typically, 400 accept the offers, and Microsoft ends up with roughly the top 2 percent of the nation's graduates.

Finally, it is also evident that companies with strong brands can more easily reach beyond their traditional market sectors and be successful at undertaking new ventures. Since most strong brands have an elasticity that allows them to credibly relay information about a new product or service—witness the Virgin brand, whose reach extends from airlines to recorded music to wine retailing—customers are more willing to try those products and, even more important, forgive mistakes. Wal-Mart recently entered the supermarket sector and quickly became the largest grocery retailer in the United States. IBM parlayed its strong brand reputation in office equipment and computers into a profitable consulting business. Online auctioneer eBay has moved increasingly away from collectibles and created a new space that is a marketplace for just about everything. Conran has extended its hip home store experience into equally hip restaurants, and Samsung is extending its global brand strength for cell phones to market its electronics. Even though not every extended venture is assured of success, the chances of succeeding are significantly increased by starting with a strong brand.

Greater Capital Efficiency

As we have seen, strong brands have greater success at generating demand than do their weaker counterparts. Given that its customer base is more loyal and more committed, a strong brand can elicit a response with practically any marketing stimulus. For years Pillsbury has dominated the profitable category of refrigerated dough. The company uses well-conceived marketing campaigns to its loyal consumers, who typically are eager to try new products when they are introduced. This loyalty and willingness to experiment have kept competitors, both national brands and private labels, at bay. Although consumers will use the private label, when it comes to trying a new product, they usually opt for the brand they know and trust.

Such a scale advantage translates into an efficiency advantage: The larger the brand, the more it can spread out its marketing costs. Whether the target is 10 million or 1 million customers, the available media—direct-mail campaigns, in-store coupons, TV advertising, and so forth—largely determine the cost of reaching them. Obviously, larger brands can reach the same customers more efficiently than can smaller brands. In grocery retailing, for example, where gross margins are thin, chains must have a large market to be competitive on marketing costs. A store circular placed in a local newspaper costs the same whether the chain has 20 or 120 stores. Spreading those advertising costs over 120 stores, however, is more economical than putting the burden on just 20 of them. Distribution and other costs act in similar ways. It is not uncommon to read that a grocery retailer is looking for scale in a new market or that it has decided to withdraw from a market when it fails to achieve scale. The grocery retailer knows that it is more capital-efficient to play big or not at all.

OVERLOOKED OPPORTUNITIES

To create a strong brand, a company has to go through the obvious steps of making a distinctive promise, executing well against that promise, and providing consistent brand communication over time. There are, however, three other areas in which opportunities are often overlooked—namely, brand measurement and analysis, treating B2B relationships as important brand components, and aligning and improving execution.

Brand Measurement and Analysis

Marketing managers who take the traditional view of brand strength (that *brand* is the name and the extent to which that name or logo commands a high place in the customer's awareness) are less likely to be open to the kinds of metrics that go beyond the traditional measures of awareness. These are the measures of the customer's total experience with the brand. But these measures are exceedingly difficult to quantify and even harder to analyze and apply to decision making. Many marketers, unfortunately, are not trained to do this sort of analysis, nor do they have much interest in it or appreciation for what it can do for improvements in decision making.

Companies that hire outside firms to do brand measurement for them often don't analyze the data well and end up underusing brand data simply because marketers don't understand how to use it for decision making. Or they understand the value, but after years of staff reductions have no time or personnel to do the analysis. In such cases, those skills are largely lost. From long experience we can say that almost without exception, the brands that are the strongest in a given category are the ones that collect the relevant data, measure the most carefully, derive the deepest insights, and use the results to make the most informed decisions.

To capture opportunities using such analytics, managers first need to assemble the brand facts about their company and its competitors—for example, in pricing, frequency, and size of transactions; in strength of partnerships; and in cobranding and brand extensions. Next, they must set forth a clear comparison between their company and the competition, noting differences that exist and in which areas. Usually this analysis reveals rather quickly that the necessary facts about one's own company are not readily available, much less facts about a competing brand. Without this information, however, it is next to impossible to determine where brand value can be leveraged.

An extremely helpful device for pointing out differences between one's own brand and those of competitors is called the *marketing funnel*. Essentially it places customers in various groups according to the depth of their commitment to the brand. At the top is the widest-ranging group, those customers who have, say, only a passing awareness of the brand. As the funnel narrows, there is a smaller group of customers who are extremely loyal and represent a highly concentrated value stream for the brand. This heuristic, or discovery, activity can help managers see in vivid form how their brand stacks up against the competition on the scale of customer awareness versus deep loyalty. The benefits of this exercise are immediate: The analysis reveals weaknesses that are unique to each brand, each company, and each market. Brand X may generate a great deal of customer awareness, but very little willingness on the customer's part to try the product. Brand Y may generate relatively little customer awareness, but a tremendous amount of loyalty among those who do recognize it. The former needs to work on encouraging customer trial, while the latter must ramp up its advertising and promotional activities.

Even more important, this analysis can reveal brand strength relative to that of the competitions' brands in such a way that suggests how a new marketing program can unclog a brand bottleneck and release the flow of value to the company and its shareholders. Let it be understood, however, that this kind of analysis requires a lot of work, both in gathering the needed information about customers' attitudes and experiences and in diagnosing problems in the marketing mix. Odds are good that other companies in the same category are already engaging in similar analyses and are that much further ahead.

B2B Customers as a Brand Value Opportunity

A lot of attention has been paid of late to the consumer or end user as the primary focus for marketers. Hence, the consumer is the object of much research and surveying, including details on purchasing habits, price points, household education levels and incomes, frequency of purchases, and so forth. For most marketing managers, this consumer's experiences are the most important in establishing a strong brand.

Few companies, however, recognize that if brand encompasses the total experience, then the rule applies as equally to business customers as to end users. The examples of Citibank and McDonald's illustrate that B2B customers increasingly are making decisions for the end user on which brand will be available. As a result, it's becoming more critical for marketers at a B2B supplier to understand how its intermediate customers view their relationship to the supplier. One easy first step in this direction is for marketers to receive and read material on the work being done by their company's market research department for the sales and customer service functions (e.g., customer service and satisfaction surveys of channel partners) in addition to poring over consumer research data. In reviewing such surveys, marketers will be able to better understand their company's relative brand strengths and weaknesses among its influential business customers, how they compare with those of its competitors, and their impact on the brand among consumers. They then can begin to identify ways in which improving the brand relationship with B2B partners will translate into a stronger brand at the consumer level. Although traditionally not part of the marketer's job, improving the B2B brand experience will certainly benefit the company's *B2C* brand efforts and add to overall brand value.

Aligning and Executing

Given that the brand is the fulfillment of the promise and that the customer has to have a positive experience with all aspects of the company, then it stands to reason that aligning all the elements in the life cycle of the brand is essential to success. Once managers understand the brand promise, they need to make sure the organization as a whole delivers consistently against that promise. In most organizations, those responsible for making the promise and setting the strategy are *not* those whose job it is to deliver on it. How many marketers or brand executives really have a chance of influencing what goes on in a customer call center? This is why alignment and consistency are so important.

Perhaps it's simply a matter of writing a script for the call center representative or of instructing retail employees on how to dress or how to interact with customers on the sales floor. What we call *brand manners* determines in large part how customers experience the brand—everything the company "says and does." These recommendations fall primarily in the province of CRM, and everyone in the organization has to take responsibility for seeing that they are carried out. Does the brand promise convenience, yet the phone recording keeps cycling people through more telephone menus? Does the brand stand for premium quality, yet marketers send out notices to customers about discount prices and second-rate models? Does the B2B side promise excellent account service, yet the sales technology is focused only on productivity? If so, there are major problems in alignment that managers must correct.

Opportunities for improving the execution of the promise are everywhere: perhaps overlap in services, inconsistencies in delivery, miscommunications between designers and producers, and the like. CRM decisions should appear at the top of the

VISA'S COMMITMENT TO BRAND
KEEPS IT IN THE TOP TIER

Marketers and brand experts around the globe consider Visa one of the world's top 10 best-managed brands. But far from resting on its laurels, the company continuously reassesses and rejuvenates its brand strategy to stay in the top tier. In the words of Caroline McNally, executive vice president of Global Brand Management at Visa International: "The best time to evolve a brand strategy is when a brand is in a position of strength."

And the brand certainly is strong. Visa has a share of the global payment card market that surpasses all other payment systems combined—despite the fact that, to many people's surprise, Visa interacts with consumers only through its member banks. Visa is a global association of 21,000 member banks which sign up merchants, issue the Visa cards, set the rates, and effectively "own" the relationships with cardholders. Visa adds value to consumers in part because of its strong brand, a brand that stands for global acceptance, reliability, security and convenience.

Brand Strategy

In 1995, the association recognized the opportunity to better integrate its brand strategy with its corporate and product strategies and embarked on a rigorous program of qualitative and quantitative research to assess consumers' perceptions of the brand and identify the roots of its strength. This strategic assessment addressed the following key questions:

1. What attributes does the Visa brand own, functionally and emotionally?
2. How does the Visa brand differ from both traditional and emerging competitors' brands? What is the strategic intent? Where are the gaps and vulnerabilities?
3. What are the brand's strengths and limitations? Can the brand support more products and services within the payment category—or even outside the payment category? If it can, does extending the products and services fit in with the corporate strategy? How can Visa address the limitations—and build on the strengths—to create future growth?

Single-Brand Strategy

The research revealed two key learnings that were integral in setting Visa's long-term single-brand strategy:

*   In consumers' minds, Visa was perceived as a global or universal brand with single-product functionality (i.e., wherever consumers live in the world, they view Visa as either a credit or a debit facility).
*   Consumers had the expectation that Visa, because of its association with reliability, security, and convenience, could be more than it is. Clearly, the opportunity for expanding the brand within the payment category—backed by a strong products and communication program—was Visa's to capture. However, while Visa learned that consumers would accept some extension *outside* the payment category, such a move would not be aligned with corporate strategy.

Building on these key learnings, Visa took its strategy to the next level. Under the umbrella of the brand, the association set out to take Visa from being "the world's best credit (or debit) card" to the "world's best way to pay." To achieve that, however, the company needed to be confident about how far it could go with new products and services—how far it could stretch the brand—before it would disconnect with consumers and the corporate strategy. Applying the single-brand strategy allows Visa to use its existing strengths to remain relevant in established and emerging markets by ensuring that future products and services link to the Visa name and imagery. This means delivering on the four objectives of the strategy:

1. *Using the existing strength of the Visa brand.* Virtually all new products, services, and programs use the strength of the brand and retain the Visa name.

2. *Delivering superior consumer and merchant experiences.* This is key to keeping the Visa brand promise. It means ensuring that products work seamlessly and reliably, are accepted where consumers would expect to use them, and that the customer experience is consistent at all points of interaction.

3. *Enabling new product and service introductions for Visa and its member banks.* Ensure, for example, that the branding system is appropriate for current and future programs.

4. *Consistently applying current brand strengths to maximize opportunities in new payment channels and payment environments.* Innovation for innovation's sake isn't what's relevant to consumers. Visa must carry the same meanings and advantages in both the physical and virtual worlds.

Visa's challenges now lie mainly in the area beyond cards, ensuring that the brand continues to thrive in the new and emerging channels of payment such as mobile phones, set-top boxes, and personal digital assistants. In these highly personalized environments, trust and reliability won't be enough. Visa knows that building deeper relationships with consumers requires the establishment of an emotionally positioned brand to which consumers can relate in this highly personalized marketplace.

Rigorous Review and Measurement

Visa recognizes that brand strength in the present is no guarantee of strength in the future. To ensure that the brand remains strong, relevant, and dynamic in the changing payment environment, Visa regularly conducts a robust, disciplined, business-focused review of the brand via the following:

- *Global Brand Monitor Study.* A quarterly, quantitative survey of 14,000 cardholders in 21 core countries that measures important brand attributes such as "best overall card," "for everyone," "global yet local." To ensure the survey remains relevant, Visa maintains a close understanding of "Brand Health," the ability of the Visa brand to create and sustain valuable growth opportunities for member banks and the ability of Visa to be relevant in new payment environments.

- *Brand Value.* An initiative that directly links the value of the brand to the bottom line and financially proves the brand's importance in achieving the business objectives of the company. The concept of brand value is what Visa describes as the "$1 + 1 = 3$ equation," wherein a member bank's brand combined with the Visa brand creates more value than either brand standing alone. Consequently, Visa's commitment to understand the value of the brand to its members' business endeavors—and measuring and monitoring the value—is consistent and ongoing.

Conclusion

Visa recognizes that "everything communicates," whether it's directly related to payment or tangential—removing a card from a wallet, making a purchase at the point of sale, standing in line at a bank branch, withdrawing cash from an ATM, reporting a lost card to a customer service representative, or paying a monthly bill. Visa manages its brand by first understanding what it stands for in cardholders' hearts and minds.

As Visa continuously strives to understand, enhance, and protect the Visa brand, the evolution of its brand strategy is constant. On an ongoing basis, the association monitors and assesses its brand positioning, the value the brand adds to the business, and the consumer-facing brand attributes it possesses to ensure the brand remains fresh and relevant in the future.

managers' agenda as they weigh the costs between preference and profit: Is it worth another $10 million in the yearly personnel budget to have a live person answer the customer's call on the second ring? Should another customer call center be built and staffed to handle an expected increase in calls once a new product is released? These are not the sorts of questions that marketers have typically faced in the past, but they are on the increase today. To ignore them is to risk the value of the brand and the marginalizing of marketing's role in brand management. Good execution means getting a clear picture of the employees on the front lines, those most likely to come into contact with customers face-to-face. If their brand manners are not superior, chances are the customer will register some dissatisfaction. If employees do not understand the brand value and their role in determining what kind of experience the customer has, it's a safe bet that the brand will falter. Consider the success that Disney has had in creating great experiences for guests at its theme parks, where every employee undergoes extensive training in brand manners. Ritz-Carlton Company recognized this simple principle long ago and has been on the forefront of hiring and training people to represent its brand (which is wonderfully summed up by the company's motto, "We are ladies and gentlemen serving ladies and gentlemen").

Managers who have trouble gathering the facts about call center behavior, sales complaints, and other such metrics might try calling the center themselves and talking to a service or sales representative. It could prove to be a lesson in humility, as well as a first step toward making real change at the company that would increase brand value. Similarly, on the personnel side, the human resources manager might conduct employee satisfaction surveys, examine each person on the extent of his or her knowledge about the brand and about customer relationships. Chances are excellent that in doing so, managers will discover major areas for improvement.

CONCLUSION

A broad definition of brand, at first blush, can appear to be a nightmare for marketers. In effect, the definition tells marketing managers, "Although you are responsible and accountable for the company's brand in the marketplace, you have formal control over only one small factor that contributes to the brand—and the smallest and least influential one at that."

On the other hand, by understanding brand in this way, marketers can move past their preoccupation with advertising and consumer awareness-building activities and start seeing branding from a much more holistic perspective. They can begin to use a more complete set of metrics to measure brand value (and compare the value of their own brand to that of competitors), and they can work with their colleagues in sales and customer service to ensure consistency in messaging and experience for critical channel partners and customers interacting with the call center.

An expanded definition of brand also makes it clear that CRM plays a critical role in the branding process and that activities formerly considered outside the scope of a company's brand are actually the principal contributors to the brand's strength or weakness. As a result, companies must fully understand their brand promise—and how they intend to execute that promise—before committing to building specific CRM capabilities.

One final note: Building a strong brand is only the beginning of the game. To maintain the strength of the brand, a company must be vigilant in its attention to all aspects of the customer experience. Activities such as constant measuring and ana-lyzing data from customers' responses, comparing the brand against competitors' products and services, making the necessary adjustments in corporate alignment—these are not one-time actions, but must be performed consistently and repeatedly as long as the brand has life and value.

5

Channel Strategy: Avoiding Channel Conflicts

Paul F. Nunes, Bruce W. Bendix, and John B. Goodman

Ｎew technologies bring new opportunities to channel designers, marketers, and business strategists. From catalog selling, which grew out of improved rail and postal technologies, through today's Internet and wireless shopping opportunities, companies continually face an array of new methods and choices for reaching customers. Yet many suppliers fail to exploit new channel opportunities for fear of creating conflict with their existing channels.

Such fears are far from groundless. Consider clothier Levi Strauss & Company. In 1998, it sought to introduce a new channel option for its end consumers by taking advantage of the emerging capabilities of the Web. It unveiled a direct-sales site that offered a much larger selection of jeans than most of its 3000 retailers. And the company prohibited its traditional retailers from selling Levi's products on their own Web sites.

Though online sales were brisk, the company quickly terminated the program. As a spokesperson explained, "We needed to get closer to our retailers. Several said they'd like to sell our products on their Web sites. Some [retailers] questioned the strategy of limiting online sales exclusively to Levis.com." Today, customers can buy Levi's jeans online, but only through retailer sites—once limited to traditional Levi's retailers JC Penney and Macy's, but now expanded to include more than 40 online sellers.

Levi Strauss denied being pressured by its retailers. But other suppliers clearly have been. A large home-improvement retailer once told its suppliers in a letter, "You can understand that [we] may be hesitant to do business with . . . competitors." And a spokesperson for a leading mass merchandiser once publicly declared, "If a supplier chooses to be a retailer, they will become a competitor." Many manufacturers have received similar warnings from their channel partners while exploring or initiating a new channel option.

Home-appliance maker Maytag once announced plans to sell direct, but scrapped the project when dealers objected. Rubbermaid had a similar experience with its plastic products for the home. Barbie.com once quietly began selling online, but quickly retreated and now sells only through links to retailer sites. According to a Forrester Research study, 74 percent of the manufacturers surveyed reported expecting to see channel conflict arise as a result of the emergence of the Internet. As a consequence of these past experiences and the stories told of them, most suppliers today hesitate to move into the uncertain and at times hostile environment of channel change, regardless of the opportunities new technologies may offer.

Finding conflict avoidance at the heart of many companies' channel strategies is not surprising in light of the evidence. Yet these strategies often disappoint because they focus primarily on minor support of existing processes—for example, online product information—rather than on leveraging technology to create new offerings and capture new markets. But there is another way.

CHOOSING TO CHANGE

Most suppliers can envision the opportunities new technologies present in the form of new channel designs—increased geographic penetration, market share growth, and higher profit margins. And many can go so far as to articulate these goals as their strategic direction or intent, only to freeze when faced with the conflicts that arise from acting on these intentions.

But such paralysis can be overcome. With the right tools, suppliers can identify the sources of channel conflict in their industries and use this knowledge to devise business-expanding strategies that do not unduly threaten the economic interests of their existing channels.

One strategy less threatening than pure online selling is targeting a small subsegment of customers who are reachable only online. For example, Timex sells watches online to a customer segment who wants more variety than most of its retailers can provide. By selling only at the manufacturer's suggested retail price—higher than most retailers charge *and* more than most retailer shoppers are willing to pay—Timex reaches a segment it could not easily target in the physical channel, and it does so without significant impact on its existing sales channels.

Another conflict-mitigating strategy is to introduce different product lines specifically targeted to draw on the capabilities of the new channel. FranklinCovey, a global professional-services firm, leveraged online interactivity to introduce its Design Your Own planner pages, binders, and cases. Customers find they can create a customized planning system tailored to their needs and have it delivered in less than two weeks, an offering not well suited to delivery through the traditional channel.

A similar approach is to save new product launches for the new channel. Toyota did this by selling its battery-and-gas-powered hybrid vehicle, Prius, online. Because production was limited, it wanted distribution to be as well. Dealers responded favorably because they retained the fulfillment portion of the transactions, and Toyota was able to generate a three-month waiting list for the car shortly after initiating the program. Volvo followed a similar strategy by creating an early online launch of the Volvo S60.

What these companies have in common is that they made the move to introduce new channel options by first understanding their channel dynamics, then conceiving of new ways to organize and group channel activities to create value down the line and thus overcome conflict. The combined experience of the authors and a broad range of experts and practitioners in channel change strategy has led to the development of two analytic tools that can help suppliers do the same—evaluate their options and exploit opportunities to create innovative sources of channel value. The first is a *channel map,* which helps managers understand and articulate the path of change. The second is the *channel conflict strategy matrix,* which informs channel strategy choice based on critical aspects of the current channel environment. Together, these tools enable channel designers to overcome channel conflict and restructure channel roles.

MAPPING THE WAY

The channel map offers a bird's-eye view of who's who and who does what in the channel. In effect, there are two maps:

- A *status quo map* identifies existing channel participants and the topography of their existing relationships. This map lays out where a company stands in relation to its existing channels and participants, and it is something every organization should create before evaluating new opportunities.

- A *future map* incorporates likely change scenarios and new relationships, roles, and interactions in the channel. This map reflects the company's vision of the future its channels.

By comparing the two maps, companies can identify where the channel-change battle lines will be drawn and where channel conflict will be most intense.

Both maps are plotted using the same coordinates:

- Customer segments served
- Basic channel functions: inform, interact, transact, deliver, and service the customer, performed either exclusively or cooperatively by traditional channel participants—suppliers, wholesalers, distributors, and retailers—particularly in the newly conceived channels, by brokers, lenders, and others

How are the maps created? First by documenting existing channels—the customer segments served and the partners employed in delivering channel value. The process is, however, not as simple in practice as it might sound in theory. Uncertainty and disagreements often arise when companies try to determine the segments currently served and identify all the players in the channel chain. After defining exist-

EXHIBIT 5-1.   Old automotive channel map (illustrative only).

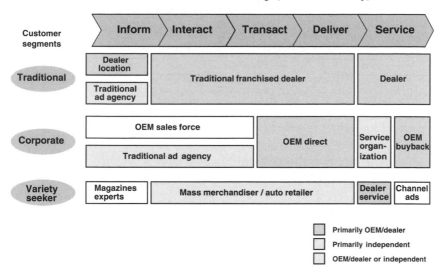

ing channels, to indicate their relative importance, the boxes on the map can be sized based on a third dimension, such as volume of customers or profitability in the channel.

Two hypothetical channel maps from the perspective of an original equipment manufacturer (OEM) in the automobile industry serve as a model (see Exhibits 5-1 and 5-2).

EXHIBIT 5-2.   New automotive channel map (illustrative only).

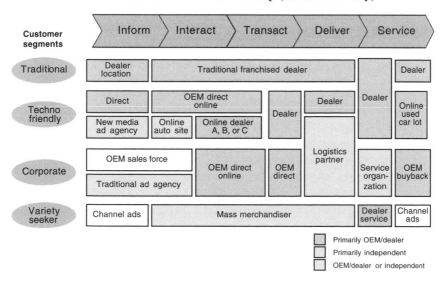

The status quo ("old") map shows who performs the five core functions for each of three original customer segments—traditional, corporate, and variety seeker. Shading denotes whether the channel participant is related to the supplier or is third-party-controlled.

The future ("new") map looks different because two things change—customer segments and process activities. Some of the new segments comprise customers who were difficult to reach through old channels but are now accessible through new technologies (e.g., those who were geographically unreachable or who demanded prices lower than traditional channels could deliver). Other new segments are ones made entirely possible only by new technologies such as the virtual aggregation of inventory and services—for example, segments defined by life events (Weddingchannel.com) or purchase intent (Move.com). This part of the map also reflects today's vision of accessible, profitable microsegments, so it generally has a significantly larger number of segments than the old status quo map.

The future map also reflects changes in process activities. The rapidly declining cost of communications and transactions, driven by technology, creates a new organizational logic where channel structures are influenced more by information flows than by inventory locations, geographies, and physical flows. These changes prompt companies to rethink core channel processes and are breaking apart the traditional wholesaler, distributor, and retailer roles. New process definitions and new channel roles reflect the disaggregation of current channel activities and their reaggregation into transformed channels.

MANAGING CONFLICT STRATEGICALLY

Moving from the old map to the new is not likely to be conflict-free. The more customer segments that are added, the greater the likelihood that the new channels will ruthlessly cannibalize the old. New segments do not always represent new customers obtained from market growth; often they represent customers culled from the old segments. This cannibalization, with the associated loss of revenue to the supporting channels, is one of the major sources of channel-change conflict.

Changes in processes require changes in channel participants. As channels specialize and form new roles, old players face continual threats, at least until their place in the new order is clear and secure.

Clearly, making the transition from the first to the second map gives rise to channel conflict. But proper analysis and appropriate strategies can go far toward minimizing the amount of conflict and its economic destructiveness. To aid this type of analysis and decision making, we have created the channel conflict strategy matrix. Companies use the matrix to assess the forces and opportunities for change in their industries vis-à-vis each existing channel and to quickly identify optimal change strategies (Exhibit 5-3).

The matrix shows the interplay between market power and channel added value.

EXHIBIT 5-3.   Channel conflict strategy matrix.

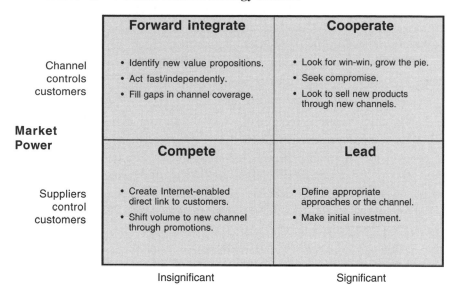

	Insignificant	Significant
Channel controls customers	**Forward integrate** • Identify new value propositions. • Act fast/independently. • Fill gaps in channel coverage.	**Cooperate** • Look for win-win, grow the pie. • Seek compromise. • Look to sell new products through new channels.
Suppliers control customers	**Compete** • Create Internet-enabled direct link to customers. • Shift volume to new channel through promotions.	**Lead** • Define appropriate approaches or the channel. • Make initial investment.

Market Power (vertical axis)

- Market power is a function of where customer influence resides—with the supplier or with the channel.
- Channel added value measures how much worth the channel creates for the customer, beyond what the manufacturer provides.

Market power rests with the traditional channel when channel intermediaries such as retailers can switch customers between competing suppliers usually by adjusting factors such as price, location in store, and displays. Channel density is one key determinant. For example, if four or five channel organizations represent 80 percent of a supplier's volume, the channel has significant power, both as a group and within each organization, and often can exert unilateral effect on upwards of 40 percent of sales. However, if 80 percent of volume resides with 30 or 40 organizations, the channel as a whole has relatively less power and is less likely to stage a successful, unified retaliation.

In addition, the power of a channel is considered low when customers place more value on manufacturers' brands than on the channel—such as is the case with top supplier brands like Nike, whose Air Jordan basketball shoes are in great demand among consumers. Market power also can result from advantageous legal contracts or government regulations. In some states, for example, regulations prohibit carmakers from selling directly to customers, giving dealers tremendous power over their OEM suppliers.

Assessing market power can be challenging, and some suppliers have gotten it horribly wrong. For example, Coca-Cola and PepsiCo believed that their strong brand image in the United Kingdom gave them significant market power. But Sains-bury, the leading U.K. grocer, competed successfully with both giants through its generic, privately labeled cola, causing both to lose market share. These suppliers seriously underestimated the market power of their channel.

The channel added-value dimension is high in the following situations:

- The channel provides valued services to the customer that the supplier does not, such as delivery or quality control.
- The channel enjoys a strong relationship with the customer, as do trusted retailers such as Macy's or Bloomingdale's.
- Customers cherish immediate access to a broad range of products. This explains the high channel added value of such large, multicategory retailers as Toys 'R' Us and Home Depot.

FOUR CORE STRATEGIES

Once a company determines market power and channel value for each existing chan-nel, the matrix becomes a framework for strategic thinking:

- Pointing to the safest and most effective strategy for each of four potential combinations of channel dimensions
- Showing where to fight out conflicts and where to mediate or avoid them

Compete

If market power rests with the supplier, and the added value of the channel is low, the supplier's best strategy is to compete with the channel. Consider the airlines. Faced with significant financial losses and a need to lower costs, they have continually reduced travel agent commissions while actively investing in electronic ticketing and supporting Web travel sites such as Travelocity.com and Expedia.com. All the while they have been building and promoting their own direct sites as well. They have gone so far as to advertise to consumers that the lowest fares are likely to be found online.

While travel agent trade groups have actively protested these moves, in 2000, American, Continental, Delta, Northwest and United banded together to form a low-price online selling site called Orbitz.com. Built partly to ward off third-party sellers such as Priceline.com, a leading name-your-own-price travel site, and partly to improve access to tickets online, Orbitz has become one of the leading sources for low-cost tick-ets on the Web. The penultimate battle between the channels occurred in March 2002 when, pressured by a business loss of $1.22 billion dollars in 2001, Delta cut commis-sions to travel agents nearly entirely. An airline analyst at a leading investment com-pany referred to this as an effort to separate "order takers" from "order makers."

Forward Integrate

When the traditional channel holds great market power, yet the value it adds is low, suppliers should consider invading the channel to increase its capacity for value creation. The supplier must create an innovative offering that the regular channel cannot duplicate and thus forestall possible conflict.

In 1998, Gateway defied the conventional wisdom that PC retailing was a dead end by launching its country stores concept, becoming the first major manufacturer to sell PCs through retail showrooms. These showroom stores have all the traditional display models and sales help, but none of the inventory. Products are ordered on location through the Web, and many services are delivered on-site. At one point, this strategy enabled Gateway to sell an average of four non-PC items—including training, Internet service, financing, and solution bundles—for every PC sold. This has been a critical enabler of its core strategy to sell "beyond the box."

Lead

Sometimes the traditional channel's added value is high, but the channel itself has little overall market power. This frequently occurs when an offering requires significant geographic coverage or adaptation or close customer contact. The result is channel fragmentation—for example, the selling of flowers through local florists and the other prevalent uses of added-value resellers. Fragmentation is a challenge for suppliers because it makes it difficult for the participants to agree on and implement new technologies and processes that can serve the customer more effectively.

In these cases, the supplier must take the lead, driving change to improve the channel. There is usually little threat of retaliation because the channel providers are too disorganized to put up a single front of resistance. But more important, resistance is slight because the supplier's moves are usually seen as being in the best interests of all parties involved.

One company that chose to lead its partners through channel change is Cisco Systems. It created a significant Web presence early on, and though it does sell some items directly to registered customers, its Web presence always has been primarily focused on providing assistance and coordination between its vast array of distributors and value-adding resellers, itself, and the customers. Visitors may perceive the online channel as owned and run by Cisco, but the independent channel partners are major users of the system and do the lion's share of the fulfillment work for the offerings presented there. In addition, the site provides online technical support and customer chat, helping Cisco's channel partners by creating a more highly valued brand and by off-loading some of their customer-care responsibilities to the manufacturer.

Ace Hardware, a dealer-owned cooperative, took a slightly different approach. It also led channel change, and as a result boosted the performance of its member stores, by going online. But instead of focusing on a single Ace Hardware site that would centralize online activity, it partnered with OurHouse.com to create Web sites for its many member franchises, free of charge to the individual stores. In addition, OurHouse put kiosks in more than 2000 Ace outlets, allowing in-store customers to research and buy more than 22,000 items typically not stocked. All the stores share the profits.

Both approaches not only greatly improved the value proposition to the customer, they also kept the focus of the solution on the existing channel.

EXHIBIT 5-4.   Strategy-based marketing policy.

Approach	Pricing	Product	Placement	Promotion
Disintermediate	Below channel price	No need for new products, but possible	Create and encourage entirely new channels	Promote new channel vigorously to reduce retaliation
Forward integrate	As appropriate to new value proposition	Increase offerings to improve value proposition	Take control of more channel activities to perform them better	Focus promotion on new value proposition distinctions to avoid conflict
Lead	Determine jointly with channel	Leverage current channels' selection	Introduce hybrid of new and best of old channel components	Cobrand new channel with current channels
Cooperate	At or above current channel price	Offer exclusive products in each channel	Design new channel with new and old channel partners	Create new brands as necessary to protect old; target ads to new segments

Cooperate

The greatest potential for debilitating conflict arises when the current channel is adding substantial value and it also has significant market power. Here, channel players view themselves as the equals of their suppliers. This compels suppliers to avoid serious channel redesign, thereby avoiding unwanted conflict and likelihood of forced compromises.

But it doesn't have to be that way. Suppliers can look to any one of myriad ways to cooperate with their channel to achieve growth for both parties. Compromise can lead to win-win situations and important benefits for the supplier and the channel. Several manufacturers have compromised creatively with their traditional channels to grow their online businesses with little conflict. Volkswagen AG, for example, got around the enormous channel power of its dealers by limiting its online selling to only special colors and models. It started by selling Beetles in Internet-only colors ("vapor blue" and "reflex yellow") and followed by limiting the sales of its eGeneration edition Golf to online orders.

Companies with large portfolios of products can often reach happy compromises with their channels simply by limiting the number of products sold online. For example, L'Oréal of France, a maker of premium beauty products, created a Web site that sells only its lower-priced brands. Procter & Gamble, also a cosmetics maker, took another approach—selling custom-made cosmetics on its Reflect.com site, effectively avoiding conflict with its traditional prepackaged lines Cover Girl and Oil of Olay.

Other ways in which suppliers cooperate with equally powerful channels range from hosting a manufacturer's product information site with built-in dealer locators and links to using the Internet as the backbone of a collaborative forecasting and planning system.

Implementing any of the four strategies described requires not just new players and processes, but changes to marketing strategy's core components as well (Exhibit 5-4).

CONCLUSION

A major contribution of the matrix is that it reveals more strategic choices than most managers believe exist. In their confusion and anxiety, many executives see only two options in applying new technology to their distribution strategies—disintermediate the channel or do nothing. The matrix lays out new possibilities, especially by presenting strategies focused on leading or cooperating.

The map and matrix are tools that offer companies a way to gauge technology's impact on channels and show how to change channel architecture to capture maximum market share. The map alone demonstrates an effective forecasting discipline, because it pinpoints an industry's vectors of channel change. Combined with the matrix, it reveals the underlying sources of channel conflict and the options for combating that conflict. The tools bring executives to the cusp of channel-change decision making. The next step is theirs to take.

CRM Strategy: Capabilities for Creating the Customer Experience

Brian K. Crockett

As the global economy lurches unsteadily through the early part of the twenty-first century, companies around the world are searching for ways to restore the growth and profitability they enjoyed in the buoyant 1990s. For many of these organizations, customer relationship management (CRM) is seen as a particularly attractive proposition. Indeed, better management of the customer base offers great potential for companies to improve their top and bottom lines—especially given how difficult it's become for businesses of all types to attract and retain loyal customers. However, as many companies have discovered, adopting the right CRM capabilities—and generating significant business benefit from those investments—is not as easy as they first thought. In fact, many industry observers and analysts are quoting failure rates as high as 60 percent for recently completed CRM projects, and they are equally bearish on initiatives currently under way.

As the cost of a typical CRM implementation continues to grow and the pressure to address the shortcomings in customer management operations intensifies, organizations will have to become more vigilant in identifying which CRM capabilities will provide the greatest financial benefit; building a bulletproof business case for the project; gaining executive and stakeholder support; creating an intelligent and comprehensive execution plan; and using the new system to develop customer insights that will fuel more effective strategies and programs for marketing, sales, and customer service.

THE CUSTOMER CHALLENGE

In the past decade, it has become increasingly difficult for companies to connect with existing and prospective customers. The reasons for this include the following: the commoditization of brands and products, with the number of items on offer to consumers expanding significantly in the past 20 years; tougher and more numerous competitors; an explosion in the amount of market noise following the huge jump in the number of messages that bombard consumers on a daily basis; proliferation of customer interaction channels, especially with the advent of the Internet and wireless devices; and customers' ever-rising demands and expectations, driven by the increased ability to evaluate offers and prices by means of the Internet and by experience with value and service leaders such as Virgin, FedEx, Wal-Mart, and Siemens.

With such stiff challenges facing them, it's no wonder that companies are increasingly under pressure to come up with better ways to manage their customer relationships. The stakes truly are high; a misstep in a key marketing, sales, or customer service activity today can be disastrous, even to a healthy company—and possibly fatal to a weak one.

CRM PITFALLS

Why are analyst groups such as Gartner bearish on the ability of today's CRM projects to be successful? What's behind the arguably checkered track record of many recent initiatives? What's to blame for the fact that, while CRM projects have improved some aspects of companies' customer-facing operations, few have generated the type of significant companywide benefits that CRM proponents tout as possible?

Several critical factors lie behind CRM's underperformance (Exhibit 6-1). One of the most prevalent is the failure of many companies *to obtain and maintain executive support* for the CRM project. Consider the typical scenario. A group within a company decides that it could benefit from new CRM capabilities. It begins to study the issue, momentum builds, and soon there's strong grassroots support for the effort. Unfortunately, when the time comes for senior management to sign off on the sizable investment required, no executive is willing to do so. Too many times, a

EXHIBIT 6-1. Principal CRM project problem areas.

- Failure to obtain and maintain executive support for the project
- Failure to align key internal functions or business units on goals and mission of the project
- Inability to accurately link the CRM project to higher-level business strategies
- Focusing on capability building instead of ROI creation
- Lack of an integrated plan for project implementation
- Failure to achieve successes early in the project

group planning a CRM effort fails to ensure—early in the process—that executives understand the initiative and the business case for it, that they are clearly convinced of the need for CRM, and that they are willing and able to proactively support the initiative, especially at critical junctures of the project (e.g., in securing funding).

Companies have also struggled with *aligning key internal functions or business units* affected by the CRM initiative. Functional misalignment is a very complex issue that often takes the form of a battle between IT and the company's customer-facing functions or a disagreement among sales, marketing, and customer service on the right priority for competing CRM recommendations.

In the former situation, a company's IT department may want to implement a particular CRM solution without having secured agreement from the functions that will have to use it. This almost always results in a waste of resources, because even though the company may end up with a good technology tool, it most likely will never fully realize the potential benefits of that tool. Why? Because the changes in business processes, strategies, and organizational structure necessary to leverage the technology were not made. An HR services firm discovered this the hard way. After spearheading the implementation of a call center system, the company's CIO found that call center employees were refusing to use it because they had never been fully coached on how the system could help them improve the way they did their jobs. On the other hand, if marketing, sales, and service decides to push ahead with a CRM initiative without IT's support and resources, the effort often stalls or derails when it comes time to implement the supporting CRM technologies.

Alignment discord among business units is also a common cause of CRM project failure. For instance, if the sales force wants to adopt automation software, customer service wants new productivity tools for its call center, and marketing is pushing for new campaign management capabilities, and all three efforts move forward without consensus, then a collection of one-offs that don't work well together will be built. The result is more money spent than necessary, a clumsy (or worse, nonexistent) technological integration, redundant or conflicting customer data gathered, and a fragmented customer experience from one interaction channel or touch point to another.

A third area that has proved to be a problem is accurately *linking the CRM project to higher-level business strategies*—in other words, identifying short- and long-term business objectives and how CRM will support them. Many companies have fallen prey to the "sexy technology" trap—becoming so enthralled with a particular CRM technology that the organization loses sight of whether the tool will actually support how the company goes to market. A simple example is the company whose marketing department wants to implement a campaign management tool to improve the efficiency and effectiveness of direct marketing. Yet the company generally takes a mass-marketing approach to customer acquisition and uses call centers as the primary vehicle for customer and prospect communications. In this instance, an investment in direct-marketing CRM tools wouldn't support the company's principal customer activities, and such an investment rightly would be deemed a failure.

A focus on "capability building" instead of ROI creation also plagues many CRM initiatives. In fact, it's not uncommon that a sponsor of a CRM project knows intuitively that a capability is needed and will create value, but doesn't spend enough time thinking through how that value will be generated. For instance, one global hospitality company was considering implementing a system featuring a handheld device that would help check in guests as they pulled up to the front door—similar to the device car-rental companies use to process customers returning cars. On the surface, the idea was attractive, but when executives were finally pressed to quantify the tangible value of the new system to the hotel (e.g., by increasing bookings or justifying higher room rates) it became clear that the project couldn't be economically justified.

A fifth problem area concerns *having an integrated plan for project implementation.* Many companies are juggling several CRM projects at once, all competing for the same limited pool of resources rather than being executed as part of an integrated CRM implementation program that ensures that capabilities are built in an order and time frame that makes sense to the organization at large. Without such an integrated plan, IT often becomes overloaded and unable to keep up with the demands of the various projects. Furthermore, such a disjointed approach can result in the implementation of a specific capability before there's a solid understanding of the key dependencies that must be in place for the company to generate value from the capability (e.g., building a campaign management system before a customer database is fully functional).

Finally, many CRM projects are considered failures because *they don't achieve early successes* that help shorten the payback time and create momentum. Instead, they are executed in such a way that the companies can't begin to realize a payback on the new systems for two or three years. This not only makes it difficult to justify the investment in the projects, but also gives the efforts the appearance of being black holes that endlessly consume valuable corporate resources. In some cases in the past, these projects have been aborted well before they were finished, resulting in a substantial waste of time, money, and opportunities.

AVOIDING THE PITFALLS:
CRM STRATEGY AND ROAD MAP DEVELOPMENT

How can organizations learn from the mistakes of others and avoid these common pitfalls? To ensure that they address these critical CRM elements—and thus improve the chance that their projects will generate true business benefits for them and avoid becoming just another statistics—companies must identify, prioritize, and build the right CRM capabilities for creating customer and company value.

This approach, which we call the CRM Strategy and Road Map, is appropriate for these typical CRM situations:

- For a company that's struggling to reconcile competing requests for CRM investments—often from different business units or departments—and must determine which requests should be funded and how each initiative will affect not only a business unit or department, but also the company as a whole

- For a company that lacks executive alignment behind a CRM strategy and plan
- For a company that's interested in proactively designing a "greenfield" CRM capability and has to pinpoint which capabilities are appropriate for its specific business requirements

The CRM Strategy and Road Map is a distinct alternative to traditional approaches to CRM capability development. It focuses on business outcomes, not capabilities alone. It is analytically rigorous, relying on an ROI focus instead of subjective considerations. Its emphasis on revenue and cost drivers links the CRM investment directly to a company's income statement. And it provides a value-based, prioritized plan for CRM implementation to ensure that the most important areas are addressed first.

There are four key steps to a CRM Strategy and Road Map project: strategic context identification, capabilities assessment, business case development, and implementation plan creation.

Strategic Context

The first step is to understand how CRM fits into the context of the company's overall business strategy. This entails first confirming the company's vision for the CRM project as well as the project's business imperative—taking into consideration the existing business environment and the company's corporate strategic priorities.

- Is the company's market growing, stagnant, or declining?
- Is cutting costs the organization's most pressing immediate concern, or is it boosting revenues the priority?
- What's the relative emphasis between customer acquisition, development, retention, and cost to serve?
- Which channels are most critical for interacting with and serving customers?
- What's the balance between product focus and customer focus?
- Who does the company see as its most valuable customers, and why?

Answering questions such as these helps determine which CRM capabilities the company pursues.

At this stage, it is vital to understand how the CRM project will fit with the priorities of key stakeholders. To ensure that the project has strong backing from the right people—and that the views of these individuals are in sync—the company must understand what key sponsors believe are the project's objectives. Similarly, the views of managers responsible for marketing, sales, and service—and those of their direct reports—must be considered to ensure that everyone is pulling for the same team as the project progresses. One technique used to help achieve such alignment and consensus is the war room, in which key stakeholders are graphically plotted on a board along several dimensions (their understanding of the project, buy-in of the initiative, willingness to take proactive action to support the effort, etc.). This helps the project team know, at a glance, which stakeholders are in their camp and which need special attention or additional information. Alternatively, a large, cross-functional input team can be created comprising numerous representatives from all functions affected by the project to ensure that views of executives, managers, and line employees alike help shape the project and the system that's ultimately created.

Capabilities Assessment

Next, the project team conducts a comprehensive assessment of the company's current CRM capabilities (e.g., marketing program execution and management, customer interaction management, and brand/message alignment). This exercise helps the company understand how current performance on these capabilities stacks up against benchmarks from other CRM practitioners (i.e., whether the company is lagging, performing at parity with its competitors, or leading its industry) and identifies stretch goals for future improvement. The team also reviews the CRM capabilities to determine which ones are most germane to the company's particular situation, assigning a weight to each capability based on how much or little it contributes to the company's ability to create customer value. The result of the assessment, weighting, and scoring process is a comprehensive report showing areas of strength and opportunity across relevant CRM capabilities and highlighting specific gaps between current and potential performance.

Business Case Development

The third step involves building a sound business case to support the CRM investment. This effort begins with estimating how the company could improve its financial position by enhancing its performance on key drivers of revenue and costs. Such drivers include customer retention, new customer acquisition, and sales per customer on the revenue side, plus average length of call center call-handling time, total number of calls handled, and direct-mail expenses on the cost side. By understanding how the company performs on all revenue and cost drivers, benchmarking this performance against industry standards or new performance goals, and quantifying the gap between current and potential performance, the company can determine where it should focus its CRM efforts to achieve maximum financial benefits.

A simple example is a company that handles 98 percent of its 10 million customer calls with live agents, at a cost of $5 per call. If the company could reduce this to 94 percent by shifting more calls to customer self-service options, it would save $2 million. Clearly, this makes a strong case for the company to invest in increasing its customer self-service capabilities to achieve quantifiable financial benefits.

With a solid understanding of where it can generate the greatest improvements in financial performance (increasing revenue or reducing costs) the company must next identify which CRM capabilities are necessary to bring about such improvement. For example, if improving the effectiveness of direct marketing is seen as a way to significantly increase revenue, two CRM capabilities—predictive modeling

**EXHIBIT 6-2.   Prioritizing CRM targets (X = short term;
O = long term).**

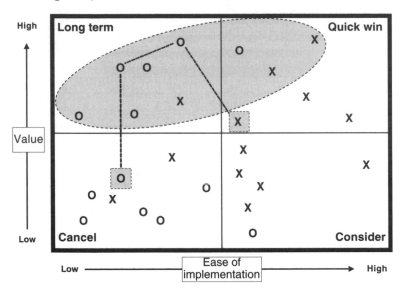

and marketing program execution—would be critical to achieving that revenue goal. By conducting this exercise for every revenue and cost driver, the company can easily identify which CRM capabilities are critical to improving its financial performance—and then map these capabilities against their ease of implementation to create a picture that clearly shows which capabilities should be pursued in the CRM project and in what order.

As illustrated in Exhibit 6-2, prioritizing capabilities in this way helps management identify which ones may represent a quick win, which require a longer-term investment, and which (because of low value and implementation difficulty) should not be pursued. With the capabilities thus prioritized, the company can then group the capabilities into logical initiatives—for example, implementing marketing automation software and improving marketing processes could be grouped into a direct marketing effectiveness initiative; adopting a customer self-care capability and improving call-handling could be bundled as a call center optimization initiative. As the illustration shows, the team can also identify interdependent capabilities (those capabilities that rely on the previous implementation of others).

To complete the business case for the project, the company must tally how much additional profit each CRM initiative can realistically generate for the company (using the revenue-enhancement and cost-reduction estimates developed earlier in this phase) and map these estimates against the high-level costs associated with completing the respective initiative (including hardware, software, training, third-party resources, and maintenance). The results of this exercise will help the company demonstrate that the project can be economically justified and secure the funds necessary to execute it. More important, it significantly reduces the company's chances of embarking on a project that will result in little or no payback.

Implementation Plan Creation

The final step involves creating the road map that clearly defines how to get there: the technical, process, and organizational elements that must be addressed to complete the CRM initiative. These include the following:

- Interdependencies between new and existing systems and processes
- Resources needed and available
- Organizational alignment
- Executive alignment
- Necessary new or redesigned processes
- Key technology infrastructure and applications
- Execution plan
- User training

The CRM Strategy and Road Map approach can help the company determine financing and sourcing options for the project as well. If, for example, the company has a high demand for capital, it may opt to explore alternatives to outright capital expenditures—such as cosourcing or outsourcing arrangements with strategic partners that can reduce the amount of company money needed to complete the CRM initiative in exchange for some percentage of the financial gains the project generates for the company. On the other hand, a company for which CRM is a core competency may prefer to build capabilities itself.

CASE STUDY: HOTEL OPERATOR

One company that is using this approach to guide the design and implementation of its CRM initiative is a large North American hotel operator. In its role as franchiser of several well-known hotel brands, the company provides a number of shared services to its properties, including a central reservations center, e-commerce support, brand marketing, and a frequent-guest loyalty program. Although the company's historic performance in delivering these services was good, there was a growing perception internally that several CRM-related enhancements were needed to improve the effectiveness of its customer interactions. Company executives—confronted with numerous uncoordinated, independent CRM investment requests from various areas of the company—realized that a cross-functional, integrated approach to CRM would provide the company with the best capabilities for enhancing its shared services organization, optimizing its customer relationships, and improving franchisee business performance. Accenture was asked to help the company develop a CRM strategy and implementation plan.

The first order of business was to develop the company's enterprisewide CRM strategy and identify and prioritize its CRM initiatives. As part of this effort, the project team first conducted a touch-point analysis of the company's operations to identify the key points of customer interaction and help the company focus its attention on those areas with the greatest impact on customers. Customer touch points were grouped into four areas: establishing the relationship, pretrip experience, on-property experience, and maintaining the relationship. The specific CRM capabilities that related to each of these each touch points also were identified.

Next, the project team conducted an assessment of existing CRM capabilities. Through this assessment, it became clear that the company was an industry leader in developing insights into its customers' needs and behaviors and running an efficient call center, but could benefit from enhancements in direct-marketing execution, call center effectiveness, and sales.

After assessing its existing CRM capabilities and identifying areas for improvement, the project team conducted a comprehensive analysis to determine the financial impact of those improvements. This effort led to a dramatic conclusion: The company could generate an estimated $65 million in additional net profit over five years by focusing on 15 to 20 key capabilities in its direct-marketing, sales, and call center operations.

The team grouped these capabilities into four distinct initiatives:

- *Direct marketing effectiveness,* which sought to improve the company's campaign management efforts and its ability to provide offers more closely tailored to individual customers
- *Call center optimization,* which involved building robust capabilities for more intelligent handling of customers' incoming calls and better access by call center representatives to customer records
- *Sales effectiveness,* which included sales force automation capabilities and an integrated channel sales approach
- *IT infrastructure enhancements,* which focused on creating more robust customer data models and enhanced guest profiles

When the CRM project is completed, the company will have in place capabilities to generate incremental improvements in business results across direct marketing, its call center, and sales. As one example, the new campaign management software and related marketing processes will allow the company to more effectively leverage its industry-leading customer analysis capabilities by creating more timely, targeted, and relevant direct-marketing campaigns.

CONCLUSION

Undoubtedly, CRM has generated value for many companies in the past several years. However, the value that's been delivered pales in comparison to what is possible. As economic uncertainty continues and customers become more demanding, organizations simply must find ways to improve the chances that their new CRM initiatives will succeed.

A major step in this direction involves adopting an ROI-based approach to CRM. This ensures that the capabilities built in a CRM project are not only the *right* capabilities (i.e., consistent with the company's mission) but are also those that support the key activities that enable the company to realize its business goals and thus have the greatest potential to provide the highest return in the form of reduced costs and enhanced revenue.

Building the right CRM capabilities is only the first part of the CRM journey. Once these capabilities are in place, it is incumbent upon the organization to take the necessary steps to ensure that the new CRM capabilities are leveraged most effectively. These steps include creating a high-level customer strategy that builds on the new CRM capabilities to improve the way the company interacts with customers and prospects; developing a better understanding of existing customers' needs and profitability and grouping customers into logical segments; creating strategies for each segment to maximize the value of those groups of customers; and identifying and building the processes, organization structures, and measures necessary to implement these strategies and optimally serve each customer segment.

By following this approach, companies can realize a significant return on their CRM investments—and subsequently attract the attention, loyalty, and business of their most valuable customers for years to come.

Gaining Customer Insights

7

Introduction: Gaining Customer Insights in a World of Change and Uncertainty

J. Patrick O'Halloran

"**K**now your customer" certainly is one of the most widely quoted maxims of business—and for good reason. However, companies often talk about the importance of customer knowledge while failing to put a lot of action behind their words. Why? Some companies are still smarting from previous efforts, such as failed data warehousing projects or unsuccessful attempts to persuade sales personnel to document customer interests. Other companies take limited measures, such as conducting a study of customer profitability or implementing a new CRM software product to improve sales force effectiveness, which provide improved efficiencies but yield little in the way of deeper customer insight. Still others may be simply overwhelmed by the huge volumes of transaction data their corporate systems are capturing and are unsure of where to start.

In years past, companies could be forgiven somewhat for failing to manage their data better. Technology solutions then were not as robust or user-friendly, often making them less than effective and difficult to use. Today, however, companies have no excuses. With the powerful CRM software and other analytic technologies now available, there's no reason for companies to remain in the dark when it comes to truly understanding their customers. Even more to the point, companies *no longer can afford* to ignore the gold mines they're sitting on. Competitive and customer pressures today mandate that managers develop the capabilities to aggregate, analyze, and use customer data to generate real business value (i.e., glean insight into how to win more customers and to increase the economic value of and more effectively serve existing ones).

To develop such capabilities, companies must attend to three critical issues:

- Creating an integrated view of each customer
- Understanding and predicting customer behavior
- Using customer insights to improve future interactions with customers and enhance the ongoing customer relationship

CREATING AN INTEGRATED VIEW OF CUSTOMERS

When beginning a CRM initiative, companies can be tempted to try to capture as much data as possible about each and every customer. In reality, the quality of the data, not the quantity, is what enables companies to build strong customer relationships and become more customer-centric. Buying and collecting ever-increasing amounts of customer data, feeding it into a data warehouse with a lot of bells and whistles, and hoping insights emerge is not the path to customer-centricity. In fact, there is little evidence to show that the mere presence of more data and more technology will lead to better customer relationships. But there is evidence that a wealth of *relevant* customer data, and some central repository to manage that data, is critical to becoming a customer-centric organization. Before pursuing either, though, companies must fully understand why they are gathering data, what data to gather to achieve the desired results, where to get the data they want, and how they will apply the knowledge they gather. Quite often, companies find that they need less—but more focused—data than they thought and that much of the data they need is already housed within their enterprise (although accessing and consolidating such data may be hampered by organizational silos).

The first step is for a company to determine exactly what kind of data it needs. This involves three basic steps: understanding what is known about customers already; identifying what the company doesn't know that it should; and determining how to fill the knowledge gaps with appropriate data.

To understand what it already knows, a company should create a profile of its existing customers based on information such as purchase history, length of relationship, purchase details, transactions with other divisions within the enterprise, demographics, credit/financial details of the transactions, and customers' most frequent means of interacting with the company.

Next, the company must define existing gaps (i.e., where more information is needed on specific customers, prospects, and markets for the company to achieve its objectives). One of the most effective ways to pinpoint gaps is to segment customers into unique groups with similar characteristics to draw a hypothesis of how they behave, what they purchase, and why they purchase. From this segmentation, further questions will arise about specific issues—such as demographic profiles of segments, differences in purchase motivation, and levels of service needed by each segment—which will help determine the data elements still lacking.

As a rule, the best source of data about customers is their actual experience with the company. To begin building a knowledge base on each customer, a company should first tap its own information systems for the following:

- Complaints/inquiries to the call center
- Credit and financial information
- Business transactions with all divisions
- Aggregate purchases/history of the relationship
- Purchase details
- Preferences based on actual purchase history/trends

Another emerging source of customer knowledge is what's being dubbed *silent commerce*. Silent commerce uses wireless mobile communications and advanced tagging and sensor technologies to enable everyday products to record and transmit important information such as how often they are handled (e.g., picked up and put down by a consumer on a retail shelf) and where they are located (e.g., to enable companies to track a particular product in transit to a customer's home or office). Silent commerce offers the potential to provide a level of customer insight never before available, because it can help companies—particularly retailers—understand customer interactions with their products, not just at the point of sale, but also at the point of decision. Making packages interactive and intelligent also will enable companies to uniquely identify, locate, and track products all along the supply chain—from the manufacturer through to the consumer and even, potentially, through recycling. Although silent commerce currently is not widely used, recent pilot implementations at numerous companies have proven the potential of this technique to significantly enhance companies' understanding of their customers.

Once these internal sources of data have been explored and exhausted, a company may find it necessary to purchase third-party data to fill in the rest of the critical gaps that have been identified. There are many sources from which to purchase data, and such information can be very useful in completing the profile of the customer. However, it is important to understand the potential limitations of third-party data before buying. Purchased data—such as that from customer-provided warranty cards, surveys, magazine subscription lists, or census list extrapolations—can be useful directionally, but also can be unreliable with low matching rates.

For instance, many reputable companies offer demographic overlays. These companies generally compile data from sources such as phone books and the departments of motor vehicles to arrive at household-level demographics. Demographic overlays are an important element of analysis, profiling, and targeting; however, their accuracy, particularly in the United States, can be compromised by the mobility of consumers (e.g., between 10 and 30 percent of people move or change jobs each year). With typical match rates of 70 to 90 percent, it becomes clear that a large percentage of purchased data may not match the records in a company's database. New privacy laws, which mandate data providers to offer opt-in rights to consumers before making their information available, also have made it difficult to obtain completely reliable information on such consumer attributes as income, home value, net worth, credit card use, and creditworthiness.

The point is that companies' own data is generally much more accurate and robust than that available from a third party. When purchasing external data to fill in gaps in customer information, companies should recognize the limitations of such data and work with vendors that understand their needs and how purchased data will be used.

UNDERSTANDING AND PREDICTING CUSTOMER BEHAVIOR

Once a company has gathered the appropriate customer data, it must combine the data to understand and predict customer behavior. This is essential to ensure that the right data is delivered to the right business functions at the right time to help shape subsequent customer interactions. To truly understand and predict customer behavior, a company must manage its customer data in ways that enable it to analyze the data and generate deep insights into what customers want and how they behave. This starts with organizing data by how it will be used by decision makers (i.e., defining the data architecture). For example, information required to drive customer interactions, such as demographic updates, will require an interactive data architecture, whereas data needed for generating customer insight will have to be accessed by data-mining and analytic tools. Furthermore, in many companies, real-time refreshing of data is very valuable. In these instances, the data architecture must accommodate such updating—for example, incorporating customer complaints or linking the use by one customer of two contact channels (such as the Web and call center) within minutes of each other or even simultaneously.

Once the data is organized, the company must identify how the data will be used to shape subsequent interactions with each customer—that is, define the rules for data use. These rules come in two principal forms: personalization and data transformation. Personalization rules shape each customer interaction by providing for consistent, timely, and relevant individualized interactions and offers across multiple customer touch points. Data transformation rules, on the other hand, govern non-customer-facing activity: merging customer data from source systems or third parties. Both forms of rules (personalization and transformation) are most effective when they address the broadest possible set of scenarios.

USING CUSTOMER INSIGHTS

After generating a solid understanding of customer needs and behavior, a company then must capitalize on those insights. The first step in doing so is understanding the *context* in which customer data is used. Context is the translation of a company's customer strategy into rules meant to deliver that strategy. Two facets of context are especially important:

- *Coordination of all activities across potential customer interaction points.*
  This is key to ensuring that customers are not, for example, instructed by a

direct-marketing piece to visit the Web site for a special offer only to discover that the offer hasn't yet been posted because the site manager was not in the loop on the campaign.

- *Understanding why a rule is being implemented or a decision made.* As more rules governing interactions and data transformation are implemented across the enterprise, it is important to understand the intended effect. Which rules are meant to contribute to which dimension of the customer strategy—acquisition, cross-selling, or retention? As the strategy is defined, rules should be defined for each dimension.

From here, companies can effectively identify particular programs and vehicles for leveraging customer insights. For example, knowledge derived from customer transaction data can enable companies to create offers for customers that best reflect past purchases, that make good first impressions with customers by demonstrating some knowledge of their preferences when they call or visit, that provide product offers and communications highly tailored to customer traits, and that improve cross-selling during key customer interactions. Similarly, knowledge gained from human interaction with customers can enable companies to foster a more conversational relationship with key customers, as well as help improve product design by listening to customers' input while also noting their mood and voice.

CONCLUSION

Achieving the Holy Grail of deep insights into customer needs, preferences, and behavior is no doubt hard work. If it weren't, everyone would be doing it. However, companies that are disciplined and approach the collection, integration, and use of customer data from a strategic perspective stand an excellent chance of generating superior customer loyalty and, in the process, strong competitive advantage. The next five chapters in Part 3 take a closer look at the issue of customer insight and how companies can put it to work for them.

8

The Critical Element: Using Data to Become a Customer-Centric Organization

Shep Parke and Holly Porter

Quality, not quantity, is the key in using data to build strong customer relationships. It's been well established how important it is for companies to more deeply understand their customers and personalize the products and services they deliver—that is, to become customer-centric. Conventional wisdom says that to become customer-centric, a company must buy more and more customer data and feed it into a data warehouse with lots of add-on software products.

However, this is not precisely true. The market for business intelligence and data-warehousing tools and services is growing at an average annual rate of more than 50 percent and is expected to reach $113 billion by 2002.[1] The race is on to develop better, smarter technologies to facilitate customer relationship management and to buy more data about customers and prospects. But there is little evidence to show that the mere presence of more data and more technology will lead to better customer relationships. The key to success in today's environment is to know what information drives customers' behavior and to apply that knowledge across the enterprise—in strategic planning, in product development, in marketing, in customer service, and in sales.

The content of this chapter originally appeared in the book *Defying the Limits: Setting a Course for CRM Success,* published by Montgomery Research.

In short, a wealth of relevant customer data is a critical element in becoming a customer-centric organization. So, too, is a central repository to manage the data. Before purchasing either, companies need to have a plan. They need to know why they are gathering data, what data to gather to achieve the desired results, where to get the data they want, and how they will apply the knowledge they gather. Quite often, companies find that they need less—but more focused—data than they thought and that much of the data they need is already housed within their enterprise.

DEFINING DATA REQUIREMENTS

In our experience, we have found it worthwhile for companies to take a structured approach to determining what data they need, particularly when third-party data is required. This approach includes three basic steps:

1. *Start with what you know.* Begin by defining what you know about your customers. Profile your current customers by using information such as purchase history, length of relationship, purchase details, transactions with other divisions within the enterprise, demographics, credit/financial details of the transactions, and customers' most frequent means of interacting with you.

   Often, companies have more data than they realize, because much of that data is hidden. As enterprises implement various CRM systems in an attempt to understand and serve customers, they sometimes blur, rather than sharpen, their view of the customer, according to a recent report by the Aberdeen Group of Boston.[2] Sales force automation, telesales, customer support, and campaign management systems typically use different keys and view customers from different perspectives. Consequently, the enterprise finds it difficult to connect these data sources and create a holistic view of the customer. The result is a weakened ability to deliver a single face to the customer and to show customers that you know how to serve them individually. Understanding the data housed within all the information sources in your organization will sharpen your understanding of your customers and of your requirements for centralization of the data.

2. *Define what you want to do with the information you gather.* Understand your objectives behind gathering more information. Do you want to retain existing customers? Sell more products or services to existing customers? Attract new customers? Tailor the delivery of services to customers based on their value to your organization? Develop new products based on your customers' preferences? Enter or exit markets based on profitability and penetration within those markets? Your objectives may include all of these and others, but for purposes of defining your requirements, treat each objective as an individual project and define the data elements required to support each project.

   This approach will help you avoid overloading end users with irrelevant information and will ultimately reduce your data acquisition costs by reducing the number of data elements you must purchase. For example, Kraft Food developed a customer knowledge system that it uses to build share in product categories. This tool enables Kraft sales representatives to obtain, analyze, and apply customer knowledge. Since sales representatives do not have the time or resources to sift through volumes of data and draw subjective conclusions, Kraft built the system to focus on the most important data elements that drive sales. As a result, Kraft sales reps use less than 20 percent of the data their competitors use, and they realize a marginal sales growth of 3 to 4 percent versus a control group.[3]

3. *Define what you don't know.* Define the gaps in your knowledge about your customers, what you want to do with the information, and what you need to know about your customers, your prospects, and your market(s) to achieve your objectives. Probably the most effective method of defining the gaps is to analyze your customers using your existing data. By segmenting your customers into unique groups with similar characteristics, you begin to draw hypotheses of how they behave, what they purchase, and why they purchase. From this segmentation, further questions will arise: How does the demographic profile of one group differ from another? What motivates a segment to purchase from you at a specific life stage? What other hobbies or interests are common within segments? What level of service does each segment require to remain loyal to your organization? Through what channel do they wish to be contacted by you? From the questions that arise, identify missing data elements you will need to answer the questions.

Once the gaps in data have been identified, the missing elements may be gathered from a variety of internal sources (customer surveys, focus groups, other systems within the enterprise, etc.), or they may need to be purchased from a third-party provider. As always, measure the importance of the data against the ultimate objective of this project.

FILLING IN THE GAPS

As a rule, the best source of data about your customers will be found inside your enterprise. Optimal match rates on purchased data are 70 to 90 percent, which means that as much as one-third of the records purchased are unusable. The source of the data you purchase can be very reliable—motor vehicle department or driver's license records, for example—or it can be inferred from less quantifiable information such as customer-provided warranty cards, surveys, magazine subscription lists, or census list extrapolations. This information can be very useful directionally; however, customers' actual experience with you is recorded inside your own four walls. Start with your internal information systems. Examples of information sources that can help you fill the gaps in your customer knowledge include the following:

- Complaints/inquiries to the call center
- Credit and financial information

- Business transactions with divisions other than your own
- Aggregate purchases/history of the relationship
- Purchase details
- Preferences based on actual purchase history/trends

The information found internally can be highly valuable in developing your customer relationships. For example, Nordstrom's department store, a renowned customer-centric organization, created the "Personal Touch" program to offer complimentary personal shopper service to customers. The program's objective is to form long-term relationships with Nordstrom customers. The store's personal shoppers have access to two systems that capture customer information: (1) a database of customers' likes, dislikes, lifestyle, and apparel needs that were gathered from telephone and face-to-face conversations, and (2) a database containing customer purchase history. Armed with both previous purchase history and personal preferences, the personal shopper is able to offer more targeted selections and truly personalized service to the customer.[4]

Following a review of internal data sources, some personal information will probably still be missing. It is likely that your customer can provide this information. Specific behavioral and buyer preference information may be more effectively gathered through primary research such as surveys and focus groups. It is also possible to simply ask the customer for information in exchange for some incentive. Many Web-based companies like Free-PC.com and E*Trade are offering incentives for customer-provided information. E*Trade offers 500 air miles for a customer's information, then follows up with a certificate for $50 toward the first investment. Free-PC.com joined with Compaq to offer free computers in exchange for personal data, distributing 10,000 computers to people who were willing to share personal information and receive targeted advertisements. About 300,000 people visited the site, and thousands who tried could not get through. It appears that, for the right offer, people are willing to exchange some of their privacy.[5]

PURCHASING AND MANAGING THIRD-PARTY DATA

After internal sources of data have been explored, it may be necessary to purchase third-party data to fill in the final critical gaps you have identified. There are many sources from which to purchase data, and such information can be very useful in completing the profile of the customer. However, it is important to understand the potential limitations of third-party data before buying.

Many reputable companies offer demographic overlays. These companies generally compile data from sources such as phone books and motor vehicle department driver's license lists to arrive at household-level demographics. Demographic overlays are an important element of analysis, profiling, and targeting; however, an understanding of their relative accuracy is critical. Census studies have shown that more than 10 percent of the U.S. population moves every year, and an even higher percentage changes jobs every year. Add to that the previously mentioned typical match rates of 70 to 90 percent, and it becomes clear that a significant portion of the information a company purchases will not match the records in its database.

In the United States, recently enacted privacy laws have made the acquisition of data more difficult. For example, under the Shelby Act, an amendment to the Drivers Privacy Protection Act, effective June 1, 2000, states must offer notice and opt-in rights to the consumer before making its driver's license and motor vehicle license lists available to direct marketers. In other words, the consumer must explicitly agree to allow this information to be sold for marketing purposes. This essentially renders two of the most credible third-party data sources far less reliable than ever before.

Similarly, Gramm Leach Bliley, the Financial Modernization Act enacted in the United States on November 13, 2000, says that before a financial institution can share nonpublic personal information (NPPI) with anyone other than affiliates, it must provide the consumer with detailed notice and the ability to opt out. NPPI has traditionally been the source data that providers use to derive such demographic attributes as income, home value, net worth, credit card use, and creditworthiness.

It is critical to understand the limitations of third-party data and to carefully test the information you purchase. To do so, choose a few vendors for evaluation based on the available data variables, their overall match rates, and their sources of data. Ask each vendor to enhance a sample of your data file and provide match rate reports. Then check the vendor's data against actual figures in your database. For example, match "age" provided by the vendor against actual dates of birth in your database, or check "home value" against the mortgage value in the customer's credit file if you house that information. Evaluate each vendor on the combined score of overall match rate, elemental match rate (the percentage of elements that are populated per customer versus the number you requested), and the accuracy of the data variables against the actuals in your database.

PUTTING IT ALL TOGETHER TO BUILD A CUSTOMER-CENTRIC ENTERPRISE

In the end, the point of gathering all of this data is to develop deeper relationships with your customers and ultimately to sell more products and services. Today's customer is accustomed to a certain degree of personalized service as a baseline—the leaders of the premier customer-centric organizations are focusing on using data that contributes to higher sales and more personalized service to the customer. Marriott, for instance, has invested heavily in a CRM system that incorporates both transaction and human data. Armed with this information, desk clerks see a display of any special needs, interests, or preferences the guest expressed when making the reservation or in past visits to Marriott properties.[6] Similarly, First Union has recently implemented an enterprisewide customer-centric data warehouse. Information from within the warehouse is first used for customer analytics, deepening the bank's understanding of who its customers are and how these customers can be served, the objective being to increase the bank's profit per customer—and ultimately to increase customer loyalty by cross-selling the appropriate products when the customer needs them. Analytics incorporate both transaction data and demographic data, prompting the bank's relationship managers to react with a targeted solution to customer events such as major withdrawals/deposits, home purchases, and so forth. By understanding the customer's complete relationship with the bank, First Union is able to introduce new services to the customer (investments, home mortgages, insurance, credit cards, etc.) at the appropriate time. The bank expects this capability to contribute $100 million in revenues annually.[7]

To understand how companies can use customer information more effectively, the Accenture Institute for Strategic Change and the Goizueta Business School at Emory University recently conducted a study of the customer knowledge management practices of 26 leading firms. The study found that while the specific tactics varied by organization, the leading firms had at least four major strengths in common:

- *They know which customers to focus on.* For example, the leaders each have made a strategic decision to apply data to identifying segments as a basis for action, such as enhancing service delivery to the most profitable segment, encouraging low-cost transaction options to unprofitable segments, and cross-selling additional products or services to segments that have the potential to become "best customers."

- *They are focused in their objectives for customer knowledge management.* The leaders in customer knowledge management know what they are going to do with the data, whether it's purchased or in-house. For instance, they may use it to increase market share in a specific market, to encourage the use of alternative channels in low-profit segments, to identify product improvements or additions, or to cross-sell products and services.

- *They aim for an optimal mix of data-driven and human knowledge.* The leaders creatively incorporate actual customer feedback into their analyses of transaction, purchase, and demographic data to complete the holistic view of the customer.

- *They manage to results.* Getting data into a repository is only the first step toward managing the customer relationship. Such efforts are successful only if they improve the company's bottom line or meet strategic objectives.

CONCLUSION
In building a customer-centric organization, information about the customer is critical—but it must be meaningful information that will help a company meet its goals. To make sure they are pursuing and using the right data, companies can follow a structured, step-by-step approach: Begin with an understanding of objectives. Study their own customer data. Identify the gaps in the information they have and the information they need. Ask customers for information. Where needed, evaluate and select the third-party companies to provide data that complements and supplements owned data. Then, and only then, build the systems and processes to support customer-centric operations.

The Foundation of Insight: Three Approaches to Customer-Centric Understanding

Brian K. Crockett and Kenneth L. Reed

ruth is an elusive thing, and nowhere is that more evident than in understanding the value, and values, of a customer. Becoming customer-centric is an increasingly popular goal for many companies, but confusion reigns regarding the best way to achieve customer understanding. Some believe that customer understanding comes from thoroughly understanding customer value and profitability. Others see customer value analysis as a means of understanding the set of buyer needs and desires that form the basis for purchase decisions. Still others maintain that customer understanding comes from behavioral segmentation.

The turf battles between adherents of customer profitability versus customer values/attitudes versus behavioral segmentation continue to rage, with each proponent claiming his or her approach is best. What is the best approach for customer understanding? The short answer is "all of the above," with all three—customer profitability, customer buyer values, and customer segmentation—having a place under the big tent of customer-centric understanding. The challenge is to understand the differences between the approaches, when to apply them, and how to derive strategic and tactical value from them.

The content of this chapter originally appeared in the book *Defying the Limits: Setting a Course for CRM Success,* published by Montgomery Research.

CUSTOMER PROFITABILITY

Why be concerned about differences in customer profitability? For many companies, it is an article of faith that all customers are important and that all should be treated equally. This makes for good public relations, but it ignores the reality of customer value and customer contribution to company profit. All customers do not contribute the same value to a company. A simple *decile analysis* of customer revenue and profitability can reveal surprising insights into relative customer value. The Pareto rule generally applies, in which a small percentage of customers represents a large percentage of total revenues and profits.

Recognizing the importance of a minority of customers translates into several imperatives. First is managing the cost to serve customers. Although a reasonable level of customer service is appropriate for all customers, it makes sense to balance the cost of serving a customer with the current or potential value of that customer. Take, for example, the significant differences in customer value among insurance policyholders. Highly profitable customers can support agent-made phone calls and other higher-cost means of communication, while less-profitable customers support white mail or call center contacts. Combining this principle with customer preferences can drive customer profitability, customer satisfaction, and company value.

The second imperative is product strategy. Too many companies make the mistake of managing product offerings based on the perceived needs of the entire customer base rather than tailoring offerings to the needs of those customers who actually drive profitability. A classic example is the mistake many grocery retailers make in allocating shelf and merchandising space to products that appeal to "cherry pickers" and other low-profit customers instead of allocating this space for products bought by their best (most-profitable) customers.

Measuring the value of customers only at the current point in time is not sufficient. What about customers who have spent a lot in the past but are not currently spending at that same level? What about customers who are not currently valuable but will likely be in the future?

Customer long-term value (CLV) analysis provides an approach to measuring customer value over time. CLV captures the net present value of the future stream of revenues minus the costs associated with a customer. The CLV formula also helps to identify the factors that create value, including the costs and benefits of acquisition efforts, upsell and cross-sell marketing, retention activities, and the impact of customer referrals. Although more easily measured when applied to a customer base in the aggregate, CLV can be a valuable measure of customer profitability. It clarifies the extent to which a company should invest in marketing, sales, and service efforts; and at the disaggregate level, it better clarifies how much should be spent on a given customer.

CLV can help companies make value-based resource allocations, especially in investments such as customer databases, customer analytics, customer interactions, and other CRM-related resource decisions. Consider one effective approach to mapping the components of customer long-term value to the supporting CRM capabilities. At the core of this approach is an estimate of the value potential derived from improvements in the key drivers of the CLV formula. These drivers may include customer acquisition rate, defection rate, products or services purchased, acquisition cost elements, selling cost elements, servicing cost elements, and customer duration. Value potential is measured using performance-versus-industry benchmarks, or potential performance against stretch goals, depending on available data. For example, assume that the current new customer acquisition rate is 20 percent and that the identified potential acquisition rate is 22 percent. This two-point gain in new customer acquisition easily can be quantified into profit impact by multiplying the 2 percent times the size of the existing customer base, then applying the current gross profit per customer. The value potential of improvements in each CLV component is thus determined, then compared to opportunities identified through assessing existing CRM capabilities, resulting in a prioritizing of CRM investments that will most directly create greater value for the company.

CUSTOMER BUYER VALUES

A second approach to customer-centric understanding is to determine why customers make specific buying decisions and incorporate that knowledge into specific marketing and service strategies. Known as *customer buyer values analysis,* it involves the following:

- Identifying the key values that influence customer behavior
- Understanding customer preferences and the trade-offs they are willing to make
- Segmenting customers based on their values and trade-offs
- Developing product, channel, pricing, and service strategies and value propositions that best serve those segments.

The resulting value-based segmentation can support strategic imperatives, including overall corporate strategy, revenue enhancement, cost reduction, process improvements, and increased customer responsiveness to offers.

Typically conducted by surveying a representative subset of customers, buyer values analysis identifies the key data elements that drive purchasing and measures what is truly important to customers by asking them to make trade-off decisions. Traditional research typically asks the importance of particular features individually; the predictable result is that customers tend to rate each attribute as important (especially price). Trade-off research, using techniques such as conjoint analysis, more effectively measures the decisions customers face in actual purchase decisions by asking them to choose between pairs of options. For example, a financial services customer may be asked to indicate his or her preference between opening an account in person at market rates versus opening an account by phone at a rate 0.5 percent above market rate, among scores of other trade-offs related to the account opening channel, wait time, interest rate, and service/problem-resolution channels. By conducting multiple paired comparisons, a company can determine weightings for each variable that indicate their relative importance in the buying decision.

When conducting trade-off analysis of this sort, it is critical to ask the right questions in the right way. The old adage "garbage in, garbage out" applies. First, include all the factors that are likely to influence the customer's decision. Second, combine the factors in ways that make sense to the customer and reflect his or her actual decision process. Some of the trade-off techniques consider variables in relative isolation, whereas others always present full product concepts to the respondent. Because different types of trade-off analysis will result in different weight being given to certain attributes (especially price), not choosing the right technique runs the risk of missing a critical driver of customer behavior (for example, not identifying a price-sensitive segment when one actually exists).

Customers are then grouped into segments based on their responses. For example, a segment of customers may value transaction speed and be willing to pay a premium to get it; another segment's behavior may be driven by channel preference; a third segment might value low price. The most important values for each segment can be identified, leading to an understanding of what matters to all customers as well as what matters to specific segments.

For example, buyer values analysis for a major bank dispelled several myths. The first was the belief that demographic factors such as age and income could be used to identify discrete segments; in reality, demographics were well distributed across buyer value segments. The second was the belief that customers valued individual relationships with bank personnel when in reality price and speed were found to be more important than personal banking relationships for most customers. The third was that customer satisfaction drives market success; in reality, understanding buyer values and acting on that understanding maximizes profitability.

Buyer values related to preferences and willingness to pay have led to customer strategies that include the following examples: a new product offering that rationalized pricing and delivery costs; a new high-speed telephone channel targeted at high-profit segments who preferred banking by telephone; a decision to build corporate strategies around the needs of a select number of segments rather than the entire customer base; and a marketing campaign that built demand by focusing on products and delivery channels that appealed to target customers. Process improvements included simplification of new loan documentation and customer information requirements that reduced loan decision time from two weeks to three days. These and other changes in organizational design and technology have led to substantial improvements in both revenue enhancement and cost savings.

A closely related approach known as *customer value analysis* also focuses on understanding customers' key buying factors, but also incorporates the choices customers make in choosing between competitors. It incorporates the relative importance of each buying factor, the rating of how well each competitor delivers on the key factors that drive the purchase decision, and how the buying factors, importance weights, and relative competitive performance are changing over time.

This approach is based on the idea that customers make buying decisions based on a complex set of trade-offs between product and service attributes and cost. It can be used to better understand customer satisfaction by looking not only at the customer's satisfaction with a particular company's offerings but how well those offerings stack up against competitive offerings. It also can serve as a bellwether indicator of competitive threats and lead to strategic measures to counter those threats.

For example, a long-distance telecommunications firm facing a potential price war with its competition used customer value analysis to address the question of whether to maintain its premium price position or to become more price competitive. By understanding customers' views on competitive price and long-distance service quality, the company found that although its quality was perceived as superior and customers were willing to pay more for quality, its price premium was perceived to be excessive and its quality lead to be narrowing. This insight led to a strategy of investments to improve quality, including infrastructure spending and improvements in billing and installation processes and an advertising campaign to address the price premium perception and highlight the quality improvements.

CUSTOMER BEHAVIORAL SEGMENTATION

A third approach to customer understanding is the use of behavioral segmentation, especially analysis of customer data residing in customer databases. Database-enabled segmentation addresses a critical challenge of customer buyer values analysis—the inability to efficiently assign segment membership to all customers.

Unless all customers can be evaluated, some believe that application of customer value metrics in a useful way is impossible. Segmentations based on surveys often cannot be acted on, except in a strategic sense, unless some method of imputing the survey results to the population is developed. This is nontrivial and usually so error-prone that the inferences made are often not reliable. Consequently, the advent of data mining of customer databases to derive customer-centric understanding is critical. A combination of data-based segmentation and customer value surveys delivers a more robust means of developing customer-centric understanding that can be put to use.

Customer database behavior analysis can generate valuable insight into customers because it reveals what customers actually do—not what they say they will do or their attitudes. This analysis presumes the capture of transactional data on products or services purchased, quantities, timing, promotional versus full-price purchases—as well as demographics, lifestyle, and life-stage data when available.

Effective behavioral segmentation starts first with a set of business requirements and an understanding of the critical business issue to be resolved. This shapes the choice of variables used for the segmentation and helps produce a meaningful outcome. For example, an online broker had demonstrated the ability to attract customers, but was challenged with driving sufficient activity and profit from its customer base. A behavioral segmentation incorporating trading levels, account value, proxies for trading sophistication, and measures of recency, frequency, and monetary value (RFM) identified six behavioral segments, ranging from novices to experienced power users. Each customer in the data warehouse was scored with his or her segment membership, then demographic and life-stage data were appended. This enabled the company to conduct a rich set of analyses of customer behavior, associated demographics, and lifestyle characteristics. A further step incorporated survey information that allowed a *universal segmentation* of the investor universe, which permitted penetration analysis, potential customer value estimates, and even models predicting potential trading levels.

The level of learning and insight developed from these models and analyses completely changed the way the brokerage viewed its customers. Products and offerings were targeted to particular segments and subsegments, and segment managers were assigned. Additional heavy use of data mining, modeling, and analysis was successfully implemented and incorporated into virtually every aspect of marketing. The differential successes in marketing were such that the payback for developing the data warehouse and all the data-mining activities was less than 18 months.

Many companies have adopted attitudinal segmentation approaches to customer understanding, and they effectively use the segmentation to drive advertising and product strategies. Some are resistant to adopting a behavioral segmentation approach in addition to their existing attitudinal segmentation, claiming to already have a segmentation. This is a common but shortsighted philosophy. In fact, attitudinal and behavioral segmentations can exist in parallel very effectively. Attitudes drive behaviors, and behaviors in turn create value for the company. Both attitudes and behaviors can provide valuable customer insight, but how they are applied differs. Attitudinal segmentation is, in virtually all instances, survey-based and supports broad strategic decision making such as market positioning. Behavioral segmentation can be either survey-based or database-driven; database-driven segmentation allows all customers to be segmented and can be used to influence all customer interactions. As a result, behavioral segmentation is an enabler of both customer strategies and tactical treatment.

The key to developing segmentations is keeping them separate. A common mistake is mixing demographics like age and gender into a behavioral segmentation. This muddies the resulting segments, often rendering them useless. Our approach is to define pure behavioral variables from the database, chosen for their business information value. Only these variables are used in the segmentation. Then other information can be analyzed in terms of the segments—called *profiling* the segments. Statistical analysis of demographic data can test hypotheses about behavioral segment drivers. The behavioral segmentation provides a powerful stratification for attitude and needs surveys: For example, what are the value drivers of the people in segment 6?

Another key to using segmentations is the ability to score every customer with segment identifiers and profile information. Segment-based treatments require identification of the people in the segment. This requires a data warehouse containing all the information used to derive the segments and the information used to profile the segments. Segment-based marketing experiments allow the development of powerful models capable of predicting customer response to marketing and other treatments and offers.

Finally, the segmentations and models must be *used*. Sales and marketing personnel must understand how to use the models, how to set up the campaigns and test cells, and how to retain and analyze the responses. This information must be stored in the data warehouse and used to train better models. Campaign protocols must enforce the use of the models and must require evaluation of all results. This often means developing a new paradigm within the corporate structure. Unfortunately, people being people, new ways must be proven. Acceptance of the new modeling approach may require careful proofs in order to obtain buy-in. Senior executive sponsorship is mandatory, as is a strong advocate capable of leading the charge. If either of these two factors is missing, the best models in the world will not be used, and the money and effort will be wasted.

The segmentations can be used as the foundation of customer portfolios that are assigned to a portfolio manager. Each portfolio may have its own set of priorities and directives. The service-oriented segment may require developing special services and treatments. The novice segments may require education and additional assistance. The low-value segment manager may need to identify a strategy to migrate the members to a higher-value segment. The point is that the segmentations provide the framework from which all CRM activities are defined.

CONCLUSION

Our experience indicates that customer segmentation is the foundation of customer insight. It is the core organizing structure from which all else springs. It enables experimental validation of marketing ideas and strategies and allows for customer portfolio managers who are tasked with segment-specific goals. Segmentations can be the platform from which new product and service offerings are designed and tested. Segmentation is not easy, nor is it inexpensive—but is the first step to a true customer-centric enterprise.

10

Silence Is Golden: The Emerging Opportunities of Silent Commerce

Timothy Stephens

hat if your products, your inventory, or any of your physical assets could sense the characteristics of their environment, know their location, and tell you about it? Just imagine what this would mean.

- You could sit at your desk and instantly take inventory at your warehouse and your customer's warehouse.
- Your products could monitor themselves and alert you when they are about to exceed temperature, humidity, or vibration limits.
- You could identify and track every package as it moves along the value chain, from manufacturing all the way to the consumer.
- Your products could interact with your customers, then report back new insights about those persons' buying habits and interests.
- You could provide in-the-field, real-time product authentication to help prevent counterfeiting.
- Your products could tell you if they are someplace they shouldn't be, thus reducing theft.

These "what-ifs" are in fact "right-nows." They represent the technology and business realities of *silent commerce.*

WHAT IS SILENT COMMERCE?

Silent commerce uses wireless mobile communications and advanced tagging and sensor technologies to make everyday objects intelligent and interactive, creating new information and value streams. It is "silent" because objects communicate and commerce can take place without human interaction.

Silent commerce will provide a level of customer insight never before available, along with the ability to more effectively manage programs derived from that insight. It will help companies understand consumer interactions with their products—not just at the point of sale, but also at the point of decision. Making packages interactive and intelligent also will enable companies to uniquely identify, locate, and track products all along the supply chain—from the manufacturer through to the consumer and even, potentially, through recycling.

HOW DOES SILENT COMMERCE WORK?

Some know silent commerce better by its enabling technologies, such as *radio frequency identification* (RFID). An RFID system uses a half-inch-wide plastic tag with an embedded digital memory chip the size of a pinhead. (It currently sells for about 30 cents.) The tag is easier to scan than a bar code, but an additional capability makes all the difference: The information on the tag can be changed as it moves down the value chain.

At first a chip on a product might contain basic information such as the date the product was created. Later, during shipping, anticounterfeiting information can be added to the chip. Finally, when the product arrives at the store, the retailer can add pricing and product information.

Other technologies can be combined with the RFID chip to provide an extraordinary range of silent commerce services. Small microsensors currently are being tested that monitor the environment around them. Do you want to make sure your fish is fresh, your beer has never been warmed, or your ice cream hasn't been thawed? Scan the chip, and sensors will reveal the temperatures your product has been exposed to from start to finish. Using another emerging technology called *e-ink,* manufacturers can dynamically change the text or writing on a package to warn consumers or reassure them about the product's quality.

Another emerging technology promises to put silent commerce on everyone's radar screens: an Object Internet standard. This potentially revolutionary development consists of an Electronic Product Code (replacing the bar code, or UPC) standard, an object naming service (similar to the Internet's Domain Naming Service that assigns unique URLs to Web sites), and a physical markup language (similar to the Internet's HTML) to describe objects. If you combine ubiquitous sensors with the Object Internet standard, you'll see new types of applications that can track and monitor objects through the Object Internet from anywhere in the world.

SILENT COMMERCE: WHY NOW?

Some of the technologies involved in silent commerce have been around for many years. RFID has been in use since the 1940s. Location-based services such as the Global Positioning System (GPS) have been in place for decades as well. Sensors that detect pressure, temperature, or the presence of a number of chemicals have been developed over the past century. So what's happening today to make these things come together in new and valuable ways?

1. *Lower prices.* Advances in manufacturing and materials science have lowered the price points of tagging and sensor technology so it really can be ubiquitous. Innovations such as power paper, e-ink, and microelectromechanical systems (MEMS) have enabled new kinds of applications. Widespread commercial use of technologies such as GPS continues to drive price points down further.

2. *The wired world.* The infrastructure of computing, communications, and storage is now in place to handle the huge amounts of data that can be generated in silent commerce applications. The ability to integrate different kinds of intercompany and intracompany systems continues to advance. Wireless communication technologies (necessary to keep the parts of the expanded enterprise connected) are evolving.

3. *Systems improvements.* Enterprise resource planning (ERP) and supply chain systems have matured as well, creating the ability to manage and improve operations based on the information that RFID readers provide. Supply chain partners are also becoming better integrated, which increases the requirements for greater product and supply chain information.

4. *Greater market need.* Companies aiming to reduce theft, diversion, and counterfeiting find silent commerce especially attractive. It has the potential to improve revenues, increase margins, and reduce costs. For example, by hindering counterfeiting, silent commerce not only helps to restore a company's brand but also protects its investment in the intellectual property that more firms are recognizing to be an integral component of a product's value. In addition, silent commerce meets the challenge of government requirements to identify and track products uniquely as they move through the supply chain.

WHERE IS THE PROFIT POTENTIAL OF SILENT COMMERCE?

The potential for saving money and creating new opportunities with silent commerce is significant. For example, the supply chain (the process that takes a product from raw materials to manufacturing to distribution) can account for as much as 75 percent of a product's cost. At each point in the value chain from the manufacturer all the way through to the consumer, silent commerce will drive value through improved efficiency in these and other areas:

- *Greater automation.* Manufacturers, distributors, and customers will be able to check all the boxes on a pallet and all the items in a box automatically without having to open the box or count the number of items manually.

- *Inventory management.* Businesses will know the inventory levels in their facilities and their customers' facilities in real time, allowing more efficient replenishment and smaller inventories.

- *Theft reduction.* Businesses will reduce theft by having systems that minimize manual intervention and counting and alert people when theft is occurring. Retailers are already painfully aware that the theft of products from stores or during deliveries is too often the work of professional thieves who are not deterred by the tagging technologies of typical store surveillance.

- *Anticounterfeiting.* Using a unique identifier or identification for each product and case, businesses will be able to pinpoint and significantly reduce losses due to diversion and counterfeiting.

Initial estimates suggest that total savings from silent commerce could exceed $70 billion in the United States alone and $155 billion internationally. Research by analysts Frost and Sullivan indicates there will be a steadily rising demand for RFID technology during the next four years, at a constant rate of 33 percent. Moreover, revenue from the RFID industry is projected to reach nearly $7.5 billion by 2006. Silent commerce will have a major impact on every industry and business process. It will affect the supply chain, manufacturing, and resources and raw materials. Implications will ripple through all aspects of companies and out to their customers.

SILENT COMMERCE APPLICATIONS AND OPPORTUNITIES: TODAY AND TOMORROW

Silent commerce is not just a vision of the future. It is a present capability, though technological developments will lead to an explosion of new business solutions in the coming years. Organizations that can move quickly and creatively to optimize capabilities enabled by intelligent and interactive objects will gain early-adopter competitive advantage.

For most organizations, the challenge will be not to find uses for silent commerce but to select the ones that provide the greatest payback.

Companies today are already creating a wealth of silent commerce applications in the areas of *customer insight* and *operations management.*

- A major packaging company has developed "smart packaging" to transform its packages from objects that merely protect and transport to actual "information vessels." The initiative is expected to bring automated identification to low-cost, disposable products for packages ranging from lipstick boxes to corrugated containers to breakfast cereal containers.

- An automobile manufacturer has been an early adopter of silent commerce technologies to develop inventory management applications. The company attaches wireless transmitters to its vehicles after production to manage its massive inventory.

- An upscale luggage manufacturer builds RFID tags right into its luggage and provides an ID registration service for customers. If a customer's luggage is lost, the company will track and recover it.

- A consumer products company is piloting a smart packaging program in which chips are embedded into each product and readers are built into each shelf. The result is that the company can record when customers pick up a product and whether they put it back. Much in the way that a cookie tracks a user's Web site activities, smart shelves can record customer interactions with merchandise. Theoretically, this will allow the company to rapidly adjust manufacturing so it is in direct proportion to actual consumer demand rather than mere forecasts.

- A Czech clothing manufacturer uses tagging technology to track items throughout its distribution process and at the point of sale. Smart labels attached to the clothing contain data that can be updated as items move through the supply chain. The labels are water-resistant and can withstand extreme temperatures and pressures.

- A company in the United Kingdom runs a warehouse that stores expensive single-malt whiskies, which are subject to theft even by warehouse employees. It created a new security system by building a grid of transponders suspended from the ceiling. In the warehouse, forklift trucks are equipped with RFID readers. Routing details are downloaded to the forklift truck from a central computer via a radio frequency communication link. If the onboard reader detects deviations in the proper routing and loading, the truck is immobilized and a supervisor is required to reset the vehicle.

In the future, silent commerce has the potential to become truly pervasive, as electronic connection and communication become ubiquitous. Every object could have a tag or sensor on or in it—which means any physical object with current or potential value, either intrinsic to itself or generated as it interacts with other objects or people, could be tracked and monitored from anywhere in the world. As sensors become cheaper (and smaller) there literally will be no limits to what can be tracked and how. A number of prototypes exist that demonstrate the long-term potential of silent commerce.

Online Medicine Cabinet

CRM is often thought of only in terms of how to build an interactive Web site or a better customer service center. In the future, enterprises will develop more creative ways to interact with their customers. The online medicine cabinet prototype was developed to show how consumers and enterprises can benefit from interactive information that is integrated into consumers' daily lives. Through a real medicine cabinet, consumers can get up-to-the-minute health-care information that is customized for them. The cabinet, equipped with sensors and recognition systems, can tell who is taking medication out of the cabinet and advise them of the proper dosage. Insurance companies, health-care providers, and hospitals can integrate services to provide customers with the personalized information they need to know—all in the context and the place where daily health care is provided.

Online Wardrobe

The online wardrobe serves as a physical interface between the consumer and the online marketplace. This new kind of wardrobe has awareness of what it contains.

Because it is connected directly to online stores, a consumer can use the wardrobe to engage in interactive shopping by selecting any physical item or items from the wardrobe. While the user is not actively interacting with the wardrobe, the built-in screen becomes a window for a personalized fashion show, which leisurely displays clothing products from various merchants.

Real-World Showroom

Using many of the same technologies as the online wardrobe, the real-world showroom demonstrates how the convergence of wireless devices, shopping services, and RFID-tagged objects in our environment will transform the world into the ultimate showroom. The prototype consists of a personal digital assistant (PDA) device equipped with an RFID-tag reader that can capture the identity of a sweater or necktie worn by another person. The PDA then immediately offers the option of purchasing an identical item through a wireless connection.

Wearable Services Platform—Package Delivery

Logistics companies are facing tremendous challenges in making their delivery people more efficient in the face of growing package volume. Lost packages, missed deliveries, and sheer volume are major problems. The wearable services platform demonstrates how technologies such as wearable computing, heads-up displays, wireless devices, the universal directory, and RFID tags can be used to increase the efficiency of package delivery as well as the customer experience.

Wearable Services Platform—Worker Safety

The wearable services platform for worker safety explores how developments in sensor technologies and their integration with technologies such as wireless networks and wearable computing will provide an enhanced level of safety and security for workers.

Autonomous Purchasing Object

The autonomous purchasing object is the prototype for intelligent products that are truly aware of their surroundings and can act autonomously and make their own purchasing decisions. The object (in the case of this prototype, a doll) uses RFID tags to send or reflect signals as part of a wireless network and must be synchronized with a host to initiate the online commerce.

Pay-per-Use Object

The pay-per-use object prototype explores how objects could be charged based on actual usage instead of fixed price. Using embedded sensors and wireless Internet connectivity, the prototype shows how pricing models could change dramatically and valuable customer insights could be gained and used as input for product development and marketing activities.

Ubiquitous Supervision Solution

The ubiquitous supervision solution is a research prototype that shows how RFID technology may be used to enable a generic container to sense its content and communicate with its exterior. The practical possibility of remotely querying a physical entity (in this specific prototype, a locked box) to get information about the status and the nature of its content can apply to a great number of situations. The following list provides just an example of the set of scenarios that are possible:

- *The bookshelf.* In this scenario, the "box" is a bookshelf. When the bookshelf is locked, it is still possible for a user to access it electronically and query it about its content (i.e., about what books are in it). This object could be used, for example, by organizations or corporations to automatically locate all paper assets that are distributed over a large number of cabinets or shelves scattered geographically around a wide area. The temporary owner of the box may still store private (not tagged) objects in it, as non-RFID-tagged items are not detected.

- *The container.* The box is a container, for example, used for goods transportation. The container may be queried periodically or continuously to check the status of its contents. In specific situations (for instance, when it is critical to monitor the temperature of the contents regularly) more elaborate RFID tags may be used to communicate the specific piece of information. Moreover, the smart container idea finds application in all cases in which it is necessary to investigate the contents of a container quickly without having to resort to examining paper manifests.

- *The room.* A room able to sense its contents makes possible a set of novel services. Consider the case of purchasing a very expensive piece of furniture that has an RFID tag. Its introduction into the smart room could prompt an alert service that warns the owner that the physical asset just introduced is not covered by insurance.

Another interesting scenario is when the room becomes intelligent enough to establish an interaction with the owner of the objects contained in it. The interaction is the result of some artificial reasoning that is based on the contents of the room itself. Suppose, for example, that the room senses some objects, such as a pair of ski gloves and a book on travel holidays. It would then be possible to automatically provide the owner of the objects with useful information or services that most likely would be relevant to the owner's profile and future intentions (e.g., a holiday break to the mountains).

- *The post office box.* Querying a post office box about its contents can speed up and automate some operations that are currently time-consuming. For example, a post office box established for a business can contain a large number of checks and remittances that must be periodically cleared and processed. The smart post office box can process its contents remotely and dynamically plan the clearance visit depending on the number of documents it contains.

WHAT SHOULD COMPANIES BE DOING TODAY TO REAP THE BENEFITS OF SILENT COMMERCE?

With an eye on the market as well as on their competitors, forward-thinking organizations are beginning to consider silent commerce opportunities from two different perspectives.

Holistic Perspective

First, organizations are taking a holistic approach, working to understand how the technology can benefit their whole business and not just one facet. Once an object is embedded with silent commerce technology, a wide variety of capabilities becomes possible. For instance, rather than focusing just on product handling, successful companies also have considered the value of addressing counterfeiting, diversion, product liability, and customer retention. One fertilizer company initially looked at silent commerce to improve product handling through automation. However, it soon realized that once the package became smart, it also could do other things: improve inventory management at key customers' sites; address issues associated with paying rebates on some items twice; and ensure that the product was being used in the correct geographic region and during the correct time of year, thereby reducing product liability and product warranty issues. This approach fundamentally changed the company's economics and interest in silent commerce.

Proactive Perspective

Second, rather than using silent commerce to solve a problem, organizations are focusing on how to use it to prevent the problem from occurring in the first place. An example: Many companies initially used silent commerce to help find things that were lost—containers, packages, cars, and paper rolls. But once they began using the technology, they realized that the real benefit was in never losing anything at all by always knowing the location of every item.

These responses barely skim the surface of silent commerce's capabilities. A complete solution is still emerging as technologies and market needs are refined. Meanwhile, it is not too soon to begin asking key questions that will encourage your organization to appreciate the value of silent commerce:

- What is your total cost of counterfeiting and diversion (including both lost sales and potential damage to your brand)?
- How much do you spend on trade promotion and market development, and how well can you manage those dollars?
- What are the potential cost and liability to your customers when they use your product improperly?
- How much do you spend to recall products?
- How often do you give a rebate twice for the same product?
- How much do you lose in sales from out-of-stock products?

- How much better would your ERP and supply chain management systems work if they had more granular data on a more timely basis?
- How often is your bar code system a barrier to how you really want to run your business?

Like the capabilities of silent commerce itself, this list just begins to touch on the challenges and opportunities these new technologies pose. However, taking action on the answers now can deliver far deeper levels of customer insight—and far greater success—to organizations that begin capturing the benefits of silent commerce.

11

Beyond the Data: Making the Most of Customer Knowledge

Jeanne G. Harris and Thomas H. Davenport

D ata, data everywhere, but ne'er the time to think. That's the state of most companies' knowledge of their customers today, as transaction systems capture unimaginable volumes of data about customer activity but create real challenges for managers hoping to glean insight into how to win more customers and more effectively serve existing ones. Despite having a wealth of transaction data, few organizations have developed capabilities to aggregate, analyze, and use customer data to generate real business value. Though the business world is witnessing an explosion of interest and investment in CRM software and other analytic technologies, many fail to exploit those technologies effectively. As a result, customer satisfaction ratings remain largely unchanged.

WHY CARE ABOUT CUSTOMER KNOWLEDGE?

"Know your customer" is one of the most widely used maxims in business. Yet many companies devote little thought to improving their own understanding of their customers. Often companies have been discouraged by previous efforts, such as failed data warehousing projects or unsuccessful attempts to persuade sales personnel to document customer interests. Many companies that do seek to improve their customer understanding take limited measures, such as conducting a study of customer profitability or implementing a new CRM software product to improve sales force

The content of this chapter originally appeared in the book *Defying the Limits: Setting a Course for CRM Success,* published by Montgomery Research.

effectiveness. Too often, these efforts provide improved efficiencies but yield little in the way of improved customer insight.

An Accenture research study suggests that the best companies in certain industries derive as much as 6 percent additional operating margin simply by having a better understanding of their customers.[1] An organization whose people have better customer knowledge can develop a deeper insight into its customers. These insights, if properly nurtured and applied, enable employees to improve their customer relationships in every interaction with the customer. It is this increased *customer equity* that leads to improved margins.

The following are the most common ways organizations use their customer insight to create value:

- *Segment and prioritize the customer base to maximize resource allocation.* Harrah's Resorts analyzes customer data to determine which customers are most likely to respond to offers to visit particular casinos. As its base of customer data has grown, more of its marketing bets are paying off.

- *Create more effective marketing messages.* Food company Frito-Lay was involved in a study that compared a retailer's total return on investment for direct store-delivered brands (like Fritos) versus warehoused brands. Having this knowledge about its customer's performance allowed Frito-Lay's salespeople to make a stronger pitch for increased shelf space.

- *Innovate and improve existing products/services.* Hewlett-Packard's laser printer, Laser Jet V, was not designed to be portable (portability is not a factor in its purchase). However, handles were added because observations of customers showed that 30 percent of users are in the habit of moving their printers. Because many of those who transport printers are women, the handles were designed to be large enough to avoid breaking long fingernails.

- *Engender customer loyalty.* British Airways analyzed customer data to discover instances in which an executive customer had flown one-way on British Airways but used another carrier on the return. It sent these valued customers a special mailing, headed "now we see you—now we don't," and offered a special incentive to use its services both ways.

- *Enhance the array of products/services.* Travelocity, the Web-based travel agency, offers customers a destination guide with useful information about their destinations.

- *Improve success in cross-selling.* Amazon.com steers its repeat book buyers to other types of products based on interests they have displayed in past purchases.

CUSTOMER INSIGHT LEADERS
In our research on 22 leading companies, we identified the multipronged approaches that allowed these companies to develop superior customer understanding. We noted that all were tackling the challenges simultaneously on many fronts, combining

approaches to managing transaction-derived and human-based knowledge. While specific tactics differed in many respects, the leaders excelled in three areas: *strategic focus, knowledge creation,* and *organization integration.*

Strategic Focus

A company's market position and corporate strategy must be defined and understood before pursuing a knowledge-creation initiative. Then, the company can choose its spots. While it would be nice to be thoroughly knowledgeable about every customer, the reality of resource constraints dictates that there be an emphasis on some highly valuable subset. Leading companies focus their resources on the most valuable customer segments. Microsoft, for example, shifted its emphasis a few years ago to understanding the needs of chief information officers because it anticipated a future in which vastly more revenues would come from corporate than from individual software purchases. A similar shift occurred at consumer goods manufacturer Procter & Gamble when it altered its focus in the 1980s to become more knowledgeable about Wal-Mart and other increasingly powerful trade customers. Until then, its efforts were largely focused on end-consumer research.

Knowledge Creation

Leading companies align their knowledge management initiatives with their business strategy. Prior to the information-gathering process, these companies define and focus their customer knowledge objectives based on their business strategies and customer relationship objectives. For example, clearly defining its objectives first, FedEx successfully undertook an initiative to increase the company's share of the small shipper market. Since this depended on being able to serve these customers cost-effectively, a related goal was to encourage small shippers to drop their packages off rather than have FedEx trucks pick them up. The clarity of these objectives made it much easier to understand what knowledge had to be gained and shared about small shippers.

These leading companies also use transaction-driven and human-based information to build a complete customer picture, fostering customer loyalty. Transaction-driven data can be obtained through systems and data warehouses/marts that include information from past purchases, ZIP codes, or income data. This data can be used to improve direct marketing and products cross-selling and to identify unprofitable customers.

Detailed databases can be helpful, but the best companies recognized that much more sophisticated human-based knowledge, gathered through personal interactions with the customer, must be managed as well. This is especially true in situations in which the past is not a particularly relevant guide to the future. For instance, for a company selling largely fashion goods, past transactions probably are not the best indicator of what will sell to whom this season.

Procter & Gamble, long considered one of the world's best marketers, exemplifies an organization that employs transaction-driven and human-based approaches to gaining consumer and retailer knowledge. Going a step further than the concept of focus groups, Procter & Gamble constructs highly detailed "mental maps" of consumers' thinking about products, such as detergents, which are based on extended, wide-ranging discussions with typical consumers. Procter & Gamble marketing people walk the floors of stores with shoppers, noting what they say and don't say, and observing what they do. With thorough mapping, a great deal of insight can be extrapolated from the thinking of a few consumers. At the same time, Procter & Gamble has been a heavy user of statistical data from point-of-sale transactions. Now the company has begun to focus on managing explicit knowledge about key retailer chains as customers, and it encourages members of customer teams to capture and share key information about retailers with other members serving the same customer.

Organization Integration

The companies that are best at managing customer knowledge also recognize that customer knowledge initiatives do not exist in a vacuum. Rather, their success is dependent on the broader context of roles and responsibilities, the culture of the workplace, and organization structure.

It is imperative that the organizational structure enforce the strategic objective of customer understanding; therefore, it must be conducive to generating and managing customer knowledge. Many companies, such as Hewlett-Packard, have undertaken reorganizations to become more customer-focused. The company's laser printer business, for example, prides itself on technological excellence. Over time, Hewlett-Packard managers realized that as its printers became more of a commodity, the company would lose market share if it relied exclusively on technical leadership. Like many great product companies, Hewlett-Packard was organized by product segments (such as midsize laser printers). Management began a major cultural shift to focus instead on the full customer experience—which included customer support, buying, upgrading, selling, service, toner purchase, and maintenance.

Getting Hewlett-Packard's development engineers to think more broadly about their products was one benefit of this approach. For example, surveys suggested that customer satisfaction could be increased if the "low toner" message were changed to indicate how many pages were left before the toner would run out. Doing this would require adding sensors to predict how many more pages could be produced. Before the new focus on customers and customer knowledge, development engineers would not have understood how adding this feature would contribute to market leadership.

Reorganizing around customers seems a double-edged sword. If a company is organized around types of customers, each type will receive significant attention, and approaches will be developed for managing knowledge about that type of customer. However, this segmented organization may mean that generalized solutions for customer knowledge will not be developed, and useful approaches may not be shared easily across different customer types.

MAKING KNOWLEDGE USEFUL

Our research shows that the companies that are most recognized for knowing their customers and getting value from customer insights (e.g., Harley-Davidson,

Hewlett-Packard, and Procter & Gamble) are making significant investments to develop transaction-data-driven analytic capabilities. But more important, they are investing in a wide variety of approaches to gain customer knowledge. In fact, our detailed interviews with the leaders in customer knowledge reveal that they give most of the credit for their success to their efforts in increasing the collection, distribution, and use of *human-based* (as opposed to *transaction-derived*) knowledge. We would argue that information from both customer transactions and human customer relationships are necessary for real customer insights, but they must be turned into knowledge to be useful.

Transaction-Derived Knowledge

There is no doubt that an organization's ability to analyze and interpret transaction data can be a source of competitive advantage. The companies in our study had many examples of using data to create customer knowledge, which led to improved business results. The following are examples of some of the leading companies' use of transaction-driven knowledge:

- *Using past-purchase or other personalized data to target and deliver promotional offers.* American Express designed four different covers for its merchandise catalog; each household got the one that best reflected its past purchases (high-tech gadgets versus jewelry).

- *Increasing customer loyalty.* Marriott invested heavily in CRM systems. Desk clerks now get a heads-up display of any special interests or needs a guest might have expressed when making the reservation or during past stays at other Marriott properties. Having such information available during those first few critical minutes following the customer's arrival can make all the difference to their lasting impression of the hotel's service.

- *Achieving a sense of relationship through personalization.* Clinique.com is designed to be a natural extension of the Clinique retail experience. The site asks users for information, such as natural hair color and tendency to sunburn, so it can tailor recommended products that are likely to be right for them. Clinique periodically sends e-mails, personalized by skin type, which offer deals on these products. To date, more than 1.1 million users have registered.

- *Improving cross-selling.* First Union, one of the largest U.S.-based banks, implemented a massive (27-terabyte) enterprisewide customer-centric data warehouse. First Union uses its customer data to improve the effectiveness of direct-marketing efforts. The bank also analyzes customer characteristics to identify unprofitable customers, with the hope of transforming them into desirable customers. Finally, by analyzing both transaction and demographic customer data, First Union relationship managers are able to react in real time to consumer events (for example, a major savings withdrawal or deposit, or purchase of a house). It expects these combined capabilities will contribute $100 million in revenues annually.

Human-Based Knowledge

As useful as transaction data can be, the truth about customer knowledge is that successfully managing it requires more than data crunching. Sophisticated knowledge, particularly human insight, must be managed, together with voluminous data. The following are examples of some leading companies' uses of this type of knowledge:

- *Promoting a higher level of interaction between employees and customers.* Fidelity Investments requires salespeople to record customer knowledge gained in sales calls, a particularly useful resource when a customer account is reassigned for whatever reason.

- *Tightly linking corporate identity to their customers' identity.* The Jeep division of DaimlerChrysler understands that it must know its customers extremely well in order to continue to introduce product improvements that are true to the brand. It hires marketing professors (with strong backgrounds in the social sciences) to observe and interpret customer behavior at rallies and discuss it with executives and marketing management—an attempt to capture subtle observations and impressions and convert them to explicit knowledge.

- *Improving product design.* At General Electric, comments from customer calls on the division's inbound toll-free number are systematically recorded by service reps and later analyzed by product developers. To get a feel for the customer's voice and mood when giving the comments, engineers and researchers are required to listen in on customer calls at regular intervals.

Our research found that the best approach to customer knowledge is a mix of transaction-driven and human-based knowledge, though even the best companies struggle with achieving the right balance and integrating different types of knowledge. Those that are most successful take a conscious, deliberate approach to transforming data into knowledge and results.

CUSTOMER INSIGHT SUCCESS STORIES

Here are two examples of organizations that use a combination of transaction-derived and human-based knowledge to develop superior insights into their customers—and use that insight effectively.

Nordstrom

The Nordstrom department store, famous for its customer service, created its complimentary Personal Touch shoppers program to build rapport and establish long-term customer relationships. The personal shoppers are fashion consultants who seek to form a long-term relationship with their customers; they are given extensive training in color, current fashions, and how to match their store's products to a customer's appearance, taste, and lifestyle. Through a close relationship with clients based on knowledge of the client's tastes and fashion expertise, Personal Touch shoppers try to sell ensembles as opposed to individual clothing items.

Though Nordstrom knows that when it comes to fashion, a human can extrapolate from a client's past choices to current styles much more reliably than a computer, Personal Touch shoppers are supported by technology. In fact, they have access to two systems that capture customer information and knowledge. The first is a database of personal profiles in which they record customers' likes, dislikes, lifestyles, and apparel needs as learned in telephone and face-to-face conversations. They can even document clothing acquired from other stores. The second database contains customer purchase histories to help the shopper understand a customer's tastes or to suggest items that might complement a prior purchase. In the purchase history system, shoppers can annotate a customer's records, noting how clothing will be used or prompting some follow-up (for example, a reminder to verify that a customer's alterations are completed on time or to notify the customer of an upcoming sale). It is easy to see how Nordstrom's combination of human-based and technology-derived approaches to managing customer knowledge leads to superior service and loyalty.

Harley-Davidson

Though Harley-Davidson finds it impossible to pin down the essence of its customers in any succinct form, it ensures that management stays in touch with customers through extensive programs in which executives fraternize with customers at rallies and owner group meetings. Particularly noteworthy is that Harley's executives also regularly ride their bikes across the country to join the customers. In doing so, they learn from the customers by meeting them, but they also develop their own tacit knowledge of the experience of riding their products over long distances.

Also, to continue to introduce product improvements that are true to the brand, Harley (as does the Jeep division of DaimlerChrysler) hires marketing professors with strong backgrounds in the social sciences to observe and interpret customer behavior at rallies. Not ignoring customer insight derived from data, Harley is developing an automated system and customer data warehouse that will track customers' purchases and their interactions with the company, and it is supporting some Internet-based relationships with HOG, the Harley Owners Group. However, the focus is and will continue to be on "high-touch" interactions at rallies and dealerships as the primary repository of customer knowledge. Harley's heavy and long-term focus on tacit customer knowledge seems to have worked; the company is in the enviable situation of selling all the motorcycles it can make, with a long order backlog. It has one of the highest levels of customer loyalty of any business.

LOOKING FOR INSIGHT IN ALL THE WRONG PLACES

Clearly, companies investing in customer knowledge management must focus on particular customer types and objectives, employ both transaction-derived and human-based knowledge, and manage the broader customer knowledge context. Most large companies have a good record of the business transactions they complete with customers. Many of these companies are focused heavily on analyzing transaction data and have forgotten that there is a world of customer knowledge coming directly from human interactions with customers. Companies must not be tempted by the easy availability of transaction data to mistake transactions for customers or to gravitate into territory where the projects are least ambiguous and where finding knowledge looks easiest.

Customers, first and foremost, are people—and building a relationship with them entails more than just tabulating their transactions.

12

More Than Data Warehousing: An Integrated View of the Customer

Kevin N. Quiring and Nancy K. Mullen

That vibration on your belt is familiar, but you're still startled when the pager interrupts your session with the *Wall Street Journal* as you wait for a flight at the Miami airport. You glance at the message, surprised that it's from your online broker. You almost delete it, assuming it's a pedestrian banner ad from the Web site that has somehow wormed its way into your pager address. Then you notice that it's a personalized message. You can have the fee waived for your next trade. No way was this message sent to everyone in their database; it would have cost them a fortune! Apparently, your online broker has noticed your conspicuous lack of trading activity since you opened the account eight months ago. The offer makes you want to act immediately. In retrospect, you decide it's not the eight bucks that is spurring you on, but the poignant reminder that your money has been earning zero-point-nothing percent interest for nearly a year in the brokerage account. You make a mental note to log on when you hit the ground in Minneapolis and take advantage of the offer.

This campaign for an online brokerage firm garnered a 30 to 40 percent activation rate, and 20 to 30 percent of those people repeated. Its value and success in terms of increased accuracy and reduced costs are attributed to having what is being commonly referred to as an *integrated view of the customer* (IVoC).

IVoC is an enabling business capability that supplies the missing link for CRM implementations: the connection between customer interaction channels and cus-

The content of this chapter originally appeared in the book *Defying the Limits: Setting a Course for CRM Success*, published by Montgomery Research.

tomer strategy. IVoC brings together demographic, behavioral, and contact data for analysis and customer scoring. It also makes those customers and their scores available to, for example, the brokerage's Web site and e-mail system for outbound campaign execution.

In addition to gaining higher value through some very profitable campaigns, the brokerage also improved speed and increased throughput. Models for predicting response that used to take 6 weeks to develop were done in 10 to 12 days because the brokerage had an integrated view of its customers.

GAINING GREATER VALUE

Many companies have embarked on CRM projects to improve their marketing and service capabilities—for example, to increase cross-selling and up-selling; improve call center routing, based on the type of customer calling in; and to more effectively target the customers most likely to be interested in what they are selling.

These are worthwhile objectives, to be sure, but the central problem remains: Neither operational CRM databases nor data warehouses meet the needs of a holistic marketing, sales, or customer service agenda. Most CRM database implementations are channel-specific; most data warehouses are not channel-centric, but they are not customer-centric, either. No CRM database integrates everything you need to know about your customers—their interactions, the products and services they've purchased, and the channels they've used—at the exact moment you need to know it. The results? Unused data and underutilized processing capability. The missing link is an integrated view of the customer that is the touchpoint for all interactions a company has with its customers. This capability is essential for companies to realize better value from their existing CRM investments.

Equally important, as companies feel their way through initiatives meant to extend CRM value across channels and product lines, they are undermining the integration of these solutions because they lack a key ingredient—*context*. Defined as the intent or purpose of the customer interaction, context determines how all of these interactions work together to shape a customer's overall experience with a company. Today's cross-channel integration efforts are usually not holistic or strategic. Efforts do not consider the breadth and depth of the overall customer experience when the scope is being defined. Instead of thinking big, starting small, and growing fast, managers are thinking small, starting slowly, and not growing because they lack a road map.

A typical result is cross-channel integration that occurs one data element at a time. Call centers gain access to e-mail addresses captured on the Web, and the Web site gains access to customer service contact data stored in the call center system. None of this takes into account the enterprise solution to such problems, nor does it address the enterprise value. Context is required to translate customer strategy into action.

A UNIFIED SOLUTION

An IVoC capability that will provide this context is composed of the following elements:

- Customer contact and marketing processes that are linked to ensure that customer insight can be generated and leveraged by the customer contact channels
- Technologies that deliver the required data to the right business function on a continual, real-time basis
- An organization and governance model, enabled by technology, that can apply the customer strategy across business units and contact channels

To achieve an IVoC, a company's customer contact channels should be connected to ensure that contact history, transaction history, demographic data, and preferences are available as needed across all channels. In addition, key information required to generate customer insight must be captured and made available to customer insight functions, such as analytics and campaign management, in a timely manner. Finally, messages and offers intended to shape customer interactions must be delivered back to contact channels such as the sales force, call centers, and the Web.

An IVoC capability is essential to ensure that the right data is delivered to the right business functions at the right time to help shape subsequent customer interactions. Not all customer data needs to be accessible to all processes at all times—only meaningful data, delivered just in time.

This is a far cry from the data warehousing approaches of old. In fact, we see the IVoC capability as the third stage in the evolution of data warehousing. The first stage, which came into being in the 1980s, highlighted virtual information access. It provided for online access to business information contained in systems of record. However, this approach was characterized by inconsistent data, poor performance, and inadequate data availability. Systems typically were locked down and inaccessible except for nighttime batch reporting. Online query and reporting software was limited. Finally, no solution could be found to the problem of inconsistent data across multiple systems.

In an attempt to correct these deficiencies, a data warehousing methodology emerged in the 1990s. Like any evolutionary process, this step solved previous problems but created new side effects. Data warehousing methodology insisted that companies define specific business problems to solve or questions that needed answering on an ongoing basis. This approach helped guarantee business value, performance, and availability for known questions. However, due to the time- and capital-intensive nature of this approach, flexibility was limited. As businesses took new directions and users changed their minds about what types of questions they wished to ask, data warehouses were slow to respond and required ever-larger development efforts.

The ultimate example of business users changing their minds occurs when they become customer-centric. This represents a huge process shift for businesses and often invalidates existing data warehouses that were built to be product-centric. Moreover, this process change brings with it two new requirements that traditional data warehouses are ill equipped to satisfy: *value* and *speed.* Data warehouses must be constructed more quickly, with less investment, and be flexible as businesses' customer-centric needs change. Analytical results must be fed back into interaction systems so they can deliver value by shaping the customer experience. A real-time feedback loop was never a requirement before, but it is a necessity now.

THREE CRITICAL COMPONENTS

Enter the integrated view of the customer, the third stage in the data warehousing evolution. The IVoC capability encompasses three vital components that produce the value and speed today's customer-centric business strategies require:

- *Data* includes the information required about the customer to extend CRM solutions across contact channels or product lines within your enterprise.

- *Rules* are the instructions for using the data to shape the next interaction with your customer. Rules define what you do with the information after it is warehoused.

- *Context* is the translation of your customer strategy into rules meant to deliver that strategy.

Data

A wide variety of data is required to drive CRM value and provide an integrated view of the customer. More is not necessarily better, however. What you really want your IVoC capability to enable is delivery of the right data to ensure the desired customer experience across channels. For instance, if preliminary analysis shows that an e-mail address plays no part in customer segmentation or is not used in any channel other than the Web, then it is unlikely that you will want to store that attribute in your IVoC data architecture.

You also should consider how the data could best be organized. Information required to drive customer interactions, such as demographic updates, will require an interactive data architecture. The data required for generating customer insight also will have to be accessed by data-mining and analytic tools.

Timing is another important consideration. For example, some businesses would find significant value in receiving real-time updates as customers log complaints. Complaint data would help drive real-time analytics and effect customer treatments applied in real time at the point of interaction. Another example: Information shared between two customer contact channels is very often required in near–real time, as a customer may use both a call center or a Web site within minutes of each other.

In addition, the quality of data and privacy issues must be considered. An IVoC data architecture also must be augmented and cleansed as appropriate and, at the same time, provide an organization with a centralized record of which data can be used for which functions. Integrating information from independent touchpoints can be very challenging, due to the absence of quality customer identification information. Growing attention to privacy restrictions further increases the difficulties in identifying customers.

Rules

The rules required for an IVoC capability come in two primary forms: *personalization* and *data transformation*. It is important to note that their development should be considered a business function and not simply be delegated to your IT department. Why? Most rules are a manifestation of business objectives, decisions, and requirements rather than technical implications of those requirements.

ASK THE RIGHT QUESTIONS

As you consider better ways to link your customer interaction and strategy, the following questions will help you decide whether you need to develop an IVoC capability or, if you already have an IVoC capability, whether it requires improvement.

Customer Relationship Management

- Can I share customer contacts across channels?
- Can I share a customer's business transactions across channels?
- Can customer service representatives (CSRs) view a customer's entire book of business?
- Can customers view their entire book of business on the Web?
- Can Marketing analyze a customer's entire book of business?
- Can Marketing analyze complete and consistent attitudinal and behavioral data for a customer?
- Can I run an integrated campaign?
- Can I run a multichannel campaign in real time?
- Can I differentiate the level of service provided based on who is calling?
- Can I consistently identify a customer on any channel?
- How many callers can a CSR accurately identify?
- How many times does a CSR have to enter in the customer number?
- Do my CSRs know my customers' Web preferences?
- How many of my customers use two or more channels to interact with us?
- How much revenue is generated from a cross-sell by a CSR?
- Can I cross-sell and up-sell on the Web?

Customer Data

- Do I have the right kind of data? Is there enough information, and is it rich enough? Could it move a metric, such as revenue per call?
- Where does all my customer data reside? Is information in the right places?
- What information is duplicated in multiple databases? How many databases?
- Is information easy to access for CSRs, marketers, and others who need to use it?
- Of the shared information available, how much is being used? For example, are CSRs using the data available?
- When the shared information is used, how are revenues affected?

Rules
(Instructions for using the data to shape the next customer interaction.)

- Are the rules consistent across multiple channels?
- Can I deliver a consistent message across our channels and make sure that I'm doing so?

- How many systems store rules that govern customer interactions?
- How many systems store rules that unify customer data?

**Context
(Translating your customer strategy.)**

- Am I meeting the goals set forth in my customer strategy?
- Am I experiencing undesirable side effects from my campaigns?

Personalization rules shape each customer interaction. They provide for consistent, timely, and relevant individualized interactions and offers across multiple customer touch points. Personalization rules govern what information is pushed to customers and how customer information is collected. Data transformation rules, on the other hand, govern non-customer-facing activity. They provide for a similarly important business function: merging customer data from source systems or third parties. Both forms of rules, personalization and transformation, are most effective when they address the broadest possible set of scenarios.

Context

Context is typically the missing piece for many CRM implementations, yet it has the greatest impact of all three IVoC components. Two facets of context are especially important:

- A holistic understanding of all the potential customer interactions within an organization, the events that make up those interactions, and how the outcome of each interaction affects subsequent interactions or the overall customer relationship
- The reason why a rule is being implemented or a decision is being made

To better understand the critical importance of context, think back to our brokerage example at the beginning of this chapter. Automated stock alerts sent by a brokerage to personal digital assistants (PDAs), cell phones, or pagers may have the unintended effect of driving trading requests to a call center if convenient Web connections are not available at the time customers receive the trading message. The call center, not anticipating such peaks, may experience reduced service levels at the very moment its customers desire and expect immediate attention. After all, it was the brokerage that notified them, not the other way around. It is at this touch point that context becomes real and urgent.

In addition, the purpose of each rule must be determined. As more rules governing interactions and data transformation are implemented across the enterprise, it is important to understand the intended effect. Which rules are meant to contribute to which dimension of the customer strategy—acquisition, cross-selling, or reten-tion? As the strategy is defined, rules should be defined for each of the dimensions. For instance, an up-selling rule implemented as part of a direct mail campaign for an automotive manufacturer may actually cannibalize a retention program currently in place at the customer service center. The company's IVoC capability should provide awareness of this conundrum and the ultimate long-term strategy. This goal is the manifestation of context, which governs which of these rules should take precedence at any given time.

LOOKING AHEAD

As customers increasingly demand more relevant and personalized interactions with their suppliers and the competition for customers' mind share continues to intensify, companies will need to do a better job of making use of the mountains of customer and transaction data at their disposal. For many, this will mean developing an inte-grated view of their customers. Doing so, however, will require first asking many difficult questions (see sidebar) to determine the scope and extent of the challenge that awaits them. The answers to these questions will help companies unlock the value of their existing CRM investments and carry those capabilities (and their cus-tomers) to a higher level of responsiveness and profitability.

4

Reinventing Customer Contact

13

Making Customer Interaction More Profitable

Philip J. Tamminga

I n the past decade, CRM gave rise to a spate of customer-facing programs in companies of all stripes. These programs were based largely on customer-centric strategies and executed through large-scale technology investments. As CRM technologies and practices evolved, companies intensified their efforts to improve customer service and provide new ways for customers to interact with them. The motivation behind these efforts ranged from spurring growth, responding to competition, and making operations more efficient. But regardless of why the initiatives were undertaken, the fact is that customer-centricity became a way of life for most companies.

Now add more fuel to the fire. Heightened pressure from Wall Street to further reduce costs and increased customer demand for new and enhanced services are making it difficult for companies to know in which direction their current and future CRM efforts should head. The inherent contradiction between *more and better service* and *lower-cost operations* reveals the limitations in the approaches most companies take to customer interaction today.

For instance, many organizations pursue the ideal of giving every customer the highest level of personal service possible. This is certainly laudable; however, the costs of doing so continue to escalate as customers become even more demanding and the financial community becomes less tolerant of miscues. Furthermore, companies' significant investments in contact center and interaction infrastructure during the 1990s have left them grappling with high fixed costs and excess capacity. Unable to relieve themselves of these costly assets without compromising service, companies take a major hit on their margins when revenue comes up short or customers leave the fold. Finally, the methods for interacting with customers in the 1990s are no longer sufficient to meet customer expectations. Today's customers expect a company's call center representative to know the same things about them that the marketing head does. However, past CRM efforts (which optimized specific areas within the organization) have resulted in a silo effect among the marketing, sales, and service functions that has made it extremely difficult, if not impossible, for companies to integrate data and processes across these areas.

To fundamentally change the economics of sales and service, companies must address a number of critical issues. For starters, they have to develop a deeper understanding of customers—particularly, each customer's business impact on the company—and use that insight to dictate specific interactions (including messages and offers and mode of delivery of them) with each customer based on his or her value to the company. They also have to do a better job of understanding the cost of serving specific customers relative to the potential revenue they generate—an exercise that will further help specify how particular customers are treated (e.g., steering low-revenue customers to self-service options while reserving live support and more conversational interactions for more valuable customers or transactions). In addition, companies must improve the performance of their customer-facing workforces to enhance proficiency and motivation. And they must work toward integrating all their customer-facing channels to ensure a consistent customer experience and an uninhibited exchange of information and customer knowledge.

TECHNIQUES FOR TRANSFORMING CUSTOMER CONTACT

The preceding challenges are a tall order, to be sure; but they're not insurmountable. In the pursuit of changing the economics of sales and service, we've identified a number of areas in which companies can take action to make their customer contact activities dramatically more effective and efficient:

- Leveraging new technology-enabled channels to interact with customers
- Using customization and personalization to transform customer insights into more meaningful, conversational interactions
- Reinvigorating and realigning customer-facing workforces
- Enhancing relationships with channel partners

Leveraging New Technology-Enabled Channels

Just as the emergence of the Web in the 1990s opened up a whole new world of customer-contact options, wireless and messaging technologies today provide companies with unparalleled opportunities to interact with customers wherever they are (often at the exact point of need) and do so extremely cost-effectively.

With wireless technologies, companies truly stand at the cusp of an entirely new way of doing business: *mobile commerce,* or *m-commerce.* The fact is that m-commerce offers huge opportunities for companies to make dramatic changes in how they relate to customers, and greater business potential than that offered by e-commerce. For example, m-commerce can enable buyers of commodities to stay constantly in touch with prices of goods—whether they are in the office, on a train, in a boat, or sitting on a tractor in a field. It can help customers and suppliers keep track of goods in transit. And it can serve as an extension of the stationary Internet terminal, allowing for mobility between sessions at the desktop while maintaining continuous contact between buyers and sellers.

However, companies must avoid the notion that m-commerce is "just like e-commerce, but on wheels." The rules for engaging in m-commerce are different, as are the challenges that companies will encounter. To meet customers' needs and capitalize on m-commerce's potential, companies must make sure that customers can use wireless phones or PDAs to actually connect with someone or something of value. Sites to be accessed with wireless devices must be easy to use and offer only the most necessary features and functions. Companies must enable customers to use their wireless devices to fill not only their downtime (consolidating and polishing off a set of tasks that would otherwise take up valuable time, such as reading e-mail, checking news reports, and the like) but also their "uptime" by providing services and information that customers know they can count on and need access to immediately. Perhaps most important, companies must ensure that customers have control over their wireless environment (such as being able to store information for later retrieval or customizing the interface) and that it is easy for people to buy via a wireless device (i.e., execute a transaction, which is different from shopping).

Similar benefits and challenges are offered by messaging technologies (which can, incidentally, also be wireless). More than 130 million people use instant messaging technology—such as AOL Instant Messenger or short-message-service (SMS) messages via mobile phones—to send more than 1.5 billion instant messages a day. These numbers (combined with projections of significant growth in the market) indicate that messaging has been established as a mainstream communications channel.

As is the case with wireless devices in general, the constant connectivity offered by messaging technologies will revolutionize communications and create new relationships between businesses and customers. Messaging technologies provide an unprecedented ability to intelligently and cost-effectively interact with customers at scale, as a number of pioneering companies are beginning to discover. For instance, a realtor site on the Web enables visitors to send a message to the mobile phone of the realtor representing a house the visitor is interested in with the click of a mouse. Furthermore, several retailers have created a "buddy" on instant messaging networks that enables customers to send messages from their instant messenger of choice to customer service representatives, who will send a response in real time to that customer's messenger address. In the near future, expect to see airlines begin to adopt messaging technologies as a way for travelers to stay in constant contact with them and get the most current updates on time-sensitive information (e.g., flight delays and cancellations) and for airlines to send alerts quickly to large numbers of customers through their communication devices of choice.

In short, wireless and messaging technologies represent the new frontier of customer contact, and companies that act now to incorporate them into their interaction strategies stand to reap the greatest benefits.

Using Customization and Personalization

As discussed in the preceding chapter, new CRM technologies enable companies to analyze customer data as never before and, in the process, develop greater insights into customers' needs and preferences. The next logical step is to use those insights to craft more relevant offers and communications, tailored to each customer or segment, to strengthen customer loyalty and increase revenue while reducing wasted effort. In fact, many companies are now beginning to use personalization in just this way via the Web, with great results.

To further improve their performance, some companies are combining personalization with *customization* (i.e., giving customers themselves the ability to define and shape the personalization). Rather than relying on some mix of artificial intelligence technologies (inference engines and collaborative filtering, for example) to surmise the needs and preferences of their customers, these companies are designing processes that solicit and use customer feedback.

There are three important actions that companies must take to leverage their investments in personalization capabilities and enhance the value of their Web sites. First, they must work within the limits of today's personalization applications to strengthen their personalization efforts where they can. This means having the right content at the right time and generating the right options, recommendations, and communications from interpretations of both personal and broader-context information. Simply welcoming a person to a site by name is no longer sufficient. Second, they must more proactively enable the user's involvement in the design and flow of a site by increasing the availability and ease-of-use of customization options. In other words, they should pay more attention to cocreating their Web sites with their users than to trying to create the perfect site. Third, where it makes sense, companies should combine customization and personalization to capitalize on the strengths of each approach. They can offer *customizable personalization*—for example, allowing customers to review and edit the data the personalization engine uses to make its recommendations so that only relevant aspects are included. Or, they can *personalize the customization* available to user by using the knowledge gained in personalization to offer users the opportunity to customize only specific, limited aspects of the Web site at one time. This simplifies the decision-making process and reduces into manageable chunks the time commitment required for customization.

Whether using personalization, customization, or some combination of the two, companies can realize a return on the significant investments they have made in customer-insight capabilities in the form of more efficient transactions, interactions that resonate more deeply with customers, and enhanced customer loyalty.

Reinvigorating and Realigning Customer-Facing Workforces

All the technology in the world will not compensate for an ineffectual workforce. That is why it is critical for companies that are serious about transforming the way they interact with customers to include the human element in their CRM initiatives.

That is often easier said than done, however. The pressure to effect critical change quickly is more relentless than ever. But techniques and approaches for improving workforce performance and linking it to bottom-line value, like many initiatives that go right to the heart of an organization, often seem to move too slowly to meet critical demands. How can companies achieve necessary workforce reductions yet maintain or even improve productivity levels? How can they keep their people focused and engaged? How can they put together the right mix of tools, rewards, training, and career opportunities to provide the job satisfaction necessary to retain their top talent? Most important, how can they do all this right now?

We have identified several keys to reinvigorating and realigning key customer-facing workforces—which, in most organizations, are what we call *mission-critical workforces* because they are particularly vital to a company's overall business performance. Incremental improvements in job performance in a mission-critical workforce can translate into discernible differences in financial results. Field-service workers, for instance, are a mission-critical workforce for many companies, because companies depend on this workforce to represent their brands to their customers and to distinguish themselves from competitors based on the services they provide. Improving the performance of this workforce can have a major impact on customer satisfaction and retention, and it can ultimately lead to increased revenue and profitability.

The first key to transforming a workforce is to understand the specific behavior the company wants the workforce to exhibit. Doing so requires pinpointing six or eight key performance objectives—identifiable as such because: (1) They are measurable, and (2) they represent clear business imperatives (and often link directly to financial outcomes).

The second key is to identify the specific business benefits derived from particular workforce improvements. For instance, in a call center initiative, the focus might be on three potential benefits: (1) increasing the number of desirable customers acquired, (2) increasing profits from each customer, and (3) fostering a longer overall relationship with the customer.

Once the key performance objectives and business benefits pieces are in place, the next step is to assess the current performance of the workforce to understand what changes must be made to bring about the improvements and business benefits sought. Finally, the appropriate training and development package (which could include a mix of process improvement, performance feedback, e-learning, knowledge management, and other such tools) must be created to raise the workforce's performance level.

By following this approach to workforce performance improvement, a company can help ensure that its critical customer-facing workforces are operating at peak efficiency and are having a measurable, positive impact on the company's bottom line.

Enhancing Relationships with Channel Partners

While business-to-consumer CRM seems to get most of the attention these days, there still are plenty of opportunities for companies that don't sell to consumers (or that do so through intermediaries) to use CRM techniques and technologies to enhance relationships with their channel partners.

One such emerging twist on CRM is *partner relationship management* (PRM), which specifically focuses on the process automation between companies and channel partners. To create greater customer value and channel partner profitability, leading companies are building PRM infrastructures that enable them to coordinate business-planning activities, share information, conduct commerce, and provide postsales support across the channel.

PRM solutions are designed to improve the efficiency and effectiveness of the interactions between companies and channel partners by allowing them to share information in routine business activities. Early adopters of PRM not only are improving channel marketing, sales, fulfillment, and service functions; they also are evolving the channel itself into a greater provider of value-added services and solutions. These companies largely are using the Internet and numerous e-business tools to eliminate most manual processing techniques that are prone to costly errors and inefficiencies, thereby promoting a seamless channel partner experience. They are also leveraging these Web-enabled capabilities to maximize the value of every channel partner interaction to deliver a consistently branded end-customer experience focused on common processes and tools.

At the leading edge of PRM, new application technologies enable manufacturers to extend collaborative business processes through the channel. Channel partners will be able to share their experience and knowledge and provide greater customer value as a network than any single channel partner could alone. Channel partners that have complementary skills, products, and services will be able to work together to come up with creative new solutions to support the companies' value propositions and customer needs.

Another variation of CRM is an approach called *customer-centric service management* (CCSM). CCSM is being used by an increasing number of original equipment manufacturers (OEMs) in the industrial equipment industry to extend relationships with their business customers and, in turn, differentiate their products, drive revenue growth, grow customer loyalty, and build competitive advantage. This approach essentially seeks to transform a company that sells products into a company that sells a wide range of services and products, bundled and tailored to each customer's needs. The driving force behind CCSM is the fact that although customers can invest hundreds of thousands to millions of dollars in the purchase of a single piece of industrial equipment, the purchase price represents just 10 to 25 percent of what the customer will spend on the equipment during the product's total life cycle. The remainder is spent on such services as maintenance, insurance, fuel, and parts, and that is where the opportunity lies: offering bundled services that capture the total life-cycle revenue.

For industrial equipment OEMs to move beyond their core manufacturing capabilities and tap into these valuable product life cycle revenues, they must be adept at generating and using deep insights into their customers' needs and operations; equipping their technicians with the tools and content necessary to skillfully, quickly, and remotely address service issues; and using predictive maintenance to identify and correct issues before they become problems.

CONCLUSION

Many organizations are facing new market pressures with outdated, unfocused customer treatment strategies, investment models, and delivery options. They currently have only a vague picture of their customers' revenue potential, and their infrastructure and service costs are increasing faster than revenues. The following chapters discuss in more detail how companies can improve their customer contact strategies and operations to address these issues so that they can not only keep up with the demands of customers but also satisfy the financial community's desire for a more robust bottom line.

14

Let's Talk: Applying the Art of Conversation to Customer Contact

Brian A. Johnson and Paul F. Nunes

B efore the age of mass communications, transactions large and small were conducted face to face, often ending with a simple handshake. Marketing consisted largely of the goodwill created over the course of a number of dialogues (sometimes spanning years) between the buyer and seller. Business, in other words, was *conversational.* With the advent of radio and television, dialogues with customers were replaced by series of monologues; messages were not presented to individual customers but broadcast to millions grouped into *target segments.*

Today, however, technology is bringing back dialogue between companies and customers by enabling message-and-response interactions on a mass scale. By using call centers and direct mail (both print and electronic), companies are once again conversing with their customers and getting to know them individually. More important, technology is helping companies make use of the knowledge gained during these interactions to customize future contact with individual customers. Although consumers have always integrated their past experiences into commercial transactions, companies have not. How often, for example, do companies try to sell customers credit cards they already hold?

GINGERBREAD AND PEARS

Business once again has become conversational: Each interaction, dialogue, monologue or discussion with a customer is being recognized and managed as part of a

This chapter originally appeared in *Outlook,* vol. 14, no. 1, January 2002, an Accenture publication. Reprinted by permission.

larger discourse. The quality of a company's conversation with a customer is therefore measured not simply by its ability to have a discussion (through a call center, for example) or a dialogue (as in an integrated direct-marketing campaign) but by its ability to integrate these customer contacts and use the knowledge gained to proactively set the direction of future interactions. For companies, conversations are the mechanics of relationships. More broadly, this means moving the core marketing process away from the *target marketing* of the mass communication era toward *conversational marketing.*

Some companies already excel at conversational marketing. Casino owner Harrah's, for example, maintains an ongoing dialogue with its gaming customers through an opt-in loyalty card program; the company determines the exact timing and value of its offers to individual customers through data mining. Inter-Continental Hotels and Resorts records the insights it gains from customer interactions with its staff, and it uses those insights to improve future customer encounters. For example, one guest always finds a plate of his daughter's favorite gingerbread cookies in the room when he arrives with her, no matter which Inter-Continental location they visit.

But many companies are not ready for the changes conversational marketing brings. They face three critical issues.

- What types of dialogues and other customer interactions must be created to support true customer conversations?
- How can the company determine and implement a conversational style that is aligned with the customer's needs and based on a cost-effective set of new technologies?
- Who inside and outside the company must participate in customer conversations to sustain them, and how can these participants be included?

At their core, these are the same questions people face every day in their attempts to be good conversationalists. Companies can use what linguists know about these attempts to improve their own conversations (see sidebar).

Most companies talk to customers for just two reasons: to sell something or to fix a problem. The result is that while many companies think of themselves as conversational, they are capable of engaging customers in dialogue at only two points in the selling cycle—at the time of purchase (through cashiers and salespeople) and while providing postpurchase support (through customer response centers). But valuable conversations require a lot of seemingly pointless small talk—snippets of dialogue that jump back and forth across various topics. Scholars in the field recognize that this exploratory banter is critical to identifying commonalities and building the foundation from which deeper discussions can emerge. The French have long known that the best time to approach difficult business topics is over dinner, but near the end ("*entre la poire et le fromage,*" as they say, or "between the pear and the cheese"); such forbearance ensures that there is time for small talk to have its effect on relationship building.

In a commercial setting, this requires developing the ability—and the patience—to talk to customers about things that might appear unrelated to pushing products, and to do so in a seemingly spontaneous manner. It means being able to engage customers in the selling process on their terms and according to their timetables—engaging them at the points at which they become aware of offerings, consider alternatives, and determine preferences.

Take General Motors, for example, which recently announced that it was developing a low-energy radar system that sounds an alarm if children are left alone in the backseat of an automobile—even though the option won't be available until 2004. In the past, car companies were reluctant to unveil such projects while they were still in the R&D stage, but now they carry on open and public conversations as a way to gain feedback and respond to customer concerns early in the selling cycle. According to Lawrence D. Burns, vice president in charge of research, development, and planning for GM, "By exposing customers to what might be possible early on, we have a chance to learn faster what might be the best solution longer term."

Home Depot has trained its associates to engage customers consistently in dialogues about their project needs (not to simply fulfill sales transactions) and has supplemented selling activities with free in-store home repair classes. Recently Home Depot has been focusing on increasing the time its associates spend face-to-face with customers: Store stocking activities now take place after hours, and call centers are being created to help take customer phone calls off the selling floor.

Environment can have a significant impact on whether conversation does, in fact, flow freely. For the most part, cavernous "big-box" retail outlet formats have not been conducive to undirected dialogue with customers. Then there's outdoor gear retailer REI, which has been particularly innovative with its store environment. The company's Seattle flagship store features a mountain-biking trail and a climbing wall where customers can test equipment. Unlike traditional retail formats, the environment encourages much longer interactions between employees and customers. This leads to deeper conversations and increased sales, as conversations help customers become aware of additional needs while they are still in the store. The key to the success of all these examples is the sharing of resources across traditional marketing silos. Sales, product development, and marketing (particularly promotions) all contribute to the conversation, and they work together to deliver new interactions with the customer.

A Matter of Style

Human conversation ultimately involves overcoming an inherent contradiction: People need to be connected to other people, yet they also want their independence and privacy. Few people can exist happily alone, but the more they bump up against the needs and desires of others, the more their independence and privacy are threatened. Successful conversationalists balance these opposing considerations by adapting their conversational styles to be compatible with those of others. One of the key reasons conversations break down is the mismatch between styles.

WHY COURTESY COUNTS

Each of us has heard it—or said it—a thousand times: Be polite.

But what does that mean exactly, especially in terms of conversations with customers? According to linguists, there is a "logic of politeness" that influences our behavior in all conversations. Three rules govern our attempts to be polite: Don't impose; give options; and be friendly.

All three are good ideas. But in defining the actual mechanics of conversation, speakers must focus on observing just one. Each rule creates a different effect—distance, deference, or camaraderie, respectively—and thereby communicates a different level of perceived relationship. The choice of rules employed sets the tone for the discourse—the degree of formality and the directness of the messages.

To understand these effects, consider the familiar conversation opener, "Would you like something to drink?" One can respond with a simple yes, but that feels somehow too abrupt and incomplete to be polite. So we answer, "That would be nice," a response that isn't an imposing request and that adds distance to the question through its indirectness. Or we might answer, "Only if you're having something," which gives options and shows deference. Or we could say, "That would be great; do you have any juice?" in an attempt to be friendly (a common American choice). Politeness fails when circumstances cause speakers to choose an unexpected or inappropriate approach. A person who is more accustomed to a "don't impose" approach, for example, might be shocked at the *demand* for juice. There would be misunderstanding, miscommunication, and, ultimately, a sense that somebody hadn't been polite.

Now that communications and responses can be customized down to individual customers, companies must give new thought to politeness, which can occur only when communications are aligned with customer expectations.

For example, stating, "I understand what you are going through" to a disgruntled customer can create a minefield for a service representative whose attempt to be friendly implies a camaraderie that might not fit the customer's expectation. Yet other customers may find "I am sorry for the inconvenience" too distant and insincere to be considered polite. While sensitive employees can often make adjustments for politeness, it is far more difficult with computers increasingly generating automated voice responses, scripts, and marketing copy.

If companies are truly going to make polite conversation with their customers, they must document their customers' politeness logic and incorporate this understanding into the behaviors of all customer touch points, such as direct-marketing campaigns and call center responses. A company that fails to do so risks forever being considered rude.

Likewise, companies must seek harmony with their customers by adopting an appropriate conversational style—an insight that flies in the face of conventional wisdom. It has been argued that companies should be as attentive as possible to customers, asking questions and reaching out. Yet every day, thousands of people bristle as cashiers, for example, ask for their phone numbers. In these cases, the customers' need for privacy outweighs their need to feel connected through an unsolicited telemarketing call. Adapting models from interpersonal communications studies, we see a set of conversational styles that emerges from two key elements (Exhibit 14-1). The

EXHIBIT 14-1.   Influencers of conversational style.

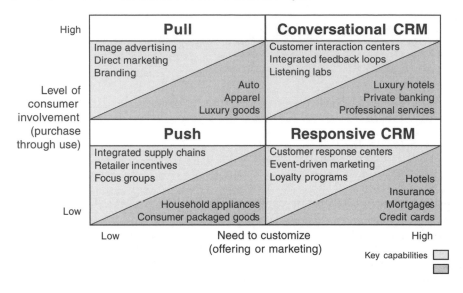

amount of information a company solicits from a customer expresses how familiar it thinks its relationship with the customer should be. Similarly, the amount of information a company volunteers about itself (from its mission to save the rain forest, for example, to its internal production costs) expresses the level of intimacy it hopes to create with the customer.

The automatic use of a single style in a heterogeneous society is a recipe for conversational disaster, linguists tell us. This is because good communication is based on *reciprocity*. Many customers recognize that information translates into power in a relationship, and they resent being given too much information for free because of the quid pro quo expectation it creates. They may feel they are being drawn deeper into a relationship than they want to be.

For that reason, conversational styles, when taken to extremes, are almost certain to mismatch and be counterproductive. Even being too open to listening can be risky. Consider NIKE iD, a Web-based offering that allows customers to order shoes emblazoned with their personal messages. This offering exposed the company to the risk that customers would request messages that might embarrass Nike. And indeed, when one customer decided to order a shoe that made a political statement about the company, Nike found itself involved in a national conversation it would certainly have preferred to avoid.

How can a company select and adopt an appropriate conversational style? By aligning the amount of information it discloses with the level of customer involvement in the product—and by aligning the amount of customer feedback solicited with the company's need and ability to customize subsequent offerings or marketing campaigns (Exhibit 14-2). Each approach relies on certain core technologies and marketing tactics, and each is likely to be more appropriate for customers in certain

EXHIBIT 14-2.   Conversational style map.

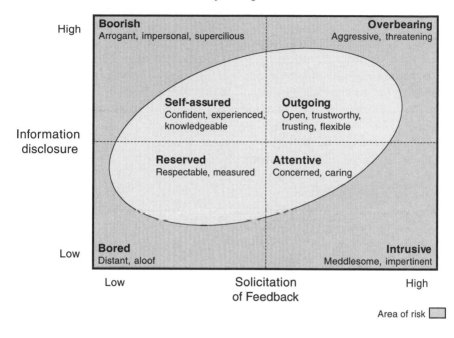

product and service categories than for others. It is essential that companies make the right investments in the technologies that best support the conversational styles they need with their customers.

USING FEEDBACK

Although technology is making it cheaper for companies to invite feedback, not every company will see great returns from this. When products and services cannot be customized profitably, soliciting greater feedback can imply a promise to change that the company may not be able to keep.

Customizing toothpaste for individual customers, for example, is possible but probably not economical. So a toothpaste maker stands to gain as much from a statistically significant sample of customer preferences as it does from expensive technologies that can test and capture each customer's individual preferences. Using such technologies can even be detrimental if they inappropriately raise expectations—asking customers for preferences that cannot or will not be delivered.

Similarly, the level of customer involvement in the purchase will dramatically affect that customer's willingness to converse. Involvement is usually a function of price, complexity, and affinity, and it is therefore quite low for many of the goods and services consumed every day. Yet companies spend millions of dollars in failed attempts to engage low-involvement customers in deep conversations; this was particularly popular in the dot-com era, when it was broadly assumed that online customers would return to a site frequently to chat about products such as pet food.

Credit card banker Capital One, on the other hand, uses sophisticated technologies to predict the nature of a customer's call, anticipate customer reaction to new product and service offerings, then route the call accordingly. The company has achieved such success that it sells its services (predicting real-time customer interest in certain products and categories) to other companies interested in having their pitches delivered at just the right moment.

Implementing an appropriate conversational style is difficult because it requires consistent behavior over time. With numerous autonomous marketing groups each taking responsibility for creating their own customer contacts, this consistency is hard to create and even harder to maintain. It can only be created by broad ownership of the topic, at the brand or chief marketing officer level.

OPENING THE DISCUSSION

Successful conversational marketers certainly value one-to-one dialogues with their customers. But they also recognize that all product discussions with customers are in the end "polylogues"—complex sequences of monologues and dialogues among numerous relevant parties. Customers discuss products and brands with countless friends, salespeople, and trusted advisors before they actually purchase, often relying on buzz to build their preferences.

Effective marketing conversations must therefore include not just the buyer but also those who influence the buyer's decision. These are typically identified in marketing textbooks as trusted advisors, end users, the media, and what are known as *gatekeepers*—people whose duty it is to keep marketers away from the customer.

Missing from the list are competitors who, it must be remembered, are also attempting to have conversations with your customers. But discussing your products with customers in the presence of competitors in an open and uncontrolled way can be risky.

Automobile company Lexus took that risk with its IS 300 sport sedan. Most automakers simply invite potential customers to test-drive their cars at a dealership. Lexus instead set up test tracks in major cities, and invited prospects and members of the automotive press to test the IS 300 head-to-head against the two leading competitors' cars. By immediately injecting competitors into the conversation, Lexus risked suffering by comparison. It was an acceptable risk, however, because it conveyed the confidence and openness necessary to win sales in a polylogue. Also forgotten in many polylogues are business partners. The best marketers make these participants perfectly at home in the conversation, partly by sharing information but often by tightly integrating operations. For example, the glass replacement company Safelite is so completely integrated with Liberty Mutual Insurance that when the customer calls Liberty Mutual with an auto glass claim, Safelite answers the phone.

EDUCATING EMPLOYEES

In the end, a company's closest business partners are its employees, which makes their performance in conversations critical. In an age in which one employee's ill-advised interaction with one customer has the potential to make the evening news, companies must educate their employees on the role they play in conversational marketing.

The complexity involved in managing polylogues (the number of participants, the risks to both sales and brand, and the difficulty of calculating a return on investment) suggests that it is a critical task demanding the attention of the chief marketing officer if it is going to be done right. Good customer conversations pay dividends. They enable better recommendations to be made to customers, which leads to increased sales—whether on a showroom floor, in a supermarket aisle, or through an online recommendation engine. They also enhance a company's ability to make innovative improvements to its offerings.

When companies mismanage conversations, however, they suffer. By failing to capture and apply knowledge gained in previous interactions, companies fall prey to fatal inaccuracy—getting facts about customers wrong (such as addresses) and losing those customers' trust. They also become irrelevant—attempting to talk about extraneous topics, such as undesired travel locations, which causes a loss of respect.

Finally, they become incoherent—not knowing enough about previous interactions, such as past related purchases, to be consistent in their dealings with the customer, which destroys intimacy. Yet being conversant with customers requires a certain level of risk taking. In any conversation, there is a chance that we will be perceived as boring, uninformed, or uncouth. Though companies can mitigate these risks through attention to conversational style, real conversational marketing is too complex and too perpetual to be constantly under control. If they are to have real conversations with real customers, companies must accept that there will be a slipup every once in a while, and then be willing to apologize for their mistake. Taking the chance, however, can lead to a world of deeply engaging and profitable conversation.

CHAPTER 15

Collaboration: Effective Personalization's Missing Ingredient

Paul F. Nunes

C ompanies have invested millions of dollars in generating the customer insights needed to personalize their customer interactions, particularly on the Internet. But as the results of a recent Accenture study show, personalization alone may not be enough.[1] By testing the perceived value of both personalization (which we defined as company-controlled modifications to Web interactions) and customization (defined as user-controlled modifications to Web site interactions), our study found a distinct preference for customization. This suggests customers desire greater control over their interactions with companies, particularly on the Web, and that they must be made more involved in creating the personalization intended to serve them. A better course of action, therefore, is for companies to find ways to integrate customization with personalization, allowing them to gain the benefits of both.

It seems obvious once stated, but how many companies view their customers as partners in the personalization process? Do they value customers' reactions to personalized offerings and marketing, viewing them as part of a beneficial collaboration between customer and company? Or, are they so impressed with the technologies and concepts that they forget whom they are serving? Rather than designing processes that solicit and use customer feedback, most companies rely on some mix of artificial intelligence technologies (inference engines and collaborative filtering, for example) to surmise the needs and preferences of their customers. Meanwhile, they forget that asking may be the simplest and ultimately fastest and lowest-cost way of learning what customers want.

As companies' CRM efforts mature and their investments continue to expand, there are new opportunities for (and rewards from) sharing control of personalization with those most affected: the customers themselves. Early results suggest that companies that view the customer as a source of personalization expertise and those that reflect their knowledge of the customer in the customization options they offer reach levels of customer relationship most companies can only imagine today.

CUSTOMIZATION OR PERSONALIZATION: CONSUMERS SPEAK

There is an old adage, "If you want something done right, you have to do it yourself." This seems to encapsulate the attitude of online users toward the commercial Web sites they visit. Instead of trusting companies to personalize Web sites to their needs, users are more confident in their own abilities to do it themselves.

This was revealed by the results of a recent study by the Accenture Institute for Strategic Change, conducted with help from an MBA team at the Owen Graduate School of Management at Vanderbilt University. The goal of the study was to better understand online users' preferences with regard to site-created *personalization* of content versus user-defined *customization* of Web sites. The study yielded several findings that, in combination, suggest online users today do not highly value the kind of site-based personalization created by recommendation engines, collaborative filtering, and dynamic page design. Instead, users seem to find much greater value in being able to customize a Web site, selecting the format and content they want presented, as can users of My Yahoo! or MyDell, for example.

That users prefer to customize Web sites in a computing environment where the machine can do the work is strangely counterintuitive. This unexpected finding points to two related conclusions. The first is that Web site personalization based on artificial intelligence is not delivering on its promise, at least in terms of creating measurable perceived customer value. The second is that user-performed customization has been underrated and underleveraged by companies seeking to connect better with their online users. To build Web sites that develop closer relationships with customers, companies need to address both of these issues head-on.

To better understand user preferences for Web interfaces and their design, our survey asked respondents to estimate the value they perceived in customization and personalization. For the four categories tested—online groceries, news, financial services, and sports—users reported a decided preference for customization over personalization (Exhibit 15-1). They reported finding "great value" in customization 2 to 4 times as often as in personalization depending on the category, and found at least "some value" in customization significantly more often than in personalization.

On average, users reported finding significant value in customization, while the perceived value in personalization netted out to no effect (Exhibit 15-2). When respondents were asked which they preferred in a head-to-head comparison, they

EXHIBIT 15-1.   Value of customization versus personalization (by percentage of respondents).

	Groceries		News		Financial		Sports	
	Custom	Personal	Custom	Personal	Custom	Personal	Custom	Personal
Adds great value	38.40	11.10	42.90	15.20	23.50	11.00	26.40	12.00
Adds some value	33.80	29.30	33.30	32.60	31.10	27.10	25.80	24.30
No effect	21.30	34.30	17.90	26.10	32.10	36.30	33.80	37.90
Detracts	2.10	13.60	3.10	14.30	2.50	10.10	2.20	11.00
Not to visit again	4.30	11.70	2.80	11.80	9.80	15.50	11.80	14.80

were roughly 5 to 10 times more likely to choose a customizable Web site over a personalized one (Exhibit 15-3). In a related study that tested levels of dissatisfaction, Indiana University researchers found that almost 50 percent of respondents objected to features in the personalization category, while less than 20 percent disliked one or more of the customization features described. Control is clearly valued by users.

EXHIBIT 15-2.   Value of customization versus personalization.

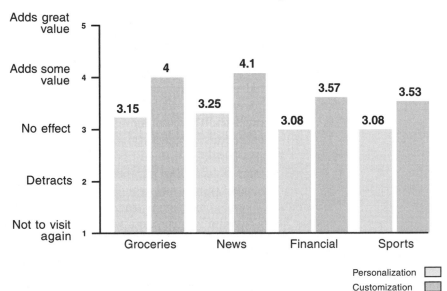

EXHIBIT 15-3.   Respondents' preferences.

	Customize	Personalize	Like both equally	Not use either one
Grocery	55.2%	5.6%	21.0%	18.2%
News	51.9%	6.9%	26.6%	14.7%
Financial	33.2%	7.0%	21.4%	38.3%
Sports	33.2%	5.0%	25.4%	36.4%

Exploring this preference for customization also yielded the unexpected finding that respondents are willing to give more information to a customized site than to a personalized one (Exhibit 15-4). This is surprising because personalized sites usually require significantly more personal data about the user in order to make linkages across data and draw the inferences needed to provide personalized service, whereas a

EXHIBIT 15-4.   Volunteering information.

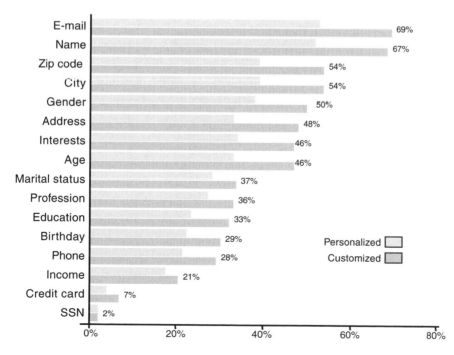

customized site can require little or no personal data, relying instead on user-reported preferences.

While all of these findings show a very strong preference for customization, it should be noted that responses varied significantly by type of site being considered. While the percentage of respondents who said that personalization added great value was consistently in the low teens across categories, those who saw great value in customization differed a great deal by category of site, with many more seeing great value in customization for groceries and news sites than for financial and sports sites. Clearly then, the nature of the site must be considered when evaluating the usefulness of customization.

IMPLICATIONS FOR EFFECTIVE WEB SITE DESIGN

The study's findings highlight two important actions that companies must take to leverage their investments in personalization capabilities and enhance the value of their Web sites. First, they must work within the limits of today's personalization applications to strengthen their personalization efforts where they can. Second, they must more proactively enable the user's involvement in the design and flow of a site by increasing the availability and ease of use of customization options.

Strengthening Personalization When and Where Possible

Clearly, users do not perceive a tremendous amount of added value from companies' current efforts to personalize their Web sites. But that shouldn't be taken as a reason to give up just yet. In our survey, roughly 40 percent of the respondents claimed a preference for sites that recognized them by name (Exhibit 15-5). And an overwhelming number of users (more than 78 percent) said they would be more likely to return to a site after disclosing personal information (Exhibit 15-6).

Yet regardless of how many users express an inclination toward personalization, Web sites must deliver real value through this capability (something more, in other words, than just a warm greeting by name) if they hope to build strong bonds with their users. The need to deliver real value is evident from the fact that 41 percent of the respondents in our survey cited "no benefit" as a reason for not giving information to a Web site (Exhibit 15-7).

Delivering user value means presenting the right content at the right time and generating the right options, recommendations, and communications from interpretations of both personal and broader-context information. It means becoming aware of and acknowledging customer life events, such as weddings and births. It also requires interpreting and reacting to users' moods, inferred from their online behavior in the moment (i.e., is their focus directed at completing a purchase, or are they simply surfing?).

Delivering value through personalization is not always an easy task, and getting help can be challenging as well. While there are currently any number of companies focused on helping online businesses personalize their sites using rules-based and collaborative-filtering software techniques, many of these companies remain rela-

EXHIBIT 15-5.   **Likelihood of returning to a Web site that recognizes users by name.**

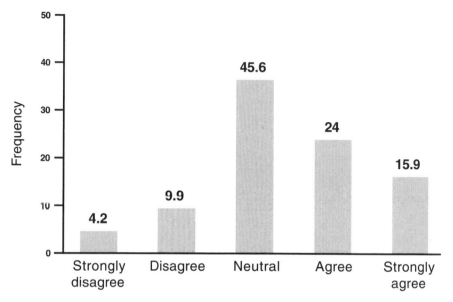

EXHIBIT 15-6.   **Likelihood of returning to a Web site after disclosing personal data.**

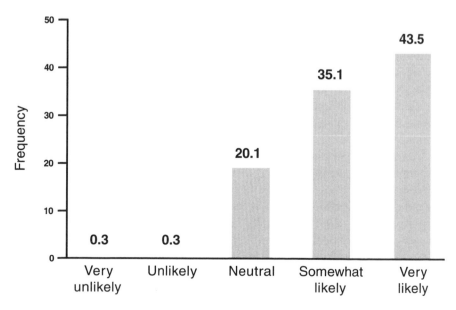

EXHIBIT 15-7.   Reasons for not personalizing Web site.

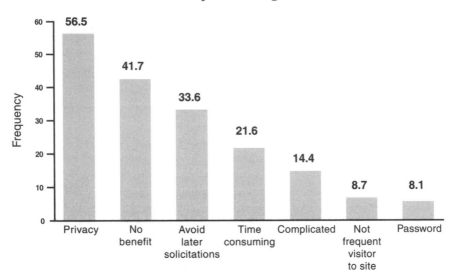

tively young. Yet others are beginning to come into their own as mature solutions and should be explored.

Exploiting Customization Possibilities

Knowing that online users value customization means that companies should pay more attention to cocreating their Web sites with their users than to trying to create the perfect site on their own. Though customization is often assumed to be a time-consuming and complicated process, the results of an Accenture survey show that 93 percent of online users have customized at least one site, while 25 percent have customized four or more.[2] And these numbers are likely to increase as consumers become ever more comfortable in the exploration and use of Web sites.

In conjunction with this finding, the prevailing preference of online users for customization across all four site categories in our survey suggests that customizable Web sites have the potential to be more attractive to users and to provide them with greater value. Given the survey respondents' professed willingness to provide more personal data to a site that offers customization, a customizable platform benefits the hosting company as well, by granting greater access to customer data. Web-based firms seeking to garner more information about their customers for use in data mining or future marketing efforts should therefore employ customization features as a bartering currency in order to collect this information.

However, customization is not guaranteed to draw or retain traffic. The time required to customize a site must not be so great as to encourage exiting rather than loyalty. And some categories of information and offerings lend themselves better to customization than do others: news, for example, where 76 percent of survey respondents perceived at least some value in customization, as opposed to sports, where only 52 percent perceived any value. The key to capturing value from customization therefore lies not only in testing user attitudes but also in effectively communicating the value proposition.

FINDING A BETTER WAY

Yet even with these efforts, personalization technology and customization choices are likely to remain several steps behind what online companies really need for them to be successful. Determining what users want still requires a tremendous amount of interpretation by site designers, and the complexity of this task is apparent in the limitations and shortcomings of today's leading search and recommendation engines. Though they are able to combine information about a user's tastes in books with data about his or her purchases in other categories, they sometimes yield confused and even humorous results. A recent search by one of the authors to purchase *Anatomy of Buzz,* a business book about viral marketing, yielded the suggestion that we might like *Gray's Anatomy,* too.

But there is a better way: *Combine the two approaches.* By adding each to the other, companies can establish a unique collaboration between personalization and customization, as well as between customer and company.

First, create customizable personalization. Customers are likely to be more receptive to and satisfied by site personalization if they have some control over it. One way to do this is by allowing customers to review and edit the data the personalization engine uses to make its recommendations. Imagine being able to tell a personalizing site which purchases were relevant to your interests and which were gifts—and do so even months after the purchase.

This has already become the operating standard at Amazon.com, where recommendations are now followed by the word "Why?" Accessing this link brings customers to a page where the data used to form that particular recommendation is laid out, and where the customer is empowered to change information that is incorrect or no longer valid. It would take a traditional system months or years of additional purchasing behavior observations to unlearn what a customer can tell it in a couple of seconds.

Another way to customize personalization is by allowing customers to control the level of personalization on a Web site. Software maker Younology has created *permission-based* personalization. Its applications allow Web sites to respond to consumers' individual requirements regarding information sharing. This approach gives users the ability to control how their information is collected, used, stored, and shared by a site, as well as the ability to change inaccurate or unwanted information.

An alternative way to combine the approaches is to *personalize your customization options* available to the user. This can be achieved by using the knowledge gained in personalizing a site to offer the user the opportunity to customize only specific, limited aspects of the Web site, one feature at a time. This simplifies the decision-making process for the user and reduces the time commitment required for customization into manageable chunks. For example, a weather site could say, "You regularly check the weather in Spain, would you like us to add a button for this feature to your home page?" rather than relying on the user to find and use the customization options offered on the site. Such a service is likely to be welcomed by customers, who frequently are overwhelmed by the countless choices they face when attempting to customize a site on their own.

This is similar to adaptive Web sites that observe usage preferences and then self-modify, but with an important difference: The site asks permission first. Many users prefer, and even require, constancy in the look and feel of a Web site and will not be pleased to unexpectedly find lesser-used features whose appearance and location they have grown used to replaced by those they use more frequently, even if the new configuration would save them time.

THE CUSTOMER IS ALWAYS RIGHT

Both our own primary data and our research of secondary sources suggest that Web sites that are adapted to individual users drive more repeat traffic and increase conversion of shoppers into buyers. Accordingly, Web merchants should incorporate interactive tailoring into their Web sites, either through customization or personalization, but preferably through both.

Yet in so doing, companies must be sure to address the fact that Internet users who decline to provide information to sites do so primarily because they fear both loss of privacy and the prospect of further solicitation from the Web site or from other companies (Exhibit 15-7). To allay these fears, Web sites with customization or personalization features must go to significant lengths to reassure visitors that their information will be safeguarded and that solicitors will not target them.

But above all, it is apparent from our research that customers really do believe that if they want a company's Web site done right, they must be involved—at some level, they must do it themselves. For Web designers, and CRM managers more generally, given the choice between customizing and personalizing interactions, the answer is yes.

16

Untethered Relationships: How Wireless Is Changing Customer Contact

John C. Beck, Patrick D. Lynch, and Mitchell E. Wade

C ompanies that missed out on the e-commerce boom or arrived too late to reap first-mover advantages, market share, and revenues are intent on not making that mistake again: They are "crouching tigers" ready to leap on mobile commerce (m-commerce). But if they leap before looking at what m-commerce is really about, they may get caught out of position again. The mistake they may make is in thinking that m-commerce will be just like e-commerce, but on wheels. But the business potential is different from and much greater than just mobile e-commerce.

E-commerce and m-commerce do share a nemesis: consumer frustration. But while consumer frustration can knock e-commerce initiatives back into also-rans, it will hammer mobile commerce into the never-should-have-even-thought-about-it category. Even on the wired Internet, a few awkward steps in the checkout process are enough to drive 65 to 80 percent of potential Web customers away.[1] In 2000, this awkwardness cost e-commerce vendors $3.8 billion in lost sales. Studies of Internet users report that two-thirds of customers named ease of navigation as one of the most important attributes of an online service[2] and that more than 40 percent will not return to a site if their first visit results in a negative experience.[3] And users say that more than half the time they are unable to find the information they are seeking.[4]

Now think of how many more steps it takes to complete a transaction over a mobile phone, and just how physically awkward each of them is. A purchase on Amazon that takes 148 keystrokes on a computer will take 183 keystrokes or Graffiti characters on a Palm device and 366 on a Wireless Application Protocol (WAP) phone. A survey of 1500 tech-savvy readers of one magazine showed that 84 percent did not have wireless Web access, and more than half of those who did never used it.[5] It's no wonder that only 16 out of the top 100 most popular retailers on the Web even have the necessary mobile site to deliver their content to wireless devices.[6] Without their buy-in and, consequently, that of the rest of us, the wireless Web will never boom to the projected $50 billion in U.S. retail transactions by 2005.[7] This is consistent with projections calling for tens of millions more in expenses than in revenues for providers of mobile content over the next two years.[8]

WIRED VERSUS WIRELESS

Wired Web sites have an advantage over wireless Web sites in every aspect but one: They are essentially immobile. Thus, to make wireless work you must capitalize on the mobile phone's advantage in mobility while working around its relative limits. Let us look, first, at some of those constraints.

Using or even creating a Web site is literally child's play nowadays. For several years now, rank amateurs have been able to create complete Web stores using drop and drag elements from off-the-shelf software. That ease of entry and the resulting huge influx of entrants fueled remarkable innovation on the wired Web. How was it possible? What would it take to get that same creative burst in wireless commerce?

One System, Indivisible

One key is standardization. In the PC world, Web site designers can assume that customers have a color display monitor, enter data with keyboards employing the QWERTY standard, and use a mouse to explore site content. Modem speeds vary, but designers can assume that any computer surfing the Internet has basic and adequate processing capacities (chip speeds, memory, etc.). On the software side, site designers can assume that customers' browser software for viewing Web sites displays the same navigation buttons (back, forward, home, etc.). Developers are, in a very real sense, working and designing for one customer.

Common design languages such as HTML or Java make possible standardized design packages that in turn make possible sites ranging from those such as HugeClick, which portrayed information using three-dimensional layouts, to those such as Yahoo.com, which uses hierarchical text links. The same standardization enables customers to view display content almost identically, no matter what Web browser they are using.

Moreover, a number of technologies have emerged that create a more enriched customer experience. Do you need to help customers evaluate goods before making a purchase? MGI's Live Picture visually represents products and allows shoppers to zoom in on every detail. Macromedia's Flash displays navigation links in a dynamic way, showing customers expanding choices for even more content. Text chats and streaming video provide customers with an experience that in many ways surpasses what they could get from talking with sales associates in a bricks-and-mortar store.

Yet as strategically powerful as these technologies are, they have become technologically routine, integrated effortlessly into the software used by developers to design Web stores. The wired Web has standards that make it easy for all kinds of developers to enhance customer experience.

Wireless devices, on the other hand, do not have standardized form factors—each one is different from the rest. Sites can display differently depending on each device's manufacturer. Imagine if each wired Web customer viewed a dramatically different site depending on whether the computer was a Dell, Gateway, Compaq, IBM, or Apple. The fact that there are varying wireless devices means hardware specifications can determine the customer's experience on a site more than ever before. An Ericsson phone's keys and functions are different from those on a Samsung phone. The Motorola Timeport screen displays four lines of text at any one time, whereas the Mitsubishi T250 screen displays 10. This is not just a problem for creative and technical types; it presents a huge business issue. Early in the growth of this market, businesses are investing in wireless to reach the small fraction of their customer bases that uses mobile data at all. Splintering that group into tiny subgroups defined by the technology and interface of individual devices sharply increases the cost of development and reduces the possible return.

Each site's display can vary according to the wireless Web device's software processing capabilities. Is the customer using a Samsung WAP phone, Motorola WAP phone, Palm V, Palm i705, HP Jornada PDA—or any number of new information appliances hitting the market weekly? Software formats can determine that the content looks great on a Palm but horrible on a PocketPC running Jornada. There could be dead links, partial images, and a user interface far from the one developers saw when they built the site. Each of these issues forces designers to offer users even fewer options and more primitive interfaces—starting from the already low base provided by the mobile form factor.

Because of these constraints vendors must rethink and recast their product and service offerings (see sidebar). Those who try to get away with dropping a shrunken version of a wired Web site onto a mobile site, including every product and category, will end up with a poor navigation structure, endless menus, and frustrated customers. When e-commerce first moved from hype to reality, businesses learned (often the hard way) that certain kinds of commerce worked well on the desktop while others failed miserably.

What is most enticing for a wired Web is often detrimental for a wireless Web site. Rich graphics, multiple navigation structures, and vast menu selections only crowd the tiny screens of wireless devices, most of which cannot take full advantage of such features. These sorts of embellishments frequently conflict with a potential customer's ability to use a wireless device to conduct transactions easily and quickly. Mobile consumers are often on the run and are much more interested in convenience and reliability than graphic novelties and endless options.

And chances are that customers are paying by the second for the privilege of viewing content and information. In a recent poll, 69 percent of respondents said

INSIDE THE WORLD OF WIRELESS

Regardless of the wireless device used to access a site, adhering to a few design principles can dramatically improve the consistency of a site's appearance and function. More is not necessarily better. Companies that hope to develop successful wireless interfaces for the current generation of devices must shift their view that sites must be everything to everyone. Customers using the wireless Web have come to expect flawlessness, and the key to flawlessness, at least in wireless's inchoate days, is simplicity. Focus your efforts on the following goals:

Providing Basic Functions

On wireless devices, interface design issues are more critical than before. You could easily lose a customer because of design factors that are device dependent and out of your control. Most Web-enabled phones have "soft keys," generic buttons that can be assigned multiple actions such as "back" or "home." By programming logical navigation functions into these soft keys, you can help customers navigate your wireless site in a manner reminiscent of the wired Web. Because soft keys are dynamic (reprogrammable), the function you assign to each key should be evaluated screen by screen for the wireless site to enable actions required by users at that particular moment in the buying process.

Providing Basic Structure

Simple and descriptive wireless designs win with customers because they prevent customers from getting lost in the wireless site. Naming menus and numbering options will prevent a great deal of customer angst. Sites that are problematic for users assume too much about the customer's knowledge of what product categories are available and how to find them. The best sites draw a road map with text-based descriptions that guide visitors through the selection and purchasing processes.

Providing Basic Content

Screen space is more precious on wireless devices than it ever was on the PC. Use every bit of it wisely. Instead of building a superstore, build a convenience store. Designers should devote screen space to the categories customers need most and can navigate to quickly. Time-pressed wireless customers have specific things in mind; they will save their browsing until later, when they have a more powerful computer at their disposal.

Setting Your Sites on Design: Cases in Good Wireless Site Design

Best Buy

Retailer Best Buy improved its wireless site function by taking the guesswork out of mobile shopping carts. Most mobile sites fail to show customers what is in their shopping carts. When an item is placed into a cart, it disappears, and there is no simple way to navigate back to what is being purchased until checkout. Best Buy puts control of the shopping carts back into the hands of customers by telling them the number of items in their carts and the value of those items. Customers also have the ability to check product availability and make changes to their orders—all before entering the checkout process.

FTD

Floral services organization FTD makes sure that its site provides an easy drive through Catalogville. Browsing for a product on a wireless site is often a painful series of wrong turns, and a number of sites force customers to surrender their purchases to confusion. At FTD, text menus clearly guide customers so that they know where they are at all times. Short, to-the-point product descriptions also make shopping for flowers a rosy experience.

Barnes & Noble

Retailer Barnes & Noble incorporated content that uses the advantages of the mobile device to help shoppers make purchasing decisions. Other sites should take advantage of the phone as a medium to deliver an experience that allows customers to sample product offerings before deciding whether to buy. Barnes and Noble's Listening Wall offers sample audio clips from a selection of CDs and verbal instructions on how to complete the purchase.

they could not find any reason they would pay for content on wireless devices. If your frills frustrate them on their dime, they may not ever come back.

MEETING BASIC CUSTOMER CONCERNS

It is most important that wireless offerings be tailored to avoid disappointing potential customers. Players will have to fashion their initiatives to meet these customer concerns:

Connection

Supply interactivity. If companies want to make money from the average mobile phone user, they should emphasize products and services that emphasize connection: text messaging and voice connections to knowledgeable customer service representatives, location services that help parents keep track of their children and vice versa, and the like.

Convenience

Supply ease and speed. Build the site around easy, limited tasks—customers' specific information requests and preset destinations. Leave complex tasks such as those requiring searching, browsing, and comparing for the desktop PC. Meet speed expectations. Wireless customers are not strolling around a shopping mall metaphorically, even if that is where they are in physical space. When using mobile devices, they are dashing in for a quick purchase or bit of information. Great vendors make it easy for them. United Airlines' mobile Internet site, for example, offers all of your itineraries on United (no matter where you made your initial reservations) simply by entering your Mileage Plus number. You just click on the itinerary you want and can access seat assignments, flight status, and other services with as little input as possible. At the desktop, this is a luxury. On the mobile, it is a necessity.

Consolidation

Wireless data users often are filling their downtime—consolidating time that would otherwise be wasted to do work or search for information. Actual users of the mobile Web tell us that they typically access these services from trains, meetings that have gone on too long, buses, rental cars, and cars stuck in traffic. The applications they actually use are news, weather, sports, e-mail (more reading than writing), and location services (electronic maps).[9] Employees who are expecting an important e-mail during an airplane flight home, for instance, can access their corporate e-mail in the taxi on the way home from the airport, leaving them free to interact with their loved ones when they get home rather than booting up the computer.

Constancy

Wireless data users also are filling their "uptime." When they are constantly online, it is often because they are in a rush and need immediate information and services: travel arrangements, updates on flight delays, timetables, stock prices, driving directions, and maps. They will expect immediate response. This is not the time for a "thanks for your e-mail, we will respond within two business days" message.

Consumption

People will not use these devices to shop—but they will use them to buy. Focus on making the purchase easy and ensuring that the products sold are popular, readily available, and easy to distribute—and leave products that require special orders for the desktop.

Control

Consumers want easy control of purchases, information, and their environment. For example, Amazon's one-click system allows users to store their credit card information, shipping addresses, and other personal information on Amazon's servers. When customers enter the Amazon Web site from a cookie-enabled PC, they need only a few mouse clicks to buy a best-selling book. On the wireless Web, with their user name and password stored, it takes only 10 button pushes.

As m-commerce begins to take shape, its potential to enhance both business-to-business (B2B) and business-to-consumer (B2C) relationships is only now being understood.

BUSINESS-TO-BUSINESS M-COMMERCE: THE CORPORATE LANDSCAPE

B2B m-commerce is still in its infancy, but there are opportunities in commodity or near-commodity industries in which the buyers rarely sit in offices hooked up to broadband networks. Using wireless technology, for example, a farmer sitting astride a John Deere tractor could stay abreast of and make buy and sell decisions in the grain or pork-belly markets. Or, in the fishing industry, a captain of a trawler in the Pacific could make a satellite connection to the Web and decide whether to continue fishing for halibut or to go after cod instead, depending on the demand for and daily market price movements of these different kinds of fish. And the captain will be able to sell the entire catch before the boat returns to port.

Wireless could mean even more to spot purchasing, whether it is done through established consumer or corporate Internet sites adapted for mobile use. Most purchasing professionals treat spot purchasing (which constitutes about 10 percent of the dollar value but 28 percent of the transactions in large organizations) with disdain. But if the promise of true B2B e-markets (meaning more and more transparency with increasingly perfect information) becomes a reality, spot purchasing might become the most efficient and least costly method of buying. In such a scenario, purchasing departments would disappear, and the buying decision would be pushed down to the final user of the product in an organization—secretaries could order the pencils they need, floor personnel could order automobile transmissions, and executives could make their own travel arrangements on the fly, using whatever mobile device they had at hand. Those who have the most knowledge and understanding of the products and services needed at the moment would be handling the purchasing.

The second way that wireless technologies can cut the cost of doing business is by improving monitoring, communication, and integration. Through monitoring and notification applications, companies can keep track of the fulfillment side of the B2B equation. Workers on the shop floor can use currently available mobile phones or text pager services to receive notification that production specifications have changed and to respond back when they have made the necessary changes. Such messages can be personalized by job function and broadcast almost immediately to factories around the globe. As location services become more commonplace, company-specific software will be developed and used to ensure that truck drivers, delivery personnel, and even key executives utilize their time and their location more effectively. One prototype for such applications gets critical information to executives wherever they are by consolidating and monitoring all the crucial back-end functions of an organization and delivering that data to a wireless device. The application also notifies the user whenever a crucial indicator is triggered or a decision is needed. Instant links can be established with assistants, sales forces, or fellow executives, so everyone can act quickly, wherever they are. One of the first enterprise applications ever developed for wireless Java, the prototype shows how this emerging wireless technology will create significant value for global business.

Moreover, the day will soon be here when the mobile phone becomes the "CPU" for all Web connections. With technology currently being developed in companies such as British Telecom (BT), the mobile phone will become the engine for always-on Internet connections. An executive who is in critical Web-based negotiations could unhook a mobile phone from a terminal in an office in Glasgow, check the phone display regularly on the drive home to Frankfurt, and on arrival hook the phone back up to a large-screen terminal without ever having to turn off the broadband flow of time-sensitive, money-making electrons. In this way, m-commerce becomes an extension of the stationary Internet terminal, allowing for mobility between terminal sessions while maintaining contact—a sort of supercompact laptop.

BUSINESS-TO-COMMERCE M-COMMERCE: LESSONS FROM SUCCESSFUL WEB RETAILERS

In addition to improving B2B relationships, m-commerce can dramatically change how companies (especially retailers) interact with consumers. Some Web retailers have learned the lessons of simplicity—to simplify the basic functions, structure, content, and customer concerns—and are successfully managing wireless customer expectations. We surveyed the top 100 Web retailers to see how they were migrating their customers to wireless.[10] We found careful tactics in place to seamlessly move customers from the Internet to the wireless realm.

Give Them Guidance

Use the Web to set customer expectations for wireless. The top Web retailers we surveyed offer their customers as much information as possible about wireless access and navigating with no wires attached. Successful Web firms provide screen shots of their wireless sites and descriptions of their wireless shopping options so that traditional Web customers can learn more about wireless access. They show consumers how wireless access enables them to search and browse product categories or manage their accounts with relative ease. As with any new technology, it has to be not only easy to use but also nonthreatening. Even for enthusiastic users, new technologies can be frustrating and embarrassing. Subliminal reassurance that their first effort will work and will be worthwhile is a great investment.

Give Them Something for Trying

Use incentives to entice customers to cross the line. In Germany, the largest transportation rental company, e-Sixt, partnered with Lufthansa to offer frequent-flyer mile incentives for customers who book their car rentals through WAP instead of a call center.[11] This was part of e-Sixt's strategy of offering real-time online booking via the Internet with immediate confirmation of reservations. SEB, a top Nordic bank, has given away Ericsson R380 smart phones (a cross between a WAP phone and a personal digital assistant) to its most prestigious customers. This is part of the bank's initiative to provide WAP access to services such as account statements and stock portfolio management. In both cases the strategy is clear: Give customers something they value to get them accustomed to new services and make WAP a routine channel.

Give Them Unique Capabilities

Offer customized, location-specific services. There are a number of European companies with a small presence on the traditional Web that have gained a solid foothold in moving customers to WAP. Some examples are alerts by ehem.com that tell subscribers when events happen in their homes (anything from unwanted intruders to thermostat adjustments); instant opinion surveys by MobileOpinion.com to find out immediately what customers think about a company's products, image, or advertising; alerts from delego.com to truck drivers when cargo awaits; and notification by

SEB when customers' stock hits its target price. Each of these takes advantage of WAP's unique time and location qualities to give customers natural reasons to use the mobile channel.

Give Them Only What They Want Most

Good wireless sites are not everything to everyone. Major airlines such as American, Delta, and United, as well as third-party services such as Travelocity and Biztravel, boast their own mobile site access. Furthermore, major brokers and banks such as E*Trade, Fidelity, Ameritrade, and DLJ Direct provide wireless access across multiple mobile devices. These companies have found success in wireless because they know exactly the services customers want most—quick and easy access to time-sensitive information. While a minority of the top 100 Web retailers have wireless sites,[12] the most successful ones limit the product and services available via wireless. For example, Best Buy limits its product offerings on its mobile site to music and movies in order to deliver a simple and easy shopping experience. Amazon.com truncates customer reviews of books to the mere title of the reviewer's posting, and Barnes & Noble limits its offerings to services such as books, music, Store Finder, and eCards.[13]

Tell Them the Whole Story—Fast

Consider the wireless medium and deliver appropriately. On the wired Web, FTD.com combines its marketing messages with pictures and text descriptions: "A jovial and vibrant display." On the wireless Web, the importance of product text descriptions is magnified. Vendors need to tell customers exactly what is present: "This is an arrangement with a minimum of four mature red roses." It must be an engaging message that conveys the whole story about the product offering.

Give Them the Right Bells and Whistles

Incorporate content that uses the mobile device as a multimedia platform. Few sites took advantage of the WAP phone as a medium that improves a value-added service. Why not allow customers to sample product offerings before they decide whether to buy? Alerts and push technologies offer another wrinkle in wireless access. Sites such as OracleMobile already offer instant notification when airline flights are cancelled or delayed, when stocks reach highs or lows, and when packages reach their destinations.

Give Them Support

Make live customer service just a touch away. Mobile shopping on a WAP phone is a new experience for many shoppers, so expect them to need assistance. Rather than cramming the Web phone with endless screens of FAQs, top vendors allow customers to ask their questions directly to service reps. Best Buy has on its WAP site a hot button that places a call directly to the customer service center to clear up questions or complete a purchase.

FROM M-COMMERCE TO U-COMMERCE

It is here, in the mobile commerce trenches, that we will really see the evolution of u-commerce. When you see the scale of change that is needed to serve customers through wireless technology and what it will take to address the emerging issues, you realize that what most companies think they are working toward, m-commerce, is really just the first step in a truly sweeping change. As the first major wave of wireless device adoption hits, you can begin to grasp how the capabilities and limitations of mobile technology create new business opportunities and customer expectations. Mobile technology enables unprecedented levels of instant, integrated, and personal content and services. This is the future we call *u-commerce: u* because it is *untethered* by the hard wires of traditional computing and telephony, *unbounded* by traditional definitions of commerce, and *ubiquitous*—taking place anytime and anywhere. It is commerce integrated into ordinary life in an extraordinary way. Individuals engage in u-commerce as they live their lives—as they work, as they relax, as they meet their friends and families. And what we have seen, in studying the very earliest generation of commerce on mobile devices, is that successful Web businesses are those that have recognized and are addressing the profound shifts in the way business is done because of wireless.

Many of the executives we interviewed were farsighted enough to know that if wireless is about making the fulfillment of anytime-anywhere needs commonplace, then sales, customer support, marketing, and operations must interact in a new way to sense and respond to market demands with stunning speed and efficiency. To capitalize on wireless, companies should be reorganizing to meet the following goals:

- Work more closely with customers.
- Identify and set standards earlier by cooperating across organizational functions (no more development and design silos).
- Integrate speed as a core company value.
- Build multiple, best-of-class solutions to serve multiple customer segments.
- Engage in new strategic alliances that enable innovation with both customers and partners.

This once sounded like just business rhetoric. These changes are necessary for survival but will not be enough to guarantee market dominance. As one executive sees it, in the aggressive world of wireless business, it "won't be easy for tomorrow's Microsofts, and there may not be a single dominant market player." Smart companies have come to see that there is no homogeneous market for mobile technologies—customized, personalized wireless services will be as diverse as the customers who use them. As one CEO put it, "In all areas of business, wireless applications are increasing companies' competitiveness more than in any other area—and there will be even further changes that we can't even guess today."

Aligned Goals: Transforming Customer Interactions

Robert E. Wollan and Paul F. Nunes

T he important trends that defined business in the 1990s—globalization, deregulation, and extraordinary technological change—made the decade's countless customer-facing programs both a way for corporations to show they cared about customers and a strategic and operating imperative.

Now businesses face new challenges. Executives are caught between heightened pressure from financial markets to increase revenue and reduce costs on the one hand and increased customer demand for new and enhanced services on the other. This situation reveals the inherent contradictions in the blueprints for customer interaction used by many companies today.

These organizations rely on outdated and unfocused customer strategies, investment options, and operating models. Executives have only a vague picture of their customers' revenue potential and an even vaguer understanding of the true cost of serving them. Infrastructure and service costs are increasing faster than company revenues. Although executives understand the scope and complexity of what they need to change, they can't effectively put new strategies in place to drive significant, sustainable benefits.

These are not minor challenges that can be handled with a series of small, tactical programs and draconian belt-tightening. Companies need to rethink their basic assumptions about how customer interactions are designed, funded, and managed.

This chapter originally appeared in *Outlook,* vol. 14, no. 2, June 2002, an Accenture publication. Reprinted by permission.

This will involve aggressive, ambitious solutions and a new, strategic attitude toward investments.

In a world in which investment and operational dollars will remain scarce, a more profitable approach to getting and serving customers requires comprehensive strategies that both reduce the cost of service delivery and improve the value of customer interactions. Simply put, companies must align how much they spend on servicing customers with how much revenue these interactions generate.

RISKY BUSINESS

The recent economic turndown cut deep into many customer care programs, causing companies everywhere to scale down, postpone, or otherwise put new customer relationship management investments on the back burner. As the economy rebounds and budgets begin to loosen up, managers will be tempted to resume spending according to old CRM models. A brief review of these outmoded plans and strategies demonstrates why this would be highly risky.

Flawed Interaction Strategies

Over the past decade, many organizations aspired to provide each customer with the highest possible level of direct, personal service; many still do. However, that vision has not been realized.

Ideally, perhaps, each customer may be a market of one. Realistically, not all markets, or customers, are created equal. Although customers are even more demanding today than they were 10 years ago, companies simply cannot afford to conduct every customer transaction without regard for whether the cost of service aligns with the value of the customer and the transaction. (Nor would they necessarily be rewarded if they could. In general, companies earn less credit from customers for a positive interaction than they are penalized for a bad experience.)

Inflexible Investment Options

In the boom years of the 1990s, companies spent large sums to build contact center and interaction infrastructures. These investments now leave them saddled with high fixed costs and excess capacity. As a result, many can now only watch as margins shrink when revenues fall or customers defect, unable to shed these assets and costs without compromising service levels.

This burden includes not only direct costs that are easily accountable (e.g., labor and facilities), but also indirect costs that fly under the accounting radar and can't be easily located or contained (e.g., support and technology). Over time, these expanding costs steadily erode the financial return from profitable customer interactions.

In addition, slowing investments in "customer capital" (e.g., customer segmentation, relationship building, and target marketing) reduces the impact of CRM capability, stifling existing programs or limiting the capacity of companies to drive transformational change.

Suboptimal Delivery Models

Traditional delivery models for CRM no longer provide sustainable solutions for satisfying customer and market expectations. Companies actually have institutionalized the costs of their CRM investments without institutionalizing their benefits.

While some organizations have optimized performance in specific areas, organizational silos prevent most from optimizing across functions—in particular, by integrating marketing and customer service. These organizational boundaries drive many of the costs associated with CRM investments, such as maintenance, staffing, and training—costs that continue to grow.

For example, customer contact agents (whether in-house or outsourced) typically are not integrated with other business functions, which limits their efficiency. In the economics of customer interaction, literally every second counts. For a typical company spending $500 million annually on customer interaction, shaving one second off the average length of a customer call can save $10 million each year—savings that can be refocused on target customer segments or new customer campaigns.

A tactical response to these issues will deliver only tactical results. Significant gains are rare. Take costs, for example. Companies often try to contain operating costs by cutting staff. However, though downsizing will reduce the number of paychecks that must be issued, it will not reduce the number of customer calls that must be handled.

MISCONCEPTIONS

Entirely new approaches are necessary. Certainly, any company would benefit from a more profitable approach to getting and keeping customers. But those serving large numbers of customers through increasingly complex interactions—communications companies, retail banking, insurance, health-care organizations, and utilities—stand to gain, or sacrifice, the most (Exhibit 17-1). For these companies, profitability can rise or fall dramatically with even small changes in the cost of serving the average customer.

However, an increase in profits seems unlikely with so many basing their CRM approach on two common misconceptions about customer interaction. One is that they can easily calculate the cost of customer service. In reality, most are measuring only direct charges, understating the true cost of service and forcing decisions to be made without facts.

The other misconception is that all customers are created equal. The reality is that investment and operational dollars are scarce and will remain so. Companies must align what they spend with their most profitable customers.

One Mexican mobile-phone operator learned this lesson the hard way, paying a stiff price for its failure to differentiate profitable customers from money-losers. Locked in battle with other providers for market share, the company was paying roughly $1000 apiece for new customers. Its monthly profit per customer was around $35. However, with phone users jumping to the latest low-cost provider every

EXHIBIT 17-1.   Market profile.

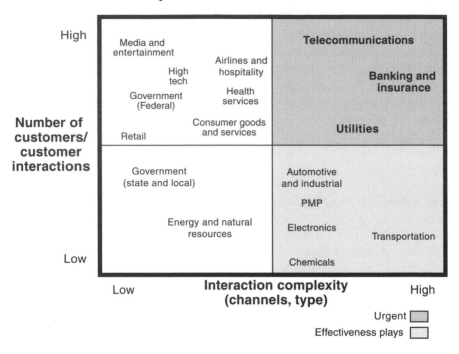

Urgent ▨
Effectiveness plays ☐

17 months, the company actually lost more than $400 on the average customer during that year and a half.

It would appear that some companies are too caught up in the myth of delighting their customers to notice this kind of gross misalignment. Datamonitor reports that only one-third of firms expect their call centers to generate a profit, and just one quarter expect them to even generate revenues. Forrester finds that only 42 percent of companies even consider selling something during a service call.

THE TIPPING POINT

When customer care is this critical to business performance, companies must transform their approaches, not fine-tune them or improve them incrementally. Accenture calls this *investing to the tipping point,* when the accumulative impact of change moves a company to a new level of performance. Parceling out investments through a series of tactical programs limits the possibility of delivering sustained, market-relevant results.

Improving the value of customer interactions in addition to reducing the cost of service delivery will produce better results than focusing on just one or the other factor. Likewise, a customer management strategy that addresses all interactions and channels is more likely to influence customer attitudes and behaviors than a piece-meal approach.

AT&T Consumer recently demonstrated this approach by announcing a program to transform sales and customer operations with an estimated investment of $2.6 billion in new technologies and workflows. By driving customer operations through a comprehensive program, rather than treating ad hoc components through incremental steps, the company expects to reduce costs by at least 50 percent.

So what will it take to fundamentally change the economics of sales and service?

Create a Customer Service Meritocracy

The first step is to escape the tyranny of the customer-as-king principle that dominates customer care. Define a customer interaction strategy based on who customers really are and what they really want, and then allocate sales and service resources according to these insights (Exhibit 17-2).

In other words, an interaction strategy based on a customer "meritocracy" requires not only deep information about customers but also the ability to differentiate customer treatment based on that information. Customer segmentation and analysis provide the foundation for proactive loyalty programs and customized offers that predict and influence customer actions. These marketing programs should be coordinated across channels and tested prelaunch to ensure that they really do reflect customer attitudes and preferences. Customer contact operations should also be designed to reflect customer preferences, and agents should be provided with the training, tools, and customer data they need to cross-sell and upsell while servicing customer requests.

Building integrated capabilities for analyzing customer data, modeling and segmenting the customer base, and creating links between customer channels—these actions will have clear impact on business results. For example, since adopting a new approach to exploiting customer profiles, Compaq gained $14 million in new rev-

EXHIBIT 17-2. A new paradigm for customer care.

	Tyranny	Meritocracy
Customer role	King	Citizen
Customer care philosophy	Highest possible level of care for every customer	Tailored care to customer needs based on the value of each interaction
Temporal orientation	Historic, including: 1. Spending patterns 2. Preferences 3. Demographics	Historic plus future, including: 1. Anticipated profit potential 2. Evolution of tastes 3. Lifestyle changes
Contact:		
Breadth	Broad based	Selective
Targeting	Undifferentiated	Highly focused
Frequency	Repeated	Timed to coincide with an anticipated need
Relationship goal	Retention	Long-term value of high-value customers

enue and generated ROI in excess of 1200 percent after only two campaigns. National Australia Bank uses predictive modeling techniques and data mining to determine how often the bank communicates with customers—via which channel, at what times, and with what offer. As of June 2000, the National had the highest share of wallet, customer satisfaction, and retention rates for high-net-worth clients in Australia. Using a similar focus on modeling customer value, Harrah's achieved a 90 percent hit ratio in turning customers worth $500 into customers worth $5000.

Know What It Really Costs

Develop a detailed and accurate picture of what it really costs to execute current sales and service models by customer segment. Although direct contact center costs for labor, facilities, and telecommunications are usually readily available, most organizations will have to dig deeper to define and measure indirect costs: operational support, technology, vendor management, integration with other business units, and other considerations.

Align Cost and Revenue

Determine service levels across the channel portfolio according to the customer needs and profitability defined by the new strategy. Typically, this will involve handling most service transactions through self-service or guided-service channels, while reserving costlier support options for the more valuable transaction types (Exhibit 17-3). Remember that emphasizing self-service still means emphasizing good service: personalized, efficient, and consistent.

EXHIBIT 17-3.   Using customer insights to reengineer the customer experience and maximize the value of each interaction.

	Low profit potential	High profit potential
High touch	Provide incentives to use low-cost channels	Focus high-touch services, high-cost resources here
Low touch	Minimize cost to serve	Find opportunities to cross-sell and upsell

Customer preference / Customer value

Experience shows that many customers prefer self-service. Some retailers have found it possible to transact as much as 40 percent of sales through self-service checkout systems.

Self-service channels also play an essential role in reducing cost to serve. Voice recognition technology, for example, helped Office Depot reduce phone interaction costs by 87 percent, and orders placed by phone have been larger on average than orders placed with human operators. Manulife Financial used similar technology to cut average call times from 12 minutes to 2 and reduce the abandonment rate, while cutting the cost by 90 percent.

Money saved by cutting unprofitable services to low-value customers can be spent making high-value customers even more valuable. Good customers deserve to be pampered. Thus, Charles Schwab clients who maintain at least $100,000 in net assets or trade 12 times a year and maintain a minimum of $10,000 in net assets never have to wait longer than 15 seconds to have their calls answered.

Boost Workforce Performance

Given that labor costs make up more than 60 percent of a contact center's operating budget, the right organizational structure and performance tools are especially important for optimizing head count and for increasing agent proficiency and motivation. According to a study by Hackett Benchmarking & Research, high-performing customer contact agents, handling 2.5 calls for every call at an average company, can reduce cost per contact to $4.73, compared with the industry average of $14.73.

Traditional performance measures such as average handling time and first-call resolution will suffice. But remember to look at the entire employee life cycle: hiring, training, speed to productivity, performance measurement tied to business results, and other factors. Incentives, for example, encourage customer contact agents to focus on performance targets during customer interactions. E-learning programs are not only effective ways to reduce training costs, they also train agents to improve sales and service.

Explore Alternative Sourcing Models

Effective partnering through outsourcing and cosourcing (the joint management of existing resources) is critical in transforming the economics of customer interaction. Outsourcing provides a flexible alternative to traditional CRM investment models by lowering the ratio of fixed to variable costs in customer care.

According to Jupiter Media Metrix, transferring contact center technologies and operations to offshore contact centers can save companies up to 30 percent of the costs of maintaining these operations in-house. United Airlines directs most customer service calls to a 100-person call center in Mexico City, whereas General Electric relies on call centers in 15 countries.

Innovative deal structures with these partners and third-party suppliers can help boost ROI by creating incentives for them to deliver results beyond traditional pay-by-the-call outsourcing arrangements. Outsourcing and cosourcing models also allow companies to launch new customer strategies with less capital spending up front and less financial outlay over the life of the investment, with the cost of strategic change amortized over a declining cost to serve. And financial markets tend to reward companies that focus on their core business strategy while realizing a better return on customer spending.

But take note: The call center outsourcing market is increasingly fragmented, and solutions are, for the most part, commodities. Historically, call center outsourcing has not been about innovation. Innovation and transformation must come from within the company. External vendors should be aligned with the company's business strategy and focused on putting that strategy into operation; they cannot be expected to define or drive the strategy.

Put It All Together

Finally, follow a basic set of guiding principles for delivering cost-effective, high-quality sales and service interactions.

* Eliminate calls at the source:
    In sales, develop more targeted sales campaigns to increase conversion.
    In service, simplify product and service offerings, eliminate unclear communications, and so forth.
* Use customer insight to differentiate sales and service channels and levels.
* Increase the use and effectiveness of self-service channels.
* Handle calls that are directed to live agents more efficiently through operational improvements.
* Balance internal and outsourced personnel to take advantage of labor arbitrage opportunities.

CONCLUSION

Since the mid-1990s, business gurus have preached that the customer is king. In many cases, though, the customer has become a tyrant, demanding high levels of service from every seller. A combination of new customer treatment strategies, more flexible investment options, and creative operating models now makes it possible to transform the old system of tyranny to a meritocracy in which customer treatment is aligned with customer profitability. However, to realize the full power of these new approaches (and the multiplier effect of implementing them all at once) organizations must be willing to substitute transformational programs for piecemeal CRM improvements.

18

Partner Relationship Management: The Next Generation of the Extended Enterprise

Marc F. Hayes and Ron Ref

During the past decade, companies have invested significant time and money in improving their internal business processes, cleaning up data, and integrating systems. As a result of their hard work, these companies now are positioned to reap the benefits of the *e-CRM extended enterprise,* which we define as the extension of a company's business model through process automation to customers and channel partners.

Partner relationship management (PRM) is the component of the e-CRM extended enterprise that specifically focuses on the process automation between companies and channel partners. To create greater customer value and channel partner profitability, leading companies are building PRM infrastructures that enable them to coordinate business planning activities, share information, conduct commerce, and provide postsales support across the channel.

STRATEGIES THAT CREATE VALUE

PRM solutions are designed to improve the efficiency and effectiveness of the interactions between companies and channel partners by allowing them to share information in routine business activities. Early adopters of PRM not only are improving channel marketing, sales, fulfillment, and service functions. They also are evolving

The content of this chapter originally appeared in the book *Defying the Limits: Setting a Course for CRM Success,* published by Montgomery Research.

the channel itself into a greater provider of value-added services and solutions. A recent survey of 50 executives from large manufacturing companies projects that on average, over the next two years, the use of extranet and PRM solutions will reduce distributor support costs by 32 percent and increase sales through channels by 17 percent.[1]

To achieve such benefits, channel managers are using PRM to implement business strategies that will help them meet the following goals:

- *Reengineer channel functions to drive costs out of the channel.* Through PRM, companies are automating customer service functions and are cutting manual processing costs in the areas of promotional funds management, order management, warranties, and returns processing. PRM also is being used to reduce collateral distribution costs and promote self-service transactions through online inquiry (for example, order status and account status) and self-study training programs. Customer service and sales representatives can serve partners more quickly, which enhances operating margins without raising prices.

- *Capitalize on growth opportunities in solutions and services.* Channel partners are critically important in providing services, product consulting, and integrated solutions. Companies are adding PRM solutions that strengthen channel partner relationships and add value to enhance the channel's ability to add value. Through the Internet, companies provide their channel partners with development tools and online starter kits that teach partners more about new and complementary revenue-generating opportunities, thereby expanding base product revenue streams. For example, a software manufacturer can provide its partners with resources such as a collection of best source code, a search interface that finds articles about bugs and corrective actions, live Webcasts, and helpful discussion forums that promote collaboration across the channel network.

- *Extend reach and increase market share.* Companies are increasing market share growth for existing partners and are providing access and reach to previously underserved or new partners. PRM enables companies to offer value-added tools such as self-configuration, detailed reporting, and transaction status. Simplifying the business relationship through value-added tools drives higher channel partner satisfaction, which can lead to improved partner retention and revenue growth. In addition, a proactive ability to support channel-inclusive e-business capabilities is often a major influence on channel partners' decisions to establish relationships with them. To increase access to new partners, companies are announcing new market opportunities, providing branded solution offerings to their partners, and instituting seamless online application and registration processes. With these strategies, channel managers are hoping to improve channel loyalty and reach. This will lead to decreased channel partner turnover, which, for companies with complex product lines, translates into less training time, greater productivity, and improved overall market presence and customer satisfaction.

EARLY ADOPTERS OPTIMIZE CHANNEL PARTNER RELATIONSHIPS

Traditionally, channels have been managed in a linear fashion, with each member of the chain handling sales and service to its immediate customers. This type of channel partner management is highly inefficient and causes companies and channel partners to experience errors and delays in their communications.

To address these inefficiencies, early adopters of PRM have focused on using the Internet to provide channel partners with several different e-business tools, including the following:

- *Product and service evaluation tools:* Channel partner Web sites that focus on Web content and that provide product as well as service catalogs and postsales support information (including methods for answering frequently asked questions and self-help guides)
- *Dynamically presented information:* Channel partner Web sites that personalize the channel partner relationship and include individualized information on authorized products, pricing, and promotion and service information
- *Transaction extension:* Channel partner Web sites that extend companies' transaction capabilities, helping channel partners directly manage their own accounts, self-configure orders, and track the status of service requests, orders, and other transactions

Internet-enabled PRM solutions have helped both companies and channel partners improve the efficiency of transactions. Manual processing techniques, which are prone to costly errors and inefficiencies, have been largely eliminated, promoting a seamless channel partner experience. Heightened capabilities offer companies a way to reliably maximize the value of every channel partner interaction to deliver a consistently branded end-customer experience focused on common processes and tools.

The following case studies illustrate the ways in which some early adopters have extended their investments in enterprise resource planning (ERP) and CRM systems by employing PRM solutions to optimize channel partner relationships. First, we look at how two companies improved their internal business operations through systems integration initiatives. Then we see how they took the next step, investing in PRM platforms that extended their business models outward into the channel. These companies succeeded in creating channel partner relationship interfaces that maximize the value of each interaction.

Case Study 1: Alcatel

Alcatel's eBusiness Group is one of three business units within Alcatel Telecom, a manufacturer of high-tech communication products and services headquartered in Paris. The eBusiness Group manufactures, sells, and supports voice and data products such as cellular phones and PBX systems.

As early as 1996, eBusiness Group executives observed the beginnings of a shift in the market for leading-edge communication products. As often happens with technology, the shift was life-cycle driven. Following an inaugural phase of red-hot demand, a steady evolution toward commodity status occurred, bringing with it the need for lower prices, increased efficiencies, and a growing emphasis on service.

To remain ahead of the curve, company leaders launched a transformation program focused on the development of a highly efficient, global, service-oriented culture. Fundamental changes to the company's business processes would anchor the program.

Group leaders also foresaw that by the late 1990s, customer contact would mean more than excellent support and easy access. Instead, marketing, sales, order management, and service would have to be integrated into comprehensive, Internet-enabled relationships with channel partners and customers. Alcatel needed new strategies and technologies that would not only support changes within the company but also enable the company to expand outward along the channel. In effect, Alcatel would create an extended enterprise and, using PRM solutions, facilitate communication between the company and its channel partners.

Alcatel's new PRM solutions would provide complete electronic product catalog display; incorporate quotation and configuration features; manage online order placement; ensure direct, full-time access to order status information; and provide entry to complementary business portals. These new capabilities were expected to increase market share within reseller/distributor channels, improve pricing controls, reduce head count in information technology and order-processing functions, and eliminate item stocks at local sales units.

To accomplish these objectives, a team of Accenture and Alcatel executives revamped several supply chain and financial processes and developed a new technology architecture to support incoming ERP applications. Concurrent with the implementation of the ERP software, the team developed the group's new e-channel, composed of a call management system and a transaction-focused Web site for serving customers and interfacing with distributors and dealers.

The group's new system presents each authorized dealer/reseller with an online catalog of orderable items, each of which is custom priced for that user. When all items have been selected and the channel partner is ready to buy, the system runs a credit check, confirms the availability of each item, and displays fulfillment details such as total price and delivery timetable. When the transaction is complete, all back-office information is processed by the ERP system. At any time prior to delivery, the channel partner can log on to the system to determine order status.

More than 2500 customers and authorized dealer/resellers are now connected to Alcatel's new extended enterprise. The result has been improved pricing controls, reduced head count, and more efficient order processing. By virtually any measure, the Alcatel eBusiness Group has attained a new level of PRM.

Case Study 2: Sharp Electronics Corporation

Sharp Document and Network Systems, the office equipment division within Mahwah, New Jersey–based Sharp Electronics Corporation, is a leading manufacturer of fax and copy equipment. Sharp was faced with rising channel partner expectations for improved sales and service support. In addition, market pressures called for improved sales productivity. A PRM approach provided a way for Sharp to improve channel relations by building a dealer Internet business system that promoted more effective channel communication, timely distribution of product and pricing information, efficient order processing, and customer support.

Though Sharp had invested substantially in an ERP system to enhance its own internal business processes, working with dealers and distributors remained challenging. Sharp could neither achieve substantial growth nor increase the level of channel satisfaction using its current manual processes, which were not efficient and did not support collaborative exchanges with channel partners. Sharp and its dealer channel needed a better way to communicate. David Lewis, director of Internet business systems for Sharp Network and Digital Document Systems of America, stated, "We wanted a scalable alternative that would streamline the information hand-offs and improve the timeliness of information delivered to the channel."

Sharp products already provided excellent service revenues, low product failure rates, and low product repair costs. To improve efficiency and satisfaction among channel partners, Sharp needed a business platform that would provide excellent support and easy access to information. Sharp's recent investment in an ERP platform, combined with a dealer Internet business system, would promote real-time information sharing and common information repositories for its channel partners. This solution would provide authorized product and pricing information for each partner, launch timely marketing promotions based on partner eligibility, ensure order accuracy, and provide timely order status checking (for example, expected shipping dates and carrier tracking information).

Sharp executives set out to design a set of business processes governing interactions along the channel—an approach that was more encompassing than simply building a Web site that communicated with the ERP system. The team addressed key business processes such as availability to promise, inventory allocation, promotion management, and freight optimization. The goal was to allow dealers to process orders seamlessly and access self-service inquiry functions at any time.

Sharp succeeded in building a dealer Internet business system that provides the following features:

- Effective channel communications
- Timely distribution of products and pricing information
- Efficient and accurate order processing
- Better customer support

Everything from placing an order to ensuring that the order was sourced from the right warehouse to viewing the order status has been simplified. Instead of relying on fax orders, dealers are able to go online, view specific product and pricing information, and place orders. In this way, information is properly recorded, and dealers receive immediate confirmation of orders. In addition, each dealer's Web site is tailored to that dealer's authorized certification, and dealers are able to view the most current promotional programs. They can quickly determine which promotions they qualify for and what they must modify to receive additional promotional benefits.

Dealers have been unanimous in their praise of Sharp's new system. Order inquiry calls to customer service teams have fallen dramatically. Uptake has been remarkable: Within nine months, more than 80 percent of the order volume was being processed through the Internet, with approximately 90 percent of dealers' sites activated. Information has been more reliable, and administrative work both at Sharp and at dealerships has been reduced.

Sharp's efforts were so successful that personnel within both the company and the dealerships were newly motivated. The success story was used as a public relations tool to promote the new PRM-inspired solutions to the channel sales, order administration, and customer service personnel. This energized and motivated personnel across the channel.

Sharp implemented a platform strong enough to support ongoing enhancements. Using PRM solutions, Sharp can now respond to technological advances. In the future, it will be able to reengineer other activities such as collaborative accounts receivable management, third-party finance company integration, electronic training/certification courses, and quota and commission/sales management. These advanced functionalities will provide greater opportunities for lowering costs and increasing productivity and sales.

THE NEXT GENERATION: COLLABORATIVE PRM

The case studies demonstrate how companies are leveraging PRM to extend their business models and transaction capability. So what is next for these companies?

New application technologies allow manufacturers to extend collaborative business processes through the channel. Channel partners will be able to share their experience and knowledge and provide greater customer value as a network than any single channel partner could alone. Channel partners that have complementary skills, products, and services will be able to work together to come up with creative new solutions to support companies' value propositions and customer needs.

Establishing a collaborative PRM relationship with channel partners will require companies to develop the following processes, features, and capabilities:

- *Closed-loop business processes that integrate manufacturers and channel partners to deliver a complete customer experience.* Companies are deploying closed-loop processes to improve the overall customer experience and direct work to the channel partner best positioned to perform that work. Through extranet workflow, companies can coordinate multiple players in the network and more effectively manage the delivery of services or solutions. For example, an end customer may have a service request that requires specialized skill or knowledge. While the field technician servicing the request may not have sufficient knowledge to address the issue, a request can be generated and routed to the most competent individual(s). Through alarms and alerts, service for the request is managed, thus reducing the response time, decreasing the resolution effort, and improving the overall customer experience.

- *Workspaces to foster communication and knowledge sharing among channel partners.* Companies are hosting forums where channel partners can find out about other partners in the channel network and collaborate to develop solutions, solve business problems and evaluate designs. A site may help members of the channel network find other members that have the competency, experience, and assets to address a specific customer situation. Other sites may support discussion forums allowing channel partners to explore broader market opportunities by either sharing proven solutions or evolving a collaborative solution design by working through multiple iterations of design documents.

- *Hybrid channel networks on which direct and indirect sales channels work together to deliver and install products and services.* Companies are supporting collaboration between their direct sales forces and their channel networks so that the most effective teams are engaging the end customers. For example, a manufacturer that maintains a direct relationship with its national account base deploys direct-account sales and service teams to the customers. However, channel partners fill the orders and install the products. A client placing an order for installation at multiple locations would benefit from the manufacturer's ability to coordinate the effort with its channel partners. PRM solutions assist in this type of complex delivery by integrating the order and installation process.

- *Syndicated application and content deployment capabilities.* Manufacturers are extending marketing, selling, servicing, and fulfillment solutions to their channel partners. The next generation of PRM will create an extended enterprise that embodies characteristics of a franchise operation. Just as franchising replicates a successful business format (business infrastructure, operations manuals, systems, and procedures) in the physical world, content and application syndication promises to provide channel partners with proven business practices in the virtual world. Syndication enables partners to operate their businesses at a much higher point on the learning curve. Rather than recreating product catalogs, customer needs assessment tools, and product diagnostics, channel partners will be able to leverage tools that have been tried and tested by the enterprise, reducing potential mistakes. An illustration of application syndication is a company sending an electronic product catalog to its distributors, those distributors in turn sending portions of the catalog to their contractors, and so on. The syndication of an enterprise's branded electronic catalog that can be used in the distributor's online environment as well as the contractor's Web site not only creates efficiencies for the channel but creates a consistent experience for all network members and customers.

GUIDELINES FOR FINDING PRM OPPORTUNITIES AND BENEFITS

Early adopters of PRM have realized substantial benefits from their extranet and PRM solutions. To identify the right opportunities for your channel network, you must align your company, channel, and customer priorities with strategic objectives. Consider the following diagnostic questions when determining if your channel is configured to generate similar benefits from PRM.

Partner Enrollment

To build a strong community of channel partners that can meet your market objectives, your company must profile channel partners and monitor sales performance. Gaps must be managed through well-defined, cost-effective recruiting processes.

- Does your channel provide adequate market coverage?
- Are you cost-effectively targeting, qualifying, recruiting, and registering the right partners that will effectively represent your product?
- Are you tracking your partners' skills and competencies?

Business Planning

After you have recruited your target channel partners, you must understand their strengths and business objectives so that you can work effectively with them. This means developing rich channel partner profiles, creating sales forecasts, allocating promotional budgets, and planning marketing programs.

- How effectively do you plan and manage your channel partners' sales goals and funding?

Channel Marketing

Understanding your channel partners' points of view and motivating them to sell your products means supplying them with the tailored information they need to sell products and routing leads to the most qualified channel partner. You must provide them with well-defined channel partner profiles, well-managed content distribution processes, and lead management. As the Sharp case study demonstrates, channel partner satisfaction grows when channel partners are given authorized product, pricing, and promotion information.

- How effectively do you train your channel partners?
- Do you provide your channel partners with opportunities through distributed lead management?
- Do you provide timely product and programs communications to enable them to close more business?

Selling

Companies must respond quickly and effectively to channel partners. When channel partners are given access to sales resources, channel partner productivity increases. As

Alcatel realized, excellent support and easy access means providing the channel with an electronic product catalog, integrated with quotation and configuration features.

- Are you achieving the sales revenue per channel partner that you expect?
- Are your channel partners satisfied with your channel support responsiveness?

Transacting

Rapid execution of orders means providing channel partners with the inputs they need to make an order decision (for example, pricing, availability, and financing terms). You also must give them tools to log onto the Web site and monitor inventory, order, and shipment status; capture and process orders accurately; and communicate directly with back-end systems for order processing.

- How cost effective are your distribution and order management processes?

Postsales Service

To increase the responsiveness of the service process while reducing administrative tasks for the service provider, you must provide the channel with easy access to service management. Channel partners need efficient ways to manage service requests, warranty claims, returns, and spare parts orders and to access service manuals and service bulletins. The channel network also needs an electronic workspace for resolving service issues.

- How well are you able to provide consistent service delivery?
- Is your channel service as responsive as it should be?
- Is your channel service under control?

Performance Management

To achieve effective promotional programs, accurate sales forecasts, and maximized channel productivity, your company must continuously refine its activities and investments. An information infrastructure and the right decision-support tools are critical to gaining insight and visibility into channel activity.

- Are you able to make informed decisions on channel activities and investments?

LESSONS FROM THE LEADERS

PRM offers companies significant value, whether by allowing the sharing of previously difficult to share information or by helping channel partners collaborate through closed-loop, cross-enterprise business processes. These opportunities can lead to increased channel profitability and greater satisfaction for customers, channel partners, and enterprises.

Understandably, organizations want all the benefits of partner relationship management. Early adopters offer guidelines on how to achieve world-class capability:

- *Build stakeholder buy-in.* Channel management, influential channel partner representatives, and sales management must buy into strategy and deployment.

System acceptance rates improve dramatically when relationships among stakeholders are strong and all parties buy into the value proposition and support its promotion and uptake.

- *Staged release rollout.* PRM is a journey, not a destination. Develop a long-term vision and a release plan that allows you to phase in the new system in a way that builds channel support.

- *Focus on the end customer.* The value proposition for each constituency is driven by improving the end-customer experience. Design your PRM processes end to end so that customer value is of primary importance.

- *Cross-functional representation.* PRM affects multiple components of the organization. Ensure that the team has representatives from sales, marketing, order management, customer service, and logistics.

For companies that consider channel partners increasingly important in the marketing, selling, delivering, and servicing of their products, forging ahead into the world of PRM is imperative, not optional.

While PRM offers significant opportunities, the challenge is to identify the channel priorities that will drive the greatest value for your company, channel partners, and customers.

WHAT CAPABILITIES SHOULD YOU LOOK FOR IN A PRM SOLUTION?

New software vendors now offer applications that address the wide-ranging business capabilities required to connect, communicate, exchange information, and transact throughout the partner life cycle. These vendors provide components of a new PRM architecture that takes advantage of the Internet while addressing the problems of channel complexity and the lack of channel partner functionality in traditional CRM and ERP vendor applications.

While there is no vendor that supports the complete partner relationship life cycle, there is a useful framework for evaluating PRM capabilities. Here is what a comprehensive set of PRM capabilities would entail:

Recruit Partners and Manage Relationships

First, companies focus on recruiting channel partners and managing the application process. To facilitate this, PRM offers solutions in applications management, partner registration, and partner profiling functions. In order for companies and channel partners to develop common goals and objectives, they must plan channel sales and marketing activities together. These processes include sales forecasting, promotions planning, and a continuous feedback loop for managing partner feedback.

Generate Demand for and from Partners

With improved information distribution, channel partners can receive personalized communications about existing and new products and services, as well as sales and marketing collateral. In addition, training and certification packages increase channel partners' awareness of products and services. Finally, armed with the right information and training, companies are routing leads so that channel partners are informed about potential sales opportunities. As product life cycles shorten, it becomes increasingly important to communicate special programs and promotions in a timely manner.

PRM systems are enabling quicker distribution of these materials. Channel partners must manage the presales process electronically by focusing on assessing customer needs through questionnaires, evaluating product and service options, generating price quotes, managing sales opportunities, and providing customers with product availability and price quote information. Finally, channel partners must track customer interaction through contact and activity managers to maximize their effectiveness.

Fulfill Demand

Using e-commerce tools, channel partners electronically direct everything about the purchase process, from placing orders to receiving products. Order management tools apply to order entry, payment and finance processing, tax and shipping calculations, management of allocated inventory, distribution of digital assets, and the ability to track order and shipping status.

Postsales Support

The postsales support process begins with product registration. Emphasizing the reduction of cost of service, channel partners electronically manage the postsales support process using self-service tools such as solution libraries, problem diagnostics, and discussion forums. Field support is managed through tools that include field service dispatch, service request management, and proactive service management. Finally, standard processes such as warranty, returns, and repairs processing are streamlined.

Account Management

By promoting self-service through ease of access to account information, companies are enabling channel partners to view and manage their account activity electronically. Without having to contact an operational staff person, partners are able to get answers to questions about accounts receivable, quota, and commissions management.

Reporting and Decision Support

Companies and channel partners can share information and tools to gain insight and visibility for improved decision making. Tools include standard report cards that measure channel performance, site performance, and usage reporting.

Site Management

This set of capabilities targets the functions required to manage and administer PRM site operations. These functions address the ability to administer both internal company operations and partner site operations. Company site operations include basic administrative procedures such as security (data access and capability authorization), content management (creation, review and approval, and staging and deployment), personalization, site navigation, and search functions. Partner site operations include functions such as syndication (the ability to deploy content and application functionality to a partner's site), distributed user administration (the ability to establish and manage user access within the partner organization), and extranet workflow administration (the ability to route leads, service requests, and promotional fund requests within the partner and company organizations).

Integration Capabilities

A comprehensive PRM infrastructure will require information exchange with internal company applications, third-party applications, and partner Web sites. To support the integration requirements, vendors are providing hooks into leading packages (ERP, SFA, and call center) and leading enterprise application interface vendors. Vendors are accommodating integration with leading third-party providers including logistics providers, training vendors, and so forth.

If your industry is served by a channel that uses a standard order management system, you should examine how a specific package might support direct integration into your partners' systems. Finally, if your company has developed a direct customer channel leveraging the Internet and you believe there is an opportunity to route customer interests to your channel partners, you should consider integration with your public dot-com presence.

19

Mission-Critical Workforces: Developing a Source of Value

Dorothy V. VonDette and Patrick Mosher

A nyone can cut costs. The question is, can you cut costs and create value at the same time?

It's an urgent question today, particularly when it comes to an organization's workforce. A lot of cost pressure these days is relieved through head-count reductions. However, unless companies balance these reductions with new kinds of employee-enabling programs, they are likely to have workforces that are not only smaller but also dispirited and less motivated, which will make hitting financial targets all the more difficult.

How can companies achieve necessary workforce reductions yet maintain or even improve productivity levels? In unsettled times, how can they keep their people focused and engaged? How can they put together the right mix of tools, rewards, training, and career opportunities to provide the job satisfaction necessary to retain their top talent? Most important, how can they do all this right now?

Today the pressure to effect critical change quickly is more relentless than ever. The trouble is, techniques and approaches for improving workforce performance and linking it to bottom-line value, like many initiatives that go right to the heart of an organization, often seem to play out at a glacial pace. As one executive put it, reacting recently to a proposal for performance improvement: "I like what you're telling me. But here's the deal: I've got to turn my sales figures around in six months. That's my window. If you've got something that can help me do that, I'm all ears. If not, then let's both move on to our next appointments."

This chapter originally appeared in *Outlook,* vol. 14, no. 1, January 2002, an Accenture publication. Reprinted by permission.

FOCUS

It is a challenge that can, in fact, be met. Remember the early days of just-in-time manufacturing? Recall how experts in the field could simply walk around a shop floor making observations and, in a matter of days, identify areas where improvements resulted in millions of dollars in savings? How did they do that?

First, they had a deep and broad understanding of the environment. They were like medical doctors with a genius for diagnosis. Second, they did not look at everything. They knew where the critical influence points were, and that's where they focused most of their attention.

Similarly, certain workforces are particularly vital to overall business performance; we call these *mission-critical workforces*. Once those workforces are identified, then a deep understanding of the influence points for a workforce can lead to the rapid diagnosis of performance issues and quick implementation of a plan for improving employee performance.

Just what are these mission-critical workforces? Think of the distinct workforces in your company. Then imagine which of them are responsible for significant revenue or costs. For instance, during a new drug launch, a pharmaceutical company's sales force is mission critical. Or think about insurance adjusters, whose job it is to settle policy claims worth millions of dollars. Increasing their ability to render fair and accurate settlements has a measurable impact on the financial performance of the company. Field-service workers are a mission-critical workforce for many companies, because they depend on this workforce to represent their brands to their customers and to distinguish their companies from competitors based on the services they provide. Improving the performance of this workforce can have a major impact on customer satisfaction and retention, and it can ultimately lead to increased revenue and profitability.

Generally speaking, look for a workforce segment for which incremental improvements in job performance translate into discernible differences in financial results.

For example, Ryder System, an international provider of supply chain and transportation management services, recently focused attention on areas of its workforce that are instrumental not only in driving sales but also in designing and implementing these services.

Ryder realized that to achieve and maintain strategic competitiveness in the twenty-first century, its employees needed the tools necessary to share best practices and innovative ideas more easily and dynamically. The solution: a state-of-the-art knowledge management center that enabled the exchange of the company's best new thinking, facilitated quick access to experts within Ryder, supplied customized news feeds on key market trends, and provided collaborative work areas for project teams.

But what lies beneath a workforce solution is just as important as the solution itself. To meet the performance needs of a particular mission-critical workforce, a comprehensive, holistic view of the performance environment is needed. This view is encapsulated in the workforce performance framework (see sidebar, "The Workforce Performance Framework").

THE WORKFORCE PERFORMANCE FRAMEWORK

The workforce performance framework (Exhibit 19-1) is based on two important premises: (1) the performance of certain workforces is mission critical, and these employees can materially affect the financial performance of the organization; and (2) by aligning mission-critical workforce performance with financial and operational goals, you can directly increase bottom-line results.

EXHIBIT 19-1. Workforce performance framework.

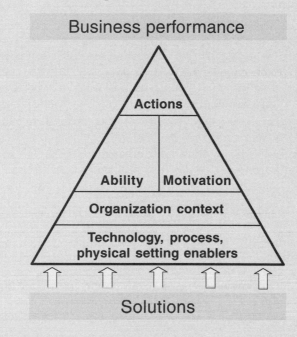

Typical programs aimed at improving workforce performance focus largely on either efficiency or cost. By contrast, this approach ties certain key target behaviors to operational performance, focusing both on efficiency and effectiveness as well as creating value from workforce performance.

Helping to identify certain critical workforce behaviors that are linked in measurable ways to business performance is one aspect of the framework. A second is tracking the particular influences on those behaviors. Those influences can be grouped under three major categories: *ability, motivation,* and *context.*

Behaviors arise out of a worker's ability (can the worker show the behavior?) as well as motivation (will the worker show the behavior?). A poorly designed context can prevent workers from exhibiting the behavior, even if they have the ability and motivation. Job design, organization structure, technologies, process design, and physical setting are all contextual elements to consider.

To achieve optimal levels, workforce performance must be supported by a comprehensive context of services. Ryder's implementation of its knowledge management center program included communications, training, policies and procedures, knowledge proficiencies, incentives, a comprehensive measurement system, and the creation of an organizational team to lead the knowledge management effort. This solution provided Ryder employees with the tools and information needed to perform at more efficient levels, as well as the motivation to succeed. According to Gene Tyndall, Ryder's executive vice president of global markets and solutions, "Ryder employees have embraced these changes to make them more competitive and better suited to deliver value-based services to its customers."

GOOD BEHAVIOR

Now that you have identified your most important workforces, you are ready to plot a course for performance improvement. But what exactly are you trying to change? What do you want to improve? If you answered "workforce behaviors," go to the head of the class: Ultimately, you are trying to change the workforce's actions.

As it turns out, persuading executives to focus on the performance objectives of their mission-critical workforces is one of the most important services a human performance professional can provide. Whittle down a broad list of performance goals to a half-dozen key performance objectives. Any fewer than that means you are not being specific enough. More than that means you are losing your focus.

How do you know if you have an effective set of key performance objectives? First, you will know because the objectives are measurable: Remember, what gets measured gets done. Second, you will know because they represent clear business imperatives. That only makes sense. If you are trying to have a quick impact on business performance, you will want workforce performance goals that are easily linked to financial outcomes (see sidebar, "Measurable Business Results").

Here is an example of how identifying key performance objectives can help a workforce meet a real business need. A major insurance company faced a number of challenges related to its call center. Market conditions had led to overcapacity and underutilization of the center's representatives. The company wanted to increase the overall capability of these representatives to generate revenue through sales and to realize full benefits from the CRM technology infrastructure it had recently installed.

The call center management identified an overall set of key performance objectives, including reducing the time it took to train workers, increasing the value of each customer contact, retaining the best call center talent, and increasing the rate of first-contact resolution for customers. Each of these general key performance objectives for the center was then translated into specific target behaviors for call center workers.

For example, the general objective to reduce training time for workers involved the following specific behaviors on the part of the representatives: Quickly learn how to perform in new situations; translate training to real situations; apply general

MEASURABLE BUSINESS RESULTS

Identifying opportunities for quick wins from mission-critical-workforce improvement has paid off at a number of leading companies. A major telecommunications company, for example, sought to transform its customer-facing network operations. Through enhanced network capabilities and a focus on end-to-end processes, the goal was to improve customer service and build new, competitive skills in its workforce.

Once the mission-critical workforce was assessed in light of the business goals, the designed solution had two major thrusts: new deployment centers that focused on improving the customer experience, and a skilled field service and call center workforce to help launch new products and services.

Measurable business results from this initiative are startling in each of three major areas: an improved customer experience, the reduced cost of operations, and an increased capacity to change.

Improved Customer Experience

• Improved customer transaction scores by 10 to 15 percent
• Increased first-time completions by 50 to 100 percent

Reduced Cost of Operations

• Increased quality by 20 to 30 percent
• Increased productivity by 10 to 15 percent
• Reduced turnover by 20 to 40 percent
• Reduced executive commission complaints by 40 to 70 percent

Increased Capacity to Change

• Reduced cycle time to train by 20 to 25 percent
• Decreased time to proficiency by 20 to 75 percent
• Increased knowledge application by 30 to 60 percent
• Increased organizationwide consistency by 30 to 50 percent
• Increased employee satisfaction by 10 to 50 percent

principles to guide decisions in specific situations; and actively use support mechanisms to improve performance. These specific objectives and behavior targets provided the company with the critical input to identify where its spending would have the maximum effect on the exact behaviors that most quickly translate either into cost savings or increased revenue.

(For another, more detailed example of key performance objectives and target behaviors—this one, for airport security personnel—see the sidebar, "Establishing Key Performance Objectives").

ESTABLISHING KEY PERFORMANCE OBJECTIVES

Discrete, measurable, focused key performance objectives create a direct link between business performance and human performance. For example, to improve the performance of airport security personnel, the set of key performance objectives noted in the following table guides the analysis of the current capability of the workforce.

Key performance objectives	Target behaviors
Minimize passenger risk.	Effectively qualify potential risks. Apply appropriate scanning techniques. Ask appropriate security questions. Apply up-to-date security policies and procedures. Pay attention to screened items. Continually review potential security risks (review most wanted list).
Minimize passenger disruption.	Minimize false detentions. Use security backups to deal with potential security risks. Treat customers with respect. Open new checkpoints to facilitate customer lines.
Respond effectively to emergency situations.	Apply up-to-date security policies and procedures. Notify supervisor immediately. Remain calm and in control. Act professionally. Act decisively.
Hire the best security talent.	Consider the company for employment. Commit to the organization. Reach expected performance targets. Remain employed with the organization.
Organize the workforce to minimize risk.	Rotate security team members to reduce monotony. Provide support mechanisms (mentoring, etc.) to mitigate job stress. Provide adequate staffing at security checkpoints. Provide adequate leadership/supervision at security checkpoints.
Improve workforce proficiency.	Complete studies on new procedures, tools, products and services. Apply training to real situations. Actively use support structure to learn new policies and procedures. Perform screening without instruction. Review, retain, and apply up-to-date security information.

Each key performance objective translates into specific target behaviors, which are checked against performance behaviors of the workforce. Based on the gaps identified between the real and the ideal, a unique program of performance enhancement for these workers is designed and implemented.

BUILDING THE BUSINESS CASE

The next step is to identify business benefits derived from particular workforce improvements. Staying with our insurance company example, the value proposition from workforce improvement in the company's call center focused on three potential benefits: an increase in the number of desirable customers; an increase in profits from each customer (partly through deeper relationships and higher value, and partly through enhanced efficiency and thus lower costs); and a longer overall relationship with the customer—that is, an enhanced lifetime value of the customer relationship.

After examining the current conditions at the call center and projecting the results of improved performance, the company set its sights on these potential benefits:

- Potential revenue growth of 5 to 15 percent through the increased retention of the best customers, the improved capacity for upselling and cross-selling, and an increased customer acquisition rate.

- Potential cost savings of 10 to 20 percent through improved employee productivity, improved channel efficiency, and streamlined customer call handling.

- Potential increased margins of 2 to 7 percent through an improved growth rate, reduced operating cost, and improved customer profitability.

Once the key performance objectives and business benefits pieces are in place, you must assess the current performance of your workforce. In other words, you cannot know where you are going until you know where you are.

It may be an obvious point, but the assessment of workforce performance is often given either too little attention or too much. The too-little part is probably obvious—people may have a tendency to jump at a solution without a clear sense of what the problem is. But the too-much assessment is just as bad: Analysis paralysis in the diagnostic stage can mean missing a key window of opportunity.

Assessment may certainly include some of the traditional, well-known survey instruments and diagnostics. But here is another, simpler assessment tactic: Observe your people at work. Not exactly revolutionary, but it's an approach that is so obvious, it is often missed.

This takes us back to the just-in-time (JIT) analogy. Just as those experts made improvements through direct observation, so does a human performance professional. Observation and analysis of current workforce behaviors can lead to quicker identification of problem areas—areas in which improvement may lead to quicker payback. Just as JIT experts had their tools (process run charts, spaghetti diagrams, and swim-lane diagrams) human performance specialists have their tools—behavior architectures, key performance objective work packets, and motivation assessments.

If you are trying, for example, to improve the performance of your mission-critical field service workers, it is essential to have experts ride along with them. Monitoring the calls made by call center representatives is another example, provided that this direct observation is done unobtrusively.

THE APPROPRIATE PACKAGE

There are many options available for raising workforce performance, including process improvement, performance feedback, e-learning, knowledge management, and mobile applications. Although the number of options is not infinite, it may appear that way to harried executives looking for help. The question at this stage is how to configure a solutions package for the particular performance needs of your mission-critical workforces.

You can use a short assessment phase to identify gaps in the performance of the workforce according to the categories of the workforce performance framework. Analyze the human performance elements and the resulting business performance to identify areas to improve. Then tailor a human performance strategy to address specific gaps in the categories of ability, motivation, and context. These strategies may involve innovative new approaches in such areas as collaboration and knowledge management, human relations process and technology, performance management, workspace portals, e-learning, and performance simulation.

Workspace portals are a new and important enabler for mission-critical workforces. They integrate, in a single interface and with personalized context, the information, best practices, and knowledge that employees need to do their best work. Unlike the traditional business-to-employee portal, the workspace portal provides a specific workforce with relevant e-learning programs, collaboration tools, and content-specific applications. Employees can not only view information but also act on it in a way that makes their jobs easier and their efforts more productive.

New e-learning solutions are also enablers of mission-critical workforces. For example, communication services provider BellSouth recently launched an initiative to energize its customer service area. The company was looking for ways to make its customer service representatives better motivated and more knowledgeable.

These representatives had to learn to handle every imaginable type of customer call, and they had to learn quickly. In an environment in which the attrition level of call center representatives was rising along with the complexity of the business, these men and women needed more than coaching—they needed empowerment. That meant being equally comfortable with both the sales and service elements of the job. It meant learning to think and act swiftly, and with confidence, on shades-of-gray decision points. Most of all, it meant proving to customers that they were in the smartest and most capable hands possible.

The solution? An e-learning program BellSouth called *BEST*, for Business Excellence through Simulation Training. BEST lives up to its name, providing a unique electronic training experience in which customer service representatives learn via simulated customer calls. Representatives get 16 to 24 hours of simulation training based on exemplary and best-practice employees. Their prior training comes into play, but beyond that they learn to use judgment and communications skills normally gained over months, sometimes years, of practical experience.

The benefits of BEST go straight to the bottom line. Some program participants have increased their sales performance by as much as 200 percent. And because of a

13 percent reduction in training time, fewer repeat calls, and a reduction in the time it takes a representative to reach proficiency, BellSouth expects to see as much as $52 million in cost savings over a five-year period.

CONCLUSION

You may ask, "Where's the catch?" If there is one, it goes back to the point about needing a deep understanding of what makes these workforces tick. Close observation and experience go hand in hand. Without the experience, it is hard to know what to look for. And without the ongoing and effective observation of real behaviors, experience quickly becomes out of date.

Call the desired state *hands-on knowledge*—with such expertise, one can more quickly diagnose a problem, design and implement a specific solution for a mission-critical workforce, and have a measurable impact on financial results. This is the new workforce opportunity today: to treat human performance not as overhead to manage but as a source of value to develop.

The Message Must Go Through: Messaging Technologies and Customer Care

Marc F. Hayes

I n April 1860, the first Pony Express rider set off from St. Joseph, Missouri, and headed west across the United States with a bag of mail. The route would take him and the other riders along the trail over the 2000 miles to San Francisco in just 10 days, a huge improvement over the usual three weeks it took to deliver mail by stagecoach from Missouri to California. The system forged a new frontier in communication with the motto, "The mail must go through." By reducing time, guaranteeing delivery, and allowing people to reach out and communicate quickly (by 1860 standards), the Pony Express revolutionized mail communications. Today we are on the brink of a similar communications and messaging revolution. This time, it is digital, wireless, and Internet enabled. Messaging technologies have the potential to completely alter the nature of message delivery and, therefore, customer care—just as the Pony Express revolutionized mail delivery more than 140 years ago.

MESSAGING TECHNOLOGIES: MOBILE AND MULTIPLYING

Today approximately 180 million consumers and business workers alike worldwide use instant messaging technology to send more than 400 billion messages a year. By 2005, the research and advisory firm IDC estimates there will be nearly 600 million

The content of this chapter originally appeared in the book *Defying the Limits: Setting a Course for CRM Success,* published by Montgomery Research.

instant messaging users sending more than 2 trillion messages a year.[1] Add to these numbers those individuals who are using voice messaging and interactive pagers to send messages to each other and it is clear that messaging has been established as a mainstream communications channel. The development of these technologies points to another area of phenomenal growth: mobile communications. Devices such as pagers, personal digital assistants, and mobile phones with Internet access are just a few of the new tools available that support the mobile messaging channel. If an individual possesses just one of these devices, that person can be contacted anywhere, at any time.

This type of constant connectivity, if effectively harnessed by businesses, will revolutionize communications with customers, employees, and business partners and will create new relationships between businesses and customers. Messaging technologies provide an unprecedented ability to intelligently and cost-effectively interact with customers at scale. However, for these changes to take place, businesses must embrace messaging technologies and promote them as tools for improving customer care.

BUILDING CUSTOMER LOYALTY

The rapid and explosive growth in messaging technologies may become a primary driver in the changing nature of communications and customer care. In today's market, customer loyalty is the key to success, and businesses must focus on developing it with each interaction. Messaging channels can serve as powerful tools for building this loyalty.

Organizations must treat their customers as individuals, from both marketing and service-delivery standpoints. By collecting customer information and gleaning insight from it, businesses can anticipate customer expectations and tailor each customer's experience to match these expectations. With this insight, companies are also able to proactively reach out to customers and business partners with personalized promotions, products, pricing, and message content. Businesses can optimize customer acquisition, development, and retention by using this information and new messaging tools to better meet customer expectations at every turn, thereby improving customer loyalty.

TECHNOLOGY TOOLS PROMOTE CUSTOMER CARE

Even as some companies have made great strides in their customer service, aggregate customer satisfaction continues to decline in many industries. For example, aggregate customer satisfaction in the airline industry has dropped from 72 to 63 percent since 1994. Since 1997, telecommunications has seen a yearly one-point decline in overall customer satisfaction, from 75 to 72 percent.[2] Enterprises can mitigate this trend by first recognizing why customers are dissatisfied, then using new technology tools to solve problems.

Many customers note three characteristics of customer service today that businesses must improve. First, customers believe that many companies are rigid because they provide only one or two ways for customers to interact within specified time periods. While many companies have worked hard to make call centers and Web sites helpful, customers want easier, more timely access to information and services. Second, customers characterize these systems as company-centric. Instead of being able to choose a communication method or call and get a quick answer, customers often find themselves on hold for many minutes, lost in a voice-mail tree, unable to find the answer in a confusing sea of Web pages, or waiting for a return e-mail. Third, companies are perceived as reactive, responding only when approached directly by the customer and asked a specific question.

What has stopped companies from being more flexible, customer-centric, and proactive until now? It was often cost-prohibitive for organizations to contact individual customers with time-critical information. In addition, the necessary technologies to automate the process simply did not exist. However, if companies are willing to take advantage of new messaging technologies, they can change their interactions with customers and alter customer perceptions. Several new technological enablers are making this possible.

- The rapid emergence of instant messaging services and their proliferation onto wireless PDAs and handhelds promotes even more efficient messaging communication, which will save both time and money for companies and customers.

- Natural language processing technologies can make systems more in tune with humans. For the first 40 years of the computer revolution, the industry focused on making humans understand computers. Now, with the emergence of natural language processing, computers are able to understand humans. For instance, a system based on natural language technologies can receive a question via an instant messaging service, understand that question, and respond to the customer in natural language without the involvement of a customer service representative.

- Advances in voice recognition and voice synthesis technologies, coupled with natural language processing, are making voice interfaces possible today. These technologies also can be utilized to create outbound alerts or voice messages to which customers can respond.

- E-commerce and the rapid evolution in database technologies make it possible for businesses to collect customer information, including preferred contact methods and billing methods, as well as purchasing patterns. This data then can be used to tailor individual customer relationships and communications.

Although these technologies are now available, most companies are not yet harnessing them. However, as the business potential of new messaging technologies comes to light, communications between companies and customers will be redefined rapidly and dramatically—and to the benefit of all participants.

EARLY ADOPTERS ALREADY RAISING THE BAR

Regardless of the industry, the multiple messaging techniques create value through timeliness, efficiency, and interactivity, thus enabling people to make better business decisions. Time-critical information can be exchanged, customers can make decisions, and then businesses can act accordingly—responding directly to individual customer needs.

Already the first examples of companies taking advantage of messaging technologies are emerging. Realtor.com, an online resource focused on helping individuals contact real estate agents and search for listings, provides a good example of how businesses can use messaging technologies to their customers' benefit. As we know, real estate agents are highly mobile throughout their working hours. Whether they are showing properties, driving around town, or stopping by the office, they are rarely in one place for more than a few minutes. When a potential customer is looking to relocate and wants to reach a real estate agent, it can be difficult, if not impossible, to track one down. Realtor.com provides such customers with a new resource. Customers can visit Realtor.com, get a listing of real estate agents in a particular region of the country, and then contact these agents via messaging technologies that send messages out to agents' cell phones. This resource makes conversations between realtors and customers simple and time-efficient.

In another example, FAO Schwarz, the famed toy store, has created a "buddy" on AOL Instant Messenger, a Yahoo! Messenger "friend," and an MSN Messenger "contact" (Shop FAO). These allow customers to send messages from their instant messengers of choice to customer service representatives, who will send answers in real-time to each customer's messenger address. While this solution does not take advantage of the most advanced technologies, it does provide yet another avenue of customer service that is personalized for individual customers.

In these two examples, businesses are working to improve their relationships with individual customers. However, these messaging technologies also can be used by businesses whose customers are other businesses. Today, freight companies such as Yellow Freight and ABF Freight are using messaging technologies to respond to customer care requests from their business customers.

THE NEXT GENERATION OF CUSTOMER CARE: UBIQUITOUS MESSAGING

While the preceding examples highlight current uses of messaging technologies, there are many examples of how messaging technologies can be exploited more fully to benefit both businesses and customers.

For instance, airline travelers want answers to time-sensitive questions, and airlines must be able to contact their customers to deliver time-critical announcements about flight delays or changes. An airline could have an "AirlineHelper" that customers could add to their buddy lists on instant messenger services. With AirlineHelper, customers would be able to get answers to many questions related to travel plans, including: "What gate is my flight departing from?" "Is my flight on time?" and "Have I been upgraded?" AirlineHelper could respond to these inbound messages from customers by using natural language processing and identifying technologies to answer questions. But AirlineHelper also could send outbound messages, notifying customers when flights are delayed or gates are changed, before customers even ask.

The shipping industry provides a useful illustration of the opportunities an industry can leverage by using messaging technologies in business-to-customer communications. FedEx and UPS combined ship 20 million packages a day, and the U.S. Postal Service handles approximately 660 million letters a day. Shipping companies that take advantage of new messaging technologies will tackle many problems, including tracking lost packages, contacting customers about undeliverable packages, and saving drivers time by ensuring that customers will be available to sign for packages. New solutions based on messaging technologies will enable these companies to contact individuals and confirm that they will be available to receive packages, thus reducing resources and time spent on individual deliveries and increasing efficiencies.

Business-to-business relationships also can benefit from the use of advanced messaging technologies. For example, with messaging technologies, chemical exchanges will be able to alert customer businesses when they have been outbid, when a chemical they are seeking goes up for auction, and when there are shipping delays or backorders. An additional example is in the high-tech industries, where messaging technologies can significantly improve the time to respond to customer service requests performed by third parties. Many business-to-business processes, such as service management, order management, account management, sales force management, and communications, can be streamlined by the application of messaging technology.

CAPABILITIES AND KNOWLEDGE CAPITAL LEAD THE CHANGE IN CUSTOMER CARE

We are on the verge of discovering the full value of messaging technologies. As companies expand into this communications arena, several key strategies will drive businesses to adopt new solutions and use messaging to their advantage and to the advantage of their customers.

One very plausible vision for the future of customer care and communication is encompassed in a cross-industry, customer-driven messaging solution that would allow customers to enter their personal profiles once, establish their preferred communications devices, and determine how they want to be contacted. Many different businesses in multiple industries including banking, travel, utilities services, and credit card companies could take advantage of such a solution. This approach promotes easy communication between businesses and customers, while protecting proprietary information (such as bank account numbers).

There are four key capabilities of this prospective customer messaging system that would help determine the success of messaging as a business communications tool:

- *Universal profile and permission marketing model.* In this model, customers are in charge, defining a communications profile for a broad audience and then setting specific criteria to determine who can use what pieces of information. This approach decreases the time customers must spend telling suppliers their preferred methods of communication while increasing efficiencies for businesses that need to send alerts.

- *Hierarchical guaranteed delivery alerting architecture.* This architecture allows customers to define exactly how they want to be contacted by the messaging solution. Each customer establishes a hierarchy of alerts. The solution then uses that hierarchy to attempt to send an alert to that customer, continuing down the hierarchy of alerts until the customer gets the message and responds.

- *Customer intent-response models.* Many companies within specific industries face the same customer questions and concerns on a daily basis. Those same companies also face the challenge of offering consistent yet differentiated responses to customers. Definable customer intent-response models can be customized for many companies within a specific industry, offering these companies an efficient and consistent model for answering customer questions.

- *Virtual agent architecture.* The customer messaging system would deliver virtual agents that are resident in the major messaging networks—including, for example, AOL Instant Messenger, Yahoo! Messenger, MSN Messenger, SMS, e-mail, and interactive pagers. These virtual agents would use the universal profiles, natural language processing, and the intent-response models to receive, interpret, and respond to customer requests and to send proactive and interactive customer alerts.

CAPABILITIES TAKE FLIGHT

These capabilities sound appealing, but will they improve customer care? The airline industry once again provides an illuminating example of how these capabilities can be utilized in a real-world scenario. As discussed earlier, travelers often seek time-sensitive information from airlines, and airlines often need to send alerts to customers quickly.

Exactly what happens when a customer has a question? A frequent business traveler is preparing for a trip later that evening but must check on the flight time. Rather than calling the airline and being put on hold, the traveler sends an instant message to AirlineHelper: "Is my flight on time?" The customer-messaging solution receives the request, and the natural language processor (NLP) interprets it as a request for flight status. Based on the traveler's instant-messaging screen name, the system is able to identify the traveler's next flight. The question is then routed to the appropriate business, in this case the airline. The request is processed by the airline's internal system, and a response is returned to the messaging system, where the answer is formatted into an appropriate message and sent back to the customer. Moments later, the traveler has an answer. Based on the answer, the traveler can then expedite plans to get to the airport or reschedule the flight.

Conversely, airlines often must contact customers with time-sensitive alerts about particular flights. For instance, weather conditions have prevented a flight from taking off, and the airline must contact the 130 passengers on that flight. Rather than hiring customer service representatives to call all of the passengers, the airline sends an alert to the customer messaging engine with the names of those individuals who must be alerted. Using the hierarchical delivery architecture, the system determines each customer's preferred contact method. The alert is formatted for each messaging method, and the system attempts to deliver the alert until an acknowledgment is received from each customer or until all methods of delivery have been attempted. Once a customer is contacted, a dialogue can be started that presents the traveler with several options, including the choice to remain on the same flight, reschedule, or cancel. Thus, the airline receives customer responses that provide critical data for improving customer operations.

Specifically, think about the business traveler. Suppose the traveler prefers to receive notification on a home voice-mail system. However, because the traveler is not at home, he or she will not receive an alert there. The system moves to option B, the traveler's mobile phone. Again, no response. Finally, the system beeps the traveler's interactive pager and receives a response indicating that the customer has received the message. After receiving a confirmation of delivery, the system notifies the airline that the customer has received the alert. This type of comprehensive messaging system is the future of customer care and communication.

A COMMUNICATIONS COUP FOR BUSINESSES EVERYWHERE

As companies implement these new technology solutions, they will find that messaging fundamentally changes their interactions with customers. Companies will become more flexible and responsive, because their customers will be able to decide how and when to interact and will be able to interact using their natural language. Companies will also become more proactive, because they will be able to anticipate customer needs and act accordingly, contacting customers with pertinent information. Finally, by doing business under each individual customer's terms, companies will become more customer-centric.

When the Pony Express first started delivering transcontinental mail, the service was a novelty. It was expensive and customers wondered how the service could really guarantee delivery, especially at such a fast pace. However, as more people took advantage of the service, they began to realize that the Pony Express could live up to its guarantee and offer the best solution available—fast, reliable delivery of important messages. Today, messaging channels are perceived as novel, but when businesses begin to harness these technological advances, customers and companies will see the results. The messaging explosion provides businesses with a great opportunity to redefine the way they interact with their customers, increase business efficiencies, and reduce costs. Ultimately, those businesses that take advantage of new messaging technologies will increase customer satisfaction and loyalty, because they will be prepared to anticipate and proactively meet customer needs anytime, anywhere.

C H A P T E R

Customer-Centric Service Management: Maximizing Life-Cycle Revenue for OEMs

Dean J. Teglia and Luis Vassal'lo

*I*t is 7 P.M. in a quiet office just outside Chicago. An alert is triggered. The oil temperature on unit number 145 is fluctuating dramatically. Indicators show that usage levels have not varied and weather conditions have remained consistent in the small South African mining community. The diagnostics reveal that the fluctuations in oil temperature are indicative of a pending compressor failure. The service administrator initiates the work order. The appropriate technician is available the next day, and the parts recommended by the diagnostic system are available at a South African distributor. The technician is dispatched with all available information and accepts the work order. Once out at the mine, the technician views the illustrated parts catalog on a PDA. The technician selects the impacted part and is hotlinked to the appropriate service bulletin and technical manuals. Unfortunately, another part is required. The technician quickly checks available inventory at the local distributor and arranges immediate delivery. After receiving the part and completing the work order, the technician records a history of the work performed, records updates to the as-maintained configuration, and completes the appropriate warranty information. In addition, the technician performs the quarterly preventive maintenance scheduled by the administrator to coincide with the corrective maintenance.*

Some will dismiss this scenario as an overblown vision grounded in unproven value propositions and immature technologies. However, we believe that such an approach—called *customer-centric service management*—is a direction of choice for original equipment manufacturers (OEMs) in the industrial equipment industry. Furthermore, we are convinced that, for many, it will introduce compelling business cases—combined increased revenues of up to $60 million for a $1-billion OEM and its dealers.

NEW REVENUE STREAM

The industrial equipment industry is a mature industry with low profit margins and even lower revenue growth that consistently underperforms other industries as well as the U.S. gross domestic product. Shareholders are demanding better returns. Aging channel partners with limited capital to invest in new capabilities are insisting on more innovative, cost-effective ways of working together. Customers are clamoring for better service, lower costs, and new ways of doing business.

OEMs have tried to boost their performance through investments in operational excellence, product and process redesign, technology, and workforce training. But these efforts have not generated the required incremental value.

Faced with questionable results, CEOs of industrial equipment companies are searching for new ways to differentiate their products, drive revenue growth, grow customer loyalty, and build competitive advantage. Growth in this environment requires new and innovative approaches to doing business.

One approach is to transform from a company that sells products to a company that sells a wide range of services and products, bundled and tailored to each customer's needs. This approach can lead to significant shareholder value creation and enhanced customer satisfaction and loyalty.

Depending on the industry sector, customers can invest hundreds of thousands to millions of dollars in the purchase of a single piece of industrial equipment. However, this initial cost is just a fraction (10 to 25 percent) of what the customer eventually will spend on the piece of equipment. The remaining 75 to 90 percent of costs associated with product life-cycle ownership are spent on services such as maintenance, insurance, financing, fuel, parts, and tires. This is where the opportunity lies—in offering bundled services that capture a greater share of life-cycle revenue.

OEMs that pursue the service management opportunity tend to increase their profit-to-earnings ratios (Exhibit 21-1) as well as augment their revenue streams with $1.50 to $3.00 of service management revenue for every $1.00 they receive in new product sales. These additional service management revenues net a 30 to 50 percent margin on parts and more than 50 percent margin on service, compared with a margin of less than 10 percent on industrial equipment new product sales.

Distributors and customers likewise benefit from the increased focus on service management. Distributors receive increased service and parts revenue and decreased administrative and technician costs. Customers benefit through reduced downtime, repair costs, and fleet management expenditures.

EXHIBIT 21-1.   Potential annual impact on a $1-billion industrial equipment organization. Estimated combined dealer and OEM benefit is about $60 million.

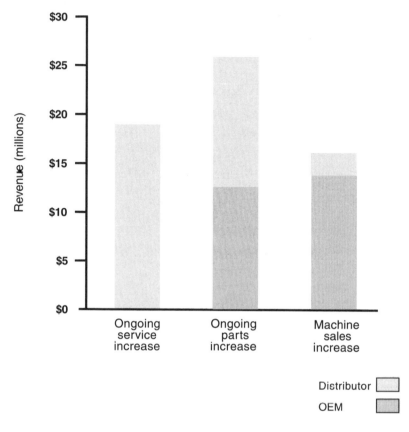

CUSTOMER-CENTRIC SERVICE MANAGEMENT DEFINED

Customer-centric service management (CCSM) encompasses the capabilities that will enable industrial equipment OEMs to move beyond their core manufacturing capabilities and tap into valuable product life-cycle revenues.

The three main components of CCSM are customer insight, technician enablement, and predictive maintenance (Exhibit 21-2). Each of these three components includes a series of critical capabilities.

Customer Insight

Customer insight includes customer knowledge management, service forecasting, service proposal development, contract maintenance and monitoring, and competitive intelligence. OEMs and distributors rely on deep customer knowledge and dependable service forecasting capabilities to generate their service management

EXHIBIT 21-2.   Three components of customer-centric service management.

proposals and agreements during and after the initial product sale. The challenge is to maintain the customer relationship during the entire product life cycle.

The revenue opportunities associated with maintaining a long-term relationship continue to increase as the product ages. According to an analysis by Accenture, the costs of maintaining heavy construction equipment will increase progressively during the first five years of a product's life cycle. The fifth year of maintenance is approximately equivalent to the first four years combined.

Competitors are aware of the ever-increasing value of a long-term maintenance agreement and actively compete for postwarranty service. Given the competitive environment, it is critical that OEMs be able to initiate, capture, and maintain customer relationships.

Technician Enablement

OEMs and their distributor networks need the capabilities to deliver the promised service levels while still generating an acceptable margin. Many of these capabilities are related to enabling the technician; they include content management, configuration management, asset management, inventory management, scheduling and dispatching, and mobile access.

Customers view the ability of the technician to fix it right the first time (FIRFT) as one of the most critical measures of success. The ability to fix it right the first time is often determined well before the technician is even aware of the work order. The service administrator reviews the problem, identifies required skill sets, schedules from a pool of geographically dispersed service technicians, confirms availability of the appropriate parts at the right location, and coordinates access to the required facilities and tools within a remote environment. The service administrator ensures that the technician arrives on time with "the smarts and the parts." When this does not happen, the number of trips per work order, travel time, and expedited parts orders increase dramatically and customer satisfaction decreases.

Once assigned work orders, technicians are supported by a content management capability that provides access to large volumes of integrated technical information, including illustrated parts catalogs, service bulletins, service procedures, and configuration information. One engine manufacturer reports that it creates 1000 engine types alone, with tens of thousands of pages of documentation.

Configuration information poses significant challenges to effective content management. During a product's 10- to 20-year lifespan, the as-built and as-maintained configuration can and often does vary dramatically. These variations are largely not captured. OEMs must provide a configuration management capability to monitor a product's bill of material and update it as variations occur.

Much of the information required by a technician can be accessed via remote handheld devices using real-time wireless capabilities or through CDs. In developing their mobile access capabilities, OEMs will determine which information should be accessible in real time.

Inventory management is one capability that is commonly considered for support by a real-time mobile capability. Occasionally, a technician will not have all the required parts to complete a work order. Using the handheld unit, the technician will select and order parts from the nearest distributor. Technicians turn to the source that provides the easiest and most effective way to order parts. The path of least resistance should not lead a technician to your competitors.

Predictive Maintenance

One way to enhance customer satisfaction with service management is to address a problem before it even occurs. "The writing was on the wall." "We should have seen it coming." "History repeats itself." All are catchy clichés that point to the fact that most failures are preceded by a warning. Most service organizations do not have the required sophistication to detect what can be minor fluctuations in performance that predict a pending failure. The capabilities they require include equipment monitoring, diagnostics, and maintenance planning.

Equipment monitoring and diagnostic capabilities involve the remote capture of diagnostic data from sensors on "smart products"—that is, equipment with monitoring devices. The data is forwarded to engineers and service administrators, who will monitor the equipment for unusual trending or deviations from the lower or upper control limits. The data is processed and converted into useful service management information, which then is used to anticipate a pending failure and trigger the appropriate maintenance. The ability to perform this type of predictive maintenance cuts costs significantly.

Increasingly, companies are finding that they can realize their service visions more quickly and cost-effectively by leveraging a set of tools and technologies col-

INDUSTRIAL TELEMATICS: AN ESSENTIAL ENABLER

Telematics refers to wirelessly enabled, two-way communication between a vehicle or piece of equipment and its external environment. By linking assets, customers, and operations, telematics enable OEMs and dealers to transform their businesses in innovative ways. Manufacturers and other entities can use and service assets more efficiently, capture a larger share of life-cycle revenues, create recurring revenue streams, and counter undervaluation by stock markets of cyclical products companies' share prices. End customers can benefit from value-added services and interactions, new business opportunities, reduced costs, and superior products.

This level of capability requires not only the know-how to optimize the maintenance of an individual product but a deep understanding of how products interact in a production environment such as an industrial plant, mine site, or construction site. Telematics can enable this capability by providing real-time information on position, loads, throughput, and other operational variables.

The supporting technologies exist today. Telematics uptake is accelerating in industrial products. According to a recent Yankee report on wireless mobile telemetry, revenue growth in the United States will triple to $3.4 billion by 2006.[1] This telematics revenue estimate reflects expenditures within the industrial equipment industry on hardware (e.g., transceiver equipment with Global Positioning System and wireless communications capabilities) as well as subscription fees (e.g., monthly service charges for communication and related services).

lectively known as *telematics* (see sidebar). Industrial telematics enable real-time data capture and communication with pieces of industrial equipment. This in turn provides equipment owners, operators, manufacturers, and dealers with the high-quality information essential to any CCSM capability.

The predictive maintenance program will not replace the need for preventive maintenance. However, the data used to build the predictive maintenance program can be used to develop a more effective preventive maintenance program. Typically, half of preventive maintenance activities are not required.

TECHNOLOGY REQUIREMENTS

CCSM capabilities are supported by a robust technical architecture comprising a data warehouse, required service applications, enterprise application integration, and a mobile commerce platform.

Data Warehouse

The data warehouse is one of the most critical components of a CCSM solution. It provides a structured data environment that supports both strategic decision making as well as daily operations associated with CCSM. The data warehouse typically includes customer data; work content, such as technical service bulletins, service procedures, and part catalogs; predictive models and engineering life-cycle data; preventive maintenance schedules; equipment configuration history; and equipment maintenance history.

Service Applications

Processing the data and turning it into actionable knowledge is performed by various service applications. The service applications perform the diagnostics, facilitate planning, enable scheduling and coordination, and provide the required content to the remote technician. These applications typically link to the company's enterprise resource planning (ERP) systems, advanced planning systems (APSs), legacy and custom applications, and best-of-breed packaged applications.

Enterprise Application Integration

Integrating these systems requires an industrial-strength interface architecture. A poorly planned environment will be plagued by unmanageable integration code and limited mechanisms to manage end-to-end integration. Access to real-time information will be constrained depending on batch load processes.

Enterprise application interface (EAI) software is an emerging class of software that makes efficient integration a reality. EAI provides a host of services that combine aspects of low-level messaging middleware, data transformation and formatting, intelligent routing, workflow and business process automation, custom and prebuilt application interfaces, and flexible development tools.

The use of EAI applications reduces interface development time, provides seamless integration between software components, and enables interfaces supported by the software vendors. EAI will allow for solutions that are independent of hardware or database platforms and contain standardized interfaces.

Mobile Commerce Platform

In addition to a well-defined integration architecture, a mobile platform is required for CCSM to be effective. The mobile platform provides technicians with access to critical enterprise information and the ability to update the information when and where they need it. Mobile commerce is conducted using a myriad of mobile devices such as cell phones, PDAs, and digital notepads.

OEMs must overcome significant challenges and limitations before fully enabling their mobile technicians. As discussed earlier, remote field service is considered a complex solution. Challenges include slower than desired bandwidth, intermittent availability, multiple technical standards, data entry difficulty, and limited screen size.

A number of existing and emerging technologies are helping to overcome these challenges and continue to fuel mobile commerce adoption. Next-generation digital cellular networks, mobile-specific architectures, advances in mobile devices, and other new and emerging technologies are playing a critical role in streamlining technicians' remote access to critical data.

CONCLUSION

The shift from a purely product-centric organization to a customer-centric services organization is a challenging transition for OEMs. As depicted in Exhibit 21-3, con-

EXHIBIT 21-3.   A new paradigm for service management.

	Conventional wisdom	New paradigm
Service and support	• Reactive • A necessary evil	• Proactive and intelligent • Drive shareholder value creation from postsales service
Postsales service	• Delay customer defections • Fix it right	• Create customer disciples • Fix it right the first time
Business model	• One-size-fits-all approach to presale and postsale	• Different business models require different solutions
Approach to CRM	• Activities are operating expenses	• CRM capabilities will drive bottom-line benefits

ventional wisdom must be transformed to a new paradigm in which service is viewed as driving shareholder value, as opposed to being merely a necessary evil.

OEMs are uniquely positioned to make the transition to delivering CCSM. OEMs know more about their products, have more content information, and understand the service requirements better than any other organizations. In addition, they and their distributors own the initial customer contact and the initial product purchase.

However, OEMs must carefully explore the CCSM opportunity before deciding to embrace it. It may not be appropriate for every organization. Important considerations include the comparison of new product margins versus service margins, the size of the installed product base, the extent of influence that an OEM can exert over its distribution channel, and the degree of customer concentration. As the benefit potential increases so does the development complexity. OEMs should evaluate the potential benefits and identify the gaps with their existing capabilities. When the gaps are identified, OEMs will need to prioritize their development efforts, as few will have the resources to implement all the required capabilities at once.

Although there may be significant efforts related to building the required capabilities for most OEMs, the road to CCSM can lead to substantial financial opportunities. The question for OEMs is no longer whether but how to increase penetration into their customer's life-cycle revenues.

Transforming Marketing

Introduction: Bringing Rigor and Discipline to Creative Pursuits

Brian A. Johnson and Steven S. Ramsey

There has never been a time when the need for better, more efficient marketing was more intense. Customers are more sophisticated. Their loyalty to particular brands and companies no longer can be taken for granted. Fierce competition continues to drive companies to earmark more resources to their marketing efforts. The financial community and key stakeholders are stepping up the pressure on companies to demonstrate greater financial accountability and return on their marketing investments. And companies must exercise increasing flexibility to be able to capitalize on rapidly emerging opportunities, regardless of their markets.

Unfortunately, there has also never been a time when marketing has been less prepared to respond to the challenges companies face. As a recent Accenture survey demonstrates, marketers today are dealing with a host of problems that limit their ability to make significant, positive contributions to the company's bottom line. This survey found that a large majority of marketing executives in the United States and United Kingdom:

- Have trouble capturing the attention of customers with their campaigns
- Are struggling to more effectively integrate customer touch points
- Cannot measure the return on their marketing investment
- Need better access to more current and accurate customer data
- Take too long to develop and execute marketing campaigns
- Need greater collaboration, both within the marketing function and with the sales and customer service departments

The fact is that most companies suffer from some serious limitations that are putting them at a serious competitive disadvantage. For the most part, companies are saddled with obsolete marketing tools, many of which have been in use for the better part of a century and no longer are appropriate to the current business environment. They are also hampered by fragmented marketing processes that limit marketers' ability to effectively collaborate with each other or with other customer-facing functions. They have little in the way of metrics that objectively gauge the performance of various marketing campaigns and activities, and tend to hold fast to the gut-feel approach to messages and media. The image of marketing as a creative pursuit that is not subject to rigor and discipline has made it difficult for companies to identify inefficiencies in campaign creation and execution. And increasing turnover among both CEOs and senior marketing executives has resulted in eroding consistency of marketing messages and a lack of a broad corporate perspective on what the company should stand for in the minds of its targets.

As global companies continue to expand their brands and marketing requirements, these shortcomings inevitably become magnified. The instances of miscommunication, poor execution, and misspent marketing funds can increase many times. In very large companies, most marketers have no easy way to share marketing information with each other and often end up reinventing the wheel many times over. The result is more and more money spent on marketing activities that are increasingly less effective.

TURNING IT AROUND

Marketing professionals are well aware that they must improve both the efficiency and effectiveness of their programs, not to mention of their function as a whole. Efficiencies, of course, can save companies money—money that then can be added straight to the bottom line or, alternatively, plowed into activities to stimulate growth in other areas (for example, taking money saved from streamlining the process of identifying targets for a direct-mail campaign and directing it to further support the launch of a hot new product). Sharing knowledge and best practices reduces marketing costs by preventing the reinvention-of-the-wheel syndrome and minimizing the cost of learning. Tasks are performed more proficiently, thus increasing speed to market and throughput capacity. The marketing organization produces more programs with higher success rates. When organizations are more effective and efficient in program development and management, nonperforming marketing spending also declines.

Improvements in marketing effectiveness make programs more successful, thus increasing revenue and profits. For instance, a redesign and automation of critical marketing processes can help increase capacity, thereby allowing companies to conduct not just more campaigns but better targeted ones. Targeting improves campaign success rates, increasing customer acquisition and retention levels. Furthermore, the use of knowledge management and best practices facilitates more effective decision making, driving greater revenue and profitability. Organizations are able to redirect spending and reallocate assets to achieve the greatest profit.

To achieve heightened levels of efficiency and effectiveness, marketers must address the shortcomings in their processes, technologies, and organization structures. A number of leading companies already are showing the way. These organizations are adopting techniques and technologies that enable them to effectively integrate marketing processes across the function; precisely determine which marketing activities are losing money, which are generating money, and how much investment each merits; create and execute just-in-time marketing campaigns that more accurately and quickly hit intended targets; and link their offline and online activities to more effectively meet the situational needs of their ever-fluid customer bases.

MARKETING RESOURCE MANAGEMENT: TYING IT ALL TOGETHER

Just as manufacturing resource planning (MRP) and enterprise resource planning (ERP) brought more holistic and integrated approaches to manufacturing and enterprise data management, respectively, a new movement promises to bring the same types of benefits to marketing. *Marketing resource management* (MRM) is a concept whose goal is to integrate all aspects of marketing across the diverse spectrum of activities—from planning, developing, and executing campaigns to streamlining core marketing processes and facilitating more effective communications among marketing team members. MRM is designed to instill order and accountability in a function that historically has lacked discipline.

Through the use of MRM concepts and technologies, companies can get a better handle on marketing expenses and help ensure that everyone involved in the marketing effort (whether a company employee, contractor, freelancer, or agency) has access to the data and knowledge he or she needs, whenever or wherever it is needed. Furthermore, by supporting the rigorous measurement of marketing performance that historically has been difficult, if not impossible, to accomplish, MRM makes it easier for marketing heads to assume responsibility for the financial management of the entire marketing portfolio.

MRM encompasses three essential components:

- The *marketing workbench,* which provides an integrated platform for marketing execution by pulling together the critical processes, technology tools, and data that marketers need to be more efficient and effective. These include the various point solutions that marketers can use to plan, develop, and execute campaigns; the technology applications that support such internal activities as knowledge management, project management, workflow, and the storage and reuse of video, audio, graphics, and documents that the marketing team uses on a regular basis; and the technologies that integrate the marketing function with other key areas of the company, such as finance, customer service, and sales.
- *Redesigned core marketing processes* that leverage the appropriate technology tools. With new marketing technologies now available, there is no reason for companies to continue inefficient practices. Using MRM, companies can

address the inherent inefficiencies of critical processes such as customer strategy development, branding, portfolio management, customer insight development, and program evaluation and measurement.

- *Realigned marketing organization* to support the new way of working, including the sharing of knowledge across the entire marketing effort. Any changes in processes depend on complementary changes in the marketing organization to be successful. Seven areas, in particular, are addressed by MRM: organizational alignment, decision-making governance, leadership development, compensation, training and development, and career path development.

By implementing a marketing workbench to provide for the support and integration of the marketing function (and making the concomitant changes in processes and organization elements) companies can bring the marketing function into the twenty-first century and give the function the kinds of tools and support that other corporate functions have had for decades.

SHOW ME THE ROI

Various estimates put the amount of money spent by the Global 1000 on marketing at roughly $100 billion annually, and growing. Unfortunately, most companies have been seeing a declining return on this investment, in the form of increasingly lower response and acceptance rates to campaigns, higher customer churn rates, and eroding brand loyalty. Not surprisingly, this is having a significant impact on the bottom line—and not a positive one at that.

Clearly, something must be done to improve companies' return on their marketing investment. The solution, in theory, is simple: Measure the costs and returns of specific activities, and ensure that time and money are being expended only to support the markets, products, and customers that offer the greatest potential for growth. In practice, however, it is a different story altogether.

Because of the fragmented nature of marketing processes, the traditional resistance of many marketers to initiatives that they believe compromise their creative license, and the historic lack of appropriate technology tools, few, if any, companies are able to determine with any degree of certainty which marketing programs are boons and which are busts. However, newer marketing techniques, including econometrics, ROI measurement, and allocation software, make such analyses possible, and the continued slide in marketing effectiveness is making marketers more willing to embrace new methods. As a result, a number of leading companies are taking a new approach that overcomes marketing's historic limitations and enables them to truly measure and subsequently improve the return on their marketing investment.

There are six steps in this approach. The first involves gathering a wider range of critical data and analyzing that data in greater detail to understand which elements of the marketing mix have proved successful and which have fallen short. Next, using the same techniques, the company creates detailed and insightful assessments of its key competitors' strengths, weaknesses, and marketing portfolios to understand how each is performing and how the company stacks up to that performance. Third, the company identifies underperforming initiatives before they become too costly—for instance, pinpointing which elements of the marketing mix are not pulling their weight or which products fail to perform better regardless of the amount of marketing support they receive. Fourth, the company establishes accountability for each marketing element by setting reasonable, reachable, and appropriate goals for each marketing activity, specifying clearly what those goals are, and rewarding each element appropriately if it achieves the desired outcome. To ensure that marketing budgets are thrown behind the right products and markets (i.e., those that have the potential for significant growth), the company complements its traditional rearview measures, such as past sales and revenues, with new data and measures that can help it more effectively forecast changes in markets, market share, and profit margins. Finally, with these better markets and products identified, the company reallocates its marketing resources to capture those new opportunities and wean itself from spending on terminal or flat markets that no amount of marketing support will revive.

With this approach, companies will be able to improve their marketing ROI very quickly—not only because they will have objective measures of performance, but also because they will have identified areas with the potential to reward marketing expenditures with increased sales and revenue.

GETTING THE MESSAGE JUST IN TIME

Change certainly is a constant these days, particularly as it relates to customers. To be able to keep pace with rapidly changing customers, companies must become more flexible and proactive in their marketing. Some leading marketers, consciously or not, have done just that, taking a page from the just-in-time (JIT) manufacturing model pioneered in postwar Japan and later adopted by companies around the world. These companies, leveraging the tools and concepts of MRM and emphasizing ROI, are able to market themselves in ways that are streamlined, collaborative, and insight-driven—and that benefit from the lessons learned by manufacturers' attempts to streamline their sourcing and production activities over the past several decades.

For instance, just as manufacturers learned that value comes from managing flow (that is, the manner in which all manufacturing processes are performed on the shop floor and not just the manufacturing process itself), marketing leaders know that simply automating various marketing, sales, and customer service activities via a large-scale CRM solution will not alone generate significant benefits. Just as the JIT revolution changed the emphasis from managing the direct labor content of a part and the variances in component costs to managing throughput and end quality, these companies are thinking carefully and comprehensively about the expected outcome and ROI of each campaign. And, just as manufacturers moved from "push" to "pull" scheduling so that they wasted no effort or money making parts unless and until someone wanted them, JIT marketers are eschewing mass or "push" marketing to insight-based conversational marketing that is more efficient and results in marketing programs and offers that more people accept.

In short, for every campaign they launch, companies exhibiting JIT marketing define the desired outcomes and marketing measures; define the process; clarify roles and organizational responsibilities for "owning the customer" and executing an integrated, end-to-end marketing process; integrate data and tools to support the process and organization; and implement technology tools to speed execution and improve information delivery to the point of need.

INTEGRATING ONLINE AND OFFLINE ACTIVITIES

Insight is an inherent element of the JIT marketing mind-set. It is also a core element of a company's ability to satisfy the needs of customers as they change, not only across time and various situations, but also across channels—specifically, physical and virtual channels. Without a full understanding of the ways in which customers buy, online and off, marketers cannot make the right decisions about which e-marketing tools to adopt and how best to use them to support their customers, wherever they might be.

To gain such an understanding, companies must avoid relying too heavily on categorizing customers by groups or segments (essentially putting them in buckets of like characteristics) to drive their marketing programs. Today, marketers must expand their thinking about segment definition if they are to respond to the *dynamic* customer segments that technology is enabling them to serve. Dynamic customer segments are composed not of a permanent subset of the customer base, but of buyers that exist in a particular set of circumstances at a particular moment in time. These part-time segment members require service and support based on their circumstances and buying behavior, not on some permanent label of who they are.

To provide this support, companies need a more holistic approach to marketing than the "one segment, one channel" model of old. They must incorporate online and offline marketing tactics across the buying-decision cycle for each pattern of customer behavior. By understanding online consumer behaviors as they pertain specifically to their products or service (e.g., how does the way consumers shop for a sweater online differ from their approach at a store in the mall, if they differ at all?), companies can design their Web sites in such a way that will maximize the potential for meeting visitors' needs, as well as determine the ways online and offline marketing efforts should be integrated.

The importance of this approach is that it recognizes that it is the *consumer* who determines the best design for an integrated marketing strategy, not the traditional value-based or demographic-based segment definition of the customer. Companies that do this, and target different behaviors through behavior-based integrated online and offline capabilities, will be able to keep pace with their customers and will realize substantial competitive advantage in the process.

CONCLUSION

In many ways, the marketing organization represents the last frontier for the type of technology-enabled change that most of the rest of the typical corporation has undergone in the past two decades. And it is high time for it to undergo such change. Without new technologies and processes, marketing will continue to see its ability to influence customers and stimulate demand marginalized—just at a time when companies need marketing most to prosper and thrive. The chapters in this section present a comprehensive picture of the challenges marketing faces today and explore how marketers can and should embrace these new capabilities to transform their organizations and help their companies realize the promise of CRM.

Market Madness: The State of Marketing Campaign Management

J. Patrick O'Halloran, Theodore Ansusinha,
Shep Parke, and Mark C. Giometti

I n recent years, many companies have embraced CRM tools and techniques for their sales and customer service functions. Although it is early in the process, these companies are beginning to see some payoff from their efforts. Many are reducing their costs to serve customers. Others are improving their responsiveness to customers' requests for help. Still others are enhancing the ability of their sales forces to manage their prospect pipelines, respond to sales opportunities more quickly and effectively, and convert more of the "right" kinds of deals. A select few companies are doing all of these.

Unfortunately, in their quest to improve sales and service, many companies have ignored a critical link in the customer management chain: *marketing*. In fact, the exclusion of marketing from CRM efforts has, in many cases, severely limited companies' ability to generate greater benefits from their CRM applications. As CRM has taken root in sales and service, it has become more obvious that new marketing processes and technologies must be adopted, and integrated with existing CRM efforts, if CRM is to fulfill its potential.

To get a better understanding of the challenges that today's marketing executives face, the effectiveness of companies' marketing efforts, and organizations' experiences with emerging marketing automation tools, Accenture conducted a survey of marketing professionals in the United States and the United Kingdom in 2001 (see sidebar for methodology and respondent demographics). The goal of the survey was to gain greater insight into five key issues:

- Challenges in creating and executing effective campaigns
- Marketing campaign effectiveness
- Measuring campaign performance
- Campaign cycle time
- Ways to improve campaign effectiveness

The findings of the survey were certainly illuminating. For instance, a large majority of marketing executives in the United States and the United Kingdom reported having trouble capturing the attention of customers, given the noise and clutter in the marketplace, and are struggling to develop a single view of the customer. Furthermore, measuring the return on their marketing investments, implementing marketing technologies in a timely manner, and increasing marketing and advertising ROI are among the challenges most frequently encountered by marketing executives in both countries.

RESEARCH METHODOLOGY AND RESPONDENT DEMOGRAPHICS

We interviewed by telephone 175 marketing and customer relationship managers in the United States and United Kingdom in the spring of 2001.

The largest group of respondents (40 percent) comprises senior marketing executives, and about one-third of participants are specialists (i.e., managers of a specific marketing function such as direct marketing or marketing analysis). Finally, about one in four is responsible for managing customer relationships or another function (Exhibit 23-1).

Respondent companies, selected in part for their size, tend to be large. More than half (58 percent) have 5000 or more employees, while just 12 percent have fewer than 1000 employees. In our sample, the mean number of employees is about 5200. For the most part,

EXHIBIT 23-1.   Respondents by job title.

Title	Respondents, %
Chief marketing officer	8%
EVP, SVP, or VP of Marketing	10
Marketing director	22
Direct marketing manager/head	30
Marketing analysis head	4
Customer knowledge/value director or manager	7
Head/director of customer management	5
Head/director of CRM strategy	2
CRM program director	2
Others	10

the senior marketing executives we interviewed are from slightly smaller companies than are the marketing specialists and customer relationship managers (Exhibit 23-2).

Participants represent a diverse mix of industries, which we broadly categorized in six groups: automotive (19 percent), consumer products (19 percent), financial services (17 percent), power and utilities (14 percent), services (13 percent), and high-tech and other companies (18 percent). Respondents also are split geographically, with 57 percent from the United States and 43 percent from the United Kingdom (Exhibit 23-3).

EXHIBIT 23-2.   Respondents by company employment.

Employment	Respondents, %
Less than 1000	12%
1000 to 3499	18
3500 to 4999	10
5000 to 7499	15
7500 or more	43

EXHIBIT 23-3.   Respondents by industry group.

Industry	Respondents, %
Financial services	17%
Automotive retail/manufacturing	19
Power and utilities	14
Services	13
Consumer products (retail/manufacturing/distribution)	19
High-tech and other	18

The survey also noted that a majority of marketing executives cited access to more accurate and fresher data, better integration between customer touch points, a better overall customer strategy, and more collaboration (both within the function and with the sales and customer service departments) as their most pressing needs.

The following sections explore these and other survey findings in more detail.

CHALLENGES TO MARKETING CAMPAIGN CREATION AND EXECUTION

Marketing executives face a number of significant challenges in their efforts to uncover, attract, and motivate prospects to buy their companies' products or services.

In speaking with our survey participants, we were able to get a better understanding of what those challenges are, how frequently they are encountered, and the severity of impact on respondents' businesses.

Frequency of Challenges

The challenges that marketers most frequently encounter when creating and executing marketing campaigns run the gamut from problems with data access and technology tools to connecting with prospective customers and identifying campaign ROI (Exhibit 23-4). A large majority of respondents (70 percent) said that capturing customer attention amidst the noise and clutter in the market today is a challenge they encounter regularly—not surprising, given the barrage of marketing messages received daily by consumers. A large percentage of executives also noted that they are often challenged by an inability to measure the ROI of campaigns, and by the time it takes to implement the technology tools and infrastructure that marketing requires to do its job (68 percent each). Two-thirds cited frequent or occasional problems with trying to increase the return on advertising and marketing expenditures, while 65 percent identified being challenged to develop a single view of customers derived from all interactions with the company.

EXHIBIT 23-4.   Most frequent marketing campaign challenges, ranked by percentage of total respondents who experience the challenge frequently or occasionally.

Challenge	Total	U.S.	U.K.
Capturing customer attention	70%	67%	75%
Measuring campaign ROI	68	65	72
Implementing technology in a timely manner	68	65	72
Increasing marketing/advertising ROI	67	63	73
Establishing a single view of the customer	65	58	75
Gaining real-time access to data	58	59	57
Leveraging statistical tools for effective segmentation	58	51	68
Lacking information on customer profitability	57	53	63
Integrating campaigns across customer touch points	57	51	65
Long campaign cycle times (creation through execution)	57	63	49
Declining customer responsiveness to marketing campaigns	57	54	60
Lacking tool to monitor the marketing process	56	50	64
Transforming large amounts of data into actionable insight	53	42	68
Diminishing campaign effectiveness	53	54	51
Applying learnings from a campaign to subsequent projects	50	48	52
Achieving anticipated ROI from marketing automation software	50	51	49
Inaccurate or outdated customer data	43	40	48

Although respondents generally agreed on the challenges that they typically encounter, there are some differences between executives in the United States and in the United Kingdom. Just 58 percent of U.S. executives said they frequently encounter problems related to a lack of a single view of the customer, but a full three-quarters of U.K. professionals cited this as a recurring problem. Similarly, 68 percent of U.K. executives said they often have problems transforming overwhelming amounts of data into actionable customer insight, compared with just 42 percent of U.S. respondents. In one instance, the reverse is true: 63 percent of U.S. respondents, compared with just 49 percent of U.K. executives, said they frequently have trouble getting campaigns from idea to execution in a timely manner.

Overall, it appears that there is more consensus among U.K. executives than their American counterparts in the types of challenges they regularly encounter.

Impact of Challenges

The frequency with which a challenge is encountered is only part of the story. The other part involves how problematic that challenge is for the business. To probe this issue, we asked participants to tell us how much of an impact each of the challenges identified earlier had on their organizations. The results are illuminating (Exhibit 23-5).

In general, the challenges that respondents most frequently encounter also cause the most trouble for respondents' organizations—with one glaring exception. Although 70 percent of respondents cited regularly encountering difficulty in cutting through marketplace clutter to capture customers' attention, just 40 percent said that that challenge has a major impact on their organizations. In essence, respondents seem to be saying that marketplace clutter is a frequent annoyance, but one that doesn't significantly impede their ability to do their jobs effectively.

Other challenges, however, *are* having a big impact on marketers' efforts, according to survey participants. Fifty-five percent cited not having a single view of the customer as one such challenge, while nearly the same percentage noted their inability to measure the ROI of their campaigns. Other challenges that hamstring marketing's efforts are the lack of management tools to monitor the entire marketing process, lack of customer profitability information to help target campaigns appropriately, difficulty of increasing the ROI of advertising and other marketing expenditures, and the amount of time it takes to implement necessary marketing technology tools and infrastructure.

As was the case with the frequency of challenges encountered, there is some disagreement between U.S. and U.K. respondents on the level of impact of these challenges (particularly in regard to the lack of real-time access to data on which campaigns are based). However, the amount of discrepancy between the two groups on the issue of impact is much less pronounced.

Severity of Challenges

To most accurately determine which challenges have the greatest influence over respondents' companies, it is necessary to consider both a challenge's impact on the

EXHIBIT 23-5. Most problematic marketing campaign challenges, ranked by percentage of total respondents who note the challenge to be extremely to very problematic to their businesses.

Challenge	Total	U.S.	U.K.
Establishing a single view of the customer	55%	52%	59%
Measuring campaign ROI	54	51	57
Lacking tool to monitor the marketing process	48	46	50
Lacking information on customer profitability	47	45	49
Implementing technology in a timely manner	46	39	56
Increasing marketing/advertising ROI	46	48	44
Gaining real-time access to data	44	51	35
Integrating campaigns across customer touch points	44	47	41
Long campaign cycle times (creation through execution)	43	41	46
Transforming large amounts of data into actionable insight	42	38	45
Inaccurate or outdated customer data	41	35	47
Capturing customer attention	40	43	36
Applying learnings from a campaign to subsequent projects	39	35	44
Declining customer responsiveness to marketing campaigns	38	39	38
Leveraging statistical tools for effective segmentation	37	33	41
Diminishing campaign effectiveness	36	43	26
Achieving anticipated ROI from marketing automation software	28	22	38

business and the frequency with which the challenge is experienced—a measure we call the *severity index.* To arrive at a severity measure for each challenge, we multiplied each challenge's frequency percentage by its impact percentage, then divided that figure by 10 to create a number suitable for a scale of 1 to 1000. The higher the number, the more severe the problem (Exhibit 23-6).

Using this method of problem measurement, two challenges to creating and executing marketing campaigns stood out over all others as the most severe: measuring the return on investment (scored at 366) and achieving a single, companywide view of the customer (360). Other key, though somewhat less severe, challenges include implementing the technology tools and infrastructure marketing needs on a timely basis (314); increasing the return on advertising and marketing spending (309); and capturing the attention of customers in a noisy, cluttered marketplace (280).

EXHIBIT 23-6. Severity of marketing campaign challenges, ranked by a problem severity score calculated as follows: $(a \times b)/10$, where a = percentage experiencing the problem frequently or occasionally, and b = percentage finding the problem extremely or very problematic.

Challenge	Total	U.S.	U.K.
Measuring campaign ROI	366	330	413
Establishing a single view of the customer	360	300	440
Implementing technology in a timely manner	314	250	400
Increasing marketing/advertising ROI	309	300	320
Capturing customer attention	280	290	267
Lacking tool to monitor the marketing process	269	230	320
Lacking information on customer profitability	268	240	307
Gaining real-time access to data	257	300	200
Integrating campaigns across customer touch points	251	240	266
Long campaign cycle times (creation through execution)	246	260	226
Transforming large amounts of data into actionable insight	222	160	307
Declining customer responsiveness to marketing campaigns	217	210	227
Leveraging statistical tools for effective segmentation	217	170	280
Applying learnings from a campaign to subsequent projects	194	170	227
Diminishing campaign effectiveness	189	230	133
Inaccurate or outdated customer data	177	140	227
Achieving anticipated ROI from marketing automation software	143	110	186

Once again, the severity of challenges differs for U.S. and U.K. executives. While inability to measure campaign ROI is the most severe challenge for the U.S. group (with a factor of 330), the lack of a single view of the customer tops the list for U.K. respondents (with a score of 440). Similarly, taking too long to implement marketing information technology tools and infrastructure received a severity factor of 400 from U.K. participants, but just 250 from their American counterparts. And although transforming overwhelming amounts of data into actionable customer insight scored 307 in severity for U.K. executives, it rang up a score of just 160 among U.S. professionals.

The top obstacles to effectively creating and executing marketing campaigns also vary greatly by industry group, as does the degree to which they challenge managers in those industries. The most severe challenge for financial services firms is length of time it takes to implement technology tools and infrastructure for marketing (533). For the automotive industry, it is the inability to integrate or coordinate campaigns with other customer touch points (383). Managers in the consumer products industry are most challenged by the need to develop a single view of their customers (455). Power and utilities companies also are most pressured by a lack of a single view of the customer, along with the inability to measure campaign ROI (417 each). For service industry executives, the most severe challenge is not having real-time access to data for designing, analyzing, and executing campaigns (392). And for firms in the high-tech and other industries group, the inability to measure the return on campaign investment (354) is the most severe challenge.

MARKETING CAMPAIGN EFFECTIVENESS

Although marketers have a difficult job, many believe they are succeeding in spite of the challenges they face. Half of the respondents described their marketing campaigns as "effective," 35 percent called their marketing campaigns "very effective," and 6 percent said their campaigns are "extremely effective." Just 8 percent rated their marketing programs as largely "ineffective" (Exhibit 23-7).

From a geographical perspective, there are some (albeit not dramatic) differences among respondents' self-ratings. Nearly all U.K. managers (97 percent) describe their marketing efforts as primarily successful, compared with 88 percent of U.S. respondents. The biggest differences can be seen in the percentages of respondents rating their efforts "effective" and "not at all effective." Fifty-six percent of U.K. respondents said their campaigns are effective, versus 46 percent of U.S. executives. And, while 4 percent of U.S. professionals said their campaigns are not at all effective, no respondent from the U.K. shared this view. These results may reflect differences in consumers and market environments between the two countries, or perhaps higher expectations for campaign performance among U.S. companies. It also may indicate that U.K. firms do indeed have more effective marketing campaigns than do U.S. companies.

Levels of campaign effectiveness also vary by industry group (Exhibit 23-8). Respondents in the consumer products group rated their campaigns the most favorably, with a strong majority (64 percent) describing their marketing efforts as "extremely effective" or "very effective." Representatives of the high-tech and other industries group are the most critical of their programs—none rated his or her company's campaign as extremely effective, and just 26 percent called their marketing programs very effective. These respondents are also twice as likely as other man-

EXHIBIT 23-7. Effectiveness of respondents' marketing campaigns.

Challenge	Total	U.S.	U.K.
Highly effective	42%	42%	41%
Effective	50	46	56
Ineffective	8	12	3

EXHIBIT 23-8.   Average campaign effectiveness by industry group: 4 = extremely effective, 3 = very effective, 2 = effective, 1 = not very effective, and 0 = not at all effective.

Industry	Score
Financial services	2.37
Automotive retail/manufacturing	2.32
Power and utilities	2.38
Services	2.43
Consumer products (retail/manufacturing/distribution)	2.73
High-tech and other	2.03

agers to rate their campaigns as downright ineffective (19 percent versus 8 percent average). Three other industry groups (financial services, automotive, and power and utilities) share similar views of their marketing campaigns, with about half of the respondents in each group describing their campaigns as simply effective. Managers in the services group stand out somewhat, with nearly two-thirds (65 percent) calling their campaigns effective and none rating them as ineffective.

Converting respondents' ratings to interval values on a scale of 0 to 4.0 (where 4 = extremely effective, 3 = very effective, 2 = effective, 1 = not very effective, and 0 = not at all effective) generates even more illustrative statistics on campaign effectiveness. With this approach, the consumer products group has the highest self-rating of marketing campaign effectiveness at 2.73. On average, companies in the high-tech and other industries group rated their campaign performance the lowest at 2.03. The remaining industry groups have almost identical average scores, ranging from 2.32 in the automotive sector to 2.43 in the services group.

MEASURING CAMPAIGN PERFORMANCE
Just how do these executives know whether their campaigns are effective or missing the mark? By and large, most respondents measure their campaigns in some way, although the techniques and metrics used vary widely (Exhibit 23-9). Four different measures stand out as being the most commonly used: response rate (cited by 79 percent of all respondents), revenue generation (78 percent), customer retention (69 percent), and profit generation (66 percent). Indicators used less frequently to measure marketing performance are level of sales activity (15 percent), brand awareness (5 percent), and cost of customer acquisitions (2 percent). Just 5 percent of respondents, all from the United States, indicated that they cannot measure the performance of their marketing campaigns. These organizations are mostly small companies and, perhaps not surprisingly, generally rated their marketing campaigns as ineffective.

EXHIBIT 23-9.   Most commonly used campaign performance measures.

Measurement	Total	U.S.	U.K.
Response rate	79%	70%	91%
Revenue generation	78	75	81
Customer retention	69	65	75
Profit generation	66	63	69

More than two-fifths (41 percent) of our survey respondents use all four of the key performance measurements (Exhibit 23-10). This practice is more prevalent in the United Kingdom, where 45 percent of respondents reported using all four measures, compared with 38 percent of U.S. firms. The top measure of marketing performance used in the United States is revenue generation (cited by 75 percent versus 81 percent by U.K. respondents), whereas the most commonly used measure of campaign effectiveness among U.K. firms is response rate, used by virtually all U.K. managers (91 percent, versus 70 percent of U.S. respondents). In general, there is greater consensus on the use of measures among U.K. participants than among those from the United States, and U.K. respondents, on average, use more measures than their U.S. counterparts. Furthermore, U.K. firms are more likely than U.S. companies to use a variety of other, less scientific measures in addition to standard financial and customer response figures. As one executive remarked, "We have an emotional attachment to what we do. Therefore we have certain [other] measures that we need to track."

Although the four most prominent performance measures in our survey are the same across all six industry groupings, preferences for their use vary by sector. Revenue generation is the most frequently used measure of marketing campaign performance in the services (87 percent) and financial services (83 percent) groups, whereas the automotive and consumer products industries favor the use of response rates (85 percent each). Reflecting the competitive pricing wars that have followed deregulation in most areas, power and utilities companies rely extensively on customer retention rates to determine campaign effectiveness (88 percent). There is no clear front-runner for performance measurement in the high-tech and other indus-

EXHIBIT 23-10.   Number of key campaign performance measures used.

Measure Usage	Total	U.S.	U.K.
Use all 4	41%	38%	45%
Use any 3 of 4	29	28	29
Use 1 or 2	23	22	25
Do not use	7	12	1

tries group, whose companies rely with about equal frequency on revenue generation (74 percent) and response rate (71 percent) to assess marketing effectiveness.
This group is also the least likely to use profit generation as a measure of campaign
performance.

Not surprisingly, the larger the company, the more performance measures it
uses—particularly financial metrics that help managers understand how their significant investments in marketing are paying off. For instance, 83 percent of companies
with more than 7500 employees use revenue generation as a campaign performance
measure, compared with 72 percent of companies with fewer than 3500 people. Similarly, 69 percent of the largest companies in our survey evaluate their campaigns
with a profit-generation yardstick, versus 57 percent of the smallest participating
companies. Interestingly, smaller and midsize companies appear to be slightly more
likely than larger companies to use customer retention as a measure of campaign
performance.

Typically, firms using three of the four key performance measures favor financial measures. Indeed, essentially all of these companies (98 percent) use revenue
generation to measure campaign effectiveness, and nearly three-quarters (74 percent) also use profit generation. On the other hand, companies using just one or two
of the four main performance measures are primarily focused on nonfinancial measures, relying on response rate (76 percent) and customer retention (49 percent)
much more than either revenue (37 percent) or profit (15 percent) generation.

TIME TO COMPLETE CAMPAIGNS

As noted earlier, nearly 60 percent of managers reported that they frequently struggle with shortening the time it takes to create and launch a marketing campaign. Furthermore, 43 percent said that the fact that it takes them too long to get a campaign
from idea to execution negatively affects their organization's ability to do its job. But
how long is too long? We asked participants to tell us how long, on average, it takes
them to create and execute a typical marketing campaign. Here is what we found.

The average participating company takes 2.5 months to conceive of and launch
a marketing campaign. However, while firms in both the United States and the
United Kingdom have similar average times, there is more variance in marketing
campaign cycle time among U.S. companies (Exhibit 23-11). Indeed, 23 percent of

EXHIBIT 23-11.   Time to complete marketing campaigns.

Time	Total	U.S.	U.K.
Less than 2 weeks	3%	3%	3%
2 weeks to 1 month	15	20	8
1 to 2 months	31	27	37
2 to 4 months	33	25	43
More than 4 months	18	25	9

U.S. organizations (versus 11 percent of U.K. companies) said they create and launch marketing campaigns in less than one month. On the other hand, 25 percent of U.S. respondents (compared with 9 percent of those from the U.K.) reported that it takes them more than four months to develop and execute a given campaign. A plurality (43 percent) of U.K. respondents said that their campaign cycle time is between two and four months.

From an industry perspective, marketing campaign cycle times vary considerably. Continually under the gun to reach today's mobile and finicky consumers with innovative items, the consumer products industry is the most adept at quickly moving a campaign from the drawing board to the streets: Just 9 percent of consumer goods respondents said their campaign cycle time is more than four months, and 21 percent noted that it is less than one month. Financial services also moves relatively quickly, while the power and utilities industry (with a much less active product-innovation engine and customers with fewer choices of providers) and the generally large and bureaucratic automotive companies tend to be the slowest in getting campaigns off the ground.

It is important to note that we have found that the time it takes to complete a marketing campaign is inversely related to its effectiveness (Exhibit 23-12). More than half (51 percent) of our respondents who have a short campaign development and execution process (i.e., taking less than two months from idea creation through execution) rate them as extremely or very effective, compared to just one-third of the managers whose campaigns are long (taking two months or more to complete). Yet, while there is obviously a point at which too long a marketing cycle time is ineffective, there is also a point at which too short a cycle is ineffective: Companies with very long (more than four months) or very short campaign cycle times (less than one month) are four times more likely to report having ineffective marketing campaigns than others (16 versus 4 percent).

One of the principal reasons that a long campaign cycle time impairs campaign effectiveness is the perishable nature of data. The longer it takes to get from idea conception to campaign execution, the less likely it is that the data on which the idea was based is still accurate and fresh—and, subsequently, the less likely the campaign will be to hit the mark. Our survey figures bear this out. A large percentage of respon-

EXHIBIT 23-12.   Effectiveness of campaigns by length of time to complete them.

Length	Highly effective	Effective	Ineffective
Less than 1 month	52%	32%	16%
1 to 2 months	51	46	4
2 to 4 months	40	56	4
More than 4 months	19	66	16

dents reported that the effectiveness of their campaigns is diminishing due to out-dated or inaccurate data. For 60 percent of these individuals, more than one-tenth of their data is inaccurate or outdated. In fact, 21 percent said that at least one-fourth of their data is suspect, making it difficult for them to craft and launch highly effective campaigns.

WAYS TO IMPROVE CAMPAIGN EFFECTIVENESS

Despite the largely satisfactory grades that respondents give their marketing cam-paigns, most also recognize that there is always room for improvement. In general, executives noted that they could improve the effectiveness of their campaigns by having access to better data, addressing a number of internal corporate issues, and adopting better tools (Exhibit 23-13).

For example, a strong majority of our survey respondents (68 percent) said fresher, more accurate data could help their campaign efforts—not surprising, given the large percentage of respondents who reported having a significant percentage of suspect data. The desire for better data seems to be stronger in the United Kingdom (79 percent) than in the United States (60 percent).

A majority of respondents also believe that several internal changes would bol-ster campaign performance. Sixty-seven percent cited the need for better integration of the various customer touch points, which would help them create a more complete view of each customer and maintain consistency among their marketing messages. Sixty-five percent believe their marketing campaigns would be more effective if they were centered on a better overall customer strategy. And 59 percent said their cam-paigns would perform better if they had a faster process for developing and execut-ing them.

While managers are aware they must overhaul their marketing strategies and processes to foster lasting customer relationships, they also recognize the important role technology plays in this transformation. Among the professionals we surveyed, more than half cited their need for specific tools to foster collaboration between departments (59 percent), to control the campaign process from creation through execution (58 percent), and to effectively segment and model their markets (56 per-

EXHIBIT 23-13.   Improvements needed for effective campaigns.

Improvements	Total	U.S.	U.K.
More accurate, fresh data	68%	60%	79%
Integration between customer touch points	67	61	75
Better overall customer strategy	65	57	75
Tools to foster collaboration	59	52	68
Tools to control the process	58	53	64
Segmentation and modeling tools	56	51	63

cent). A minority of respondents (about one in three) believe better creative design will help them get customers' attention.

CONCLUSION

In today's world, customers are becoming less loyal to brands. They use new sources of information to build impressions and make decisions in buying a product or service. Yet, as is clearly indicated by the survey results, marketing executives are not equipped with the tools they need to keep up with changing customer expectations, achieve greater share of wallet, and maximize the lifetime value of customers. To achieve the level of efficiency and effectiveness in marketing that customers and the marketplace demand, companies must address their shortcomings in marketing campaign management and their ability to collaborate with other customer-facing functions.

It is time for companies to embrace the new organization structures, processes, and technologies that are needed to help marketing executives improve the way they do business—and, in the process, take yet another step toward fulfilling the promise of CRM.

24

The Next Frontier:
Just-in-Time Marketing

J. Patrick O'Halloran and Todd R. Wagner

The theories, buzzwords, mantras, and missions that have streamlined successful manufacturing over the past 30 years are familiar even to casual students of business, let alone those deep in the trenches. Terms such as *quality circles, make-to-order, just-in-time,* and *push versus pull* have become so common to the business vernacular that few can remember a time before these terms were coined—and before they defined the ways in which any successful manufacturer had to view its business.

The movement toward a just-in-time (JIT) environment had its roots in postwar Japan, where survival required nothing less than a total reinvention of the nation's manufacturing processes. Thirty years later, Japan's success in manufacturing forced American industry to adopt the same principles. It became inordinately clear that by cleverly harnessing the available technology, boldly reworking their processes, systematically reprogramming their mind-sets, and helping their people adjust to a new way of both thinking and working, American corporations could gain an important competitive edge. Not to mention the fact that they would avoid the disaster they knew awaited them if they did not advance in this direction along with their competitors.

We are at a similar point in the evolution of marketing. Intense global competition, emerging technology, incredible reservoirs of data, less loyal but more sophisticated customers demanding personalized, permission-based attention and service, and a growing corporate emphasis on CRM have given corporations the imperative to do marketing faster, cheaper, and better. For many corporations, however, this

This chapter originally appeared in the *Journal of Business Strategy,* May/June 2001. It is reproduced here by permission.

insight has been little more than insight. They have not been able to turn it into customer-focused action. One way to do that is to find the parallels between just-in-time manufacturing and marketing, and then to apply these principles to marketing that is enabled by technology, empowered by insight, and informed by history.

WHERE'S THE RETURN?

During the past several years, with the evolution of a CRM consciousness and CRM software, many companies have purchased expensive suites of CRM software, hooked them all together—and realized little or no benefit. They are not getting the ROI they expected. They are frustrated. They may even be further behind than they were before embarking on these initiatives.

What went wrong? Too many corporations bought the tools without rethinking organization, process, and integration around the customer. They automated first and then began considering simplification and integration across customer-facing groups. By viewing technology as the solution, not the enabler, and by automating before they integrated, they did not really know what it was they were actually automating. They were not extracting the value. While the software applications themselves might have been integrated, their use throughout the company was not. Rather than looking at automation from an enterprise (and a customer) perspective, companies took a more traditional, siloed approach and simply automated discrete functions such as sales or call centers, using unconnected software applications. Taking this approach can often limit the value of the applications. Beyond that, employing software silo by silo often can keep companies from using the technology not only to serve customers but also to better target the marketing campaigns that bring them customers in the first place.

Lesson 1 from Manufacturing

The rush to implement large-scale CRM solutions has a parallel in manufacturing in the 1970s. At that time, manufacturers viewed technology as the solution to managing manufacturing-floor inventory. Companies bought high-capacity, large-production machines such as multiaccess milling machines, programmable logic controllers, and inventory movement robots to provide flexibility. They invested in manufacturing resource planning (MRP) solutions and applied them to complex shop-floor processes. But what they ended up with were disconnected islands of automation. They were not getting efficiencies. The lesson manufacturers learned was that the value comes from managing the flow (that is, the manner in which all the processes are performed on the manufacturing floor) and not just the manufacturing process itself. Eliminating non-value-adding activities reduced the complexity and made the tools more effective.

CAN WE TALK?

The head of marketing at a major company was asked when he had last spoken to the head of call centers. He never had. Think of that: The head of marketing had never had a conversation with the head of one of the major customer-interaction points. While this lack of communication might not have been unusual in the old siloed organization, it is clearly counterproductive in the modern corporation. Not having a dialogue has kept this bank from effectively exploiting some key opportunities and issues. The head of marketing, for one, was missing the chance to get insight into customers that could feed into future campaigns and potentially cross-sell or upsell products and services. The head of call centers was going about his job without a clear understanding of what the bank's marketers were trying to sell to the customer.

Another bank has embedded face-to-face meetings (marketing-style quality circles) into the culture. Each time the bank mounts a campaign, the head of marketing pulls together a cross-functional team consisting of marketing, technology, analytics, customer service, and creative communication people—everyone whose work has a direct impact on the customer experience. The marketing manager who convenes the meeting serves as the facilitator, making sure the group understands what the manager's vision is from a marketing standpoint and then opening up the discussion to solicit ideas about how this vision can be developed, altered, improved, and executed. The call center people discuss what they have been hearing from consumers that might affect how the program is designed or executed. The analytics experts explain what they have been seeing in the data that ought to be considered before the team jumps headlong into the campaign. The information technology and business application representatives talk about how the team might execute the ideas they have come up with given the tools and capabilities available—whether the Web or the call center or the field is the most appropriate channel to use. And finally, the creative folks reflect on what sort of spin they might put on this campaign, based on everything they have heard so far. This approach has proven quite successful. Concurrence is usually reached. The team comes away from the meeting with not only program content but also a plan for action and specific assignments, and the campaign is off and running.

However, there is clearly room for significant improvement. Although their communication is well established, and they leave the meeting with the processes and their next steps mapped out on paper, team members do not have the tools and enablers in place to integrate and automate the process. They also lack real-time access to campaign and marketing performance data. These capabilities would enable the bank to shorten marketing cycle time, automate feedback and learning from campaign results, and support more proactive management of marketing programs.

Lesson 2 from Manufacturing

One of the key lessons learned in the transformation of manufacturing was to get the voice of the customer in all processes. A critical design concept was the manufacturing cell, which linked all production processes for a component in a small, contained area. This created a chain of customers from one machine tool to the next. Each customer could quickly provide quality feedback for each individual part as he or she received it. The feedback was quick, direct, and required no intermediary or system to make it work. The value of eye-to-eye communications on the spot quickly eliminated the need for complex data-gathering and -processing systems.

WHERE ARE WE GOING?

Many corporations embarking on a marketing campaign simply push ahead without thinking carefully and comprehensively about the expected outcome of each campaign, not to mention what the ROI must be. First, it is important to determine who the campaign's core customer is, how many people fall into this target group, what the content of the campaign is, and what channels will best deliver the intended message to the intended audience. It is critical, too, to look at the cost of delivering to the number of people targeted, what the expected consumer reaction is, and how many people can be expected to read the marketing piece, respond to it, and ultimately buy a product or service as a result. Understanding this allows the marketers to predict the financial margins the program will achieve.

However, the tendency to pursue the campaign before predicting the end result is of course part of what created problems for companies rushing headlong into CRM initiatives before they had taken a broader view of their organization's goals. Only after you have decided what you want your outcomes to be and defined a process, and a means for supporting that process, can you really start applying technology to the process and developing a tool that will enable everyone to understand the goal of each campaign, the measures of success for each campaign, and the individual metrics that contribute to a campaign's success.

Lesson 3 from Manufacturing

The JIT revolution established a new mind-set in the factory. The change from managing the direct labor content of a part and the variances in component costs to managing throughput and quality was a key to making the results happen quickly. "Lead time, quality, and cost are the only competitive weapons" became a popular mantra. Companies that focused on only one of these legs failed. Initiatives that were "the right thing to do" but did not have a solid business case and sponsorship took resources away from valuable efforts and typically failed as well.

WHY DOES IT TAKE SO LONG?

How does a marketing program get launched today? The typical scenario works something like this (Exhibit 24-1): A marketing manager working for a large bank wants to do a preapproved credit card offer. The marketing manager has some assumptions about the target of the campaign, but knows it is necessary to look at the data. The manager calls up the information systems (IS) department and says, "Why don't you do an extract on these types of customers, who have x number of accounts and x volume," and so forth. IS does an extract. The marketing manager looks at the report and says, "That isn't really what I want." It goes back to IS. They modify the extract. They run it again, and the marketing manager says, "I think this is close."

**EXHIBIT 24-1.   Anatomy of a marketing campaign: 26 weeks versus
26 minutes.**

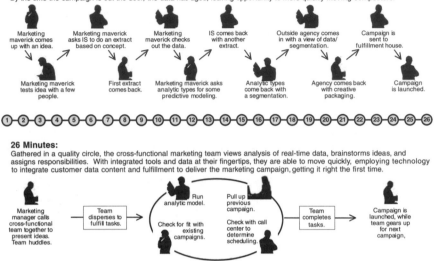

26 Weeks:
For many companies today, moving from marketing idea to campaign execution is a long, laborious series of steps.
Collaboration is hindered by functional silos. Data is gathered in batches from external departments and outside agencies.
By the time the campaign is out the door, the data has aged, leaving opportunity to more quickly moving competitors.

26 Minutes:
Gathered in a quality circle, the cross-functional marketing team views analysis of real-time data, brainstorms ideas, and
assigns responsibilities. With integrated tools and data at their fingertips, they are able to move quickly, employing technology
to integrate customer data content and fulfillment to deliver the marketing campaign, getting it right the first time.

Then the marketing manager gets the analytic-model PhD types involved and says, "Start segmenting this stuff." They start iterating through the data, and they segment, and this goes on for awhile.

Then the marketing manager says, "I think we have some good segments defined here. Let's do some predictive modeling." It goes back to the analytic modelers. They model. They figure out what segments they want to send this campaign to, and they modify the segments slightly for each different grouping of people. The marketing manager then takes this information over to the campaign analyst, who uses a variety of spreadsheets to analyze cost versus expected response rate and purchase rate. This cost analysis exercise drives some tweaking of the offers and channels used to contact the targeted customers. Then everything goes to a fulfillment house, and they launch the campaign.

The data comes back and has to be analyzed by another group of people. Finally, the data is filtered back into the database so that the company can get a historical view of the results. However, that historical view is limited in nature: The marketing manager has been functioning in a virtual vacuum, disconnected from other marketing managers pursuing similar paths in other silos, with little or no knowledge or understanding of what initiatives are going on elsewhere in the same company. What was lost in this process? Why did it have to take so long? Isn't there somewhere along the way that the process could have been coordinated and streamlined and the cycle time reduced?

Lesson 4 from Manufacturing

The manufacturing cell eliminated many queues and stacks of inventory between operations. Optimizing throughput versus focusing on individual steps got products through the cells more quickly and with significantly higher quality.

HEARING YOUR CUSTOMER OVER THE NOISE

We are continually bombarded with information about the tremendous wealth of data now available on customers. The truth is, much of the data is inaccurate, some of it is not available when you need it, and all data is extremely perishable. When you are relying on data to create a marketing campaign, time is not on your side. This is where taking the information you have gathered through marketing quality circles and applying the appropriate integrated technology can allow you to mine the data quickly, accurately, and effectively to achieve your clearly identified goals.

So it was for Xelector, a U.K.-based business-to-business-to-consumer online marketplace through which Europeans can compare, select, and purchase a wide range of financial services and utility products. The company wanted to identify the best and most profitable customers, determine their demographic, geographic, and behavioral characteristics (by asking them a series of fact-finding questions about their purchase requirements, for example), and then use that information to create relevant, differentiated customer offers. The challenge was to turn that concept into an operational business. Meeting that challenge meant creating a database business capable of supporting multiple financial services and utility products across Europe. This meant choosing the right data-warehousing, data-mining, and reporting tools, and then complementing those with sophisticated data analysis tools that would generate ranked lists of purchase options tailored to meet customers' needs. The result: the opportunity for Xelector's product providers and Web site partners to understand market trends and customer behavior, to test products on the Internet, and to tailor customer offers appropriately.

Similarly, when Germany's Commerzbank wanted to offer the best-tailored products to differentiated customer groups, it had to reengineer its entire retail banking business. The new marketing approach includes utilizing a real-time data warehouse and data analysis tools that allow efficient online analysis and targeted campaigns. At the click of a mouse, a call center employee can now display the customer's entire history with the bank. As a result, Commerzbank can offer each customer products that fit his or her individual needs.

Lesson 5 from Manufacturing

A key element of JIT outside the factory was a proactive relationship-building effort with the suppliers that sold parts and subassemblies to the factory. By doing this, manufacturers and suppliers were able to share information on quality metrics processes and eliminate waste that occurred between the two organizations.

HOW DO WE START THE CONVERSATION?

To reach these customers, companies at first relied on mass marketing, which *pushed* messages out to everyone. Then came targeted marketing, which focused on groups of customers, attempting to respond to their interests in a *pull* approach. The next level of customer-focused marketing requires moving beyond pushing and pulling by seeking permission from customers and paying close attention to the information derived from various touch points so that marketers can have a needs-based, responsive conversation with the customers. In a shotgun marketing approach, you push a lot of information out to the market at large (by placing banner ads on the Web, for example) and see who bites. This is the *finders* approach, and if you are lucky, you might get a 0.5 percent response. Alternatively, if you use e-mail or direct marketing to customers and targets (a *seekers* approach) you might get up to a 5 percent response. Much better, however, is moving to a conversation orientation, a dialogue, an interaction. This *partnership* approach, in which you provide highly targeted, customized information, can increase response rates by upwards of 40 percent.

Lesson 6 from Manufacturing

The move from push to pull scheduling helped reinforce the message, "make no parts or products until someone asks for them." By using the customer pull, companies wasted no effort in making components and products that might sit on a shelf until needed—if they were ever used. Pull scheduling eliminated the need to be a perfect forecaster by leveraging the responsive manufacturing cells. The process was built to support the pull scheduling mind-set.

A HOLISTIC APPROACH TO MARKETING

Where does all this lead us? For a sense of marketing's future, consider these recent experiences.

When a large agricultural company wanted to mount a copromotional campaign with its parent, an industrial/service corporation, that would capitalize on the affinity between seeds and crop chemicals, the challenge was: How do you launch an effective comarketing program when your data is in more than 20 different places and your dealers are distrustful? The answer drew on virtually every tool discussed earlier, from keeping the end in sight to integration before automation, from tearing down the silos to using technology effectively.

In this company's case, this meant starting by interviewing employees to gain insight into their needs for serving customers. Then it meant building a data warehouse that consolidated, cleansed, and standardized existing customer information from a host of sources. By consolidating all the data, rather than relying strictly on demographics, which do not generally describe purchasing behavior, the company could blend transaction history and contact and customer feedback history with demographics to create a richer, more powerful data source to predict customer behavior. Once the warehouse was built, the company leveraged it with marketing analysis and operations tools that enable marketing analysts to optimize offers and promotions to farmers and perform aggregate analysis for dealers to provide business leads on new or existing customers in their area. In the wake of this program's success, measured in sales growth and the increased provision of data by no longer hostile dealers and distributors, the company has built a suite of sophisticated data analysis tools for customer offers that can be differentiated by segments—groups of customers defined by particular needs and behaviors.

Similarly, E*Trade, the online investment service, knew that successful competition in an increasingly crowded field required better segmentation of its customer base and a heightened ability to analyze customer behavior. The goal: to move from quantity of customers to quality of customers. The method: building deeper relationships with customers, whether they were long-time core customers or first-time online investors. The solution: a marketing environment that, by taking lessons learned from previous campaigns and applying them to new initiatives, turns customer activity into insights. These insights, in turn, fuel targeted marketing campaigns and foster the deeper customer relationships the company is seeking. This happens because the customer experiences that come from campaigns driven (and thereby leveraged) by insight are more personalized, more fun, more conversation based, and more rewarding.

Data warehouses enable these companies to trap and store more information gained through interaction with customers, and this data, once accessible and usable, can be analyzed more readily. With data at marketing's fingertips that is easy to use and easy to transform into marketing campaigns, along with treatments that are truly focused on customers, companies can tailor treatments to specific customers and specific distribution channels.

Whether consciously or not, these companies have clearly taken a page (several pages in fact) from manufacturing and developed an approach to marketing that is streamlined, collaborative, and, most important, insight-driven. For every campaign they launch, customer-focused marketers such as these perform the following steps:

- Define the desired outcomes and marketing measures.
- Define the process.
- Clarify roles and organizational responsibilities for "owning the customer" and executing an integrated, end-to-end marketing process.
- Integrate data and tools to support the process and organization.
- Implement technology tools to speed execution and improve information delivery to the point of need.

The logical extension of this process (maintaining the manufacturing metaphor here) is to coordinate all this activity through what could be seen as a "workbench." Working at this workbench, all the different people who participated in the quality circle would have access to the same information, albeit tailored to their own view and their own responsibility, within the entire length of the program and the complete set of desired tasks and outcomes. In their own view of the workbench, they could see their role in the process and everything else that goes on so they would not be blindsided when someone throws something over the wall. In addition, they would have access to specific modeling tools which then, depending on which assignments they have finished, would update the workflow so that everyone involved in the process would know what is getting done—and what is not getting done. That would enable the frustrated marketer described previously to extract the data, commingle it with external data, and personally do some high-level segmentation. Then the marketer could pass it to the analytic modeler, who could work through it fairly quickly.

The result: Time, tasks, and people are pulled out of the process. The task is no longer a tedious operational chore. Value is added. And marketing, like manufacturing before it, moves into the modern age.

25

The New Integrated Marketing

Paul F. Nunes

I t certainly seemed logical at the time: Why not use the same online technologies that were revolutionizing retailing to set off a companion revolution in marketing?

But many marketers found that employing such Web-enabled marketing capabilities as e-coupons, banner ads, opt-in e-mail, e-reminder services, and permission-based marketing did not deliver the value they expected. Sure, through trial and error or sheer luck, some marketers achieved impressive results with these powerful online tools. But between their rush to adopt these tools and their overreliance on expected online purchasing, marketers tended to ignore some fundamental truths about consumer behavior. Without a full understanding of the ways in which customers buy, online and off, marketers cannot make the right decisions about which e-marketing tools to adopt and how best to use them to support their customers, wherever they might be.

Marketing has evolved around the notion of categorizing customers by groups or segments—essentially putting them in buckets of like characteristics. Marketers must now expand their thinking about segment definition if they are to respond to the *dynamic* customer segments that technology is enabling them to serve. Dynamic customer segments are composed not of a permanent subset of the customer base, but of buyers that exist in a particular set of circumstances at a particular moment in time. These part-time segment members require service and support based on their circumstances and buying behavior, not on some permanent label of who they are. To provide this support, companies need a more holistic approach to marketing than the "one segment, one channel" model of old. They need a model that links electronic and offline marketing tactics across the buying decision cycle for each pattern of customer behavior. That approach is the new integrated marketing.

ONE CUSTOMER, MANY SEGMENTS

Suppose a particular consumer bought your product every week for the past four weeks. Would you conserve time and marketing costs by ignoring this customer? Or would you contact this customer immediately, sending an electronic coupon to encourage the fifth buy?

The correct answer: It depends. Many would assume that four weeks of repeat purchasing signals loyalty and therefore little need for marketing intervention. But for certain customers in certain situations, repeat purchasing indicates impending burnout and the urge to try something new. Guessing wrong is expensive, hence the old marketing adage, "We know we waste half of our expenditures, we just don't know which half."

Before a customer's behavior can be predicted and cost-effectively supported in a channel, companies must identify and understand the context of the immediate purchasing situation—the details surrounding prior purchases, the consumer's current frame of mind, the environment in which the decision is occurring, and the intended recipient of the purchase.

How can companies adopt behavior-based approaches to customer interactions and marketing? They must begin by recognizing what happens when they fail to adapt to customers' circumstances.

EXTENUATING CIRCUMSTANCES

Failing to understand and respond to consumer behavior yields particularly disappointing results online. A shop.org study indicated that at one point, 65 percent of online shopping carts were abandoned. While some customers may simply change their minds, others feel stymied online. According to a Jupiter Research survey, one of the top reasons visitors leave Web sites is the inability to find the information they need.

Poor site design is partly to blame. Many Web sites are little more than online catalogs or brochure-ware. They disregard the Internet's capability to easily morph into a tool that meets a customer's immediate, circumstantial needs. When a customer's first action on a site is a keyword search, for example, sites might infer that they are there not to browse but to buy. Based on such circumstantial evidence, sites should be designed to modify and sequence follow-on screens accordingly.

Failing to align e-marketing tools to the immediate need also contributes to poor online marketing performance. For example, many consumers are simply not involved enough in the purchase of the products being advertised in online banner ads to want more information (i.e., to click through). Yet, new research from the Marshall School of Business indicates that banner ads *are* effective in creating brand awareness, with 50 percent of online users noticing banner ads and 11 percent recalling them the next day. Companies must therefore align the use of banner ads (as one example) with the behavior of customers and the goal of the marketing plan, either awareness building or deeper consideration.

Heavy reliance on online communities as a source of customer influence is another example of an online marketing tool that often is misapplied. Many products are simply too complex and expensive for people to trust nonexpert opinions. In a recent Accenture survey, chat rooms were the lowest rated source of online advice, far below even retailers. Time and again experience confirms that online tools, like offline tools, must correspond to the consumer's actual behavior to be effective.

UNDERSTANDING ONLINE CONSUMER BEHAVIORS

To make online marketing tools responsive to consumer behavior, marketers must first seek to understand online consumer behaviors as they pertain specifically to their products or services; how do consumers shop online and off in *your* offering's category? A grave and all too common mistake is generalizing the findings of online behavior studies across the many categories of offerings sold online. No one would dispute the importance of considering differences in consumer behavior when shopping for a car versus toothpaste offline, yet online shopping discussions seldom make such distinctions. Marketing managers must also recognize that behaviors change based on circumstances; a customer taking the time to make a thoughtful decision today might value a different experience and make a different decision when in a hurry tomorrow.

Although consumer behavior can seem overwhelmingly complex, marketing scholars have worked to simplify the effort to understand it. One key framework that allows us to generalize consumer behavior and thus act on it comes from Henry Assael's book, *Consumer Behavior and Marketing Action* (Exhibit 25-1). Though this framework was created to explain offline behaviors, recent research findings suggest that these behaviors remain intact online. The framework describes four generic buying behaviors: *dissonance reduction, complex buying, habitual buying,* and *variety seeking.* These behaviors are distinguished by customer involvement in the purchase (which tends to be higher for more expensive purchases) and the degree of perceived product differentiation.[1]

Within this framework, the level of customer involvement is not fixed within a particular product category. For example, some books are bought on impulse, whereas others are bought after great consideration. The difference comes from the circumstances under which each purchase occurs, for example, the difference between late-night browsing and gift buying.

The degree of product differentiation also is not fixed; consumers decide. Their perception, not an objective measure of the category, determines whether a good or service is a commodity. As such, the degree of differentiation changes with customers' changing perceptions, influenced by such factors as advertising exposure and mood.

These two axes have broad implications for how customers learn, form beliefs about products, and ultimately choose. For low-involvement products, such as cereal, a trial purchase helps them form an opinion about the product. For high-involvement purchases, such as autos, beliefs typically are formed long before customers enter the showroom, even before they are old enough to drive. While customers typically research highly differentiated products, the opinions and behav-

**EXHIBIT 25-1.   Consumer behavior types. (*Adapted from Henry Assael,*
Consumer Behavior and Marketing Action, *6th ed.* [*Cincinnati, OH: South-
Western College Publishing, 1998*].)**

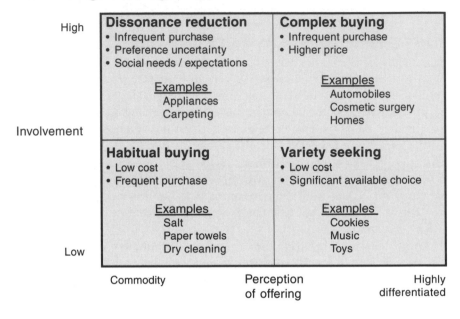

iors of friends, relatives, and close associates shape their opinions of commodity
brands.

These implications about learning and belief formation engender generic
descriptions of behaviors across the buying cycle. Exhibit 25-2 describes aspects of
each behavior type at each of the five stages in the buying cycle: *awareness, consideration, preference, purchase,* and *loyalty.* For example, the consideration phase of a
habitual buying decision requires only easily acquired information, whereas a complex buying decision warrants significant search and evaluation.

An understanding of buying behaviors at each stage of the buying process ought
to inform a Web site's design. Therefore, marketers must invest time and effort up
front in segmenting customers according to these behaviors in real time. Primary and
secondary research into consumers' exhibited behaviors in the product or service
category is the necessary starting point. Online research tools such as Speed-Trap,
which captures information about online consumer behavior at the source computer
(allowing even mouse movements to be monitored), greatly illuminate consumers'
behavior and the difficulties they experience in site usage.

But take care when assessing consumer attitudes or intended behaviors; consumers may behave differently online and off. For example, offline channels may be
used for thoughtful purchases, browsing, or gathering information, while online may

EXHIBIT 25-2. Buying behaviors across the buying decision process.

Buying process / Buying behavior	Awareness — Needs recognition	Consideration — Information search	Preference — Evaluation of alternatives	Purchase — Purchase decision	Loyalty — Postpurchase evaluation
Habitual	• Often originates from an out-of-stock situation	• Uses only information provided or easily available • Discovers new products in passing	• Often uses long-held preference beliefs • Brand loyal, but susceptible to spurious change	• Is reminded • Both planned and unplanned • Inertia driven	• Performs only moderate evaluation, unless switching
Variety seeking	• Often impulse driven by shopping as entertainment	• Performs on-the-spot comparison • Looks for sales	• Often spontaneously created • Must meet minimum standards • Willing to try it	• Purchases on impulse • Purchase on suggestion	• Most evaluation occurs here • Asks if astounded or disappointed
Dissonance reducing	• Recognizes need based on life event or external influence (e.g., salary increase)	• Trusts the evaluation set created by retailers • Relies on sales assistance	• Seeks out advice of friends • Uses heuristics, brands to form judgment	• Waits for the right time, (e.g., limited-time sale) • Often necessity driven	• Significant reevaluation postpurchase • Likely buyers remorse
Complex	• Often driven by life goals, longtime interests • Sometimes based on event or influence	• Performs significant search/needs evaluation • Considers numerous attributes	• Seeks the advice of experts	• Thoughtfully selected time and location	• Conducts little immediate reevaluation

be the place to go for impulse or simple repeat purchases. This is certainly true for some consumers' clothing purchases. Identifying the types and locations of these kinds of behaviors goes a long way toward capitalizing on them.

ALIGNING SITES TO BEHAVIORS

Once companies have created ways to identify customers' purchasing behaviors, they must evaluate how well their online and offline channels are aligned with those behaviors. Is the company's online presence prepared to give customers what they need, given their exhibited shopping behavior? What about less likely behaviors, such as impulse purchasing of an expensive stereo? Does it provide support across the entire buying decision process, from the creation of awareness through the rewarding of loyalty?

Aligning Web sites with consumer behaviors requires expanding the Web site concept to include the company's overall marketing presence. This new view encompasses all of the ways the Internet engages customers in a dialogue to serve their purchasing needs, including new Web-enabled marketing tactics such as opt-in e-mails and viral marketing, as well as existing channel and marketing capabilities.

One of the most critical challenges marketers face today is identifying the e-marketing tools that merit investment. Many assume that all of these tools can be valuable to their businesses—a belief the media reinforced for a long time. The reality, however, is that each e-marketing tool is best used for a certain consumer behavior type at a certain point in the buying decision process. Exhibit 25-3 identifies some of the most commonly used e-marketing tools and maps them to the behavior and buying process stages they best serve. Marketers can use this matrix to choose the tools that are most likely to show a return on investment. For example, sellers of

EXHIBIT 25-3.   E-marketing tactics in context.

Buying process / Buying behavior	Awareness — Needs recognition	Consideration — Information search	Preference — Evaluation of alternatives	Purchase — Purchase decision	Loyalty — Postpurchase evaluation
Habitual	• "Billboard" banner ads • Permission-based marketing/opt-in e-mail	• Advertorials promotional sponsorship • Search engine and directory positioning	• Online loyalty programs- rewards/points • Personal accounts (MyYahoo!, MyDell)	• E-continuous replenishment • One-click switching • E-reminder services (gift giving)	• Automated response systems (voice and E-mail) • E-returns
Variety seeking	• Funnel pages/referral hyperlinks • Highly targeted online ads	• Search engine and directory positioning (e-slotting allowances) • E-direct mail (broadcast and targeted e-mail)	• E-couponing • Interactive banner ads • E-cross-selling • E-recommendations	• Single-click purchasing • Transparent associates program (online vending machine)	• Virtual shelf presence • E-personalized customized product
Dissonance reducing	• Referral hyperlinks/ commissions • Online community sponsorship	• Online community- based selling • Online community- based testimonials	• Online expert communities (eg., ePinions) • Online service reps/Web call-through	• Dynamic pricing • Exploding deals (limited time offers) • JIT promotions	• E-follow-up • On-call service
Complex	• Event-based marketing	• Active site search support • Intelligent agent support • Brochure-ware	• Comparison engines • Configuration tools • Interactive needs assessment tools • Online training/tutorials	• Solution configuration • E-financing links/instant credit	• E-service (eg., online repair reservation)

ultra-high-end stereo equipment, a product largely bought through a complex purchasing behavior, need to improve their opt-in and event-based marketing much
more than they need banner ads, which are unlikely to create much additional awareness or persuasion for this kind of shopper. Yet few companies evaluate online marketing tool expenditures in such a systematic way.

MAKING THE CONNECTION

The matrix also clarifies which e-marketing tools should be linked together to support the entire process. One company that connects the pieces throughout the process
is Amazon.com. Amazon starts by supporting awareness through virtual storefronts
on affiliated Web sites. Using an associates program, Amazon provides graphics and
links that site owners can embed on their Web sites to connect users to Amazon. It
then pays a small fee per transaction to the site owners when their customers come
to Amazon and purchase. These links seamlessly move customers from awareness of
their book needs and desires to consideration of a purchase, as they find themselves
presented with editorial and customer book reviews on Amazon's site. Amazon then
moves the customer from consideration to preference building by recommending
similar or related books. And preference turns to purchase with the omnipresent Add
to Shopping Cart and Buy Now With One Click buttons.

Linking in postpurchase activities, such as tracking of orders, helps to complete
the integration of the cycle but also yields an additional benefit. Many companies
(booksellers, hotels, airlines, and brokerage houses, to name just a few) report
increased sales from customers who visit their sites to check the status of previous
purchases.

Anticipating and serving the customer's real intentions encourages further and faster progression through the buying cycle. One company that has acted on this insight both online and offline is Home Depot. It has trained its associates to engage customers consistently in dialogues about their project needs, not to simply fulfill sales transactions, and has supplemented selling activities with free in-store home-repair classes. Likewise, on its Web site, it has scrupulous instructions for a vast array of home-improvement projects, with detailed lists of the tools and materials required. These can be easily purchased right on the site, or the list can be printed separately from the instructions for use in shopping at the local store.

Anticipating multiple behavior styles creates additional value. FTD.com supports multiple behavior styles by prominently featuring both photos of likely desired products and menus allowing customers to shop by selecting an occasion or category. The product photos, however, are no ordinary laundry list. Each item represents a different category, such as Flowers Only or Bouquets with Cookies and Plush Toys. And each item is followed by a More Like This link to a next-level consideration set. To smooth and speed the transition to purchase, each option in the set has its own ORDERNOW! button, eliminating the need to search a crowded page for an add-to-shopping-cart button.

While several success stories of online buying process integration exist, these linkages tend to fall apart when behaviors cross industries. For example, a number of leading sites for direct online car sales lack support for insurance pricing—a rather natural customer consideration when purchasing a sports car or luxury vehicle. Online customers therefore are likely to leave the site to get this information from an insurance site or their agent, making their return to the auto site uncertain and costly at best. It is unclear whether a lack of insight into the buying process or an inability to form partnerships across industry boundaries is to blame, but as leading companies continue to evolve into expert buying process enablers, consumers likely will not tolerate this failing for long.

Creating sites that serve multiple customer behavior segments requires defining a clear path for each behavior, from awareness through to loyalty. First, a diagnostic of existing capabilities and linkages on the current Web site(s) and of future requirements should be performed, and scenarios should be created for each likely behavior.

A great way to define and test usage scenarios is to employ focus groups in usability labs. Simply gathering click-stream information is insufficient because it only tells *how* customers behave, not *why*. Focus groups should emphasize observation of behavior, which now can be supported with any of a number of online capture tools. Focus groups taught SmarterKids.com, for example, that it should step up its editorial features and intersperse advice throughout the site.

Companies do not have to look far for good focus groups. Employees can be great focus group participants. They helped Getpowercareers.com identify job-seeker category buttons for its human resources Web site, for example. In a clever twist on focus groups, Office Depot studies the questions posed to its search engine to determine customers' difficulties with the site.

Although these approaches capture customers' online behavior, what about their offline performance? The new integrated marketing requires seamless connections to be made across online and offline behaviors—a far more challenging task.

INTEGRATING OFFLINE WITH ONLINE

Most companies already recognize that the Internet is not sufficient for all consumer behavior-based needs. It was this observation that led to the popular "bricks-and-clicks" movement that closely followed the dot-com explosion. The desire to integrate channels has led to innovations such as the ability to buy online and make returns in the store. But how many companies have trained store employees to process online returns? More important, how many have designed a process that corrects the cause of the return, either online or in the store, without significant customer intervention?

One company that attacked this problem head-on is REI, the Seattle-based outdoor clothing and equipment retailer. Every night, REI transfers online sales information to its legacy systems, which also run the catalog business. As a result, customers can discuss returns over the telephone or via e-mail, and can return items either to a store location or through the mail.

Ultimately, a fluid system with numerous connections between online and offline channels is needed. Dodgeville, Wisconsin–based apparel retailer Lands' End allows users to search its site by the item numbers in its home-delivered catalog. GMBuyPower.com allows consumers to view and hold vehicle inventory on dealer lots, and even schedule test-drives. Colonial Braided Rug sends consumers swatches at the click of a mouse. And rare is the billboard, shopping bag, or print ad that does not list a dot-com address. All of these are important linkages to offline marketing that promote the new integration.

Establishing these links, however, is sometimes not enough. Customers must be directed to use the online or offline tool that best serves their behavior and the successful completion of each step in the buying process. Some products simply demand physical touch to convey their attributes. Reed & Barton, one of America's oldest silversmiths, addressed this need by providing low-cost samples through its Web site. By enabling customers to build their silverware preferences in their home, away from the competition in a department store, Reed & Barton creates a closed loop from awareness through purchase and eventual loyalty, driven by its Web site but integrated with offline behavior.

MAKING BEHAVIOR WORK FOR YOU

The new integrated marketing brings with it certain strategic opportunities. For one thing, it enables companies to influence consumer behavior throughout the buying cycle. A number of traditional strategies, enhanced by e-marketing, can be used to influence consumer behavior to a company's advantage (Exhibit 25-4). If a com-

EXHIBIT 25-4. How to modify consumer behavior.

Lower Involvement
- Enable easier returns (e.g., Lands' End's Guaranteed Period)
- Promote easy resale through new resale markets (e.g., eBay)
- Reduce purchase commitment (e.g., Application Service Providers, leasing)

Increase Involvement
- Report side-by-side comparisons (e.g., Pricescan.com)
- Increase reported-on attributes (e.g., site speed, privacy policy)
- Increase price volatility (e.g., cheaper online airline tickets)

Reduce Perceived Differentiation
- Reduce versions offered (e.g., automobile options packages)
- Increase reporting on customer experiences (e.g., ePinions)
- Provide free samples (e.g., Amazon.com's CD track download)

Increase Perceived Differentiation
- Bundle offerings (e.g., products with products, products with services)
- Increase service component of offerings (which are almost always more experience based and therefore highly differentiated)

pany's product has distinct attribute advantages—it works better or has more features, for example—it should strive to increase customer use of complex buying behavior. If the product has favorable buzz but dated technology, the company should attempt to drive dissonance-reducing behavior.

The new integrated marketing also brings to light underserved customer segments. Most companies' natural inclination is to serve their most familiar segments, but the opportunity represented by underserved segments should not be ignored. For example, although millions of customers need medications occasionally, others repurchase the same drugs year after year to alleviate chronic illnesses. The latter group is better served by Drugstore.com's continuous replenishment option, called Your List. After customers add prescriptions (easily done at time of each initial purchase) they are notified by e-mail when it is time to refill. Having Drugstore.com refill their orders is as easy as a click of button, creating tremendous value for both customers and company. A similarly underserved segment exists in autos. Seventeen percent of French car-buyers buy habitually, but how many dealers target or serve that type of behavior?

Charles Schwab & Company continually takes advantage of strategic opportunities in integrating its marketing efforts. First, by moving quickly into low-cost online brokering, Schwab became one of the first to profit from the change in online brokerage behavior, namely, the increase in customer trade volume (including the boom in day trading). Subsequently, the firm made research available online and broadened its services to target goal-based investing. Lately, Schwab continues to integrate new technologies that enable and support new behaviors, recently with the wireless Pocket Broker offering—a service that lets customers check account balances, program alerts, and perform trades from pagers, personal digital assistants, and cell phones.

CONCLUSION

In the end, it is the consumer who determines the best design for a newly integrated marketing strategy—not the traditional value-based or demographic-based segment definition of the customer. This is the customer as defined by circumstances, in all their myriad forms: the hurried business executive running to catch an airplane, and that same executive half-heartedly flipping through the plane's in-flight magazine; the housewife grocery shopping with three kids in the store during the day, and shopping online at night after they have gone to bed.

In a world with more actionable segments than customers, those who recognize and target different behaviors through behavior-based integrated online and offline capabilities have the advantage. But the greatest advantage is reserved for those who use these capabilities to move buyers quickly through the decision process, in any circumstance. This is a feat accomplished only through the new integrated marketing.

Marketing by the Numbers: How to Optimize Marketing ROI

Jeffrey Merrihue

Consider this figure: $100 billion. That is the amount of money the Global 1000 spends on marketing and advertising across all media. It is no small amount, but it is apparently not enough to halt the erosion of customer loyalty that has been accelerating during the past decade. According to CNW Marketing Research, actual customer loyalty (i.e., repeat purchase of the same brand) in the auto industry has dropped 5 percent from 1990 to 2000 and continues to decline. More than one-third of all brands analyzed dropped in customer loyalty by double-digit percentages—some by more than 30 percent.[1] In the North American automobile market alone, this decline in loyalty accounted for nearly $25 billion in sales that switched hands.[2]

To quote an old song, "Something's happening here; what it is ain't exactly clear." Certainly, today's customers are a fickle lot. When their demands and needs are not readily met, they will not hesitate to shift brands, find a new distributor, partner with another manufacturer, or seek out an alternative service provider. But shouldn't $100 billion be enough to help persuade customers to demonstrate more loyalty to brands and companies?

The problem is not necessarily the amount of money being spent (although CEOs and CFOs may beg to differ). The real dilemma is how and where the dollars are allocated. Obviously, some amount of marketing expenditures are hitting their mark, because companies are still in business. However, few if any companies are able to determine with any certainty which marketing programs consistently return genuine business benefits to the company and which simply siphon away profits, and that inability to determine the ROI of each marketing activity undermines the entire marketing effort—precisely at a time when companies need a highly effective marketing function the most.

EFFECTIVE MARKETING IS ESSENTIAL

Nothing about today's customers or markets is certain, a fact that marketers know all too well. With change now a constant, marketing managers recognize that they have to develop effective marketing programs in order to grow—not only to keep existing customers and bring in new ones, but also to open unexplored markets and create new opportunities in those markets thought to be mature. Well-designed and well-implemented marketing activities, they know, are key to generating sales and revenues. For many companies that sell fast-moving consumer goods, a major marketing effort (including new-product development, distribution, advertising, and promotion) can generate as much as 40 percent of short-term sales. In the consumer electronics industry, the introduction and promotion of new products can stimulate as much as 80 percent of those sales.

Even old products can find new life in rapidly developing markets with the support of an effective marketing function. For example, the introduction of a new technology into certain markets can send the old products into a tailspin—witness the fate of products such as rotary telephones, personal digital assistants, and computer processors. However, when DVD players hit the mainstream in North America, sales of VCRs in such places as Indonesia and Latin America actually *increased* by double-digit percentages, because savvy marketers discovered there was still significant unfulfilled demand for such old technology in these new geographies, and they supported the products accordingly.

In addition to capturing value from previously untapped sources, an effective marketing campaign is invaluable in maintaining and increasing customer satisfaction and loyalty. Marketing is the principal communicator of a company's brand promise and customer experience—everything the company says it will provide through its products and services, including customer satisfaction, support, technical solutions, guarantees, price points, discounts and coupons, prompt distribution, and the like. Effective marketers that ensure that there is no mismatch between what the company promises and what it delivers are much more likely to experience strong customer loyalty and repeat business than competitors that frequently let customers down or confuse them with conflicting messages and experiences. Nordstrom, L. L. Bean, and Home Depot, for example, have spent decades crafting their image as companies that offer no-hassle service—and they continue to delight loyal customers by accepting product returns smoothly and with a smile, no questions asked.

WRONG MARKET, WRONG MESSAGE

To be sure, an effective marketing program is essential to business success today, regardless of industry. However, many companies, even the leaders, are discovering that their marketing capabilities are letting them down just when they need them most. And they are paying for it at the cash register and on Wall Street.

Some companies' marketing limitations have manifested themselves in missed opportunities. Clothier Levi Strauss is a classic example. The purveyor of jeans that were once the epitome of cool and the object of desire by teens and young adults everywhere, Levi Strauss badly lost its way in the 1990s. Confused by the new wave of customers with different needs and values, the company struggled to develop relevant new products. While selected Levi's ad campaigns have been memorable, others have been flops, and campaigns are changed on a regular basis.

One year, Levi's astounded J.C. Penney, its largest customer, by delivering its back-to-school line to the retailer 45 days late. Such stumbles would have been easy to shake off in the old days, when Levi's jeans were essentially the only option. But in a decade that spawned dozens of competitors, these miscues threatened the viability of the entire enterprise. According to estimates by *Fortune,* the market value of Levi Strauss (a privately held company) has been halved since 1996, from $14 billion to approximately $7 billion.[1]

Likewise, General Motors continues to struggle with market share because consumers under 35 have abandoned the company, and GM's established customer base is aging. While GM ignored younger consumers (referring to Generation X and Y customers as "unprofitable"), Ford, Honda, and Volkswagen catered to the segment's needs. Honda developed an aftermarket program designed to help youths customize their cars. Ford began a young-teen marketing campaign. And VW, perhaps the hippest of car makers today, made huge inroads among 20-somethings with a series of fun, quirky ads featuring hip music and characters. Only recently has General Motors recognized its error and begun to embrace the younger crowd. But youth-oriented products such as the Pontiac Vibe, Sunfire, and Azteck—the last of which GM's own head of product development, Robert Lutz, has publicly derided—show that GM still has a long way to go. Honda, on the other hand, launched the CR-V, with its extra large door openings and a low SUV price, targeted at the sporty youth market. In its marketing efforts, Honda boasts, "Plus, with even more headroom inside, you can chauffeur lots of your friends." Meanwhile, the long-suffering Cadillac brand is about to go through a makeover. It will be interesting to see if lessons have been learned from its own styling errors and the successes of its competitors.

Other companies placed their bets on poorly conceived marketing strategies and campaigns, often overestimating their markets and making promises they could not keep, despite their best intentions to do so. Retailer Kmart, for example, developed a strategy of emphasizing low prices and went head-to-head with Wal-Mart, even though that losing proposition was evident to just about everybody except Kmart managers. This strategy, "supported" by a sharp cut in advertising, sounded the venerable retailer's death knell. Similarly, retailer Gap Inc. spent 20 years building a base of loyal customers, but then ignored their tastes when it decided to pursue a younger group more interested in trendy (some say ugly) clothes than in classically styled, high-quality apparel. The results have been disastrous. The company chalked up a stunning 18 consecutive months of declining same-store sales and saw its stock price plunge 71 percent from its high in February 2000. "We have disappointed some of our core customers," admitted Gap CEO Mickey Drexler. "We misread some of the market."[4]

Ineffective marketing also has resulted in inconsistent customer experiences for patrons of many businesses. A number of companies suffered setbacks from their ill-conceived plans for Internet shopping. They created sites where customers could make purchases, touting how easy and convenient it was to shop over the Web. But customers who tried to return items were disappointed. Web-only retailers clearly had not thought through how they would deal with returns, and the resulting expense and confusion customers endured eventually drove them away. Many retailers with brick-and-mortar stores fared no better in the early days. They confounded customers who tried to return Web-purchased items to a store in a mall by refusing to accept such returns. Stung by the experience, many customers took their business elsewhere.

Even a venerable company like Coca-Cola has not been immune to marketing missteps that can inflict considerable damage on its brand, masterfully crafted for decades. Seeking to restore earnings growth a few years ago, Coca-Cola embarked on a major reorganization that pushed decision making out of its company headquarters into business units around the world. The move backfired, however, as the company's talented headquarters marketing team left the company. Left to their own devices, the business units disbanded the global agency network and created a number of embarrassing, conflicting, and ineffective ad campaigns, resulting in two years of lower growth in sales volume, a reduced market share, and a loss of ground to PepsiCo in the brand space.[5] Coca-Cola is now reconstructing its global approach.

WHY MARKETING ROI IS IN DECLINE

What is the problem? Why have once-proud companies begun swinging back and forth from global to local or modern to traditional positioning as they struggle to find the right concept, the right message, and the right market for their products? Why are businesses of all types finding it so difficult to keep pace with customers that admittedly have become more mobile, sophisticated, demanding, and fickle? Why have so many marketing efforts produced such poor results despite the investment of significant company resources?

Five factors are largely responsible for the current state of affairs:

- Obsolete marketing tools
- Fragmented marketing processes
- Lack of objective measurements
- Lack of rigor and discipline
- Lack of consistency and broad perspective

Obsolete Marketing Tools

One of the most significant problems with marketing is that marketing professionals in many companies are using outdated practices and tools to plan and execute marketing programs. In fact, marketing today still is largely based on the brand management principles pioneered by consumer goods company Procter & Gamble in the 1920s. Clearly, these principles have been successful in the past. However, they alone no longer can be counted on to generate value for the company in today's marketplace.

A prime example is how ineffectual marketing techniques can become institutionalized. Many mass-marketing techniques, such as broadcast advertising, continue to be very effective, whereas others, such as couponing and excess price promotion, have spiraled out of control. Historically, brand building accounted for more than 50 percent of a budget; yet, in the 1990s, most brand-building investments dropped to between 20 and 40 percent of total investments, with the rest going to trade and price promotions. Numerous studies, including the trade-driven Efficient Consumer Response initiative in the grocery industry, have confirmed the wastefulness of promotional tools such as couponing. Yet their use continues to grow.

Not surprisingly, as the use of ineffectual techniques has grown during the past 10 to 15 years, the return on marketing investment of these efforts has declined steadily. Econometric analysis has shown couponing, for example, to return only 29 cents on each dollar invested—one of the lowest returns of marketing-mix items. Yet companies continue to pour millions into the medium. One executive at a major American auto manufacturer recently said, "70 percent to 80 percent of all new-car incentive dollars spent and incentive advertising is wasted on people who were planning on buying the car anyway and didn't even know they were getting an incentive, or the incentive is too low to sway their purchase decision."

Fragmented Marketing Processes

A second problem is that many companies have fragmented marketing processes. The typical marketing function takes control of the creative aspect of marketing, but rarely the analytical aspect. Thus, a lot of time and money are spent on developing ad campaigns, but not on managing and analyzing customer data or on improving the company's ability to interact with its customers. This is one of the primary causes of the inconsistent customer experiences noted earlier, especially in companies where the creative marketing efforts are top-notch, but the practical details of communicating with customers (or enabling them to communicate with the company) are rarely provided for. In an Accenture survey of marketing executives in the United States and the United Kingdom, more than half of the respondents (57 percent) reported that their marketing campaigns are not well-integrated and coordinated with other areas of their companies, particularly information technology (IT) and CRM.[6] The results are a low return on marketing investments and a high frustration level for creative managers in developing effective campaigns and giving customers the consistent messages and experiences they want.

Lack of Objective Measurements

A third major problem in a company's ability to devise an appropriate marketing campaign is that it typically lacks the objective metrics that gauge the performance of its marketing programs. The Accenture survey revealed that 68 percent of marketing executives have difficulty measuring the ROI of their marketing campaigns.[7]

This does not necessarily mean that they do not measure anything. Many companies still use the classic tools and metrics—focus groups, usage and attitude surveys, awareness tracking, and market share—to help them gauge their effectiveness. While these measurements are important, there is rarely a process to aggregate this information into accurate return on marketing investment calculations. As a result, measurements do not prevent these companies from pouring time and money into ineffective vehicles and unprofitable markets.

Most companies bemoan the lack of widespread marketing accountability but then fail to take action. Others actually take pride in applying "instinct-driven marketing." We endorse the use of experience and judgment, but believe these should be deployed on an accountable ROI foundation just like the other areas within a company (see following section).

Lack of Rigor and Discipline

A fourth problem is that, in many companies, marketing still is viewed (both by marketers themselves and by those outside the field) largely as a creative process or an art that is not subject to the same discipline and rigor as other business functions. As a result, many marketing departments are allowed to function with less scrutiny and less accountability than other departments, and marketers often resist the use of tools or technologies that they believe impinge on the creative process. The fact is that marketing has been given a free ride for years by everyone, both inside and outside the company, and has not (at least until very recently) felt the same pressure for accountability from the financial markets as most other areas, notably purchasing, manufacturing, and logistics.

Lack of Consistency and Broad Perspective

Finally, there are the problems associated with the dwindling numbers of executives who remain loyal, long-term employees of one organization. Executive churn has set in at all levels of most major companies managerial teams. This churn has destroyed long-term experience and learning, and led to a serious shortfall in the ability to take a broad perspective on business issues. And the problem is even worse at the top. Since the 1990s, churn has hit the boardroom, leaving few CEOs in place. Historically, these executives would have managed their corporations for years or even decades. A recent *Business Week* article revealed that since 1997, 65 percent of the Fortune 500 companies have had their CEOs replaced (Exhibit 26-1).[8] In many cases, these leaders are lasting fewer than 12 months in the job.

The net result is that the cultivation of *brand memory*, which was passed from manager to manager and kept alive by the long tenures of those involved in the historic success of the company, has been obliterated.

REINING IN MARKETING ROI

It is clear that the time has come for companies to measure and improve the return on marketing investment. But how? The first order of business is to adopt a new approach to marketing that consists of six major steps:

EXHIBIT 26-1.   CEO turnover.

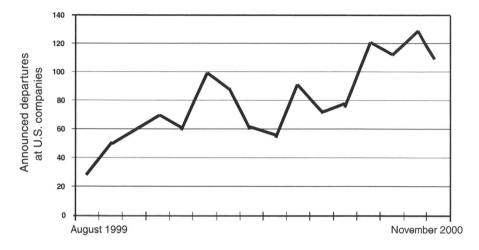

1. Quantify the effects of past marketing efforts.
2. Analyze competitive performance.
3. Identify underperforming initiatives before they become too costly.
4. Establish accountability for each marketing element.
5. Identify products and markets that offer significant growth potential.
6. Reallocate marketing resources to capitalize on new growth opportunities.

In the past, such an approach would have been impossible to adopt due to the lack of both the necessary technology and the willingness of the marketing community to embrace it. However, better access to data and newer marketing techniques, including econometrics, ROI measurement, and allocation software, make such analyses feasible; and the recent difficulties that many companies have experienced are providing the impetus for senior executive scrutiny of marketing performance (and, subsequently, grudging acceptance among marketers that new methods are called for).

Step 1. Quantify the Effects of Past Marketing Efforts.

Marketing executives are finally coming under pressure from CEOs, CFOs, and shareholders, among others, to quantify the effects of past marketing campaigns. Most companies conduct an annual marketing analysis, relating marketing investments to top-line sales and market share. Then they make decisions for the next year's campaign without having adequately quantified the effects of each individual marketing element's impact on growth and profitability. Now, however, it is much easier to gather all the data and measure that effort in great detail. Most consumer industries have good access to monthly or weekly industry sales data. For example, Supermarket Scan data can provide weekly transactions of fast-moving consumer goods, while two main national pharmacist-report systems, IMS and Scott Levin, provide similar high-quality data for pharmaceuticals. Traffic to Web sites can be measured on a daily basis in terms of the number of visitors and their purchasing behavior.

Similarly, marketing activities can be recorded with increasing specificity and granularity. Whether a campaign reaches its audience by way of television, radio, cinema, print, or billboard, reliable estimates of the number of "eyeballs" that see an ad are readily available for both companies and their competitors.

Once the data is collected and organized, marketers can use time-series analysis to determine which elements of the marketing program have delivered results and which elements have underperformed. Then the marketing mix can be reallocated to accelerate growth or cut costs. Given today's technology, marketing directors have no excuse not to be able to explain the return their marketing investments have yielded.

Judgment, experience, and creativity will always play a leading role in marketing, but they should not be applied to the exclusion of a disciplined approach to ROI.

Step 2. Analyze Competitive Performance.

It is easier for a company to quantify the effects of its own marketing efforts than to estimate those of its competitors. Managers clearly do not have all the resources they would like when it comes to evaluating how the competition is performing. Nevertheless, it is possible, using the same techniques just described, to examine competitive performance and assess its effectiveness.

Thus, it is possible to track most competitors' results and activities in terms of advertising and price promotion, perform the same time-series analysis, and piece together a fairly detailed and insightful image of key competitors' strengths and weaknesses. A full marketing-mix analysis should be part and parcel of any company's assessment, as should a holistic view of the entire industry and all its players. Such an analysis can yield deep insights regarding the nature of competition and give the company undertaking the review a clear competitive advantage. Not only will company managers learn more about their own marketing processes, they may come away with a better understanding of the competition than their competitors have of themselves.

Step 3. Identify Underperforming Initiatives before They Become Too Costly.

Time-series analysis reveals important insights into how different parts of the marketing mix are performing. For example, it can track the base sales of a product or a brand as an indicator of how loyal customers are, regardless of special promotions or marketing blitzes. In addition, it can show how effectively various elements of the marketing mix are contributing to the overall effort. If television ads are having a 25 percent greater impact than, say, radio or cinema, which cost 60 percent less, managers can carry on a debate grounded in hard numbers rather than impressions or prejudices as to which media channels merit increased investment.

Marketing-mix analysis can highlight those activities with the highest ROI at the same time that it flags the ones that are likely to show negative or mediocre returns. Especially in difficult economic times, it is essential to know which activities are working well. All too often, a downturn in the economy is taken as a signal to make drastic cuts in the marketing budget without conducting a disciplined review of risks and opportunities. Numerous studies have shown that cutting marketing investment during a recession can cause more harm than good. These decisions should be analysis driven, not reactionary.

Step 4. Establish Accountability for Each Marketing Element.

Some marketing activities are designed to increase awareness of a brand; others, to introduce a new product; still others, to encourage repeat buying and build brand loyalty. Despite this division of labor, many companies evaluate their marketing campaigns by looking solely at sales, as if the marketing effort were a single-faceted activity.

Here is one area where marketing executives can take a lesson from human resource personnel. Just as key performance indicators (KPIs) are established, measured, and validated for people working for a company, so the elements of a marketing campaign must be put to the test. Just as the KPIs are established and people are rewarded for reaching or surpassing performance goals, so the various activities of the marketing campaign can be linked to incentives. For instance, managers can link an investment in television advertising to shifts in brand awareness. If the brand currently has 60 percent awareness, they might specify that the TV advertising must increase that awareness to 70 percent. Once that goal is reached, they could continue to set incremental increases, accompanied by appropriate awards.

Alternatively, suppose that marketers plan to attach an instant-purchase coupon to the larger-sized packets of their products to encourage greater consumption. If the average family's consumption of a product is 1.5 kg per month, a special consumer promotion activity could be held responsible for increasing this amount to 2 kg a month. Similar links could be established, say, between direct-mail activities and household penetration. The important matter is to establish reasonable, reachable, and *appropriate* goals for each marketing activity, specify clearly what those goals are, and reward each element appropriately if it achieves the desired outcome. In combination with ROI analysis, tracking interim "brand health" measures will create a more robust program.

Step 5. Identify Products and Markets That Offer Significant Growth Potential.

Many executives direct their companies as if they were driving a car while looking in the rearview mirror. That is, they look primarily at past sales and revenues—where they have been, not where they are going. Given that companies have to demonstrate growth, the quantifiable methods now available can prove very helpful in showing managers where they should place their company's future efforts. For example, improved forecasting changes in markets, market share, and profit margins can point a company toward competitive advantage and market dominance.

Data on demographic makeup and market profiling can help marketers forecast a brand's future household penetration, frequency of purchase and consumption, replacement rate, changes in weight and packaging, and so forth. Such measures can guide them in planning a brand's future category size and setting its market share. Manufacturers could use such information to better predict future sales and profits of their major brands and invest against a future rather than past view. In turn, more robust consumer-driven forecasts will drive down supply chain costs by reducing stock-outs and excess inventories.

While this kind of marketing data is highly quantitative, the analysis can be used to strengthen conclusions of a strategic nature. The more complex a company's operations, the more value this approach has. Today, companies evaluate markets by category or geography. A single view is now required. Take, for example, a company that sells 50 different products in 80 countries. It must be able to view results continuously during the year, both by brand or category and by market; evaluate its marketing efforts globally as well as locally to determine where the greatest opportunities lie; and be able to reallocate across categories. Once those determinations are made, resources can be aligned and reallocated to drive growth and higher profits.

Step 6. Reallocate Marketing Resources to Capitalize on New Growth Opportunities.

Some companies allocate resources based on who shouts the loudest. Others conduct detailed planning exercises at the country or category level, but few look across countries and categories. This fractured view prevents optimization. How does the country manager from France compare the opportunity there to better or worse opportunities in Germany or Spain? How does the toothpaste category manager compare the opportunity in toothpaste to better or worse opportunities in shampoo or deodorants?

Many companies find this step the most difficult to implement, in part because they rely on ineffective ways of allocating resources. Too often it is a matter of rewarding business units on the basis of last year's sales (another case of the rearview mirror approach to driving). Or managers allocate resources on the basis of a brand's current market size. Neither approach achieves its full potential as the investment (too much or too little) hinders proper growth. To make matters worse, an underrewarded business unit may find that the resources it receives actually fall below a minimum threshold of required investment and that, accordingly, the investment is wasted.

Systems and processes must be put in place to quantify and compare investment opportunities in an apples-to-apples fashion. The practical side of this equation is often hard to implement, because reallocating resources may mean the loss of jobs, products, plants, or even an entire brand. Managers rewarded for growing their own business will fight for higher than appropriate resources. If, for example, a business unit currently accounts for only 3 percent of the company's profit, but it can be shown that this unit *should* and *could* account for 6 percent in the near future, the forward-looking manager will direct an appropriate amount (perhaps as much as 6 percent) of marketing resources to that opportunity now rather than waiting for growth that depends on that investment. The problem is that this investment will probably come from a larger business with less future potential. The current larger business can, however, defend today's budget more easily than can a growing (probably less profitable) business. A data-driven process is required to ensure that growth is optimized.

A system and process based on investing today proportionally to future profit growth potential would represent a radical improvement for most companies.

CONCLUSION

Marketers rightly say that intuition, experience, and judgment play a big role in their marketing allocation decisions. While these factors will continue to serve important functions in designing and directing a marketing campaign, they alone cannot ensure a high and reliable rate of return on the marketing investment. Every part of the marketing mix—television advertisements, print, packaging, rebates and promotions, incentives to distributors, coupons for consumers, and the like—must undergo the rigorous examination that an advanced econometric analysis provides. Otherwise, its contribution to the success or failure of the marketing campaign cannot be determined with any validity.

For global allocation, a similar quantitative system and process should be deployed to facilitate the decision-making process.

In contrast to widely held opinion, the marketing process is not mere guesswork or gut reaction, nor is it purely a creative or artistic pursuit. Rather it can and must be quantified and optimized in ways that most companies have not yet taken advantage of—just as companies have streamlined their manufacturing processes or made their logistics activities more effective and efficient. Given the challenges that all companies face today in being heard above the market noise, it is essential that they begin to take a more disciplined and rigorous approach to marketing—one that not only makes their activities more effective, but also identifies where money is being wasted or misspent. The ultimate goal should be to eventually embed an ROI mindset, system, and process into the overall marketing infrastructure to help ensure that scenarios such as those that struck Levi Strauss, Gap, and Kmart are avoided.

The Case for Marketing Resource Management

Naveen K. Jain and Marianne Seiler

As global companies continue to expand their brands and marketing requirements, the instances of miscommunication, poor execution, and misspent marketing funds can increase many times. Most marketers would lose a lot of sleep as they considered the marketing problems of any large company—say, a Procter & Gamble, which has approximately 250 brands in 130 countries. If the U.S. managers for a P&G brand develop a creative way to launch a new product, their counterparts in Asia may have no easy way to get the necessary marketing information. In fact, they may end up reinventing the wheel in their local territories. Marketing teams are frequently involved in such wasteful efforts and often, because of time pressures to meet deadlines, approve marketing programs without proper due diligence for quality.

Moreover, Global 1000 companies are finding that their marketing expenses seem to know no limits. All told, these companies devoted $910 billion in 2001 to marketing spending, allocating an additional $268 billion to producing and managing the marketing output. By 2003, that output is expected to surpass $1 trillion.[1] Why so much money? Why is marketing spending ever on the increase? The answers lie predominantly in the rapidly changing global marketplace and the rise of technology.

For one thing, customers have grown a lot more sophisticated, thanks in large part to technology, and their loyalty to particular brands or companies can no longer be taken for granted. Fierce competition continues to drive companies to earmark more resources to their marketing efforts, despite the fact that marketing productivity is declining. This equation forces marketing organizations to demonstrate greater financial accountability, become more creative in setting strategy, exercise greater flexibility, and provide a more rapid response to changes in the marketing arena. They are pressured to better integrate the message and the medium in every marketing effort, however local or global it may be.

The most promising solution to marketing's problems appears in the form of *marketing resource management* (MRM). Nowadays it can be called by any number of names, including *enterprise resource management* (ERM) and *marketing process management* (MPM), but whatever name is used, the objective is still the same. Simply defined, marketing resource management seeks to integrate all aspects of marketing across the diverse spectrum of activities—from planning to developing to executing and assessing every marketing campaign, team member, communication, and tangible result. By means of this integration, managers take the chaos out of marketing, which has heretofore been excused from accountability because the process has been deemed to be creative and subjective. What used to be the province of finance and supply chain areas has now been extended to the very people who have traditionally prided themselves on their "creativity" and their exclusion from demands that they answer to the same requirements to be financially responsible.

MRM can keep tight reins on runaway expenditures and make sure that everyone who participates in the marketing effort, whether internal or external to the organization, has access to the data and knowledge they need, whenever or wherever it is needed. Furthermore, MRM insists that managers take full responsibility for the financial management of the entire marketing portfolio, that they ensure the execution is timely and profitable, and that they set rigorous measures for performance.

SEARCHING FOR A DEEP SOLUTION

Researchers at Accenture's Institute for Strategic Change interviewed numerous chief marketing officers across a variety of industries and business units to uncover the primary obstacles to improving marketing effectiveness and efficiency. The survey revealed four key problem areas:

- *Inefficiency.* Recent environmental changes have left marketing managers with little time or resources to focus on building clarity and consistency of marketing efforts across the enterprise. Pilots conducted among consumer goods and consumer electronics companies demonstrate that $30 million to $70 million in annual benefits could be realized by enhancing the productivity of marketing teams, eliminating redundancy across various internal and external participants, and increasing the speed to market of new initiatives.

- *Noncollaboration.* Creating and executing an effective program requires that marketers work and communicate with thousands of geographically dispersed internal and external participants. Collaboration efforts suffer significantly from wasted time and unnecessary duplication. Accenture's survey of one set of companies' experiences focused on a revamped platform in trade marketing to improve communication with 725 sales representatives and 25 customer service representatives across three major business units. This system, we found, increased selling time, sales revenues, and promotions effectiveness, while providing $10 million to $12 million in identified cost savings. Similar savings can be realized by addressing collaboration opportunities in developing new products and offerings, advertising, promotions, events management, campaign management, and the like.

- *Inaccessibility.* Marketing organizations spend millions each year creating huge repositories of information and data such as direct-mail copy, photos, point-of-sale materials, videos, and music. Although they may count as tangible assets, these data banks collect dust and remain largely inaccessible to the people who could make the best use of them. Marketing teams simply do not have access to the tools they need to locate, share, and direct those assets to achieve the maximum benefits. Most are not able to manage knowledge effectively and standardize best processes. Thus, they spend considerable amounts of time and money reinventing the wheel. By developing a repository of marketing knowledge and digital assets, integrating these assets with the marketing execution workflow, and collaboratively sharing these assets, however, a manager can offer significant benefits to marketers. Large expenditures in these areas by automotive companies and other consumer goods companies clearly show the benefits of this opportunity.

- *High turnover rate of employees.* For any number of reasons, the high number of departing employees inhibits marketing groups from effectively leveraging past marketing lessons. As a result, they have to spend scarce resources on training. But even that money, we found, is being wasted. Accenture's research shows that many companies have created knowledge intranets that are not being used frequently because they lack context and integration with the work being performed by marketing teams. Thus, considerable time and money is wasted in relearning, retraining, and reinvention.

Recognizing the magnitude of these problems and sensing the potential for value in being able to solve them, many organizations have in the past relied on custom-developed solutions. For example, marketers today frequently resort to e-mail, spreadsheets, online calendars, team spaces, and even basic project management software to help them do their jobs more efficiently. They use software designed to handle specific activities such as campaign management, e-mail marketing, digital asset management, and customer data analysis. However, these solutions have had limited success, chiefly because they address problems only on the superficial level. Most efforts have dealt with the problems of a single marketing channel (Web, retail, etc.) or function (direct marketing, promotions, etc.). They do not offer solutions that go the depths of the problem. Lacking integration across disparate systems, they are not usually tied to other pertinent or supporting systems such as marketing data warehouses and lead management. Providing a limited application of technology solutions, these initiatives have redesigned some key processes, but failed to install supporting technology to cement improvements. They are not sophisticated enough, in fact, to address deeper problems in the company such as organizational structure, career path development, compensation, performance management, training, or leadership development to support new marketing processes.

It is no wonder, then, that many Global 1000 companies now acknowledge that these complications must be overcome and are searching for a deep solution.

CREATING ORDER OUT OF CHAOS

The benefits of streamlining the marketing effort can be felt almost immediately. In many industries (for example, consumer goods companies, electronics, pharmaceuticals, and financial and credit card organizations) we find that more than 80 percent of marketers' time today is spent managing the various activities associated with executing a marketing program or campaign. Most of these people are "firefighters," working to control the conflagrations that flare up continually in marketing activities. This leaves them little time to do such critically strategic work as brand architecture development, portfolio management, and new product development. As a result, the quality of their output and the success rate of their marketing activities suffer.

To improve efficiency and effectiveness, MRM solutions have begun to emerge, thanks in part to highly sophisticated technology. Typically, this support improves marketing performance through enhancing the collaboration among participants, both internal and external to the marketing program per se. It accelerates and coordinates in real time the scheduling of activities, management of marketing financials, approval processes, and execution of marketing projects. Furthermore, it provides effective, online leveraging of marketing knowledge and assets integrated across all activities. In short, marketing resource management initiatives can generate both revenue enhancement and cost-reduction benefits.

THE BUSINESS CASE

Based on our experience in pilot programs with many companies, we have identified major benefits associated with MRM solutions, as presented Exhibit 27-1, which depicts a marketing value creation framework.

Efficiencies in marketing execution can result in large cost savings for organizations. For example, eliminating non-value-added activities from marketing processes reduces the costs those organizations incur to create and implement programs. Companies can either use this to reduce costs or leverage the increased capacity to drive growth through new products. Shared knowledge and best practices reduce marketing costs by preventing the reinvention-of-the-wheel syndrome and minimizing the cost of learning. Tasks are performed more proficiently, thus increasing speed to market and throughput capacity. The marketing organization produces more programs with higher success rates. When organizations are more effective and

EXHIBIT 27-1.   Marketing value creation framework.

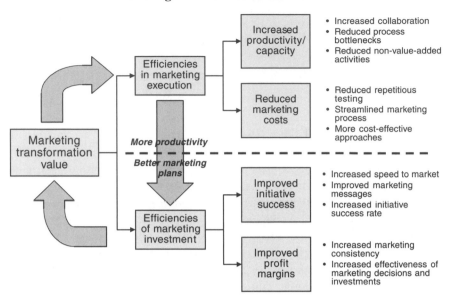

efficient in program development and management, nonworking marketing spending also declines.

Improvements in marketing effectiveness affect program success, increasing revenue and profits. For instance, redesign and automation of critical marketing processes can help increase capacity, thereby allowing companies to conduct not just more campaigns but better-targeted ones. Targeting improves campaign success rates, increasing customer acquisition (market share) and retention levels (lifetime value). Further, targeting allows for more refined pricing strategies, much as Gap Inc. has done with its Old Navy stores, which aim at a young clientele interested in lower-priced fashions. A company often can increase prices without negatively affecting acquisition or retention rates.

In addition, the use of knowledge management and best practices facilitates more effective decision making, driving greater revenue and profitability. Organizations are able to redirect spending and reallocate assets to achieve the greatest profit.

Accenture's research of global marketing companies shows that $35 million to $70 million in annual benefits can be achieved from a typical $1-billion brand by addressing the marketing efficiency and effectiveness areas. The specific components of this benefit case are set forth in Exhibit 27-2.

Our experience with clients suggests that efforts to enhance enterprise marketing execution management can provide a return ranging from 6 to 12 times the investments made in technology applications, technology hardware, and related professional services.

EXHIBIT 27-2. **Marketing transformation benefits (illustrative example).**

Transformation value drivers	Range of benefits
Increased productivity/capacity	• 10–13 percent increase in marketing capacity
Reduced marketing costs	• 2–6 percent reduction in marketing related expenses
Improved initiative success	• 0.02–0.03 percent increase in profit margin (as percentage of sales)
Effective resource allocation	• 1–2.5 percent increase in profit margin (as percentage of sales)

THE MRM SOLUTION

An effective MRM solution must include three essential elements: (1) what we call the *marketing workbench,* a design for and the implementation of an integrated marketing technology platform; (2) a transformation of the marketing process, specifically one that redefines the way work is done by redesigning the core marketing processes and leveraging the appropriate technology tools; and (3) a realignment of the organization to support the new way of working, including the sharing of knowledge across the entire marketing effort.

Marketing Workbench Vision

Unlike single-channel or point solutions, the marketing workbench provides an integrated platform for marketing execution (Exhibit 27-3). It incorporates three components:

Marketing Process Workspace. This component focuses on providing a place where the marketers come to create, develop, and implement specific marketing campaigns and programs ranging from developing advertising strategy to creating direct-mail pieces to managing the implementation of promotions to analyzing the effectiveness of sales leads. Marketing process workspace solutions assist organizations with all stages of a program, from data gathering to program creation to execution, analysis, and procurement. Typically, the marketing process workspace comprises multiple technology or software programs, each of which is dedicated to a single aspect of the marketing mix—for instance, media planning and buying, mass media campaign management, targeted campaign management, sales channel communication, promotions, point of sale, market research, and lead management.

EXHIBIT 27-3.   Marketing workbench vision.

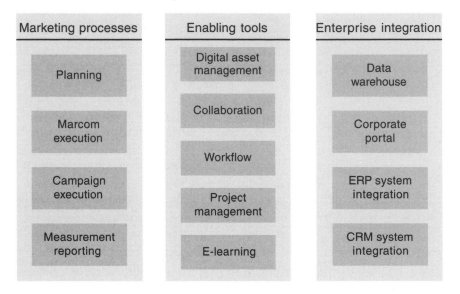

The workbench solution provides templates for critical marketing activities, allowing marketing teams to select the right project from pull-down menus and to see instantly the recommended steps for completing the project. Each step includes a suggested time frame, resource requirements, and templates for content creation, best-in-class examples, and required digital assets. With minimal effort, a marketing team can customize these suggestions to fit its particular needs and create a real-time work environment that can be shared with both internal and external participants.

Robust solutions provide marketers with the know-how (principles, tools, case studies, best practices, and the like) necessary to maximize program success. New marketing knowledge and assets are added to the solution in real time, so it is always current. In addition, the solution is flexible and can be easily customized to each organization's specific circumstances and needs.

Enabling Technology Tools.   Solutions in this area provide a foundation for work across the marketing organization to be streamlined. They assist marketers in managing and coordinating work across functions and channels. Unlike marketing process workspace solutions, these technologies can be used by all functional areas in marketing. Key technology tools include the following:

- *Digital asset management.* Marketing assets can exist in a variety of digitized forms, such as video, audio, graphics, and documents. To use them effectively, the team has to be able to search extensively and retrieve items, often converting or reformatting them from one form to another. Using this robust technology, a marketing team can access those assets in its process workspace and collaborate with internal and external participants. It can establish online working sessions so participants can check in to share their ideas in real time and refine assets.

- *Collaboration.* Marketing teams have to be able to interact with geographically dispersed internal and external participants on a real-time basis. Nothing is so infuriating to collaborators as the discovery that the item they have been working on for the past four hours is actually an old document, already revised many times by their colleagues. To prevent such wasted effort and frustration, a robust collaboration software application has to provide collaborators with a means of checking in and checking out the digital assets. This can include an automatic e-mail notification for all changes to a document. Team members are immediately made aware of project assignments or changes in status. The technology can include built-in approval and review tools for online meetings, as well as the ability to collaborate around a work in process in order to make sure it is executed accurately and efficiently.

- *Project and workflow management.* This is an easy-to-use tool that manages the workflow of many users. Team members can create and leverage best-in-class project templates, achieve a close integration of projects, and determine which items are actionable and which document repositories can be accessed. In addition, users can define a portfolio of projects, customize their associated calendars, and manage the project's budget and allocation of monetary assets. This solution tool sets milestones and measures progress across project portfolios, assigns roles and activities across internal and external participants, tracks financials across those projects, establishes a project calendar, and dynamically manages the project's execution.

- *Knowledge management.* It goes without saying that an online repository of marketing knowledge and intellectual property (for example, marketing plans or best-practice templates) can provide marketers with key information and insights in real time. From the marketer's perspective, a robust knowledge management system must push the right knowledge at the right point in the marketing activity to the correct user. It must allow the marketing teams to access online how-to guides, performance simulation training tools, and the online classroom training environment. In addition, it must be customizable, allowing organizations to tailor templates, guides, simulation tools, and training materials as needed.

Enterprise Integration.   Powerful MRM solutions are worthless if they are not user friendly and do not allow for the import and export of critical information from enterprise systems—what might be called the organization's data warehouse. This is why the simplicity of the MRM user interface is more important than any single marketing process workspace or enabling capability tool. If it cannot access the legacy systems an organization has in place, it obviously cannot integrate their contents and programs.

Marketing teams often need sales and financial information from internal systems, scanner data, information from major retail customers, competitive intelligence information—in short, all the enterprise resources. The ability to share information with these systems, to access the information easily from the marketing data marts, and to import or export the desired information is critical. Because so many solutions today cannot provide that capability, marketing teams must depend on system integrators working with them to create this customized solution for their clients.

Emerging analytical tools and dynamic access to customer information require that marketing teams evaluate their marketing programs frequently. They must have access to those tools so that they can manage the changes to their marketing process workspace on a real-time basis. In addition, the MRM solutions must provide the flexibility to integrate with the preexisting corporate portals, including the Internet and intranets.

Finally, the effective solution must consider CRM and sales force effectiveness (SFE) systems if it is to provide true integration of marketing, sales, and service functions. Enterprise marketing requires tight integration of those functions. During the past few years, strong CRM systems have been implemented to manage the 360° view of the customer and integration of messages across channels. Integrating these systems with the MRM solution will provide for end-to-end integration of marketing activities in an enterprise.

As marketing teams are being pressured for increased financial accountability, they are increasingly concerned not only with managing the marketing activities but also with tracking the financial performance of those activities. This dual responsibility requires them to integrate financials with the projects and keep tight integration with the enterprise financial systems.

APPROACHING THE IDEAL SOLUTION

Today, MRM vendors fit primarily into one of three categories: integrated marketing application suite providers, point-solution providers, and customer relationship management system or analytic suite providers. Unfortunately, no MRM vendor at present offers a complete technology solution. Those technology solutions that are commercially available to marketers, however, are likely to be more complete than most in-house solutions. Although still relatively small (but starting to gain momentum), integrated marketing application suite providers such as Aprimo are expanding the breadth and depth of their solutions. They take a holistic vision of MRM, and their solutions integrate many of the components of marketing process workspace and enabling technology tools.

A second group to address MRM concerns comprises the point-solution providers, such as Assetlink, Artesia, Documentum, and Webware, which offer solutions for managing projects, digital assets, and collaborative work environments. Many of these players have started to expand the depth and breadth of their solutions through targeted acquisitions. Other providers, such as Siebel or Kana, are CRM-focused, whereas still others, such as E.piphany, Inc., or SPSS Inc., provide analytic suites. While these vendors previously have been focused on consolidating their positions in the CRM and analytic space, they have now started to expand their current solutions to include MRM solutions.

Although creating a technology platform, redesigning key processes, and realigning the organization are not new dimensions of a process transformation effort, they are indeed more difficult to implement successfully in the marketing space. Changing the habits of marketing teams who thrive on flexible ways of working is not easy and often meets with resistance from the teams. However, companies have begun to realize the potential for adding value. They are all experimenting with new ways to make marketing execution more rigorous.

Transforming Marketing Processes through Technology

Thanks to the vast changes in technology, enterprise processes including finance, supply chain logistics, and CRM all have undergone major redesigns in the past 10 years. As a result, they have become much more effective and efficient. Marketing processes, however, have not been so fortunate. Sweeping environmental and competitive changes have made it difficult for marketers to find the time and resources to undertake similar changes. Today that situation is changing, as smart marketers at companies as diverse as Procter & Gamble, Coca-Cola, Philips Electronics, and London-based Diageo PLC are starting to understand that their tactical marketing can benefit from such an undertaking. That said, it is our experience that most companies still are focusing only on some targeted processes rather than on the entire marketing suite.

Anyone redesigning marketing processes must look at all aspects of the value chain. Primary attention should focus on the technology that enables best-in-class processes rather than today's inefficient practices. Having an understanding of the best practices for process redesign across the entire value chain is critical to leveraging full value. Exhibit 27-4 shows a typical architecture of marketing processes, including certain subprocesses that could be redesigned and supported with enabling technology.

EXHIBIT 27-4.   Marketing process architecture.

Strategic direction	Execution management	Customer management	Measurement and reporting
• Customer strategy • Branding • Product management • Portfolio management • Planning/ budgeting • Procurement	• Program management Marcom management Campaign management Internal marketing Lead management • Channel management	• Customer insight Valuation Segmentation Predictive modeling	• Tracking/ reporting • Marketing scorecard

As with any complex revision, addressing marketing processes in some areas can provide immediate returns, whereas those in other areas surely will take longer. For example, highly tactical marketing processes such as marketing communications (marcom) or lead management often see the fastest returns from process redesign and technology enablement. More strategic processes, such as developing brand strategy, are likely to have longer payback periods. A first step, in any case, is to understand where the pain is likely to occur when changes take place, and then to prioritize those processes for improvement.

Companies that take fast but structured steps in transforming marketing tend to have the greatest success with the change. They first develop the value case and prioritize high-opportunity areas. Then they develop a pilot plan that focuses simultaneously on process redesign and technology enablement. After the pilot has proven successful, rapid customization and deployment of the solution across multiple brands, geographies, and business groups follow.

Experience with many of the clients in this area has demonstrated a need for this integrated approach. An international bank, for example, found itself slipping behind its competition, particularly in key marketing and sales capabilities. As a result, it was losing its most valued customers to local and foreign competitors. To address the situation, the company transformed itself through key strategic initiatives, invested in the necessary technology to restructure marketing activities to improve profitability and long-term growth, and implemented an organizationwide, phased program to introduce the required skills, tools, processes and information systems that provided quality customer information, sales tracking, campaign management, and segmentation capabilities. The program aims to deliver a net present value (NPV) of $32 million and an investment rate of return (IRR) of 129 percent in four years. In addition, benefits from identified quick wins, implemented within six months, are sufficient to finance longer-term changes.

Realigning the Organization

Because MRM initiatives are holistic, changes in organizational enablers must accompany process and technology redesign if full value is to be realized. It will come as no surprise that people who prefer the traditional, relaxed ways of marketing and believe that this comfort is important for their creativity are among the chief resistors of MRM innovation. As some of these individuals have experimented with an MRM solution, however, they have begun to realize its benefits even as they discover it does not threaten their creativity. Building this degree of comfort with a new technology, not to mention fundamentally changing how work is done and decisions are made, requires a strong focus on organizational alignment.

Managers undertaking this level of change must be sensitive to seven aspects of the organization where MRM can have some of its greatest impact:

1. *Organizational alignment.* Managers must separate core activities from non-core ones and ensure customer or segment alignment across the enterprise.

They must assess all outsourcing opportunities and the marketing procurement process alignment.

2. *Decision-making governance.* MRM can significantly affect how decisions are made and how governance processes work. Addressing these areas will be critical to implementing the necessary changes in processes.

3. *Leadership development.* Managers must ensure that top performers are aligned with strategic businesses and that succession candidates are identified, trained, and tracked. This development requires a deep understanding of skills necessary for succession.

4. *Compensation.* It is a given that compensation drives the right behaviors; both financial and nonfinancial metrics have to be incorporated into employees' rewards.

5. *Performance management.* MRM managers should set clear performance expectations, tying performance to compensation.

6. *Training and development.* Roles and responsibilities must be in alignment, gaps in skills must be identified, and a curriculum to address those gaps must be established.

7. *Career path development.* Cross-functional team members should be aligned, with their career paths clearly articulated and communicated.

These areas figured prominently in the case of an international package goods company that recently underwent a complete marketing organization reinvention. The company wanted to redefine its marketing department's structure and roles to improve efficiency and productivity, reduce costs, and refocus on its primary value-added activities. The company began by eliminating all activities that produced little or no value. It then conducted scenario planning sessions and what-if analyses to determine the most effective and cost-efficient marketing organization for the company. This work resulted in new roles and functions for marketing personnel, and it led to the creation of centers of expertise in areas such as research and packaging. With a refocus on pure marketing in which certain activities were outsourced to the centers of excellence or external providers, the project resulted in a 4 percent reduction in marketing overhead. Not only did the project save the company a great deal of money; it also made its marketing processes much more efficient and productive.

CONCLUSION

As we have seen, today's marketing environment—the demand for financial accountability, speed of execution and decision making, and globally integrated marketing activities and messages—makes it imperative that companies streamline the execution of their marketing activities. They must search for the creative solutions that can transform their marketing execution and management processes. Typically, these solutions are technology-enabled, integrating applications such as digital asset management, project management, collaboration, and e-learning. When combined with the marketing activities and enterprise data sources, these solutions can provide a comprehensive marketing workbench to enhance efficiency and effectiveness of marketing. Only by developing the integrated marketing workbench—and redefining the way marketing processes are executed while aligning the organization and its culture—can companies generate the benefits and drive their competitive advantage.

CRM at Work

Communications:
Recovering from the Fall,
Repositioning for the Future

Julie F. Nelson

I n recent years, reports from the telecommunications industry have read like something out of a Dickens novel—"It was the best of times and the worst of times."

Fueled by optimistic projections of growth and widespread adoption of innovative communications technologies by businesses and consumers alike, telcos around the world spent heavily to build the infrastructure and capacity to capitalize on the anticipated emerging market. Investors and financial institutions rewarded this optimism with a steady stream of venture capital (banks alone invested $320 billion in telcos between 1999 and early 2001)[1] and dramatic boosts in stock prices. And telco executives and industry observers everywhere were talking about the new world that would dawn (with telcos at its center) when ubiquitous broadband Internet access would finally make the convergence of communications, computing, and media a reality.

Few, if any, telcos could have anticipated the harsh environment that awaited them as the new millennium dawned. Not only would the significant growth in consumer and business uptake not materialize, banks and investment houses would suddenly turn off the venture capital tap. Instead of rushing to rewire their homes for broadband access, consumers would turn off their landlines and begin taking advantage of the free long distance and cheap minutes offered by wireless providers. Saddled with expensive overcapacity and huge debt from the years of spending, telcos were forced to resort to price slashing just to keep afloat.

Further complicating the situation was the fact that over the years, as telcos added a plethora of new products and services, customers became increasingly confused. As a result, many customers either ignored the new offerings because it was easier than trying to sort through the complexity or played the game of musical providers and switched every few months to a carrier with a better price.

Today, telcos are faced with a steep challenge indeed: differentiating themselves in the view of increasingly frustrated and demanding customers in an industry characterized by intense competition, vicious price wars, and complex offerings.

A SILOED APPROACH

Seeking to stabilize their customer bases and restore some loyalty to their customers, many telcos have spent heavily on new CRM technologies for their customer service functions—particularly billing and call centers. The motivation for these efforts is compelling: Research published in the *Harvard Business Review* found that increasing customer loyalty by just 5 percent could increase a telecom's profits by more than 50 percent.[2] Another study, by e-business service provider ICL for a U.K. service provider, revealed that a 10 percent churn in a telecom's most profitable customers would result in a drop in profits of more than 25 percent.[3]

In addition to billing and call center technologies, many telcos have begun directing considerable effort toward serving customers better via the Web by installing self-service options, online chat, and other such features. The move by many carriers to beef up their e-CRM efforts is no surprise. The Web provides an opportunity for service carriers to differentiate themselves with 24/7 access and support at a much lower cost than that of employing live service representatives. WorldCom has, perhaps, been one of the most aggressive in this area, having moved the majority of its CRM focus online.[4]

Other telcos also have expanded the services and tools available to customers online. Ameritech, Sprint, Southwestern Bell, and Pacific Bell Web sites all feature a virtual assistant designed to make customers feel as though they are interacting with a real person,[5] while Ameritech and Net2Phone, among others, use tools that enable customers to ask questions in natural language and receive appropriate answers.[6]

Service providers also are expanding online services for their business customers, which typically represent higher margins and require more complex interactions. AT&T, for example, consolidated its CRM functions targeting large and midsize businesses into a single organization called the Web-Based Interactive Advantage CRM service, which it introduced in 1999. The system handles 140,000 customers and performs 1.5 million transactions per month, enabling customers to place "orders, change or delete service, change network configuration by rerouting calls or service, and view and dispute bills online in real-time."[7]

Germany's Deutsche Telekom also was an early adopter of Web-based service programs for its business customers. The large telco introduced an Internet bill presentment application that enabled business customers to access their monthly invoice and billing data online. With this application, businesses could check their phone bills; group, sort, and filter call detail; validate phone activity; allocate communications cost across business units; and analyze their usage of telecommunications services to budget for the future.

Some telecommunications providers are also moving their CRM efforts into other channels. SBC Communications, for instance, uses the wireless channel for its award-winning field sales force automation system. More than 27,000 installation and repair technicians use this tool, the "intelligent field device," to access service requests online, search repair databases and conduct diagnostic testing.[8]

All of this focus on service does not mean that telcos ignored sales and marketing. On the contrary, most telcos found themselves in a continual race to add new customers, and they implemented aggressive mass-mailing and telemarketing campaigns.

MOVE TOWARD INTEGRATION

The track record of recent CRM initiatives among telcos has been mixed, however. Despite significant outlays of money for billing, call centers, and other service technologies, telcos still rank at or near the bottom in customer loyalty and satisfaction ratings, and continue to bleed customers. The "blanket-the-earth" sales and marketing programs of many telcos resulted in extremely high costs to acquire customers— many of whom shortly left in favor of a sweeter deal from a competitor.

Recognizing this, leading telcos have begun to shift their focus from treating marketing, sales, and service as stand-alone functions to integrating their CRM efforts across these three areas. In the process, they are reorganizing themselves around the customer (instead of around specific products or business units, such as wireless, long distance, and Internet services). These efforts, which will be increasingly critical to the success of companies such as telcos, which have extremely large customer bases comprising individuals with widely varying tastes and preferences, are beginning to bear fruit for companies hungry for good news.

Verizon, for instance, is taking this path, adjusting the company's infrastructure to allow a single view of its customers from which it can establish a customer's preferred channel of interaction and identify customer needs. The telco plans to replace its traditional product focus with a customer focus.[9] Similarly, AT&T also has begun to rework itself around the customer, establishing an enterprisewide CRM strategy based on the integration of customer information across numerous lines of service, each of which previously had a separate CRM strategy, channels, and touch points. The company's goals are many: increased customer loyalty, improved profitability, reduced costs and time to revenue for new services, and the establishment of a cost-effective method to provide targeted offers to distinct customer groups.[10]

Working hand in hand with such integration efforts is an emphasis on customer data analysis and segmentation. Increasingly, telecommunications carriers are looking for methods to identify and retain their best customers through the use of analytical tools. Indeed, many of the telcos seeking to attain a single view of their customers are adopting analytical techniques to segment customers by their value to the company and to predict customer behavior.

Sprint's Global Markets Group, for instance, integrated its data and, with the use of analytical tools and automation software, sought to increase the amount of business Sprint does with its business customers and to identify customers who may be about to defect. The company determined that customers who subscribe to two or more services are 25 to 50 percent more likely to stay with Sprint than are customers who use only one service. The system, which went live in October 2000, has saved the company a significant amount of money by enabling the company to conduct its own analysis and database marketing, which was previously handled by a third party; this has enabled the company to conduct the analysis quicker, allowing for faster reaction to changes in the marketplace. With its new predictive ability, Sprint was able to reduce customer churn significantly.[11]

BellSouth, too, has established data-mining and analysis capabilities to support upselling and cross-selling opportunities and to increase retention. The system offers personalized incentives to its high-value customers and enables BellSouth customer service representatives to provide different levels of service based on a customer's value. For instance, high-value customers are routed more quickly in the company's call centers and are directed to the most skilled representatives.[12]

BOUYGUES TELECOM: CATCHING THE WAVE

Perhaps one of the best examples of a telco capitalizing on the next wave of CRM is Paris-based Bouygues Telecom. The situation Bouygues faced recently was not dissimilar to that experienced by telcos in many other parts of Europe and North America. France's mobile telephony industry grew enormously around the turn of the century as eager new users embraced mobile technology in droves. This growth, however, did not come cheaply. The costs to acquire new mobile phone users in France are among the highest in Europe, because carriers heavily subsidize handset and retailer costs to make it easier for new users to sign up for service. As a result, carriers face a pressing need to maximize their average return per user (ARPU) by retaining their best customers for as long as possible. This challenge is particularly acute in the face of slowing growth due to market saturation and the impending expiration of many original customers' service plans.

Bouygues's experience mirrors that of the industry at large. With more than 5 million wireless customers, Bouygues rapidly increased market share in the past five years. However, the company recently recognized that it no longer could count on significant new-customer acquisition to maintain or increase its 18 percent share of the French mobile market. Instead, the company felt the key to future success would be its ability to meet the following goals:

- Increase each customer's mobile phone usage.
- Increase the sales of additional services to each user.
- Increase the length of each customer relationship to generate greater customer lifetime revenues.
- Steer customers to other Bouygues products and services if all efforts to keep them as mobile customers fail.

Achieving these goals, however, would require a significant change in how Bouygues operated. For example, to more effectively match service offerings to existing or emerging customer needs, the company needed to learn much more about each customer. And to increase the chance of converting a marketing lead to a sale, the company had to be more targeted with its marketing messages. None of this was possible with the mass-marketing, mass-acquisition model Bouygues had adopted to capitalize on a growing market.

Bouygues began the project by defining the data it would need to effectively analyze and predict its customers' behavior, identify consumer trends, and pinpoint patterns that would indicate needs for particular products or services. With more detailed customer data, the company reasoned, it could get more granular views of specific customer groups or clusters and, thus, better understand their needs and preferences. For example, simply by specifying a handful of variables in different combinations (such as amount spent per month, types of products or services purchased, geographic location, length of time as a customer, annual income, etc.), the company found that its customer base could be segmented into 600 to 700 smaller clusters with similar characteristics.

The team also developed a marketing plan and supporting processes that would enable Bouygues to shift its efforts from mass marketing within a few large segments to real-time marketing that addresses the current needs of each customer cluster. This real-time marketing would maximize the use of the myriad communications channels that Bouygues has with its customers—including customers' mobile phones, monthly bill inserts, the Bouygues company magazine, postal letters, e-mails, and personalized Web sites. To be able to execute such campaigns, the company had to enlarge and reorganize its marketing department into dedicated teams—some focused strictly on marketing products and services to prospective customers and others on promoting retention of existing customers.

Rounding out the project, the team developed a data warehouse and marketing automation system based on a commercially available software package. This system is critical to the success of the project because it helps analyze customer data, orchestrate marketing campaigns, and manage the complexity of Bouygues's new marketing approach.

As a result of the project (which took just 10 months to complete) Bouygues has significantly bolstered its ability to develop and execute more effective marketing campaigns, and do so much more frequently and more quickly. With its new processes and system, Bouygues can target a much more narrowly defined range of customer clusters. As a result, the company can make more accurate predictions of customer behavior and thus personalize its marketing campaigns and messages.

In the past, the company conducted four marketing campaigns per month, principally in the form of direct mail, to its three main customer segments (high value, medium value, and low value). Now it executes 70 campaigns each month to various customer clusters via voice or text messages directly to customers' handsets. An important feature is that these campaigns can be designed either to boost revenue from a particular customer cluster (e.g., promoting a particular value-added service such as caller ID or voice mail) or to extend the lifetime of the customer contract (e.g., providing an incentive for customers to renew their wireless contract).

These new capabilities have translated into a number of quantifiable business benefits for Bouygues. Customer contacts are up 450 percent, the accuracy of segmentation has tripled, and the time needed to create and execute a marketing campaign has been reduced by 75 percent. Since the project was completed, Bouygues has boosted the average time a customer stays with the company from approximately four years to five, and the company has dramatically increased the revenue it gets from each customer—so much so that Bouygues' ARPU has gone from last to first among telecom companies in France.

But despite the success of the project, Bouygues cannot rest on its laurels. The third-generation (3G) mobile networks being rolled out across Europe will make it necessary for Bouygues to change its marketing approach once again.

"In the future, our campaigns are going to have to be more and more targeted," noted Olivier Laury, postpaid customer marketing director. "Before our current project, we did four campaigns a month, and each campaign was directed to approximately 300,000 people. Today, we conduct about 70 campaigns a month and each one targets 30,000 people. When 3G is fully operational, we'll be able to offer an even greater range of products and services. At that time, we plan to be conducting approximately 150 campaigns a month to even smaller audiences, getting us much closer to the 'one-to-one' marketing approach we are striving for."

GVT DIALS IN CUSTOMER SERVICE

A South American telco also is using integration as its mantra, but is taking it a step further: Instead of just integrating customer databases across marketing, sales, and service, it is integrating all of its CRM applications with key business systems across the company to ensure superior responsiveness to customer requests and more efficient customer acquisition.

Global Village Telecom (GVT), headquartered in Brazil, is a telco start-up that likes a challenge—or several challenges. The young company, formed in 1999, has taken on a huge, well-entrenched competitor. It has laid stakes in an area of Brazil in which a former wireline start-up has already failed. And it has created a CRM environment designed to provide immediate knowledge of the telco's area of coverage, support two call centers, back up a cutting-edge Web site, and support a database of marketing information and sales leads. On top of all that, GVT has had to work fast, installing a total network infrastructure for its services in just six short months.

Ruy Shiozawa, GVT's chief information officer, also likes a challenge. Launching the service, he says, was a "very important and emotional moment." Shiozawa started the company's CRM project with the larger goal of making information technology (IT) a strong business enabler. He also was charged with overseeing a long list of complicated projects. He needed to create teams of consultants, vendors, and employees; select flexible, easily maintained software; and integrate several software packages for billing, workforce management, and provisioning. Furthermore, these IT projects also had to support the best practices identified by GVT's various business group executives.

Above all, GVT had to implement a fully integrated online platform to enter the market quickly. To achieve that, the company pulled together 17 projects that involved more than 240 people at its peak, working together over a six-month period. The projects included system implementation, a data center, two call centers, new local- and wide-area networks, and software suites including billing, enterprise resource planning (ERP), business intelligence, provisioning, geographic information system (GIS), and CRM. The cost of all this work was substantial. To build its network of 860,000 telephone lines (both wireline and wireless) GVT planned to invest the equivalent of $840 million in 2000 to 2001, with funding to be obtained from four equipment vendors.

The GVT challenge actually began in 1999. That year, the start-up won its first telco license from Brazil's National Agency of Telecommunications, better known as Anatel. Earlier, as part of Brazil's effort to reform its national telecom system, the government had divided Brazil into four sections for fixed-line telephony, and Anatel was chartered to open the country's telecom market to competition. Prior to deregulation, all Brazilian phone service was handled by two state-owned monopolies: interstate and international long-distance service by a company called Embratel, and intrastate and local service by another called Telebrás. Now, under an interim plan, each region is to have local telephone service provided by two telcos: the incumbent and a newcomer, also known as a "mirror" provider. (Similarly, long-distance service has an incumbent provider, Embratel, and a mirror, Intelig.) Anatel has defined annual operating targets for the telcos, with the provision that those that anticipated the target for 2003 would be allowed to compete in other areas by 2002, or as soon as they met the target.

GVT's license allowed it to act as the mirror provider in Brazil's Region II—a huge area, nearly 3 million square kilometers in all, spanning Brazil's entire southwestern border and part of the northern border, extending into the interior. Region II encloses 9 of Brazil's 27 states and includes the country's capital city, Brasília. Despite its size, however, the region is home to fewer than 39 million people. Put another way, while Region II represents roughly a third of Brazil's total land area, it accounts for only a fifth of the total population.

That said, telco revenue from Region II is large, the equivalent of $2.5 billion a year, according to Anatel. Nearly 45 percent of that, or roughly $1.13 billion, comes from local service, the single largest sector. Other large-revenue sectors in the region are long-distance service, which accounts for 18 percent of total revenue; interregion networks, accounting for 14 percent; and data, 10 percent.

New Telco Type

In keeping with its charter, GVT represents a new kind of telco. For one, it is coowned by three international groups: Magnum Group, IDB Group, and Merrill Lynch Group. Together they will have invested the equivalent of $1.4 billion in GVT since 2000. GVT also places a high priority on social responsibility. To that end, it has invested in local educational, cultural, and arts programs to help produce concerts, plays, and art exhibits and to provide Internet service to school classrooms.

But GVT's incumbent competitor in Region II, Brazil Telecom (BrT), has good performance. It enjoys one of the highest quality ratings from Anatel as well as deep coverage of the market, especially among affluent residential customers. In fact, prior to GVT's entry in the market, BrT already had some 8 million customers and served every major city in the region.

GVT realized that its competitive advantage would have to be based on sheer speed—both the speed of its network and that of its own people to implement new services. So GVT designed its network to be 100 percent digital from the start. This enables the company to offer integrated voice, data, and image services. For example, the company's Next Generation Network (NGN) service offers several telephony and Internet Protocol (IP) services that are new to Latin America. These include video on demand and interactive video games. For the future, GVT is developing new services that include desktop videoconferencing, video-based caller ID, and caller self-provisioning.

Two other aspects of the GVT project were the creation of two call centers with more than 180 seats and the development of a comprehensive communications network that links 45 remote sites and includes retail stores, call centers, and switch sites. All this information technology does not come cheaply. GVT estimates it spent the equivalent of $50 million on IT in 2000 alone.

Steep Challenges Loomed

At the project's start, CIO Shiozawa and his IT team at GVT faced several challenging goals:

- Create a centralized billing system to handle both voice and data services, and to provide a single invoice to all customers.
- Establish seamless integration between the various systems.
- Ensure that all customer care, billing, and provisioning systems are scalable and upgradeable.

As they dug further into the project, the IT team identified five more detailed challenges—and, for each, unique solutions:

Time.   GVT had just six months to build a complete set of systems, integrate them, develop the business processes, and train its staff. The deadline corresponded to the timing of the Anatel operational goals, which GVT wanted to hit so that it would be eligible to expand into other regions of Brazil.

Solution: To move this quickly while still guaranteeing quality and integration, GVT adopted a project management office (PMO) concept. This involved creating a series of teams led and managed by a PMO team. This master team ultimately was responsible for managing the complete launch; none of the other teams could change a milestone or timeline without the PMO team's approval. The PMO team also met weekly with all secondary teams to review their projects.

Teamwork.   With the launch effort so enormous—17 project teams manned by 240 professionals—many of those working on the project would not be GVT employees. Instead, the teams would include employees of consulting firms and both hardware and software suppliers. How could GVT make these people, many of whom had never met before, feel and act as if they were part of a single team?

Solution: To encourage teamwork and help break down organizational silos, GVT found it necessary to employ a variety of techniques that generated a feeling of being part of a single team and that rewarded the team for accomplishments. For example, GVT printed business cards for all participants that identified them as part of the IT launch project, rather than as representatives of consulting, software, or hardware companies. Further, the PMO organized and sponsored parties, soccer games, and other fun events for team members after they had achieved major project milestones. "Let's keep working hard, but also smiling and celebrating," CIO Shiozawa reminded his staff.

Software Selection.   GVT needed software that was flexible and easily maintained, so it would not have to depend on the vendors for ongoing maintenance. But it also needed proven solutions.

Solution: GVT set a seven-point checklist that it used to select vendor partners. To be approved, vendors had to demonstrate flexibility, to improve time to market; self-sufficiency, so GVT could maintain its software on its own after implementation; expertise on both systems and start-ups; localization for the Brazilian market; "future-proofed" solutions, that is, flexible, convergent solutions; a package approach, instead of in-house development; and tools for integration with software from other vendors.

Integration.   GVT wanted best-of-breed applications for each important area, including CRM, billing, and workforce management. But how should the company integrate these different packages?

Solution: Middleware emerged as a way to ensure a seamless flow among the various packages. In this way, one package could automatically initiate a process in another package. For example, closing a work order in the workforce management system would automatically close the order in the CRM and provisioning systems and prompt the billing system to bill the customer.

IT as Business Enabler.   CIO Shiozawa was committed to making information technology essential to the telco's business. That meant that any technology selected had to support the best practices of a given business function. For example, GVT's marketing group determined that one of its best practices would be speed of delivering a telco line to a client. This, in turn, required a high level of integration among GVT's computer solutions.

Solution: The key to making IT a business enabler was the creation of a state-of-the-art suite of products (CRM, billing, workforce, GIS, and provisioning) all of it held together by enterprise application integration software. Shiozawa also ensured that GVT was a Web-powered company with business intelligence supporting decision making.

Starring Role

CRM technology played a huge role in enabling GVT to get an immediate leg up on its competition. Specifically, the GVT solution used CRM in four capabilities: coverage area information, call centers, Web site, and opportunity database.

Coverage Area Information.   GVT realized that its representatives would have to know whether wireline or wireless technologies were being used to service a particular area when potential customers would call for service. This would require tight integration between the call center package and the outside plant management system. With the system in place, when a customer calls and provides his or her postal code, the call center can tell whether the customer has coverage, and if so, whether that coverage is wireline or wireless. Then, when a customer wants to buy a line, the call center representative also can assign and schedule a technician immediately, then tell the customer which technician will be coming and when. This boosts customer satisfaction—and gives a competitive kick to Brazil Telecom, which cannot match that level of service

Call Centers.   GVT established two call centers, one for customer service, the other for sales. So customers with questions about their bills, for instance, can call the customer service call center. There, a representative will pull up a screen image of the customer's bill to determine how many unbilled calls the customer has already placed. Also, because the call center is integrated with the private branch exchange, the representatives have access to anything they might need to serve the customer, including predictive dialing, an automatic telephone system that improves representatives' productivity by dialing from a list of numbers, then turning the call over to the representative when a human responds; online access to the status of service requests; access to the GVT product catalog; and an interface for credit validation.

Web Site.   From a competitive standpoint, GVT's site simply had to be better than Brazil Telecom's, so GVT was the first Brazilian telco to offer online shopping carts. These allow customers to browse the site and fill their virtual shopping carts with type of phone service, type of line, and type of phone. While that is common enough on the Web, GVT added an innovation: When a customer closes the shopping cart, the system generates an e-mail message containing the customer's order and sends it directly to a GVT sales representative in the sales call center. The representative then uses that information to call the customer on the telephone and process the order.

Opportunity Database.   This was the final CRM challenge. GVT did not invest as much money as BrT in marketing and generating leads, though it knew these activities would be crucial to its success. The company ran some advertisements on television and in local newspapers, but it knew there was pent-up demand for its services. When GVT receives requests from potential customers in areas where it does not yet offer service, it adds their names and contact information to an opportunity database that is part of GVT's data warehouse. As coverage is added to new areas, the staff generates an opportunity list by cross-referencing the database. This list is then loaded into the CRM system, which delivers an automated message informing residents that GVT coverage is now available in their area and telling them how to order service.

New Milestone

Launched from scratch in six months in an industry that has recently been savaged by overcapacity, price wars, and lack of funding for new initiatives, GVT has been a big success. The company not only came on line in time to meet the operational targets set by Anatel; it surpassed them by 30 percent in 2001 and also expanded its service to 54 cities. GVT also has already bested the track record of the other mirror company (which in itself qualifies as a victory in the minds of many market watchers in Brazil) and is on track to report positive earnings in 2002, an impressive achievement for any start-up. "I am sure that this IT project will become a new milestone for the industry," says Amos Genish, GVT's vice chairman.

The company's early growth has stemmed largely from its commitment to building highly advanced and integrated CRM capabilities that enable GVT to deliver products and services in ways that customers have never before experienced. In fact, GVT's robust IT infrastructure and processes gives the company a solid base on which to build its business in the corporate market and among affluent residents— which hold tremendous revenue growth potential for GVT and, not coincidentally, represent the next battlegrounds with Brazil Telecom.

No one knows how long the global telecom industry will remain depressed or when venture capital will once again begin to flow. Then again, challenges are nothing new for GVT, which has already proven to be a keen innovator and formidable competitor that can handle nearly anything thrown its way.

CONCLUSION

Although Bouygues Telecom and GVT opted to address their competitive challenges with a big-bang approach, many telcos do not have that luxury. Either because of budgetary constraints or the sheer size and scope of their businesses, some companies are opting to make a gradual shift to customer-centricity. They are combining vendor solutions with homemade approaches and techniques to meet their CRM goals.

For example, BellSouth uses a combination of turnkey solutions customized to its needs in addition to solutions built in-house.[13] Cox, SBC, and Sprint also use implementations they have built themselves.[14] British Telecom is developing a CRM system from scratch that will support the merging of its broadband and narrowband Internet services by allowing the company to be more focused and targeted in interactions with customers. The system will include e-CRM and CRM packages that will facilitate the use of an existing database of 1.5 million customers, plus names gathered via a Web campaign.[15]

Finally, AT&T opted for a gradual and self-built approach to integrating customer data among its many lines of service. Rather than create an enterprisewide customer information database across all five service lines, the company decided to build a software layer on top of two key customer information systems to integrate the data stored in each. This approach enabled AT&T to begin the process of integrating data with much less time and money than it would take to directly integrate all its customer information.[16]

Regardless of approach, however, the key for telcos is that they just do it: Make the investments in technologies and processes that enable them to understand their customers better; develop more relevant and appropriate offers and marketing campaigns for individual customers or customer segments; improve the ability to serve these customers (and upsell and cross-sell to them) by creating a single view of each customer; and create a consistent customer experience from unit to unit or product line to product line. The telcos that are able to make this transition will be the ones at the center of the convergence universe. Those that are not will be in danger of following in the footsteps of NorthPoint Communications, VoiceNet USA, and other such companies whose innovative ideas were not enough to sustain them in a hypercompetitive market.

Government: Giving the People What They Want

Sean Shine and Craig B. Cornelius

F or years, businesses have explored the idea of CRM as a competitive differentiator—the thought being that by giving customers what they want and when they want it (rather than giving them what and when the *business* wants), a company could increase customer acquisition and retention and, ultimately, profit. Yet the appeal of CRM has only recently attracted the attention of the largest service provider in the world—government.

According to the analyst firm Gartner, the U.S. government, which has more than 281 million citizen-customers, accounted for only about 3 percent of CRM spending in 2000.[1] And a recent Accenture study of the state of CRM in governments across 11 countries found that, although the majority of agencies had invested in some related technology, most were not applying these tools to improve the delivery of services.[2]

This is a growing problem for government agencies around the world. Regardless of country, agency, or type of customer (e.g., private citizen or business), pressure is intensifying for government to change the way it does business. A number of forces are driving this call for change:

- *Rising expectations among citizens and businesses.* As the service bar has been raised in the private sector, citizens and businesses are increasingly demanding better treatment from and interaction with government agencies. Constituents are asking that government be organized more around their needs, or "customers' intentions," and less around what makes sense to bureaucrats. For example, citizens and businesses are demanding one-stop service from agencies, around-the-clock availability of government products and services, and simpler and more convenient options for paying taxes and fees.

- *Budgetary constraints.* Many government agencies find themselves in the unenviable position of being asked to provide more services and assistance on a shrinking or stagnant budget.

- *Mandates for improved access.* In many countries, better service is being mandated by legislation, such as directives to provide Internet access to underprivileged citizens or reduce the amount of paperwork associated with various governmental activities. For instance, the U.K. prime minister introduced an e-government initiative to have all government transactions online by 2005.[3]

- *Call to leverage past investments in e-government.* Governments in many countries have spent considerable tax dollars building Internet infrastructures and streamlining various activities (such as paying taxes and applying for licenses or permits) via the Web. Now these agencies are being called on to build on their e-government initiatives by linking their Web sites to additional interaction channels (especially call centers).

For their part, most governments thus far have made little progress in making themselves more customer-friendly. Citizens still must deal with multiple agencies and payment requirements to resolve even the simplest issues. Exacerbating the situation is the fact that agencies rarely coordinate activities among each other, typically do not agree on common standards, have information systems with only modest functionality, and still deliver patchy customer service at best.

It is clear that government could dramatically improve its relationship with citizens and businesses if it adopted some of the CRM principles that are helping so many private-sector companies more effectively serve their customers.

REORGANIZING AROUND CUSTOMER INTENTIONS
To be sure, there is considerable awareness among government executives that CRM can be a boon to their agencies and constituents. In a survey of the public sector in Australia, Canada, Finland, France, Germany, Ireland, Italy, Singapore, Spain, the United States, and the United Kingdom, Accenture found that a majority (76 percent) of government agencies believe that applying CRM principles to public services could significantly increase service levels.[4] Echoing these sentiments is Mark Forman, the U.S. federal government's information technology (IT) policy czar, who states that his goal is to make sure that the user of government services (whom he calls "the customer") is empowered to transact business with agencies via streamlined tools. "My job is to make the federal government more customer-centric," said Forman. "It's what citizens expect."[5]

Gradually, the notion has taken root among many within government that they no longer can treat citizens and businesses poorly simply because the customers have no alternatives. Instead, they have come to recognize that government indeed has a responsibility to provide superior service at a lower cost—hallmarks of which include the following:

- "Low-touch" or "no-touch" dealings with government
- Easy-to-access services (no waiting or queues)
- Easy-to-use service (provides choice of method)
- Timeliness (getting to the right person quickly and resolving the problem quickly)
- Confirmation of status or contact history quickly and accurately
- Service with a personal touch
- Knowledgeable staff who have access to relevant information
- Flexibility and understanding of different situations and special circumstances

There is no doubt that transforming organizations as large, bureaucratic, and philosophically entrenched as government agencies can be a huge challenge. In fact, building the types of capabilities just mentioned requires new mind-sets, not to mention huge shifts in how government agencies carry out their day-to-day duties. But several leading organizations are serving as excellent examples of how government agencies can improve their relationships with citizens while reducing their operating costs by using CRM principles to guide the organization, process, policy, and technology changes necessary to reorganize their services around *customer intentions.*

For instance, California is integrating services targeted around a specific citizen segment. The state just launched an online initiative called the E-Business Center to provide a high level of service to the business community.[6] The initiative enables business owners to go to one place for business-related transactions, cutting across government agencies to add value to the services provided to this key customer group. Similarly, the Middlesbrough borough council in the United Kingdom is integrating all of the council's services. The move is aimed at eliminating the existing departmental "stovepipe" orientation that requires citizens to pass from department to department, asking for the same information from each one.[7]

In Spain, the Ministry of Labor and Social Affairs has implemented an innovative remote electronic data (RED) interchange system that electronically links employers with the central Administration for Social Security. The ministry is in charge of collecting contributions from workers and companies, as well as keeping a lifelong register of each worker's job situation. It is one of the most important administrations within the Spanish state, responsible for 40 percent of the state's total budget. Approximately 40 million citizens deal with the ministry for benefit payments or in search of information or employment.

The RED initiative allows information regarding workers' social insurance that is held on individual employers' computers to be transferred electronically to the administration department. Once the documentation has been processed, automatic electronic controls are activated to approve or reject the information, and the appropriate answers are sent electronically back to the employer.

This effort has had a tremendous impact within the Ministry of Labor and Social Affairs: Costs associated with information manipulation have been reduced, processing time for recording data has been reduced, and information that previously took months to retrieve is now available immediately. For example, before implementation of the RED system, the management of retirement lending took several months; now it takes only a few minutes.

The companies using the RED system have experienced multiple benefits as well: Turnaround time to process claims has been reduced, the need to go to the administration office to present information and complete paperwork has been eliminated, and mistakes have been dramatically reduced.

A number of agencies have discovered how new interaction channels can play a major role in reorganizing around customer intentions. A recent survey of U.S. government entities revealed that more than one-third (34 percent) of federal sites offered some kind of electronic services, while 24 percent of state sites did.[8] Increasingly, government sites offer enhanced opportunities for citizen's self-service and enable customers to complete entire transactions online (such as filing taxes, registering motor vehicles, paying for traffic violations, and acquiring permits for everything from hunting and fishing to licenses and marriage certificates).[9] In addition to providing citizens with greater access to public services, new channels also provide governments with a more direct way to reach their citizens.

But government agencies should look beyond just putting services online. For instance, when the Spanish Ministry of Labor and Social Security sought to reduce administrative costs, improve customer service, and modernize its image, it decided to implement a new social security smart card and open a new channel of self-service terminals or kiosks around the country. The smart card allows citizens to manage their own benefits more conveniently by processing routine transactions and accessing their personal government records at self-service terminals rather than government offices.

Citizens use the cards to take care of routine administrative tasks as well as more personal business. The terminals interact with citizens through touch screens, while a narration provides information about the functions of each screen. Online bulletin boards post information about government agencies, job offers, and courses for the unemployed. As a security measure, the terminals use fingerprint identification technology so citizens can access sensitive information. The new capability increases government staff availability for other activities and makes information about government programs and policies more accessible to the public. The system also improves control over fraud, particularly for unemployment and incapacity benefits.

Similarly, a new multimodal interaction infrastructure was critical to improving operations at Centrelink, an Australian commonwealth government agency responsible for linking citizens to a range of government services. The new infrastructure, called *e-Services,* allows Australian citizens the choice of accessing services through various electronic channels, including the Internet, kiosks, and call centers. By offering integrated access to services via electronic channels, Centrelink provides citizens with one-stop service, delivering a range of government services including job assistance, unemployment benefits, family and child assistance, and retirement, disability, and youth benefits. The multimodal aspect of the new infrastructure means that customers can begin a query via the Internet and then switch to the telephone.

The Centrelink representative taking the resulting telephone call is able to view the customer's progress on the Internet and assist accordingly.

FLORIDA BUSINESSES AND PROFESSIONALS GET ONLINE, NOT IN LINE

Perhaps one of the best examples of the application of these two critical CRM principles to government operations is the initiative under way at Florida's Department of Business and Professional Regulation (DBPR). Florida state officials are rethinking the operations of the DBPR, which licenses and regulates businesses and professionals. Their goal: Replace the department's confusing maze of rules and forms with a streamlined operation that relies heavily on innovative information technology, including CRM systems. In so doing, they hope to lower the state's internal costs for licensing local businesses and professionals, provide better information to their own managers, and create new career paths for state employees.

This innovative project quickly caught the attention of Florida's governor, Jeb Bush. "As the primary interface between the people of Florida and the state's nearly one million regulated professionals and businesses," Governor Bush said at the project's start, "I am excited for DBPR to take this revolutionary step forward in e-government technology."

Adds Kim Binkley-Seyer, secretary of the DBPR, "By bringing electronic business practices to our licensees and the people they serve, this single, effective point of entry will dramatically raise the bar for superior customer service."

"Our priorities are clear," Binkley-Seyer continues. "We are improving the way we deliver services to our customers—while ensuring maximum protection to the public."

A Tall Challenge

The size and scope of the Florida program are impressive. DBPR's core mission is to license and regulate the state's 1 million professionals and businesses in some 200 industry sectors. Its larger goal is to ensure quality service for both Florida's 15 million citizens and the tens of millions of tourists who visit the state each year. Unfortunately, in the course of fulfilling this mission, DBPR had grown into an unwieldy entity with an annual budget of $1.5 billion and a payroll of some 1700 employees. In fact, far from being a streamlined, unified operation, DBPR had come to resemble 30 separate agencies, replete with all the redundancies, miscommunications, and inefficient practices one might expect from such an enormous government bureaucracy.

At the same time, DBPR's computer systems had become fragmented and out of date. As of 2000, the department was running more than 60 systems, with three of the most important each more than 20 years old. Telephone customer service was suffering, too. The department's telephone network had swelled to more than 200 published phone numbers, resulting in misplaced calls that required some 200,000 transfers a year. Worse, more than a million customer phone inquiries, or one-third of all such calls, were missed entirely each year—that is, they were never even answered.

The net effect: Florida state employees spent more time processing paper and navigating among their 60 licensing systems than they did serving local businesses.

Then there was the case of Edna Biggs. A Florida real estate broker of 30 years standing, Biggs worked in a fast-paced, high-pressure field—until she tried to renew her brokerage license. Then her world ground to a painful halt. Biggs filled out endless forms. She mailed or personally delivered them, back and forth, to DBPR's offices. Finally she received her new license, but only after the passage of 45 days. Unfortunately, that period of time was not unusual for the DBPR, but was instead typical of how long the old Florida system took. Clearly, a major change was overdue.

That change finally began in February 2000, when DBPR launched a massive effort to completely reengineer itself. DBPR's goals for the project fall into four general categories:

- *Improved customer service.* DBPR will be able to answer a greater number of customer inquiries that it can now, and it will handle them through just two points of contact: one phone number and one Web site.

- *Expanded service options.* Internet services and an automated telephone system will be available 24/7 for license renewals, inquiries, and filing both applications and complaints. A customer contact center will help complete transactions and provide a single point of contact.

- *Shorter processing times.* The use of Internet and telephone services, as well as reengineering, will reduce backlogs.

- *Simplified interaction with the state.* DBPR will replace literally hundreds of forms with just eight departmentwide standard forms.

The agency determined that the best way to achieve these goals was to reorganize itself into five centralized offices, each of which will handle functions that were formerly spread across virtually all DBPR divisions:

- *Customer Care Center (CCC).* This office will handle all customer service functions, including voice and online information requests, license verification inquiries, and correspondence for the entire department. The CCC should reduce the number of phone calls that are transferred or dropped, provide a single contact point for customers who need service, and enhance the department's ability to track customer satisfaction.

- *Central Intake.* Here DBPR will handle all applications and records maintenance processing. All paper-based customer service will take place here. Central Intake will also provide application processing and records maintenance services for all divisions. This aims to reduce the number of handoffs, speed approval turnarounds, and shorten the time needed to review complex applications.

- *Education and Testing.* This function will "own" DBPR's relationships with all testing vendors. It will schedule examinations, post and report on exam scores, work with training consultants, and monitor future training needs. Centralization here should reduce duplicated efforts throughout DBPR and provide a single point of contact for testing vendors.

- *Compliance.* This function will process complaints, handle required licensee reports, process contractual and monetary disputes, conduct drug testing, track evidence, handle audits and inspections, look into unlicensed activity, and conduct both background and facility investigations. By centralizing these functions, Compliance promises to improve customer service and shift the trainers' workloads based on staff skill sets, certification, and areas of expertise.

- *Program areas.* These offices will provide subject matter expertise to the other four areas. By centralizing this expertise, this group will foster relationships with business boards, associations, and special-interest groups. Also, because lower-level inquiries will be filtered by the CCC, program area experts will be able to spend more of their time on high-level projects.

Reengineering the Agency

It was clear that to make these changes (and thus more efficient operations and better customer service) a reality, significant restructuring was needed in two critical areas: the agency's business processes and its information technology capabilities. There was no doubt that the myriad processes that had evolved across the agency over the years had to be streamlined and consolidated. Similarly, there was broad agreement within the agency that a new technology infrastructure and associated systems were required to integrate all of the agency's data and support the new business processes.

To address the first issue, business processes, the agency began by conducting a detailed analysis of how each of its 30 "silos" did business. This included identifying the different terminology, organization structures, and technologies used by each. As a result of this exercise, the agency was able to pinpoint enough redundancies and irrelevant activities to reduce the number of processes agencywide to just nine. These nine processes will enable any agency employee to serve any Florida business or professional, regardless of industry.

On the technology front, the agency focused its efforts on three key IT initiatives:

- A single departmentwide licensing and permitting system (replacing the existing 60 disparate systems) to handle all 200 of the agency's licenses and various permits, as well as house all relevant licensee data

- New CRM and customer self-service software, integrated with the licensing system, to support the agency's call center

- Application service provider (ASP) operations to provide for ongoing maintenance, support, and hosting of all technology components

To keep the overall reengineering project manageable, the work has been divided into six "releases" that have been scheduled for a gradual rollout, culminating with a final release in February 2003. All six releases will involve the same four activities—development, testing, training, and conversion—but each will provide these four activities for a different business area and license type. For example,

Release 1 in the autumn of 2001 dealt with real estate and parimutuel wagering. Later releases will cover professions and businesses including alcoholic beverages and tobacco, hotels and restaurants, and boxing.

DBPR does not expect all state businesses and licensees to use its new systems all the time. In fact, it has identified three adoption categories and the industries likely to fall under them. For example, in the low-adoption category, only 10 to 20 percent of licensees will prefer to use the Web to conduct their business with the state; these include boxing and wagering. In the medium-adoption category, which includes the majority of the professions and most business areas such as hotels and restaurants, the share increases to as much as 30 to 40 percent. And in the high-adoption category, which includes real estate and accounting, Florida officials estimate that as many as 40 to 50 percent of all licensees will use nontraditional channels to conduct their state business.

Capabilities and Benefits

The new systems and processes offer capabilities that agency employees and customers, until recently, only dreamed about. For starters, the licensing system presents users with several options for interacting with the agency: over the phone with a live call center representative; over the phone with the call center system, using a combination of interactive voice response (IVR) technology and the telephone keypad; or via a secure Web portal. Once the user has input the relevant data in one of these three ways, the information is passed along to a central hub for processing. Using any one of these methods, professionals and businesses can access forms and documents, renew licenses, apply for new licenses, and receive information on relevant industry rules and regulations. If they opt for the IVR or Web route, users can do all of this at any time of the day or night.

The integration of the CRM solution with the licensing system gives agency employees unparalleled and unfettered access to license data that significantly improves the way employees interact with customers. Such integration allows the CRM software to pull relevant data from the licensing system and organize and present the data to call center representatives so they can understand everything about a particular caller and that caller's dealings with the agency. For instance, if a person calls to ask about the status of a license application, the call center employee can immediately retrieve information on exactly which steps have been completed and what still must be done to complete the process. Because the IVR system is similarly integrated with the CRM software and the licensing system, a person calling after business hours can access the same information within minutes.

To help ensure that customers are connected to the most appropriate agency employee quickly, a tier approach was used in the customer service, central intake, education and testing, and compliance functional areas. Each tier allows for increasingly complex operations. Tier 1 handles the most common transactions, where only a broad understanding of the department's business rules is required. Tier 2 handles more complicated transactions, those that require a higher level of subject matter expertise. What is called Tier N will offer the in-depth subject expertise to handle even the most complex transactions. So, for example, a Tier 1 call center representative would in most cases handle a person calling for information on renewing an existing license. Conversely, a construction contractor seeking guidance on the types of permits required for various activities (scope-of-work issues) would be directed to a Tier N subject matter expert.

This tiered approach offers several benefits. By channeling inquiries, it both reduces the number of experts needed to handle complex situations and frees them from working on lower-level inquiries. By centralizing all calls onto just one phone number, it provides customers with a single point of entry, eases the tracking of customer-service levels, and lowers the number of calls transferred or dropped. By handling broad inquiries at a cross-organizational level, it lets state specialists focus on their core business functions. And by enabling inquiries to be handled at the lowest level possible, the tiered approach promises to reduce Florida's costs.

Another capability that makes life better for both agency employees and their customers is the licensing systems' mobile commerce feature. Half of the agency's staff is responsible for going out into the field to inspect a business's facilities, ensure compliance with regulations, and follow up on complaints about a particular business or professional. Before the reengineering project, these field workers would visit a site with their clipboards and paper forms, record what they found, then return to the office and key all the information into the system. Now field representatives responsible for conducting inspections are equipped with handheld personal computers that are connected via a hot-sync feature to the main system. Before leaving for the field, the representative downloads all pertinent data and forms (e.g., information on the business being visited, results of the site's last four inspections, and any outstanding complaints or violations). While on site, the inspector enters the inspection findings in real time and, using a small mobile printer, prints out the results of the visit before leaving (something that is particularly important to restaurants, which must display the results of inspections somewhere on their premises before they can legally operate). Upon returning to the office, the field representative uploads the new data into the system, thus updating the records in the relevant licensees' files—ready to be viewed by anyone at the agency with access to the system.

Ahead of the Pack

The DBPR project vaults Florida to the head of the pack of government entities trying to bring a sharper business focus to their operations. In fact, Florida is the first— and only—state to offer a totally integrated, one-stop licensing and permitting transactional solution. It is also the first state in the nation to combine private-sector and public-sector expertise with CRM principles.

Already, the results have been dramatic. In late 2001, just seven months after the project started, DBPR unveiled a new integrated licensing and permitting system for real estate and parimutuel wagering professionals. These two groups comprise a quarter of a million professionals, making them the state's largest business-licensing categories. Within nine months, the agency experienced more than 300,000 unique visitors to the Web portal (averaging nearly 20,000 visitors per week) and more than 400,000 inquiries to the call center (40 percent of which were conducted via self-service). The answer rate in the call center is higher than 95 percent, compared with 66 percent prior to the introduction of the new CRM technology and processes. Furthermore, the round-the-clock operation of the licensing system was proven to be appreciated by users: Nearly as many licenses were renewed or applied for in the evening or on weekends as during the agency's regular business hours. For the latest real estate renewal cycle, the Web site and automated phone system were used to process nearly 30 percent of all license renewals.

Looking ahead, DBPR has a six-year system outsourcing agreement that is expected to help the department develop additional capabilities and ensure that the systems run smoothly. Furthermore, the arrangement allows other Florida agencies to piggyback on the solution. This would have the added benefit of reducing ongoing costs for all participants.

Over a 10-year period, DBPR projects that the system and the reengineered business processes will result in a net $100-million return on investment.

And what about Edna Biggs, the harried real estate broker? In February 2002, with Governor Bush looking on, she had the chance to test the new system by actually renewing her broker's license online. The task, which formerly took her 45 painful days, was this time completed in less than five minutes. "This is wonderful," Biggs proclaimed. "It's so simple."

For Florida state officials and business owners alike, sweet words indeed.

CONCLUSION

Of course, success stories such as the one in Florida are largely the exception, not the rule. There is still a long way to go until CRM is embraced by the government sector to the extent that it has been in business—and an even longer way to go until CRM begins to generate huge returns in cost savings and service improvements across the government landscape. Indeed, Accenture found that although most government agencies in its study are collecting customer data through their interactions with the public, almost two-thirds are not using the information captured to improve service levels or internal processes. Moreover, only one in five respondents reported having plans in place to develop a greater understanding of customer (citizen) needs, and only 7 percent noted plans to improve their ability to educate customers and promote awareness of heightened service capabilities.[10]

While current government CRM initiatives are focusing on improving service at lower costs, future efforts are likely to incorporate another CRM concept that, until now, has been the exclusive province of the private sector: attraction and retention of customers. For instance, countries, states, and cities all must attract and retain business and citizens to maintain a solid tax base. In many countries, the armed forces must attract citizens to serve and retain them for as long as possible. And if one extends the customer concept to employees, government agencies have a pressing need to sell themselves as excellent employers and hold onto productive employees (something that is especially critical to the U.S. federal government, 50 percent of whose current workforce is eligible for retirement in the next five years).

Perhaps time is all that it will take before CRM principles and technologies are firmly entrenched in government's way of doing business. Citizen and business demand is too strong to ignore, and savvy politicians, like their business executive counterparts, recognize that giving customers what they want is the shortest path to career and organizational success.

Manufacturing: Gradual Shift from Product to Customer

Gregory J. Supron

Manufacturers face a unique challenge when it comes to CRM. Because the prevailing mind-set among manufacturers has always been products first, customers second, determining the best course toward more customer-centric operations—while minding the core business of making goods—can be tricky. Furthermore, manufacturers that sell to customers primarily through intermediary companies (e.g., distributors, retailers, and wholesalers) face an even stiffer challenge in trying to carefully balance the needs of these immediate customers and the ultimate user of the products, whether they are consumers or another business.

To be sure, CRM has been slow to take root among manufacturers, who have focused the greater part of their attention in recent years on optimizing their supply chain operations. Manufacturing was identified as among the three industries with the lowest deployment of customer relationship management systems in the 2001 InformationWeek 500. Furthermore, a recent survey of manufacturers conducted by *IndustryWeek* established that, on the whole, manufacturers are not using automated cross-selling and upselling to build sales and drive profits.[1]

One manufacturer that has consistently bucked this trend is computer storage device maker EMC Corporation of Hopkinton, Massachusetts. From the beginning, EMC has made customer service its primary strategic objective. By differentiating itself through superior customer service, EMC has developed an extremely loyal customer base even in the face of its premium pricing and, as a result, has become the overwhelming leader in its market.[2]

How has it done this? The company's CRM philosophy emphasizes teamwork, data sharing, responsibility, and employee enablement, as well as using data proactively to prevent problems before they happen. This approach provides for quick reactions to problems, and thus quick resolutions. And in addition to authorizing field service personnel to take action to solve problems on the spot, EMC's philosophy also reaches to upper management. Key executives are updated frequently on the status of the company's service issues so that they do not lose sight of customers' experiences and needs. The company is so focused on customer service that it locates the service technicians' call center between the offices of the company's software and hardware engineers, encouraging their participation in especially acute service issues.[3]

In addition to involving every level of the company in efficiently and effectively serving customers, EMC is also known for going above and beyond to satisfy customers. This level of devotion to customers also has contributed to customers' loyalty. Indeed, EMC has the unusually high customer retention rate of 99 percent.[4]

EMC provides hard evidence to support the findings of a recent survey conducted by Accenture on the role of CRM in high-tech manufacturers' financial performance. This study revealed that CRM performance accounts for 64 percent of the variation in a high-tech company's return on sales (ROS), defined as "earnings (before interest, taxes, depreciation, and amortization) divided by sales." Thus, if a typical $1-billion high-tech business could improve its CRM capability from average to high performance, it could gain as much as $130 million in profits.[5]

Given the success of EMC and others, manufacturers have begun to understand how a product company can, indeed, be customer-centric. Many manufacturers now acknowledge that improving customer service can be a powerful method of differentiating themselves from competitors. In addition, some manufacturers see improved customer service as the best strategy for increasing sales, driving market share, and improving profitability.[6] Gradually, as manufacturers adopt customer-centric tools and practices, the industry is becoming more customer focused.

BETTER RETURN ON MARKETING INVESTMENTS

One area of CRM that is gaining attention among manufacturing leaders is return on marketing investments. Manufacturers, particularly those that produce branded goods, collectively spend hundreds of millions of dollars annually to market their products. Yet few if any of these companies are able to measure marketing performance in any great detail—principally because marketing always has been viewed as a creative pursuit that is not subject to the management rigor and discipline that have guided other corporate functions for decades. As a result, most manufacturers are not able to get a good handle on which marketing activities are effective and which are consuming resources that could be better allocated to other markets or customer segments or directed to support new or high-growth products.

As the cost of marketing continues to climb, and customers become increasingly difficult to reach using traditional marketing tactics, it is imperative for manufacturers to improve the return on their marketing activities. To do so, they first must quantify the effects of their past marketing efforts to understand what has worked and what has not. They also must establish explicit goals and accountability for each marketing element (whether direct mail, advertising, couponing, or trade promotion) to ensure that the marketing function has a structure in place to help guide their efforts and that the performance of these efforts can be measured against objective criteria. Finally, to keep precious marketing resources focused on the right initiatives, companies should identify the products and markets that have the potential for significant growth, then reallocate marketing resources to capture those new opportunities.

One company that has adopted this approach is now institutionalizing measurement across diverse categories in countries around the world. These techniques are playing a crucial role in transforming the brand from a traditionally low-cost proposition to an innovative brander depending more on advertising than price discounting.

SINGLE VIEW OF THE CUSTOMER: INTEGRATING DATA

Some manufacturers have opted to set their initial CRM sights on getting a better handle on the vast stores of data they have throughout their organizations. In the business-to-business (B2B) arena, many manufacturers have been investing time integrating existing information silos to gain a single view of each customer. AlliedSignal Aerospace, before its 1999 merger with Honeywell, integrated sales and service information from its four business units and 40 product lines. The company had faced serious customer complaints from its large corporate customers, some of which were being contacted by a number of different AlliedSignal sales people within the same week.[7]

Since the merger, Honeywell Aerospace has taken an even broader approach to integrating customer data, establishing a common customer information system for use by individuals in sales, field service, and product line functions and also by response center agents across business units, providing opportunities for cross-selling opportunities and helping the company present a consistent face to the customer across its interactions.[8]

In addition to sharing customer information across functions, Honeywell Aerospace also altered its sales process to create a single point of contact for the customer, strengthening the consistency of customers' experience with the company. Rather than organizing sales by product line or business unit, the company instituted a team-based sales process. Typically managed by a single person, each customer-centered team consists of sales reps and service engineers.[9]

In developing its ability to mass-customize pneumatic industrial valves, Ross Controls also takes a cross-functional approach to customer management. The close customer contact involved in customizing valves allows Ross to develop strong relationships with customers, thus building trust and loyalty. The key to the system's success, however, is the creation of a strong cross-functional workforce in which the company's engineers coordinate everything from product design to production planning to marketing.[10]

Customer data integration also was at the core of a challenge faced by the agricultural products subsidiary of a large chemical manufacturer, which was grappling with how to generate greater business value and synergy from its purchase of a company that produced a complementary array of goods. After the acquisition, the new entity decided to develop a joint marketing program to capitalize on the affinity between the two companies' seeds and crop chemicals. To do so, the entity needed greater insight into all customers' needs, preferences, and buying behaviors so it could craft relevant, compelling customer offers.

However, in trying to tap existing information to improve customer insight, the entity immediately ran up against some high hurdles. Besides the usual data consolidation issues associated with any acquisition, the acquiring company had to contend with a complex conglomeration of more than 20 customer data feeds from its own internal systems, as well as from the acquired company and third-party sources. It also had to reckon with differing definitions of what a customer is, as the acquired company generally dealt directly with farmers and growers, whereas the acquiring company typically sold to distributors and dealers. Making matters worse, dealers were wary of sharing information about end customers, worried that they could be cut out of the process (and the profits) if their supplier made direct contact with growers.

The merged company decided to create a sophisticated data warehouse, not only to help develop the most effective customer offers for the comarketing campaign, but also to ensure ongoing support for future promotional programs. Following design and development of an appropriate data architecture, the company implemented a data warehouse that consolidated and cleaned information from all 20-plus systems sources to provide details on growers, dealers, and distributors. The warehouse also was designed to capture new data from future transactions and to permit updates of its architecture and processes as necessary.

Using the data warehouse and the newly integrated customer data, the new entity designed and executed a highly successful comarketing program that generated significant sales growth in the product lines featured in the campaign. Perhaps even more important, the new capability was embraced by dealers and distributors, who overcame their initial distrust and began collaborating with the company on critical customer data. This development is expected to help the company, and its dealers and distributors, to continue to generate deep insights into their customers over the long term, thus improving revenues for all involved.

CONTACT CENTERS GET A BOOST

Another area that is receiving significant attention from manufacturers is the contact center or call center. Although manufacturers tended to minimize the importance of such facilities in the past, they now are recognizing the call center's potential to further support their branding efforts, reduce customer service costs, and provide an effective means for generating revenue.

For instance, the Philippines unit of U.K.-based consumer goods giant Unilever recently implemented a CRM solution to help improve its call center capability and boost the productivity of its customer service and consumer advisory representatives. The system automates the help desk processes of Unilever's two call centers: customer service and consumer advisory. According to Efren Samonte, Unilever Philippines commercial director, the system now enables "faster response time to queries and needs raised by consumers, provide[s] for effective maintenance of our customer database, and [gives] the company easy access to customer information for analysis and strategy development."[11] Samonte says the new system also has increased the call center's capacity from 3000 to 5000 calls per month.[12]

Automaker DaimlerChrysler also has embraced call center solutions to improve responsiveness to technicians at its dealer customers. A short time ago, the company implemented a new system that significantly streamlines the interaction between technicians and the technical service agents that serve as resources for mechanics with specific questions about a vehicle or part. When mechanics call the call center, they use the phone keypad to enter the vehicle identification number of the car in question and the type of service needed. This information is automatically routed to a call center employee's monitor screen. The system cuts one minute from each call—which may not seem like much, until one considers the fact that DaimlerChrysler receives 37,000 such calls a month. By slicing just 60 seconds off each call, the company saves 600 hours monthly. To further make the call center employees more productive, the call center system provides linkages to 26 other databases within the company that contain vital information and specifications. All told, the system saves DaimlerChrysler $225,000 a year in personnel and equipment expenditures—and enhances the relationship with its customers by enabling call center representatives to more quickly solve technicians' problems.[13]

One of the world's largest producers and distributors of soft drink beverages also realized significant business benefits by revamping its call center. The company, which sells to supermarkets, convenience stores, retail outlets, restaurants, and other small suppliers, had opened a service call center in the United States in 1995. With 280 agents taking orders to replenish customer stock and answer inbound customer calls, the center supported some 140,000 customers and $5 million in annual sales. Yet the center was not operating at its best. Agents had to check three different systems to find customer information. Inconsistent customer information prevented agents from cross-selling, upselling, or proactively marketing sales campaigns. Although the call center was operational, service and profit performance fell short of customer and company expectations.

To boost the performance of the center, the company redesigned and redeveloped the center into a new customer interaction facility. The new facility delivers more robust call center capabilities focused on building stronger relationships with customers and providing service and sales departments with leading-edge tools to do their work, including the following

- *Agent desktop,* a single, customizable, scalable application that provides easy, advanced navigation and promotional prompts. Robust configuration and custom extensions help improve sales and operational effectiveness via dynamic order and date validation, upsell capabilities, and call queue management.
- *A centralized dashboard* with a common set of performance measurements and automated reporting helps monitor and measure customer service, and ensure consistent performance.

- *Integrated marketing* expands the agent desktop to enable personalized one-to-one selling, with enhanced customer and product data, real-time promotion statistics, and trend analysis.

- *Computer telephony integration* functions link the new system with existing telephony tools, giving inbound and outbound agents greater ability to make and handle calls and automatically identify inbound customers by name.

- *Skills-based routing* of inbound calls helps determine the needs of callers and route calls to the right agent at the right time.

- *A voice response unit* (VRU) gives customers the option of handling information requests or even creating a new order on their own, as well as the option to transfer to an agent.

The redesigned facility opened in July 2000 and made an immediate impact on the business. In the first six months of operation, the facility helped contribute to a sales volume increase of 13 million cases. In 2000, the company served 145,000 customers and generated $850 million in revenue. Additional benefits include the following:

- Sales volume of 20-ounce cans is up 28 percent while the production cost per case has decreased 13 percent.

- Deliveries of fewer than 10 cases per order are down 50 percent, realizing distribution costs savings of $6 million.

- 250 agents make at least two upsell offers in 93 percent of calls, with 30 percent of these converting to actual sales. These agents drive greater revenue through high-performance selling.

- Customers are pleased with the new service and their wide range of customer interaction choices. The company is saving time and money and increasing customer loyalty with enhanced call routing and customer self-service.

The redesigned service center is now the nucleus of the company's global and evolving CRM strategy for highly effective operations, customer satisfaction, and revenue growth. In essence, the company is more competitively positioned to excel at providing great service to customers.

An electronics and high-tech manufacturer significantly improved the way it manages customer inquiries by redesigning its contact centers. Situated around the world, these contact centers support the company's growing customer base and expanding product lines. However, each center had developed its own unique method for handling customer requirements. While this point-solution strategy was aligned with the organization's global expansion efforts, executives recognized that the next step was to provide a consistent customer experience along with scalability in the face of exponential growth. In short, the company had to rethink its global customer care strategy by focusing on operational efficiency and effectiveness and begin to operate as one truly connected company.

The company set out to achieve four principal goals:

- *Improve the customer experience by integrating products and locations.* Because each center supported a varying roster of products and services, customers with numerous products often interacted with more than one contact center. Multiple interactions, in turn, added to the likelihood of an inconsistent customer experience. The company wanted to establish an integrated global network of sales and service functions, so that every customer interaction would be consistent, regardless of the center's location.
- *Drive revenue.* Executives saw an opportunity to maximize sales effectiveness by enabling the independently operated contact centers to better coordinate, gather, and instantaneously share customer data. Customer service professionals needed a tool that would provide them with a complete view of the customer, which would in turn help them to identify and pursue sales opportunities.
- *Propel continuous operational efficiencies.* With contact centers offering support on diverse products, and facing the challenge of operating in multiple time zones around the world, each center had over the years established its own customer care orientations and processes. The company wanted to realign its organization, reduce duplication of effort and inefficiencies in personnel utilization, improve new-hire ramp-up time, and streamline hand-offs between customer organizations.
- *Prepare for customer-to-the-Web thrust.* The company recognized that it needed to build a strong contact organization for customers who needed support beyond the Web.

The organization planned to upgrade its current technology by implementing Web-based tools that would replace the point solutions developed by the independently run contact centers and enable rapid deployment of applications to the customer-facing organizations throughout the company. These tools also would provide the foundation for new external processes and ultimately help ensure a consistent customer experience.

Guided by the vision to optimize the customer's experience and drive costs down, the company first embarked on a two-month assessment and planning project to outline its vision for the future. This effort defined the desired customer experience and created a road map leading to business process improvement. The result was an operating model that defined how the contact centers should interact to provide a cost-effective, efficient, and satisfying customer experience.

Convinced that this operating model presented a viable solution, the company then launched three key projects within the program:

- Realign business processes across all contact centers around the world.
- Design and build a CRM technology application to support the new contact center processes.
- Design and build a new tool to help customer service representatives retrieve product information quickly.

Focusing first on the business processes project, the project team identified the customer care processes used by contact centers around the world, defined areas for improvement, and then worked with each center to implement the newly defined processes.

The team then designed, built, and deployed a contact management system for all centers across North America and Europe that incorporated specific geographic customizations that enabled customer service representatives to capture customer requests and manage and capture interactions with customers. The system was supported by a technology architecture that integrated the CRM solution with the company's back-end enterprise resource planning system and the company's pricing configuration tool.

To complement the contact management system, the team built a knowledge management system, based on natural language processing, that gave customer service representatives a consistent tool for retrieving product information. This system is available to internal employees and provides rapid access to more than 1400 product documents while reducing call center traffic and generating a significant cost savings. The solution also increases customer response time frames and accelerates the ramp-up for newly hired representatives. The system currently is being deployed to the company's business partners and end-user customers as well.

As a result of the project, the company now has an integrated global network of sales contact centers in place that provides a consistent experience for customers, increases control of and follow-up on customer requests, and upgrades the uniformity of processes and quality across global contact centers. Each center is equipped to emphasize solution selling, has in place an automated process for lead follow-through, and practices standardized selling behaviors.

The project has had a noticeable impact on customers, who have commented on better and faster response, improved follow-through, and enhanced self-help capabilities. Furthermore, contact center representatives are more efficient and have access to more helpful customer profiles and tracking systems, and they have a higher degree of confidence in the sales and support services they provide. Statistical projections done by the company show that the project has resulted overall in improved productivity, increased customer routing accuracy, more aggressive cross-selling, and additional revenue.

WEB IS CRM TOOL OF CHOICE

Many manufacturers have made their initial forays into CRM via the Web. In addition to providing a cost-effective channel for customer interaction and data collection, the e-channel also offers obvious synergies with online supply chain management systems adopted by many manufacturers.

Such is the case with U.S. automaker General Motors. The company has made important inroads in e-CRM through BuyPower, its dealer referral Web site. In the United States, the site allows consumers to select a set of options for a GM vehicle, access information on incentives and financing, locate the vehicle in dealer inventories, and e-mail dealers for competitive price quotes. Outside the United States, GM is expanding BuyPower's coverage to 40 countries, enabling the site to service half the world's population. The site has proved to be a great success, receiving many hits in the United States, while successfully supporting complete online transactions in other countries.[14]

Ingersoll-Rand is also using Web technologies to improve customer interactions, taking an indirect approach to customer relationship management using supply chain technologies and involving its distributors. The company established an online portal in April 2001 that allows Ingersoll-Rand dealers to place and track orders and check inventory at the company or at other distributors. The system, which lets the company and its dealers collaborate on marketing and service, also gathers customer data and allows the manufacturer to interact with customers for the first time.[15]

Scotts, the maker of lawn care products, recognizes the potential the Web has to serve both its retail customers and end consumers. Its home page has areas dedicated to both segments and enables all visitors to conduct research on everything from environmental issues to where to purchase products.[16]

Manufacturer Emerson is taking a different approach to customer relationship management. The company implemented CRM software which enables it to conduct online marketing, account management, and order taking directly with business customers, circumventing its distributor and wholesaler network. The company hopes to reduce the margins it pays distributors, currently 20 to 25 percent, by using the e-channel to approach customers directly.[17]

A number of manufacturers of consumer products are using the Web to fuel mass-customization efforts aimed at giving personal attention to consumers—and, in some cases, highly personalized products. Procter & Gamble created a new Web-only brand, Reflect.com, which is an "interactive beauty service," according to Alex Zelikovsky, Reflect.com's vice president of operations and chief logistics officer. By providing in-depth information on hair, skin type, and lifestyle, customers can get beauty products custom formulated for their needs.[18] Nike Corporation launched NIKE iD, a Web site through which consumers can order shoes tailored to their specifications and personalized with an eight-letter identity on the back of the shoes.[19] And Dell Computer Corp. built one of the most successful PC businesses ever on the ability of its customers to custom build a system on Dell's Web site.

Of course, such efforts can create sticky situations for manufacturers if they impinge too much onto their relationships with their retailer customers. Indeed, many consumer goods makers experimented in the late 1990s with consumer-direct selling—mostly to the dismay of retailers—only to find the fulfillment challenges to be insurmountable. Most manufacturers of consumer goods now recognize that, in most instances, the Web and other similar channels (including wireless devices and kiosks) are more suitable to brand building, customer insight collection, and supporting the bricks-and-mortar outlets that sell and service their products—just as DaimlerChrysler did recently when it leveraged Internet and kiosk technology to improve the interaction between customers and its dealers before and during service calls.

When an automobile owner notices a potential problem with a vehicle, it is often only the first of a series of frustrations typically encountered as the owner embarks on the service and repair process. The owner must phone the local dealership and provide a description of the problem to the receptionist or service advisor to schedule an appointment. Upon arrival at the dealership for the appointment, the owner reviews, or in many cases restates entirely, the problems for the service advisor. Often, after a technician examines the car, another discussion or even a visit is required, potentially wasting a great deal of time prior to the actual vehicle repair.

DaimlerChrysler wanted to find a solution to this repetitive, often inconvenient, time-consuming and ultimately frustrating process. To enhance its customers' experiences and its dealers' reputations, DaimlerChrysler sought to automate the process of gathering the customer's description of the vehicle concerns. Specifically, the automaker wanted to make it easier for its dealers' customers to directly provide valuable information to be used for troubleshooting — and, just as important, to place the problems in the complete context in which they occur.

For example, an owner notices the car pulling to the right and decides to go to a DaimlerChrysler dealer for service. But is this a steering problem? Or perhaps a matter of the car's alignment? Does the car pull only when braking, only during acceleration, or all the time? The customer may not have ever thought to analyze how and when the problem occurs, but the answers to these (and additional) questions are necessary to place the problem in a useful diagnostic context.

So while DaimlerChrysler's goal was to improve the customer service experience and increase overall customer satisfaction, the company also was looking to realize ancillary benefits (in terms of both expense savings and goodwill creation) by the following means:

- Enabling customers to participate in the solution (helping them "buy in" to the process)
- Enhancing and refining the information-gathering aspect of repair service
- Helping the dealer's service advisors focus more on the customers and their concerns, rather than being order takers between the customers and the technicians
- Identifying concerns and improving quality more efficiently by leveraging the data for downstream quality analysis
- Reducing the amount of data entry performed by service advisors that the service center historically has completed

The result was the creation of an efficient data collection tool—the Service-Analyzer—that can serve the needs of customers, dealers, and DaimlerChrysler.

By providing customers with access to the ServiceAnalyzer, an easy-to-use tool that helps customers navigate through the initial diagnostic questions and answers, DaimlerChrysler is able to focus service advisors on its customers' concerns and clearly convey these concerns to service personnel. Whether a customer accesses the tool online (via a dealer's Web site or a DaimlerChrysler branded site) or at a kiosk or workstation at the actual dealership, the ServiceAnalyzer can smoothly and intuitively walk the customer through a series of questions that describe and isolate the potential service problem and put it in the context of when or how it occurs. This can greatly streamline the information gathering as well as the technician's diagnostic process during the repair visit. The tool does not perform a diagnosis or routinely suggest what the technician should do, but rather fully qualifies the concern so that the technician can begin structured procedures to determine cause and correction.

The ServiceAnalyzer is, in effect, a structured set of pertinent questions and answers, presented in a graphically appealing and user-friendly format. The customer can indicate the problem (e.g., "pulls to the right") and the tool will begin focusing the answers into more detail and context by building a dynamic tree of intuitive questions, such as: Does this happen only after a certain event? Only when braking? Or only in rainy conditions?

The customer's own description, captured via this series of intelligent, focused questions and answers, then is used to help the technician efficiently and accurately diagnose the problem. The tool aims to reduce hassles and delays for customers, while enabling DaimlerChrysler dealerships to differentiate themselves from the competition through improved customer satisfaction and increased efficiency. On a corporate level, DaimlerChrysler also can use the ServiceAnalyzer's descriptions to identify and repair vehicles and to aggregate data during the early-run production of new vehicle makes or models.

In an industry in which even fractions of a percent improvement in warranted repair work expense can mean considerable cost savings, the ServiceAnalyzer can help increase profitability while improving the overall customer/repair transaction. By enabling more complete, fix-it-right-the-first-time repair jobs (where problems, rather than merely symptoms, are truly fixed), the ServiceAnalyzer can save DaimlerChrysler time and money. This will significantly impact the customer's satisfaction level—ideally leading the customer to prefer the dealer's services, even for future nonwarranted work. Savings also can be realized by avoiding overrepair, in which, for example, an entire (and more costly) seat assembly may be replaced instead of the single seat part that actually needs replacement. By streamlining the repair process and making it more customer friendly, DaimlerChrysler is seeking to make and keep customers for life, establishing not only brand loyalty but also repeat business at the individual dealer level.

As David Li, DaimlerChrysler's dealer service process and technology manager, noted, "The solution places DaimlerChrysler *in the service process* versus downstream of the repair waiting to analyze warranty claims. The corporation is now strategically placed to capture and influence not only warranty concerns, but also retail repair concerns, which account for the majority of a dealer's service."

CONCLUSION

It is unrealistic—and certainly impractical—for manufacturers to abandon their focus on their products in favor of a pure customer-centric organization. The heart of a manufacturing operation will always be making and moving goods. However, as companies such as Peugeot, EMC, and others have demonstrated, embracing CRM to provide better service to one's customers (whether they are other businesses, consumers, or both) and gathering and analyzing the data necessary to help ensure that the company's products truly meet customers' needs, can have a significant positive effect on the bottom line.

31

Resources: CRM Is a Competitive Necessity

James O. Etheredge

A s a whole, the resources industry (which includes oil and gas producers and energy providers such as electric and gas utilities) is undergoing a period of intense change. Oil price volatility, massive consolidation, deregulation, and sector convergence are just a few of the factors contributing to the industry's business environment, which might best be characterized as hypercompetitive. Although energy production will continue to be dominated by oil and gas in the near term, research into and promotion of renewable and alternative energy lingers on the peripheries of the industry as a looming threat.[1] Faced with ever-increasing competition, energy companies around the world are relying on advances in technology to differentiate themselves and reduce costs to attain market dominance.

Among oil and gas producers, a wave of consolidation has globalized the sector and increased the industry footprint of major players to encompass multiple sectors. The rush to consolidate has resulted in the mergers of Exxon and Mobil, Chevron and Texaco, and BP Amoco and Atlantic Richfield—with others on the horizon.[2] As oil companies have evolved into mammoth vertical enterprises, spanning the supply chain from exploration and the recovery of crude to refining to the retailing of fuel and consumer products and services, many have embarked on programs to capture more of the individual consumer's business by developing relationships centered on personalized services, loyalty, and fuel/credit cards.

For utilities, the greatest competitive factor is privatization and open markets, as nations around the world deregulate their energy industries. In the United Kingdom, which deregulated its utilities sector a decade ago, companies still are grappling with how to act like market-driven companies, while in the United States, states are just now beginning the deregulation process. Even China recently announced plans to break up its giant State Power Corporation's near-monopoly, with eventual plans to promote competitive power pricing.[3] Those companies operating in a deregulated environment for the first time are realizing the importance of satisfying their customers.

In addition to heightening competition, another direct result of consolidation and deregulation is that many energy companies now are saddled with numerous incompatible legacy systems, dispersed customers, and operations spanning multiple channels or "touch points." Adding to this complexity is the rise of energy exchanges and marketplaces. In addition to increasing the efficiency of business-to-business (B2B) transactions for participant companies, their advent has upped the ante for energy firms to get online.

CRM BECOMES COMPETITIVE NECESSITY

Clearly, the impetus is growing stronger for energy companies to turn their attention from the supply side to the demand side of the business. And, in fact, many companies are in the early adoption phase of CRM, although the level of maturity in implementing customer-centered systems and practices varies by sector. More advanced tools and techniques are in evidence among the industry's downstream operations, where end users and consumers come in direct contact with oil companies through their B2B marketing and retail operations or interact with local utilities for business or residential energy needs.

However, while not all aspects of CRM make sense for energy companies, the industry does stand to benefit greatly from applications that streamline customer service over the phone or via the Internet, capturing more detailed customer information to develop deeper insights into customer needs and preferences and integrating field service personnel with the home office. Even within upstream operations, systems for online collaboration with business partners can be leveraged for efficiencies in B2B customer interactions and service.

Getting Online

Many energy companies have looked to the Internet as a first step in building better customer relationships. In the exploration and production sector, the focus has been on Web-enabling transactions and information exchange to facilitate collaboration with business partners and suppliers. In distribution, energy companies are using the Web more to interact directly with business customers in an effort to generate better relationships. Duke Energy, a $59-billion gas and power marketer based in Charlotte, North Carolina, launched personalized Web pages for its largest business customers to provide a direct link to billing, product, and services information. San Francisco–based Chevron provides online ordering for its 8000 service station business customers and recently extended the capability to permit 406 general aviation base operators to order everything they need for their operations, from jet fuel to food.[4]

Utilities also have been embracing the e-channel, especially in the United States, where the double whammy of deregulation and its resulting reorganization of the sector have pressed many utilities to embark on major Internet initiatives, albeit after a slow start. Most have limited such CRM projects to online account management,[5] although a few utilities have established more innovative systems. One example is the unusual program rolled out by Maryland-based Allegheny Energy, under which the company's residential customers can set their thermostats online. Once the customer enters this data, an Allegheny Web site sends out a signal to a device embedded in the customer's thermostat to maintain the temperature. This allows customers to lower their monthly bills by conserving energy. In addition, the utility may acquire the right to adjust thermostats during high-demand periods to avoid buying expensive wholesale power on the spot market.[6]

As have other industries, the energy industry also is leveraging the e-channel to provide more efficient customer service. American Electric Power, for example, contracts with an application service provider to help the utility more effectively track customer questions on the Internet; features include self-service through a bank of frequently asked questions and opportunities for automatic e-mail query or live chat support. By reducing the need for human intervention in the service process, AEP increased the speed and capacity of service while decreasing the costs per inquiry from $5.00 to $15.00 before deployment to a range of $0.25 to $1.00 afterward.[7]

A much more ambitious online effort to redefine customer service for the oil industry in Europe was executed by TotalFina, a company formed as the result of a merger in 1998 between Total of France and Belgium's Petrofina. TotalFina is the world's fifth-largest oil company; it is engaged in all sectors of the oil and gas business as well as in petrochemicals, uranium, coal, minerals, and solar energy. TotalFina's business is both upstream (prospecting, drilling, and production) and downstream (refining crude oil and delivering semifinished oil products, including direct sales and marketing).

The merged company faced a major challenge in France. The business-to-business trade in the downstream market was characterized not only by a low service level in the sales ordering processes, but also by an emphasis on price competition. Resellers and wholesalers visited TotalFina terminals and load terminals for transportation at will, without prior ordering. TotalFina recognized that this was a less-than-efficient way to operate because it made product forecasting difficult, caused confusion over responsibility for oil transportation, created security problems, and produced long waiting times at the terminal.

To remedy the situation, TotalFina initially decided to launch an e-commerce initiative to gain better control over the sales order process. However, the company quickly realized that the new system would in fact allow it to meet that objective as well as significantly enhance its customer relationships by introducing a new extranet-based sales ordering system—an enterprise portal—that controls the access of resellers and wholesalers to TotalFina's products at the point of loading while also guaranteeing product level availability and a high service level.

The results of the portal have been significant. Using the portal, customers can process orders within one minute and track order status through the whole process, from initial order to loading. Furthermore, the portal enables resellers and whole-salers to automatically check invoices received from TotalFina by comparing the original order with the invoice received after delivery. Waiting time at terminals has been reduced. And TotalFina can quickly and effectively monitor daily changes in market demand and adjust prices and procurement forecasts accordingly.

Overall, the new approach reduces customers' administrative costs, improves the availability of supply information, and makes product transportation more effi-cient. For example, by optimizing logistics and reducing administrative workloads across the industry, the new system has delivered a reduction of 20 to 30 percent in order management costs for TotalFina and its resellers and wholesalers.

Perhaps the best example of how an energy company can use the Web as a tool to help to transform itself is British Gas in the United Kingdom. In the late 1990s, the com-pany (which is a subsidiary of Centrica PLC, a company that also owns the U.K. Auto-mobile Association, the Goldfish credit card business, and One-Tel) faced a major challenge: how to change the way it did business in the face of industry deregulation and the subsequent onslaught of competition. New entrants in the market were aggressively attempting to eat into British Gas's market share by adopting a price-led approach.

Fortunately, the company had a number of advantages that the new competitors did not. Because of its history, British Gas was viewed by consumers of all ages as a reliable and trusted brand, and the company enjoyed a good reputation for quality and dependability. Furthermore, British Gas had a huge base of existing customers— some 19 million before the advent of competition in the gas market.

To prevent the loss of customers to new competitors and capitalize on its brand value and installed customer base, British Gas executives decided to transform the venerable yet essentially commoditized utilities business into a consumer-friendly offering that could win the attention and loyalty of a new generation of customers. British Gas embarked on a program to revamp its products and services and market them in innovative ways. In common with most companies at the time, British Gas developed a Web site (gas.co.uk) to provide information and, eventually, interactive capabilities for customers to check their gas and electricity accounts.

But as time went on, research undertaken by the company provided feedback indicating that it was not yet making the most of Internet technology as a customer-focused vehicle. In fact, customers overwhelmingly told the utility that there was a significant need for a single, online source that could save them time and eliminate frustration by giving them integrated access to all products and services needed to maintain a household. Heeding the feedback from customers, the company decided to take the best elements of gas.co.uk and incorporate them into a completely new Web site: house.co.uk, the United Kingdom's first comprehensive online home man-agement service.

The project took a two-pronged approach: developing the brand and visual design for the site and building the technical infrastructure on which the site would

operate. Working with commercially available CRM and content management software, the company built the customer-facing technical infrastructure that it needed
to offer a rich, personalized online experience. It also linked the infrastructure with
six third-party Web sites that enabled British Gas to integrate information on services the company itself did not provide, but that were an integral part of managing
a household: Consignia for postal services, Rightmove for house purchases, Char-
colonline for mortgages, Experian for local information, Improveline for tradespeo-
ple, and Easier2move for online conveyancing.

While the infrastructure was developed, British Gas attended to branding and
design to create a consumer-friendly Web site with strong visual appeal. This was an
iterative process that included repeated tests with consumers to gain their feedback
on the site, as well as the implementation of a full content management system to
support the management of more than 1300 pieces of copy.

The result was a broad, deep, easy-to-navigate site that would help British Gas
retain current customers and attract new ones by offering time-saving, no-hassle, one-
stop service for discounts on bundled utility and home-management products and
simple access to a wealth of estate agents and home-repair and other related services.

To prepare for implementation, the company established a dedicated House contact center, hired and trained staff, and set up all other business processes and supporting services that house.co.uk required to operate. These facets of the business
were linked as needed with British Gas's processes as well as integrated with its network of contact centers and other traditional sales and marketing channels.

The project team finished its work in just nine months, on time and under
budget, and house.co.uk launched ahead of schedule in October 2001. A national
marketing campaign began in November to support the launch.

Besides beating all its competitors with the industry's first comprehensive
online service for home management, British Gas stands to gain several other benefits from house.co.uk:

- The site's CRM and content management components help to enable marketing
  staff to gain a 360° view of customers, increase use of segmentation and personalization, reduce mass advertising in favor of more effective targeted campaigns, and create much stronger one-to-one relationships with customers.

- Over time, British Gas will increase revenues through its ability to cross-sell
  and upsell both its own products and services and those of its six third-party
  participants.

- The online self-service aspects of house.co.uk are expected to reduce the cost
  to serve customers.

- The new infrastructure gives the company the strong technical foundation it
  needs for future enhancements such as links to digital television or mobile
  devices.

- The site helps to provide a point of differentiation for British Gas in the minds
  of customers.

Company executives are confident that the combination of the British Gas brand and advanced Internet technology, working in concert with many other initiatives the company is undertaking, will not only help the company to retain existing customers but also serve as a potent tool in the company's efforts to acquire new customers. The company already has expanded its services from its traditional gas business into electricity, telephone and Internet access, home security, plumbing, heating, and kitchen appliance servicing. Internet technology is expected to make a valuable contribution to the company's aim to become a fully integrated home services provider.

Analytics and Segmentation

The majority of utilities that have implemented CRM have done so to reduce costs or to make a few services more convenient (e.g., offering online access to account information), with little or no focus on establishing a more meaningful, value-added relationship with customers. Taking customer relationship management practices to this next level requires a proactive approach to serving individual customers or groups of customers based on their specific needs.

To identify these needs, energy companies not only need to have real-time access to integrated customer data but also must use analytical tools or techniques. For instance, Nordic, an independent power supplier based in Michigan, analyzes its customer accounts to identify dramatic changes in customers' energy use and notify them of the probable causes. Nordic was thus able to identify a problem caused by a faulty motor at an industrial customer's plant and was able to suggest how a chemical and construction material supplier could reduce its electric bill by 20 percent by staggering the times it turned on machines in the morning. This sort of proactive approach builds stronger relationships with key customers, improving retention and loyalty rates.[8]

Going further, energy companies can promote stronger and more profitable customer relationships by leveraging customer data through segmentation. Very few U.S. energy companies have taken such a strategic approach to CRM practices, reflecting the monopolistic roots of the utilities sector and the isolation of the large oil companies from end users, being farther upstream and separated by a broad network of distributors and retailers.

However, there are a few instances of energy companies approaching this next step in CRM, including Southern Company, the largest U.S. producer of electricity and the parent company of five regional utilities. The company is targeting different customer segments with specific online customer service programs. Large industrial customers, for example, are able to access real-time pricing information on the utility's Web site and can view their energy usage patterns across company locations. The company is developing an electronic bill presentment and payment system for its residential customers and an integrated system for reporting power outages. The latter functions through the company call center to identify the location and expected duration of the outage for customers contacting the call center during an outage.[9]

New York–based petroleum company Amerada Hess also is investing in technology to segment its customer base. The segments will provide the basis for targeted marketing offers to increase customer acquisition rates and add greater value to existing customer relationships. The company gathers extensive customer data through its many e-business programs for use with sales force automation, data mart, and analytic tools.[10]

One European utility company that provides energy solutions for industrial, professional, and residential customers is a pioneer in the use of customer insight and segmentation. The company recently faced deregulation and its implications for the company's business. In preparation for the gradual deregulation of the country's energy market, the company began exploring how it would have to change its way of selling to and serving its customers in a market that would soon be awash in competition. It sought to avoid the experiences in other countries, where deregulation had led to the outbreak of price wars and high levels of customer turnover. But to do so, it recognized that it would need to develop customer-insight capabilities that are not common in the utility industry. These capabilities would enable the company's marketing executives to better understand the following points:

- Customers' expectations for service and their perceptions of how well the company was meeting those expectations
- Customers' intentions to switch to other energy providers and their reasons for switching
- New products and services that customers wanted from their energy provider
- The current and future value of specific customers and customer segments to the company
- The image and positioning that the company had among its customers

Such information would enable the company to determine the appropriate mix of products, services, and pricing for its various customer segments, as well as understand how to maximize the return on investment in its customer bases. The company's goal was to be viewed by its customers as providing such superior products and services that they would not only stay with the company, but also would pay a premium to do so.

Executives decided to focus initially on a key market—the small and medium-sized enterprise segment. The team began by developing a data warehouse that integrated existing data resident in three different billing systems in the company, externally purchased customer trend and demographic data, customer data from a sales force automation system, and information obtained from customers directly through an extensive customer survey.

After the data warehouse was installed, the team analyzed the newly integrated data to determine the following:

- *Customers' intentions to switch.* Cluster analyses identified which customer groups were most at risk of switching to a competitor, why they were considering switching, and what products or services would make them remain customers.
- *Future and current value.* The team was able to pinpoint the current value of various customer groups and project these groups' value to the organization in

the future. Combining these results with those from the switching analyses, the team could define the most cost-effective approach to retaining the right (i.e., most valuable) customers.

- *Customer preferences and opinions of the company.* The results of a customer survey were analyzed to help the company understand its strengths and weaknesses in customer care and customer preferences in the areas of new products and services, pricing, and customer service.

The new system has given the company the ability to gain a robust and comprehensive understanding of its small and medium-sized enterprise market. Such an understanding enables the company, for each customer segment, to develop the optimal strategic positioning, create a cost-effective marketing plan that ensures the right market positioning, and determine the best mix of marketing activities that maximizes the company's return on its marketing investment. It also enables the company to define and deploy new customer service and customer care processes (e.g., complaint handling, technical questions, and outage correction) that more closely meet customers' needs.

The new insight into customers has given this utility an innovative approach to marketing and customer service—an approach that positions the company well to compete and grow in the opportunities provided by the deregulation of its energy market.

Call Center Improvements

Many energy companies (especially utilities) also are implementing customer management systems in their call centers. Like Web-based CRM programs, call center projects typically are focused on capturing channel efficiencies and reducing costs. Recently, for example, U.S. utility Southern California Edison went live with a set of call center applications designed to reduce costs and help the company overcome mounting debt. The implementation, which was deemed a success based on subsequent cash flows, was projected to reduce the length of each customer call by 35 seconds, resulting in a $3-million annual improvement.[11]

Some utilities, however, are using CRM technologies in their call centers to improve both the efficiency and effectiveness of customer service. For instance, Entergy, an electric utility with 2.5 million customers in Arkansas, Louisiana, Mississippi, and Texas, implemented a system to make its proactive phone calls to customers more efficient. To replace its former mail-notification system, the company established an outbound calling program to notify customers that their power was about to be disconnected for nonpayment. The utility hoped to avoid disconnections, having noted that more than three-quarters of customers whose service was stopped almost immediately paid and contacted the utility for reconnection—which resulted in two trips by one of the company's field crews, thus costing the company twice as much to retain each customer.[12]

Once the program was a smash hit with customers, Entergy implemented a customer interaction management (CIM) solution that provides service representatives with customer information and an account profile when the outbound call is answered, then guides the agent through the call. With the new system in place, agents are able to make twice as many calls per hour, reaching 6000 to 10,000 customers a day. The service program itself has been extremely successful: 80 percent of customers reached by answering machine pay their bills, and about 95 percent of customers with whom Entergy representatives are able to speak pay their bills.[13]

Totalgaz, part of the France-based oil company TotalFinaElf, has found its new call center system to be a major force in helping the liquid propane gas (LPG) supplier to more quickly and effectively deal with customer inquiries—which not only saves the company money but also fosters customer loyalty and longer-term relationships.

Supplying bulk LPG to customers' business premises and homes is a complex and price-competitive business. Customers and prospects interact with multiple contacts at Totalgaz, including sales representatives and installation, customer service, and delivery staff. In addition, identifying new business often involves working with external partners—architects, property developers, and installation and safety specialists. Totalgaz recognized that to build customer loyalty, it had to improve the quality and consistency of its service across all contact points. Doing so would help offset the price competition in the LPG market—people are prepared to pay a premium for enhanced service—and improve the return on sales investment. Acquiring customers is expensive, and it is particularly important in a low-margin business to recover the costs through long-term customer relationships.

Totalgaz's solution was based on the premise that every member of the Totalgaz team who might interact with customers and prospects needed instant access to comprehensive, up-to-date customer records. This translated into the need for a customer interaction center at the Paris head office with a direct link between the front- and back-office functions—that is, between the customer service staff and support functions, like accounting, that traditionally had stayed behind the scenes.

The new system in use at the customer interaction center instantly recognizes incoming telephone numbers, accesses the caller's customer file, and displays all relevant customer information (current and historical) on the screen of the customer interaction center representative answering the call. This ensures that the call can be handled in the most efficient manner by customer interaction center personnel: The company estimates that the system has reduced the average length of customer calls by 30 seconds and has enabled 80 percent of inquiries to be dealt with on the first call. Also, by giving representatives access to critical customer data, the system provides for a much more effective and pleasant experience for each customer.

Mobile CRM for the Field

Finally, wireless technology also is providing energy companies with opportunities to increase efficiency and improve customer service, primarily through its use by field technicians. Although this application is not common in the energy industry, one innovative natural gas utility, Southern Union Gas (SUG), implemented a wireless system for its field service team in the early 1990s and since has expanded the system to help the company achieve even greater business benefits.

The system was adopted initially as a way to establish a paperless office and thus to reduce errors and make the company's operations more efficient. Of SUG's nine operating regions, five now have access to mobile devices and computer-aided dispatching (the other regions are not busy enough or big enough to warrant use of the system).[14]

The system is small enough for a technician to carry around to a customer's site, providing the technician with a detailed history of the customer's account before providing service and enabling the real-time updating of the company's customer database with details of the service call upon its completion. The system also includes an autorouting feature that allows the utility's dispatcher to keep track of a field technician's progress and update the customer service schedule accordingly. From a customer's perspective, the utility can schedule service calls within a two-hour window and is able to inform customers immediately if the technician is delayed in keeping an appointment.[15]

A LONG WAY TO GO

The success of the energy industry's CRM efforts varies by location and project. Generally, those companies that are in the downstream sectors of the energy industry (primarily utilities) have invested most heavily in CRM and reaped the greatest benefits. Likewise, utilities in Europe are far more advanced in applying CRM tools and practices than are U.S. utilities, with those in Canada falling somewhere in between.[16]

According to a March 2001 survey by industry analyst Forrester Research, only about one in four U.S. utilities had completed a CRM implementation, with another 14 percent in the process of doing so.[17] The vast majority of these programs focus on cutting costs and are primarily point solutions, frequently doing nothing more than moving specific services to a new channel (typically the Internet). Even with the sector's emphasis on the e-channel, the majority of U.S. utilities (about two-thirds) do not offer online access to account information, and those that do rarely offer advanced applications such as electronic account payment.[18] Although there are pockets of U.S. energy companies that have invested heavily in CRM—as California's utilities have, to enable customers to deal with power blackouts—most are not powerful enough to satisfy customer wants and needs.[19]

On the other hand, in Europe, where utilities deregulation is well along, organizations such as British Gas are setting the standard for CRM. These companies, and others like them, are evolving beyond their traditional products and markets, aligning with other players in other industries. They are cultivating new kinds of relationships and CRM capabilities that enable them to position themselves as retailers that provide energy rather than utilities that provide retail products.

It is important to recognize, however, that CRM capabilities are not built overnight. Many energy companies have made investments in key capabilities only to struggle to see a return. Today, there are ways to quantify the value and benefits of investments made in CRM capabilities that help determine where to invest further to reap the highest return or how to justify new investments. There are also ways to reduce the risk involved in implementing large CRM initiatives based on lessons learned from other industries. In essence, taking an approach that reduces risk and measures value will enable utility executives to determine which improvements or changes to the plan should be made and capitalize on new opportunities to leverage CRM for increased competitive advantage. If the trends in Europe are any indication of the future for energy companies around the world, CRM capabilities will soon become a competitive necessity.

Retail: Customer Demands Intensify the Pressure for CRM

Brian Kalms and Dennis A. Mullahy

Fierce competition has always been a hallmark of the retail industry. In recent years, it has become even tougher, as innovative new entrants have upset the status quo and existing retailers have become more efficient.

But perhaps the greatest challenge faced by retailers is consumers' rising expectations. It is no secret that today's consumers—whether they are in Ohio, Oslo, or Osaka—have continued to evolve into elusive, finicky targets who are harder to please and who have many options. Consumers are more highly informed than ever before and more able to compare prices and products with little time, effort, or interaction with a retailer. In fact, it is safe to say that never before have consumers expected more from a retailer and exhibited so little loyalty to specific brands.

Logically, technology has become a driving force in helping retailers differentiate themselves. Companies that invested early in key technologies and continue to embrace new advances to support their strategic visions have been among the most successful in the past decade. Wal-Mart is a great example of this. On the other hand, late adopters of technology have fallen behind and now face an uphill battle. Those retailers who have made fairly significant technology investments have directed them toward streamlining their operations or product management—improving visibility to inventory levels, communicating with vendors, and capturing point-of-sale data, for example.

However, leading retailers recognize that they must go beyond their historical product-focused operations and become more customer focused if they are to be successful in the twenty-first century. This requires some significant changes.

Retailers will need to develop an understanding of customers that is based on customer behavior rather than on geography or demographics, and they will need to learn how to use this information across the entire organization, not just in marketing. The truly customer-focused retailers of the twenty-first century will use customer behavior and attitudinal information to make decisions in everything from individual store assortments and space allocation to pricing, promotions, store layout, service strategies, sales support, and replenishment practices.

CRM IN SHORT SUPPLY

The urgency to become customer-focused stems from the fact that retailers generally lag other industries in their adoption and use of CRM and customer-centered processes and strategies. In part, this can be attributed to the fact that the traditional scope of CRM (that is, to help companies develop unique, one-to-one relationships) is much more pragmatic and economically feasible in certain other industries than in retail. For example, it is much easier to identify and track customers in utilities, financial services, and travel where the numbers of customers and transactions are smaller and the customers tend to identify themselves with each interaction. Nevertheless, Research by Gartner revealed that retailers recognize that CRM is crucial to retail success, and more than half (56 percent) rated CRM as their highest priority for 2001.[1] Yet few retailers are actually implementing CRM systems.[2]

Although the vast majority of retailers are not specifically implementing CRM software packages, a growing number of retailers have embraced retail-specific technologies that improve the experience for customers. For instance, many supermarkets are introducing self-service checkout stations that enable shoppers to scan, bag, and pay for their purchases without assistance from a cashier, or with very limited employee oversight to assist customers only when needed. Similarly, Ann Arbor, Michigan–based Borders Group is an early adopter of kiosks, which the company has placed in its Borders bookstores as an alternative to the often-crowded information counter. Customers have access to a much greater selection of book titles on the kiosk than what is available on the store shelves, and the kiosk enables customers to order items that are not in inventory.[3]

Wireless technology is making greater inroads among retailers as well. The Home Depot, WHSmith, and Wal-Mart use wireless handheld devices to scan items and process transactions for shoppers while they are waiting in line, so that on reaching the cash register the sale is almost complete.[4] Associates in the stores of Paris-based luxury retailer LVMH Fashion Group exclusively use a wireless handheld point-of-sale system. The application (which supports customer checkout, customer preference data capture, receiving, and price and inventory lookup) enables staff to be with the customer continuously.[5]

Retailers deploying these technologies in support of customer-facing activities have made strides in strengthening bonds with their customers. However, it appears that many of these efforts are insufficient or ineffective, because customer loyalty rates continue to fall. In fact, over the past decade loyalty has been eroding steadily.

Consumers today are less likely to purchase a specific brand or patronize a particular company simply because the brands are well known. The percentage of consumers who claim that they tend to stick with well-known brands when purchasing products and services dropped dramatically for all age groups from 1975 to 2000. Even the percentage for individuals over 60 years old—typically among the most loyal consumers—dropped 20 points over those 25 years.[6] Clearly, retailers still have not gone far enough in adopting CRM.

MOVING TOWARD PROFITABLE CUSTOMER RELATIONSHIPS

The opportunity for retailers to use customer data and information to build more profitable, lasting customer relationships is tremendous. The problem is that although gathering this data can be fairly easy, making sense of it is an entirely different matter. Cleaning and organizing this data can be a daunting task in itself, let alone developing the analytical framework to make strategic use of it throughout the business.

In many if not most cases, customer and transaction data tends to be housed in separate databases. This creates "silos" of data, each of which can provide only limited insights, depending on the product line or channel in which it was generated. The greater the number of channels, brands, categories, and products involved, the more difficult the task of integrating, managing, and analyzing the data. Thus, the first step for many retailers is to create a single view of the customer by combining these information silos. This enhances a retailer's ability to cross-sell and upsell, develop more personalized marketing campaigns and product offers, and present a consistent "face" or experience to customers regardless of the channel they use to interact with the company.

The Limited, a Columbus, Ohio–based retailer, recently undertook such an initiative with the objective of creating a 360° view of customers across its multiple distribution channels. The Limited has an extremely complex business structure comprising multiple brands that are marketed and sold across numerous channels. The company's Victoria's Secret brand, for instance, is sold online, through a broad network of stores, and by catalog (some 360 million catalogs are mailed each year). Without an integrated view of the customer, however, executives could not be sure if a catalog customer who stopped ordering through the call center or online had begun shopping in the stores or stopped shopping at Victoria's Secret entirely. To solve this problem, The Limited is installing a central data warehouse to combine store and catalog data into one database for analytical and testing purposes. The system will begin to help managers understand customer cross-channel buying behavior so they can promote cross-selling and up-selling and conduct more targeted direct mail campaigns.[7]

London-based online wine retailer Virgin Wines has successfully built its business using customer information to drive its operations. While many retailers continue to pursue a product focus, Virgin Wines has taken a different tack: helping customers sort through the mind-numbing spectrum of choices available and decide what is best for them. Virgin Wines has developed a site with customer-friendly features, including the following:

- A vast selection of wines, which gives shoppers access to a wide range of styles, price points, and varietals
- Simple wine descriptions, void of the often-confusing terminology preferred by wine connoisseurs, so that regular consumers can more easily understand what type of wine they are buying

The most innovative (and vital) feature on the site is the Wine Wizard, which personalizes the shopping experience by helping customers define their individual preferences and tailoring the offerings presented to each customer. As customers continue to shop, the Wine Wizard uses purchase data and feedback customers provide on the wines they have sampled to further refine each customer's preferences and provide even more tailored offerings for future visits.

To date, the results of Virgin Wines' customer-focused efforts have been dramatic. The rate of converting Virgin Wines prospects to customers is three times higher among individuals who have used the site's personalization features than among those who have not. Even more impressive is the fact that customers who use the personalization tools are nine times more likely to be repeat buyers than those who do not. In addition, Virgin Wines' cost to acquire a new customer is among the best of direct marketers and is significantly lower than most Internet companies'. And the company's cost to generate a repeat order is nearly one-tenth of the average for a traditional mail-order company.

THE FUTURE: USING CUSTOMER INFORMATION THROUGHOUT THE ENTIRE BUSINESS

Clearly, creating a single view of the customer is critical for retailers who seek to build lasting customer relationships. However, the full potential for adopting CRM in retailing encompasses more than making better marketing decisions and applies to all retail channels. A few savvy retailers are defining what may be the future of the industry. They are aggressively working to change from being product-centered organizations to become customer-centered organizations. This is a fundamental step for many retailers that is based on two central ideas: (1) adopting an analytical approach to developing customer insights based on customer behavior, and (2) using these behavioral insights to drive decisions in all areas of the business.

Adopting an Analytical Approach to Customer Insights

An analytical approach to developing customer insights based on customer behavior differs significantly from traditional retail CRM methods. This approach uses methods and associated tools to analyze customer behavior in three specific ways:

- Purchasing behavior, such as frequency of visits and market basket size
- Behavior response to merchandising and marketing levers, such as reaction to changes in pricing, promotions, and category locations

- Store behavior, such as the stores at which they shop and the areas of the store in which they shop

It is worth noting, however, that although purchasing and loyalty card data is extremely valuable in the analysis, it is not absolutely essential. In its absence, retailers still can take a much more fact-based approach to developing customer insights through customer segment and attitudinal analysis using existing data and customer observation.

Either way, these dynamic behavioral insights help retailers identify which merchandising and marketing levers likely caused each customer group's behavior in each store. This approach is very different from the customer research and demographic segmentation approaches that many retailers have leveraged, because it is driven by actual customer behavior (not how consumers say they will behave), and it predicts the factors that will motivate customers to make future purchases. With this information, retailers are prioritizing customer segments and developing detailed strategies to influence them to buy more products, more often, and in ways that are more profitable for the retailer.

For one retailer, the benefits of this method are staggering. It identified a segment that visited frequently but did not spend much per visit—an ideal group to target to increase spending and margin contribution. This type of insight is fairly common—it is what this new method and associated tool helped the retailer discover next that is so powerful.

It turned out that this group commonly shops the video game and action figure categories. The retailer found that this group responded well to coupons for juvenile and infant care products but did not respond well to coupons for video games. It also found that this group expressed some interest in newly released die-cast models. What should the retailer do with this information? The new approach suggested cross-promoting action figures with video games, reconfiguring the end caps in the video game department to include action figures, reducing coupons and discounts in video games because they had been ineffective, and exploiting the interest in new die-cast models by merchandising attachment and convenience items nearby. The result? An opportunity to increase incremental revenue generated by this group shopping in these categories by more than $17 million and increase gross margin by nearly $5 million—close to a 10 percent improvement.

As this example illustrates, customer insights alone cannot drive improved business performance, but they can drive fundamentally different decisions in key areas of the business, as described next.

Using Behavioral Insights to Drive Decisions

In-Store Optimization.   All too often, retailers fall into one of two traps. Either they make false assumptions about the profile of their most profitable customer groups, or they have a fairly accurate profile but have not made the critical changes in their business that impact these customer groups' in-store experience. Either way, retailers miss huge opportunities to increase the number of times these customers visit the store and the size and profitability of each transaction.

In the past two years, consumer electronics retailer Best Buy has leveraged the new approach to customer insight to change its in-store strategy with far-reaching success. Historically, Best Buy approached its business in a product-centric way and did little to capture and leverage customer information. As a result, Best Buy carried a wide assortment that was hindering its profitability and the effectiveness of its sales force.

Best Buy began changing its focus by using fact-based analysis of historical purchases and primary research to find out who comprised its most profitable customer group, how these customers shopped, what they bought, what their lifestyles were like, and so forth. The company discovered that it did not need such a broad assortment. On the contrary, this group wanted fewer, select items with better sales support and more solution-oriented offerings. This fact-based approach to understanding its most profitable customer group drove the transformational changes across Best Buy's entire business—everything from its brand position and marketing messages to its merchandise selection, pricing strategies, space allocations, and labor attitudes and strategies.

This major change is perhaps best reflected in Best Buy's newest stores. The music selection, which had taken center stage for the entire history of the chain, was moved from the front and center of the store. In addition, appliances were relocated between two of the highest-traffic departments. In these new stores, Best Buy showcases emerging technology and entertainment with DVD software, wireless communications, and personal digital assistants up front. And Best Buy has created a transaction center where customers can sit down and have employees review service plans and delivery and sale information for the more complex purchases. The average ticket at new stores has increased. Meanwhile, store costs have decreased and profits have shot up. Beginning in fiscal year 2003, all of Best Buy's new stores will feature this new layout and service strategy.

The transaction center also highlights the business improvement opportunities that customer insight can have when used to influence sales associate activities and behaviors. Using customer insight to change the way store labor is organized and the way it regards select customer groups is a clear means of differentiation.

Optimized Space and Assortment.   Offering the same merchandise at every store used to be the accepted norm for retailers. But now, retailers recognize that to satisfy the different needs of local customers, they must offer tailored assortments. The challenge is doing so in a manageable and profitable way—that is, without having to determine a unique assortment, space allocation, and planogram for each and every store.

This is where the power of customer insight comes into play. It uses an analytical approach to determine category-level assortments and space allocations, minimizing the complexity inherent in merchandising millions of items or stock-keeping units

(SKUs) at hundreds or thousands of stores. Rather than trying to identify different demand patterns for each item and each category at each store based on geography or demography, this approach identifies different demand patterns at the category level and assigns an assortment, category by category, to a group of stores whose customers purchase the category in a similar way. Then, advanced algorithms account for differences in local customer demand at each store within the group of stores and recommend the shelf space to give each item.

A leading retailer of clothing, foods, home furnishings, and financial services in the United Kingdom is a pioneer in this approach. The experience of this retailer illustrates the power of combining valuable behavior insights with a much more fact-based approach to tailoring product assortment and space allocation at the store.

The retailer adopted a new customer insight strategy that would better match each store's product offering with the desires of its local customers. The retailer began analyzing customer behavior (e.g., how customers shopped, what they bought, their lifestyles and work patterns, how valuable they were to the company) in tandem with the more traditional demographic and geographic information. This fact-based analysis revealed several customer groups, with detailed profiles on buying preferences, level of spending, typical purchases, frequency of spending, and likes and dislikes. Stores then were grouped according to those that had like customer groups instead of those with the same square footage. The retailer then allocated products to stores based on the buying and lifestyle behaviors of those customer groups.

Having determined what merchandise should be in each store, the next challenge was to maximize profitability within each store. The retailer developed a process and tool to model scenarios for allocating space at each store. With these facts in hand, the company piloted a program with select product groups in several of its stores.

The retailer has generated significant benefits from its new approach. Some areas of its women's department in the pilot store have delivered a fivefold increase and some men's areas have shown more than a 40 percent increase. Many of the pilot store sales increased significantly, with many of the average market basket values going up by as much as 30 percent. The pilots were so successful that the retailer quickly rolled the program out to all of its nonfood categories in all of its stores. Clearly, the move to an insight-driven customer strategy has been a smart one for this retailer.

Walgreens represents another excellent example of using an analytical approach to tailor its store assortments to meet local market needs. Not long ago, Walgreens employed the same assortments, store layout, and labor strategy across all of its more than 3500 stores. Now, using its basic department management (BDM) program and tools, Walgreens determines store assortments at the category level and allocates them to stores that have been grouped together based on like purchasing behavior for a particular category. Then it recommends shelf placement at the individual store level to account for store-to-store variations in shelf space and variations in local customer demand.

For example, a downtown Chicago Walgreens likely will end up with smaller-count products, such as single-use pain relief tablets, whereas a suburban Chicago Walgreens will stock up on larger-count merchandise. Or, in Miami, where there is a large Cuban-American population, Walgreens store managers may get a suggestion to stock up on additional shades of darker hair coloring. The changes are subtle to the customers. They only know that it is easier and faster to find exactly what they need.

Precision Pricing.   Store- and item-level pricing decisions can be overwhelming and are all too often left to intuition. When Best Buy applied an analytical approach to pricing, it achieved the following results over a two-year period from 1997 to 1999:

- 21 percent increase in revenue in key categories
- 36 percent increase in gross margin in key categories
- $50 million profit improvement in key categories
- 18 percent increase in consumer price perception

These incredible results underscore the impact a more fact-based customer approach can have. The new, more precise method works as follows: First, an analysis is performed using customer data that assigns a strategic role to each category and item—whether that role is to deliver incremental profit, drive increased store traffic, or support the brand image. Then, fact-based methods and tools create pricing strategies and tactics based on the category- and item-level role. The outcome is twofold: The retailer's pricing strategy is aligned with the company's overall objectives, and its return on pricing investments is maximized.

Here are two valuable examples of these methods and associated tools at work. Best Buy, whose results were highlighted earlier, had a best-in-market or lowest-price pricing policy in place for all of its items. By using fact-based analytic tools that utilized price elasticity, competitor profiling, and category role designation, it discovered that only a small percentage of its product categories created the desired consumer price impression. This meant that the remaining categories could adopt a more moderately priced strategy and generate a great deal more profit without sacrificing consumer price perception. The results over a two-year period, as highlighted previously, were outstanding.

Another specialty retailer applied an analytical approach to more than 1600 items in one of its departments and uncovered well over 100 opportunities to increase its price and still maintain its competitive pricing image. The price changes that were made in just this one department delivered $2 million in gross margin annually.

Promotion Effectiveness.   Many retailers say they "know" their promotions increase sales. But did they increase gross margin? Could other items have been featured that would have generated higher sales and margins? Leveraging customer insight can help retailers measure the effectiveness of their promotional programs and significantly increase the gross profit earned from these efforts.

One specialty retailer offers a great example. Historically, this retailer selected and priced items for its circulars based on its merchants' instincts or vendor recommendations, which were often accompanied by allowances. Recently, however, using an analytical approach, this retailer began to measure the incremental gross margin return on advertising spending and corresponding sales productivity for promoted items and categories relative to the amount of circular space and dollars allocated. With this fact-based information in hand, the retailer assigned a classification to each item and category and redesigned its circulars to maximize the "winners" (high profit, high sales), get rid of the "losers" (low profit, low sales), and balance the mix of "profit generators" (high profit, low sales) and "traffic drivers" (low profit, high sales). The results from applying these new techniques were significant, reaching more than $25 million in incremental gross profit over approximately a nine-month period.

Best Buy also employed a similar approach to its promotions. Previously, it did not measure the effectiveness of its promotions and relied heavily on vendors, gut instinct, and historical practices to determine how, what, and when to promote. However, Best Buy adopted an innovative advertising allocation and selection analytical tool that analyzes customer behavior and response to changes in promotional activity, such as ad item selection, placement, timing, media, and market. It used this information to help determine the most profitable mix of advertising spending across all of its print and electronic media. Best Buy's marketing group developed a new capability and process for selecting the items, categories, and events that would yield the greatest profit. The initiative generated results very quickly:

- 25 percent increase in holiday comparative store sales in 1997
- 7 percent increase in annual comparative store sales in 1997
- $80 million profit improvement in 1997

This approach has worked for apparel retailers as well. One large department store used analytical tools to determine what items and categories to feature that would drive the highest sales and gross margin. For example, it found out that promoting accessories in addition to tops and bottoms lifted sales and gross margin. This application of an analytical approach in conjunction with applications in merchandising and in-stock management allowed this department store to win during a critical time of year for its business. After four years of negative comparable store sales, this division delivered an impressive double-digit increase in comparable store sales and inventory turns, and a high single-digit percent increase in gross profit.

CONCLUSION

Competition and demanding customers are facts of life for retailers today—and for the foreseeable future. Retail leaders such as Best Buy, Walgreens, and Virgin Wines certainly have recognized this and are aggressively pursuing retail-specific CRM strategies as a way to become more customer-centered organizations. They are utilizing an analytical approach to sort through their data and turn it into actionable information. They are sharing this information across the business. And they are leveraging this information to drive decisions regarding personalized marketing campaigns, store layouts, product assortments, and space allocations. In a few years, it will be rare to find a major retailer making a critical business decision without the benefit of leveraging customer insights. The benefits are simply too compelling.

Notes

CHAPTER 1

1. David Lipke, "Pledge of Allegiance," *American Demographics,* November 2000, pp. 40–41.
2. Will Pollock, "Retailers Gear up for Zealous Expansion," *Shopping Center World,* December 1997.
3. Steve Schriver, "Customer Loyalty: Going, Going . . . ," *American Demographics,* September 1997, p. 23.
4. According to the 2001 *Mutual Fund Factbook,* published by the Investment Company Institute, there were 8200 mutual funds available at the end of 2000.
5. The National Restaurant Association's *Foodservice 2001 Report* noted that there were 844,000 total outlets in the United States serving food, including single-location and mom-and-pop restaurants. The Franchise Finance Corp of America's 2001 *Chain Industry Review & Outlook* reported that as of December 31, 2000, there were 217,917 chain restaurant locations in the United States.
6. Naomi Wolf, *The Beauty Myth,* New York, Anchor/Doubleday, 1992, pp. 78–79; Mark Munro, "A New Era of Eros in Advertising," *The Boston Globe,* 1989.
7. David Shenk, *Data Smog,* Harper San Francisco, June 1998.
8. Direct Marketing Association's *Statistical Fact Book 2000,* Direct Marketing Association
9. Statistic reported on antitelemarketer.com.
10. Source: Jupiter Vision Report, "E-mail Customer Service: Taking Control of Rising Customer Demand," August 31, 2000.

CHAPTER 4

1. Accenture presentation, "Brand Manner Market Offering."

CHAPTER 8

1. 1999 Business Intelligence/Data Warehousing Program Competitive Analysis Report, World Research Inc., San Jose, California.
2. Duncan S. McClain, "Customer Data Integration: The Essential Component of Effective CRM," *DM Review,* January 2001.
3. Thomas H. Davenport, Jeanne G. Harris, and Ajay K. Kohli, "How Do They Know Their Customers So Well?" *Sloan Management Review,* winter 2001.

4. Ibid.
5. "Information: The Newest Currency," *Target Marketing,* July 1999.
6. "How Do They Know Their Customers So Well?" *Sloan Management Review,* winter 2001.
7. Ibid.

CHAPTER 11

1. "How Much Are CRM Capabilities Really Worth? What Every CEO Should Know," Accenture, 2000.

CHAPTER 15

1. This article is based on a study sponsored by the Accenture Institute for Strategic Change and Accenture's Customer Relationship Management Service Line. The results were compiled from 333 survey responses from a sample of 3942 online U.S. consumers. The survey recipients were selected from a broad range of categories of online users, provided by Postmaster Direct, an online mailing list provider. Both the recipients and the respondents closely matched the demographics of the general online U.S. population.
2. This is a finding from a study of Web site "stickiness" sponsored by the Accenture Institute for Strategic Change with help from a team of MBA students at the Owen Graduate School of Management at Vanderbilt University. The results were compiled from 185 survey responses from a sample of 3084 online U.S. consumers. The survey recipients were selected from a broad range of categories of online users, provided by Postmaster Direct, an online mailing list provider. Both the recipients and the respondents closely matched the demographics of the general online U.S. population.

CHAPTER 16

1. Randy Souza, Harley Manning, Hollie Goldman, and Joyce Tong, "The Best of Retail Site Design," Forrester Research Report, October 2000; Steve Ulfelder, "Opting Out of the Online-Buying Labyrinth," *Boston Globe,* November 9, 2000, http://digitalmass.boston.com/columns/ecommerce/1109.html.
2. Anya Sacharow and Mark Mooradian, "Navigation: Toward Intuitive Movement and Improved Usability," Jupiter Research Digital Content Vision Report, March 1999, www.jup.com.
3. Harley Manning, John C. McCarthy, and Randy Souza, "Why Most Web Sites Fail," Forrester Research Report, September 1998.
4. Jared M. Spool, Tara Scanlon, Will Schroeder, Carolyn Snyder, and Terri DeAngelo, *Web Site Usability: A Designer's Guide* (San Francisco: Morgan Kaufman Publishers, 1999).
5. Scott Spanbauer, "The Ultimate Wireless Buyers Guide," *PC World,* October 2000, www.pcworld.com/resource/printable/article.asp?aid=18102.

6. Although hundreds of wireless sites may be available in the United States, the majority of them are not retail oriented. See Elinor Abreu, "Wireless Internet: Still Ahead of Its Time," *The Industry Standard,* February 28, 2000.

7. David Bishop, "An Introduction to Mobile Commerce," Yankee Group Mobile Communication Strategies Report 1, February 2001.

8. Dylan Brooks, Eric Horowitz, Michael Sadaka, Robert Hertzberg, Seamus McAteer, and Zia Daniell Wigder, "Mobile Content and Applications," Jupiter Research Wireless Applications Vision Report 8, February 14, 2001, www. jup.com.

9. "Wireless: Who Wants It?" *The Industry Standard,* October 11, 2000, www. thestandard.com/article/0,1902,19063,00.html. See also Joe Laszlo, Jeff Makowka, Ken Allard, Ken Kryda, Seamus McAteer, and Zia Daniell Wigder, "Mobile Revenue Models," Jupiter Research Wireless Applications Vision Report 2, April 14, 2000, www.jup.com.

10. Sample of the top 100 e-commerce sites based on unique page views according to Nielson Net Ratings. Each site discussed employed a best-practice strategy observed in the survey of top sites. Retailers had to fit one of the 10 categories of Web retailers identified using data from Harris Interactive, www.harrisinteractive. com/pop_up/si/categories.asp, and featured in "The Web's Great Order Disorder," *Business 2.0,* September 29, 2000.

11. e-Sixt services 32 European countries with car rental and other services. It also has partners in the United States, Canada, Australia, and Central and South America.

12. See John C. Beck, Patrick D. Lynch, and Lawrence Tu, "What mCommerce?" Accenture Institute for Strategic Change Global mCommerce Research Note 3, November 15, 2000.

13. The Barnes & Noble mobile site no longer enables customers to search for specific books and music.

CHAPTER 18

1. "Surviving the Internet Shakeout," Forrester Research.

CHAPTER 20

1. IDC, "Messaging Applications: Market Forecast and Analysis, 2001–2005, IDC 24855, June 2001.

2. American Customer Satisfaction Index—by Industry Sector, 1994–2000.

CHAPTER 21

1. Wireless Mobile Telemetry Forecast, Yankee Group, April 2001.

CHAPTER 25

1. Henry Assael, *Consumer Behavior and Marketing Action,* 6th ed. (Cincinnati, OH: South-Western College Publishing, 1998).

CHAPTER 26

1. "Brand Loyalty," CNW Marketing Research.
2. 2001 sales numbers were obtained from the National Automobile Dealers Association (2001) and www.Autonews.com.
3. Nina Munk, "How Levi's Trashed a Great American Brand," *Fortune,* April 12, 1999.
4. Julie Creswell, "Confessions of a Fashion Victim," *Fortune,* December 10, 2001.
5. Betsy McKay, "Coke Hunts for Talent to Re-establish Its Marketing Might," *Wall Street Journal,* March 6, 2002, p. B4.
6. Statistics are drawn from "Insight-Driven Marketing: Using Customer Insights to Build Brand Loyalty and Increase Marketing ROI," a research report released by Accenture in 2001. The report is based on a telephone survey of 175 marketing and customer relationship managers at companies in the United States and the United Kingdom.
7. Ibid.
8. Anthony Bianco and Louis Lavelle, "The CEO Trap," *Business Week,* December 11, 2000.

CHAPTER 27

1. "The e-Marketing Report," Morgan Stanley Dean Witter, May 2000; "Outdoor Advertising Association of America e-Marketing Report: Web Advertising Grows Outside the U.S.," McCann-Erickson, Wilkofsky Gruen, and Jupiter Communications, December 14, 2000. Accenture calculations are also used in making this estimate.

CHAPTER 28

1. Steve Rosenbush and Heather Timmons, "Telecom Lenders: Standing in Line for What?" *BusinessWeek,* February 11, 2002.
2. "CRM for Profit," *Telecommunications,* December 2000.
3. Ibid.
4. Mary Thyfault, "Web-Based Care Aids Telecom Customers," *Interactive Week,* April 3, 2001.
5. Sheila Flynn, "The Customer Is King," *Telecom Business,* March 1, 2001.
6. Ibid.
7. Mary Thyfault, "Web-Based Care Aids Telecom Customers," *Interactive Week,* April 3, 2001.
8. Greg Jefferson and James Aldridge, "SBC Snags Moby," *San Antonio Business Journal,* December 14, 2001.
9. "Living with a Perfect Stranger," *Telephony,* October 1, 2001, p. 24.
10. "Window on the Real World: AT&T," *Internet World,* September 15, 2001.
11. "CRM for Profit," *Telecommunications,* December 2000.
12. Deborah Young, "The Information Store: CRM Is Thrusting Data Mining Back to the Future," *Wireless Review,* September 15, 2000.

13. Ibid.
14. "Living with a Perfect Stranger," *Telephony,* October 1, 2001, p. 24.
15. "BT Plans CRM Strategy for Merged Net Brands," Curtis Brown, *Precision Marketing,* September 28, 2001.
16. "Window on the Real World: AT&T," *Internet World,* September 15, 2001.

CHAPTER 29
1. Ed McKenna, "Over 281 million served," *Federal Computer Week,* May 14, 2001.
2. "Customer Relationship Management: A Blueprint for Government," Accenture, November 2001.
3. "Microsoft Helps Turn Britain's E-Government Vision into Reality," *Information Superhighways Newsletter,* May 2001, p. 1.
4. "Customer Relationship Management: A Blueprint for Government," Accenture, November 2001.
5. Mark Forman, "Empowering the Customer: OMB's Mark Forman Leads the Bush Administration Effort to Make the Government More Customer Centric," *Government Computer News,* November 19, 2001, p. S2(3).
6. Rishi Sood, "CRM Is Focus of E-Government Transformation," *Washington Technology,* April 16, 2001.
7. Karl Cushing, "Middlesbrough Outsources its CRM," *Computer Weekly,* November 1, 2001, p. 64(1).
8. Kevin McCaney, "Survey Finds Federal Sites, While Not Perfect, Are Showing Progress," *Government Computer News,* March 4, 2002, p. 15(1).
9. Rishi Sood, "CRM Is Focus of E-Government Transformation," *Washington Technology,* April 16, 2001.
10. Liam Lahey, "Government Barriers Hinder CRM Adoption," *Computer Dealer News,* December 28, 2001, p. 16(1).

CHAPTER 30
1. Tonya Vinas, "Customer-Order Management—Out Of Order," *Industry Week,* April 1, 2002.
2. Paul C. Judge, "Customer Service: EMC Corp.," *Fast Company,* June 2001.
3. Ibid.
4. Ibid.
5. "How Much Are Customer Relationship Capabilities Worth? What Every High-Tech CEO Should Know," Accenture report.
6. Antone Gonsalves, "IT's the Tiger in Their Tanks—Technology Adds Octane for Drive to Speed Delivery and Build to Order," *InformationWeek,* September 17, 2001, p. 61.
7. "Cleared for Takeoff," *CIO,* April 1, 2002.
8. Ibid.
9. Ibid.

10. Carol L. Karnes and Larry R. Karnes, "Ross Controls: A Case Study In Mass Customization," *Production & Inventory Management Journal,* summer 2000, p. 1.
11. "Unilever Goes Live with mySAP Customer Relationship Management," SAP company news release, April 1, 2002.
12. Ibid.
13. Karen M. Kroll, "Bigger Role for Call Centers," *Industry Week,* February 21, 2000.
14. John Teresko, "Technology Leader of the Year—Transforming GM," *Industry Week,* December 1, 2001.
15. Alorie Gilbert, "IT Helps Fight Year of Decline: Manufacturers Turn to Technology to Cut Costs and Reduce Inventories," *InformationWeek,* September 17, 2001.
16. Kit Davis, "CRM Tools Work Many Ways," *Consumer Goods,* November 2001.
17. Alorie Gilbert, "IT Helps Fight Year of Decline: Manufacturers Turn to Technology to Cut Costs and Reduce Inventories," *InformationWeek,* September 17, 2001.
18. Jeff Zygmont, "Mass Customization + The Web = Intimacy with Millions," *Consumer Goods,* March 2000.
19. Ibid

CHAPTER 31

1. Samantha Low, "The Energy Industry in the 21st Century: Addressing the Challenges Ahead," *Chemistry and Industry,* November 5, 2001, p. 5(1).
2. Aaron Ricadela, "Pay Dirt: Petroleum Companies Tap IT to Help Sustain Them Through a Tough Economy," *InformationWeek,* March 18, 2002.
3. James Kynge, "China Plans Break-up of State Power Corporation," *Financial Times,* April 11, 2002.
4. Jennifer Maselli, "Full Power for Online Efforts: Energy Companies Drill Deep into Internal and External Collaboration," *InformationWeek,* September 17, 2001, p. 119.
5. Marc L. Songini, "Dimmed Utilities Plug into CRM," *ComputerWorld,* August 6, 2001, p. 1.
6. "IT Now More Than Ever," *Utility Business,* November 1, 2001 p. 40.
7. Ethan L. Cohen and Eileen Joseph, "Making a CRM Match," *Public Utilities Fortnightly* (1994), June 15, 2001, p. S66.
8. Heather Herrald, "What a Switch," *CIO,* May 15, 2001.
9. Ibid.
10. Jeff Sweat, "Information: The Most Valuable Asset. IT Is Critical for Energy Companies That Want to Expand Their Reach," *InformationWeek,* September 11, 2000.
11. Marc L. Songini, "Dimmed Utilities Plug into CRM," *ComputerWorld,* August 6, 2001, p. 1.

12. Candace Berman, "Comprehensive Customer Interaction Management (CIM) Solutions Powers Entergy," *Call Center CRM Solutions,* November 2000.

13. Ibid.

14. Angela Karr, "CRM Hitches A Ride," *Customer Interface,* September 2001.

15. Ibid.

16. Heather Herrald, "What a Switch," *CIO,* May 15, 2001.

17. Charles W. Thurston, "CRM Deployment—or Bust?" *Public Utilities Fortnightly* (1994), June 15, 2001, p. S60.

18. Heather Herrald, "What a Switch," *CIO,* May 15, 2001.

19. Marc L. Songini, "Dimmed Utilities Plug into CRM," *ComputerWorld,* August 6, 2001, p. 1.

CHAPTER 32

1. "Retailers Identify CRM as Top Strategic Initiative for 2001," *Call Center,* October 1, 2001.

2. "Retailers Say CRM Is Crucial but Few Are Implementing Initiatives," *Direct Marketing,* October 2001, p. 12.

3. Stephanie Roussel-Dupre, "Kiosks: The Latest Chapter in Customer Service," *Integrated Solutions for Retailers,* May 2001.

4. Denise Power, "Wireless: Unbound Passion," *Executive Technology,* April 2002.

5. Denise Power, "Speedier Service in Fashion at LVMH," *Executive Technology,* March 2002.

6. David Lipke, "Pledge of Allegiance," *American Demographics,* November 2000, pp. 40–41.

7. "The Limited: Uniting Multiple Channel Views of the Customer, *Software Magazine,* February/March 2001.

Glossary

attitudinal segmentation   The practice of segmenting customers based on their needs and attitudes (survey information). Attitudinal segmentation quantifies the unobservable.

behavioral segmentation   The practice of segmenting customers based on all available customer information (transaction, product ownership/purchase, sociodemographic, promotion history, channel usage, customer research).

brand   The sum total of a customer's experience with a company; as such, it encompasses the entire range of the company's products, services, behaviors, distribution channels, technologies, and processes.

brand loyalty   The tendency of a customer to choose one business or product over another for a particular need because of the brand.

brand manners   Everything the company says and does. Determines in large part how customers experience the brand.

brand value   Directly links the value of the brand to the company's bottom line. It financially proves the brand's importance in achieving the business objectives of the company.

business intelligence   The practice of analyzing an organization's accumulated raw data and extracting useful insight from it.

business-to-business (B2B)   Any business or organization that sells its products or services to other businesses, vendors, or distributors.

business-to-consumer (B2C)   Any business or organization that sells its products or services to consumers.

call center optimization   Initiative which involves building robust capabilities for more intelligent handling of customers' incoming calls and better access by call center representatives to customer records.

campaign management   Technology that aids in the management of marketing campaigns by automating the tasks associated with developing, launching, and monitoring campaigns.

channel added value   Measure of how much worth the channel creates for the customer, beyond what the manufacturer provides.

channel conflict strategy matrix   A matrix used to analyze the effectiveness of each channel in order to shed nonperforming channels and adopt new ones.

channel density Wavelength channels on a fiber. The effect of a high channel density is greater profit potential, through a higher revenue per wavelength and a lower cost per incremental service.

channel functions Informing, interacting, transacting, delivering, and servicing the customer.

channel intermediaries Organizations that mediate exchange utility in relationships involving two or more partners (e.g., wholesalers, agents, retailers, the Internet, overseas distributors, and direct marketers).

channel map Map that helps managers understand and articulate the path of change. It offers a bird's-eye view of who's who and who does what in the channel.

channels An array of exchange relationships that create customer value in the acquisition, consumption, and disposition of products and services (e.g., sales and order capture, call centers, customer service, third-party channel operations, field service contact and management, e-CRM.)

channel strategy Selecting the most appropriate and effective channels for reaching desired customers.

conversational marketing The marketing practice in which each interaction, dialogue, monologue, or discussion with a customer is recognized and managed as part of a larger discourse. Success at conversational marketing is measured by the ability to integrate these customer contacts and use the knowledge gained to proactively set the direction of future interactions.

conversational relationship Listening to customers' input while also noting their mood and voice.

CRM strategy and road map An approach to help identify, prioritize, and build the right CRM capabilities for creating customer and company value.

cross-selling A means of steering repeat buyers to other types of products based on interests they have displayed in past purchases.

customer acquisition Initiatives by a company to obtain new customers.

customer acquisition rate The rate at which a company obtains new customers.

customer analytics Methods to produce dynamic customer understanding and behavior prediction. Customer analytics are a key to creating intelligent offers and differentiating customer service.

customer buyer values analysis An approach to determine why customers make specific buying decisions and incorporate that knowledge into specific marketing and service strategies.

customer-centric continuum A continuum with six stages, ranging from a pure product focus on the left and a total customer focus on the right. The approach recognizes that every company will have a different point on this continuum that is best for it.

customer-centricity Popular goal for many companies to more deeply understand their customers and personalize the products and services they deliver.

customer churn When a customer stops purchasing from a business and starts purchasing at a competitor. Also called *customer defection.*

customer contact center A location or facility that houses an organization's remote customer contact operations. A contact center often supports multiple modes of customer interaction (i.e., e-mail, telephony, and Internet) and may include multiple CRM functions (i.e., marketing, sales, and service).

customer database behavior analysis Reveals what customers actually do—not what they say they will do or their attitudes.

customer defection See **customer churn.**

customer defection rate The rate at which customers leave a business. Also called *customer turnover rate.*

customer delight experience The sum of everything a company says, everything it does, and how it says and does it.

customer duration The length of time a business retains a customer.

customer experience The sum total of all experiences that a customer has with a company and its products or services.

customer insight The collection and analysis of customer information and design of information-based processes to support superior customer treatment decisions across all channels.

customer interaction Creating value by delivering a seamless customer experience at any touch point, more effective selling and revenue generation, improved customer equity and brand value, improved customer loyalty, and more effective customer operations, resulting in an improved bottom line for clients.

customer interaction points See **customer touch point.**

customer long-term value (CLV) An approach to measuring customer value over time. CLV captures the net present value of the future stream of revenues, minus the costs associated with a customer.

customer loyalty The tendency of a customer to choose one business or product over another for a particular need.

customer meritocracy Practice of understanding who customers really are, what they really want, and how valuable they are to the company and then allocating sales and service resources accordingly.

customer mindshare The attention, commitment, and competence of customers. The goal of many organizations is to capture a leadership market position in the minds of the consumers.

customer profiling Generating a detailed view of the customer. Profiles can be based on demographics, attitudes, behavior, or value.

customer profitability An analysis of customer revenue and profitability to ultimately determine customer value.

customer retention Initiatives by a company to keep existing customers from leaving the company or its product for another.

customer scoring Using data to apply scores to customers. This allows businesses to more effectively identify top prospects for targeted marketing campaigns, tailor call center services and scripting, and increase efficiency of direct sales efforts by improving lead qualification.

customer segmentation Placing individual customers into groups based on like characteristics (behaviors, demographics, geographies, etc.) for the purpose of driving targeted marketing programs and differentiating service levels.

customer segment management The practice of segmenting groups of customers based on like attributes and managing those segments in a way that maximizes both the benefits to customers and the long-term profit potential of the company.

customer segment manager Position in an organization that is responsible for determining which product offers customers or prospects will receive and through which channels they will be delivered.

customer service representative (CSR) Position in an organization that is responsible for helping and assisting customers by whichever method the customer chooses (telephone, e-mail, fax, letter, or in person).

customer strategy Strategy that helps define and prioritize a CRM action plan designed to expand customer relationships to build sustainable customer loyalty and bring improved business value to an organization, enabling it to show ROI on CRM investments.

customer touch point The intersection of a business event taking place via a channel using a medium (e.g., billing statements, e-mail promotions and messages, directory assistance, operator messaging, voice mail, direct mail, and telemarketing).

customer value analysis A means of understanding the set of buyer needs and desires that form the basis for purchase decisions. Focuses on understanding customers' key buying factors. Also incorporates the choices customers make in choosing between competitors.

data Facts, concepts, or instructions that a computer records, stores, and processes.

database marketing The practice of building, maintaining, and using customer databases for the purpose of contacting and transacting business.

data mart A department-specific data warehouse.

data mining The practice of finding hidden patterns and relationships in data.

data transformation The modification or alteration of data as it is being moved into the data warehouse.

data transformation rules Rules that govern non-customer-facing activity. They provide for a similarly important business function: merging customer data from source systems or third parties.

data warehouse A subject oriented, integrated, nonvolatile, time-variant collection of data. The data warehouse contains atomic-level data and summarized data specifically structured for querying and reporting.

data warehousing An enterprisewide implementation that replicates data from the same publication table on different servers or platforms to a single subscription table. This implementation effectively consolidates data from multiple sources.

demographic data   Age, gender, address, income, home value, net worth, credit card usage indicators, and credit worthiness, among others.

demographic overlay   Compilation of data from sources such as phone books, the department of motor vehicles, and the division of driver's licenses that is used to arrive at household-level demographics.

demographic segmentation   The practice of segmenting customers based primarily on overlay data (census), at the neighborhood level.

digital asset management   Technology that automates the management of marketing assets that exist in a variety of digitized forms, such as video, audio, graphics, and documents. Functions provided include storage, search and retrieval, reformatting, and check-in/check-out capabilities.

direct mail   Marketing technique used to reach customers through printed matter (as circulars) mailed directly to individuals.

direct marketing   A marketing practice of communicating directly with customers, often for the purpose of presenting an offer, via the postal service, e-mail, or other direct channel.

direct-marketing effectiveness   Initiative to improve a company's campaign management efforts and its ability to provide offers more closely tailored to individual customers.

dynamic customer segmentation   An approach to segmentation that dynamically creates groups of customers based on a particular set of circumstances that exist at a particular moment in time. These dynamic segmentations allow offers, service, and support to be based on the customers' circumstances and buying behavior, not on some permanent label of who they are.

e-business   See **extended enterprise.**

econometrics   The quantitative analysis of actual economic phenomena using statistical methods. Econometric modeling is the collection of techniques utilized to estimate the parameters of economic systems.

e-CRM   Leveraging electronic channels as a means to acquire, develop, and retain the customer in a personalized and differentiated manner.

e-learning   A learning application that integrates the power of the Internet with individualized learning approaches. E-learning applications often encompass a combination of the following attributes: individually tailored content, individual performance measurement, and innovative learning methods.

enterprise resource management (ERM)   See **marketing resource management.**

enterprise resource planning (ERP)   A suite of software tools designed to assist organizations with all facets of operational planning.

extended enterprise   The extension of a company's business model through process automation to customers and channel partners.

extranet   A secure Internet site accessible only to approved users. Often established to provide suppliers and customers with access to up-to-date information.

Financial Modernization Act   Law in the United States—before a financial institution can share nonpublic personal information (NPPI) with anyone other than affiliates, it must provide the consumer with a detailed notice and the ability to opt out.

future map A map that incorporates likely change scenarios and new relationships, roles, and interactions in the channel. This map reflects the company's vision of the future of its channels.

Global Positioning System (GPS) A worldwide radionavigation system based on a constellation of 24 satellites and their ground stations. GPS uses the satellites as fixed reference points to calculate positions on the ground that are accurate to a matter of meters.

inference engine A software mechanism that arrives at a conclusion to a specific task by applying rules against a knowledge base.

integrated view of customer (IVoC) An enabling business capability that supplies the missing link for CRM implementations. An IVoC is the connection between customer interaction channels and customer strategy.

integrated view of customer (IVoC) context The translation of a company's customer strategy into rules meant to deliver that strategy.

integrated view of customer (IVoC) data The information required about the customer to extend CRM solutions across contact channels or product lines within the company's enterprise.

integrated view of customer (IVoC) rules Instructions for using the data to shape the next interaction with the customer. Rules define what the company does with the information after it is warehoused.

interactive voice response (IVR) A telephony technology in which a customer uses a touch-tone telephone to interact with a company. IVR technology does not require human interaction.

knowledge management An application that aids in the capture and management of an organization's knowledge assets.

lead management An application that aids in the tracking, monitoring, and distribution of sales prospects and the company's interactions with them.

lifetime value (LTV) The measure of potential income streams and costs over the lifetime of a customer.

marketing automation Real-time, intelligent offer creation and customer service differentiation are key to building customer loyalty, creating new business opportunity, and gaining competitive advantage.

marketing funnel Device for pointing out differences between one's own brand and those of competitors. It places customers in various groups according to the depth of their commitment to the brand.

marketing mix Price, place, product and promotion. Also known as the *Four Ps.*

marketing process management See **marketing resource management (MRM).**

marketing resource management (MRM) The practice of integrating all aspects of marketing across the diverse spectrum of activities—from planning, developing, and executing campaigns to streamlining core marketing processes and facilitating more effective communications among marketing team members.

MRM is designed to instill order and accountability in a function that historically has lacked discipline.

marketing workbench   An integrated platform for marketing execution which pulls together the critical processes, technology tools, and data that marketers need to be more efficient and effective.

market power   A function of where customer influence resides—with the supplier or with the channel.

mass marketing   Advertising to large market segments through mass media and other public forums. One-to-many approach to targeting customers.

m-commerce   Mobile commerce. The approach of leveraging wireless technologies, such as cell phones and PDAs, to enable new channels for an organization to communicate and transact business with customers.

Microelectromechanical systems (MEMS)   Tagging and sensor technology for silent commerce.

mission-critical workforce   The distinct portions of an organization's workforce which are particularly vital to overall business performance—for example, a portion that is responsible for significant revenue or costs.

multichannel campaign   A marketing campaign that reaches a customer through multiple interaction channels, such as e-mail, direct mail, and telemarketing.

Object Internet standard   Standard used for silent commerce. It consists of an electronic product code, an object naming service, and a physical markup language to describe objects.

one-to-one marketing   The practice of delivering personalized communications and offers to very small customer segments, often a segment of one.

Pareto rule   General rule that a small percentage of customers represents a large percentage of total revenues and profits.

partner relationship management (PRM)   The integration of processes and data between companies and channel partners. A PRM technology infrastructure improves the efficiency and effectiveness of the interactions between companies and channel partners by allowing them to coordinate business planning activities, share information, conduct commerce, and provide postsales service across the channel.

permission-based marketing   The practice of obtaining a customer's permission prior to including the customer in any marketing communications or offers.

personal digital assistant (PDA)   A lightweight palmtop computer designed to provide specific functions for personal organization (calendar, note taking, database, calculator, and so on) as well as communications.

personalization   Differentiating marketing, sales, and service interactions with customers based on the ability to recognize the customer or prospect as an individual. Often the personalized interactions are based on the customer's circumstances, buying behavior, or preferences.

personalization rules   Rules that provide for consistent, timely, and relevant individualized interactions and offers across multiple customer touchpoints. The rules shape each customer interaction.

predictive modeling A data-mining technique that uses statistical methodologies to predict prospect or customer behavior.

push marketing See **mass marketing.**

radio frequency identification (RFID) An enabling technology for silent commerce. It uses a half-inch-wide plastic tag with an embedded digital memory chip the size of a pinhead.

real-time analytics Immediate, detail-oriented applications that monitor business changes as rapidly as they occur.

recency The most powerful predictor of future behavior. The more recently a customer has done something, the more likely the customer is to do it again.

recency, frequency, monetary (RFM) segmentation The practice of segmenting customers based on their purchasing history.

relationship marketing Engaging in indirect conversation with customers through analyzing their behavior over time.

sales force automation (SFA) Practice of automating the sales function in order to improve sales force effectiveness and increase customer loyalty.

segmentation Grouping customers based on like attributes to determine the most effective ways to manage those groups—maximizing both the benefits to the customers and the long-term profit potential of the organization.

Shelby Act Law in the United States—states must offer notice and opt-in rights to consumers before making its driver's license and motor vehicle license lists available to direct marketers.

silent commerce Use of wireless mobile communications, and advanced tagging and sensor technologies to enable everyday objects to record and transmit important information.

single view of customer See **integrated view of customer (IVoC).**

status quo map Map that identifies existing channel participants and the topography of their existing relationships.

target marketing The practice of dividing the pool of potential customers into discrete subsegments based on actionable criteria, then customizing the marketing campaigns individually for each subsegment.

third-party data Data purchased from another party outside the organization (e.g., demographic overlays).

touch point See **customer touch point.**

transaction data Data on purchase details, complaints and inquiries to the call center, and credit and financial information.

ubiquitous supervision solution A research prototype that shows how RFID technology may be used to enable a generic container to sense its content and communicate with its exterior.

u-commerce The future of e-commerce—*u* because it is *untethered* by the hard wires of traditional computing and telephony, *unbounded* by traditional definitions of commerce, and *ubiquitous*—taking place anytime and anywhere. It is commerce integrated into ordinary life in an extraordinary way.

upselling Attempting to persuade a customer to purchase a more expensive item.

value-based segmentation   The practice of segmenting customers based on a calculated value score. The goal is to retain the most profitable customers, as well as increase the value of other customers.

viral marketing   Word-of-mouth communication in the marketplace.

wearable services platform   Platform that demonstrates how technologies such as wearable computing, heads-up displays, wireless communications, universal directory, and radio frequency identification tags can be used to increase the efficiency of package delivery as well as the customer experience.

workflow management   An application that aids in the tracking and management of all the activities in a process from start to finish.

workspace portal   A user interface that integrates, in a single location and with personalized context, the information, best practices, and knowledge that employees need to do their best work.

Contributing Authors

Theodore Ansusinha is a partner in Accenture's customer relationship management practice and specializes in helping companies use customer insight to provide significant improvement in marketing outcomes. He has worked with clients in a variety of industries, including financial services, communications, retail, and energy. He obtained his BS in industrial engineering and MS in quantitative analysis from the University of Wisconsin at Madison.

John C. Beck is the director of research at Accenture's Institute for Strategic Change in Palo Alto, California, where he is currently leading research projects on globalization, the future of wireless communication, and multitasking. He earned his BA in East Asian studies and sociology summa cum laude from Harvard University, and was the first graduate of Harvard's integrative PhD program in business studies. He is a visiting professor at the Anderson School of Management at UCLA and an adjunct professor at the Ivey School at the University of Western Ontario, where he teaches courses on e-commerce, management consulting, globalization, and leadership. He has published more than 100 books, articles, and business reports on the topics of business in Asia, strategic management, globalization, leadership, and organizational behavior.

Bruce W. Bendix is an associate partner in Accenture's strategy and business architecture practice. He is based in Chicago, Illinois.

Craig B. Cornelius is a partner in Accenture's government industry operating group and leads the government CRM practice in the United States. He has experience serving clients in both the commercial and government sectors and specializes in helping organizations improve performance in selling and customer service across all customer interaction channels. In addition, he serves on the board of directors for the Syracuse University School of Information Studies and Technology and on the board of the Foundation for Future Technology Leaders. He graduated from Syracuse University with a degree in aerospace engineering.

Brian K. Crockett is an associate partner in Accenture's customer relationship management practice with a focus on strategic CRM issues. He specializes in helping clients identify, prioritize, and plan CRM investments based on value potential and an assessment of existing CRM capabilities. He also focuses on leveraging customer insight to drive strategic business decisions and customer-specific strategies. He has spoken at industry conferences on the topics of CRM strategy, online shopping, and loyalty programs. He has experience in CRM and customer strategy development across a number of industries, including retail, consumer goods, communications, travel and transportation, automotive, and media and entertainment. He obtained his MBA from Dartmouth College's Amos Tuck School.

Thomas H. Davenport is the director of the Accenture Institute for Strategic Change, and a distinguished scholar in residence at Babson College. He is a frequent author, and his recent publications include "How Do They Know Their Customers So Well?" (*Sloan Management Review,* Winter 2001) and "Data to Knowledge to Results: Building an Analytic Capability" (*California Management Review,* Winter 2001). His latest book, published by Harvard Business School Press, is *The Attention Economy.*

Stephen F. Dull is a partner in Accenture's customer relationship management practice and leads the company's brand practice. He specializes in brand and marketing strategy, marketing capability building, pricing, and segmentation. He is a frequent speaker on the topic of CRM and business strategy and is quoted frequently in such publications as *USA Today, Financial Times,* and *Investor's Business Daily.* He is also an active author and thought leader in the area of CRM; he recently completed a landmark study on B2C and B2B e-branding and a study of how CRM capability drives financial performance. He received his MBA in marketing from the University of Michigan and BA in international relations from Michigan State.

James O. Etheredge is the lead partner for Accenture's customer relationship management practice within the company's resources industry operating group. He specializes in strategic visioning, organizational performance, and enhancing customer experience through marketing, call centers, field sales and service, and Web channels. He has worked across many industries, including chemicals, energy, utilities, industrial equipment, retail, pharmaceuticals, and medical products. He is an active author and thought leader in the area of CRM. His articles have been published in *Sales and Marketing Management* and *Sales and Field Force Automation.* He also contributed to the Economist Intelligence Unit research initiative entitled "Managing Customer Relationships: Process Excellence in Identifying, Attracting, and Retaining Profitable Customers." In addition, he authored the paper "Human Performance in the Customer-Driven Enterprise," published in *Defying the Limits,* Vol. 1. He obtained his industrial engineering degree at Georgia Tech.

Mark C. Giometti is a partner in Accenture's customer relationship management practice. He specializes in marketing automation, helping clients dramatically reduce the cycle time to create and execute their marketing campaigns. His recent focus has been on bringing customer insight on a real-time basis to key points of customer contact. He has spent the past 13 years consulting to clients in the financial services industry, including brokerage, wealth management, consumer lending, credit card, retail banking, small business, and commercial and investment banking units. His views have been published in *American Banker* and *Future Banker,* and he has spoken at a number of industry forums, including the BAI conference. He holds a BSC in finance from Santa Clara University and an MBA from Harvard University.

John B. Goodman is a partner in Accenture's strategy and business architecture practice. He is based in Washington, D.C.

Jeanne G. Harris is an associate partner with Accenture and is the director of the Chicago location of the Accenture Institute for Strategic Change. She specializes in CRM, customer insight, human performance and management decision making. She is a frequent author, and her published articles include "How Do They Know Their Customers So Well?" (*Sloan Management Review,* Winter 2001) and "Data to Knowledge to Results: Building an Analytic Capability" (*California Management Review,* Winter 2001). She obtained her undergraduate degree from Washington University at St. Louis and a master's in information science from the University of Illinois.

Marc F. Hayes is an associate partner in Accenture's customer relationship management practice. He specializes in assisting companies in maximizing the value of the electronic marketplace as a customer channel to market, to sell, and to serve the customer in a personalized and differentiated manner. He has worked with clients in a variety of industries, including telecommunications, airlines, insurance, consumer packaged goods, and high-tech manufacturing. He is a respected authority in several technology areas, including e-commerce, large-scale solutions development, enterprise technical architectures, and technical operations. He is also an active author and speaker in the area of CRM, and he authored the paper "The eCRM Extended Enterprise: The Myth of Disintermediation," published in *Defying the Limits,* Vol. 1. He obtained his BS in computer science from Clemson University.

Naveen K. Jain is an associate partner in Accenture's customer relationship management practice and specializes in assisting clients in the transformation of the marketing function and organization to enhance the efficiency and effectiveness of marketing spend. He is a respected authority in many aspects of marketing and customer strategy, including marketing resource prioritization, marketing-mix optimization, marketing process redesign, customer-centric marketing organization alignment and governance, marketing automation and enabling technologies, and brand positioning. He is an active thought leader and has developed Accenture's point of view around marketing transformation, a key offering that addresses all marketing capabilities across the enterprise. He has worked in a variety of industries, including consumer goods and services, wholesale and retail distribution, and communications and high-tech. He holds a BS in mechanical engineering and an MBA in marketing.

Brian A. Johnson is the lead partner for Accenture's marketing strategy practice; he focuses on the intersection of marketing, technology and strategy. He is a trustee of the Marketing Science Institute and has helped clients develop and implement marketing strategies for companies in a variety of industries. His work has been published and written about in many publications, including the *Wall Street Journal, Financial Times, Australian Financial Review,* and *Harvard Business Review.* Based in Chicago, he is an adjunct professor of marketing at Northwestern University's Kellogg School of Management.

Brian Kalms is a partner in Accenture's products industry operating group. He specializes in helping companies effect sustaining change, particularly in the areas of customer related merchandising and supply chain, and has expertise in utilizing newer technologies to increase effectiveness and customer focus of marketing, buying, pricing, merchandising, and logistics decision making. He has worked across a variety of industries, including food retailing, apparel retailing, specialty retailing, food and packaged goods manufacturing, and hospitality. He is also an author and thought leader in the area of CRM. He has been published in a South African retail journal and has spoken on the subject of customer-supplier relationships at the Institute of Logistics conference. He obtained a BA with joint honors in economics and econometrics at the University of Nottingham in the United Kingdom.

Patrick D. Lynch is a research fellow at the Accenture Institute for Strategic Change. He investigates global e-commerce strategy topics such as organizational behavior, attention management, and most recently the psychology of technology (including Internet and wireless consumer behavior, customer experience, and usability). He earned his PhD in organizational behavior and has instructed courses in statistics, industrial-organizational psychology, and social psychology. His work has been published in the *Journal of Applied Psychology, Applied and Preventative Psychology,* the *Journal of Advertising Research,* the *Journal of International Business Studies, ePlant,* and *eCom Magazine.*

Jeffrey Merrihue is a partner in Accenture's customer relationship management practice. He specializes in marketing economic value effectiveness and is the global lead for Accenture's marketing return on investment practice. He has worked with companies across a variety of industries, including consumer packaged goods, automotive, electronics and high tech, financial services, and chemicals. He has deep marketing strategy experience based on 15 years in international marketing and joined Accenture from Initiative Consulting, a firm he founded and where he served as Chairman and CEO. He obtained an MBA in international business from Babson College.

Patrick Mosher is an associate partner in Accenture's communications industry operating group. With experience in industries including telecommunications, publishing and advertising, he leads initiatives for large-scale organization change in large enterprises. He is based in Minneapolis, Minnesota.

Dennis A. Mullahy is a partner in Accenture's products industry operating group. He specializes in leveraging customer information to increase the effectiveness of the merchandising organization, including optimized pricing, assortment strategies, advertising and marketing, space planning, in-store presentation and store format, and productivity analysis. He has worked across a variety of retail segments, including soft lines, hard lines, department stores, and specialty retailers. He has also worked with several consumer product manufacturers. He obtained his BS in electrical engineering from Ohio State University.

Nancy K. Mullen is an associate partner at Accenture and is the global lead of the company's data architecture practice. She specializes in data warehousing, information modeling, data architectures, applications architectures, data administration techniques, and database management systems. She has worked with companies across a variety of industries, including government, banking, electronics, consumer products, communications and insurance. She is also an active author and contributed two chapters to *Netcentric Computing,* as well as contributing a monthly column to *DM Review* called "Information for Innovation." She obtained a BS in mathematics from Michigan State University and a MA in business and economics from Appalachian State University.

Julie F. Nelson is the lead partner for Accenture's customer relationship management practice within the company's communications, electronics and high tech, and media and entertainment industry operating group. She has a strong commercial background and leading-edge technology experience and specializes in driving innovation and transformation for market leaders. She has worked in a number of industries, serving as client partner to a number of market leaders, including Consolidated Edison, Federal Express, and Frito-Lay. She holds an MBA and a BFA from the University of Iowa.

Paul F. Nunes is a senior research fellow at the Accenture Institute for Strategic Change and an associate partner in the Accenture strategy and business architecture practice. His research focuses on the impact of advancing technology on business strategy, including work on the changing nature of channels and market forms, and the challenges of profitable customer interaction through IT-enabled business processes. His work has appeared several times in *Harvard Business Review,* as well as in the *International Journal of Electronic Commerce, ComputerWorld,* and *Wired.* The results of his research have also been featured on several news wires and have appeared in publications ranging from the *Los Angeles Times* to *Yahoo! News* to *USA Today.* He is a trustee of the Marketing Science Institute and has presented frequently at industry conferences and the world's top business schools.

J. Patrick O'Halloran is a partner in Accenture's customer relationship management practice and leads the global customer insight practice. In this role, he develops and directs the operations of the company's customer insight market offerings in the areas of data management, customer analytics, marketing automation, and consultative marketing services. He has worked with clients in a variety of industries, including products, communications and financial services. He has also been published in the *Journal of Business Strategy* and focuses CRM work in the areas of strategy, process, technology, and organization and human performance. He holds an MBA in management information systems from the University of Minnesota and a BS in accounting from Arizona State University.

Shep Parke is an associate partner in Accenture's customer relationship management practice. He specializes in customer-driven operational assessment and solution design, with expertise in helping companies establish a clear, pragmatic and shared senior management CRM vision. He has worked with companies across a variety of industries, including electronics and high tech, communications, chemicals, and travel and transportation. He is also an active author and thought leader in the area of CRM. His articles have been published in *Siebel Magazine* and *Sales and Field Force Automation*. In addition, he provided advice and guidance on the groundbreaking report, "How Much Are CRM Capabilities Really Worth? What Every CEO Should Know." He graduated from Duke University with a degree in economics.

Michael Payne is a senior manager in Accenture's customer relationship management practice and leads the marketing and customer strategy team for the company's U.K. financial services practice. He specializes in the analysis and interpretation of consumer behavior and developing customer acquisition and retention strategies. He works primarily in the financial services industry, working in the retail, private banking, and life and general insurance sectors. He has authored a number of academic and industry articles and papers on customer management and on consumer behavior. His current work is focused on helping clients develop new approaches to engaging and interacting with customers in the digital economy and helping clients develop and execute customer and CRM strategies.

Holly Porter is an experienced manager in Accenture's customer relationship management practice. She specializes in customer insight and works primarily in assisting clients to define and solidify their corporate marketing objectives, then defines the CRM solution that will serve their short-term and long-term goals. She has been actively involved in developing CRM and database marketing technology, as well as consulting with corporations, primarily in the financial services industry, in the development of enterprisewide strategic marketing planning. She has worked with clients in a variety of industries, including financial services, automotive, telecommunications, and software development. She obtained her BA in communications from the University of South Florida.

Kevin N. Quiring is a partner in Accenture's customer relationship management practice and specializes in assisting clients in the identification and creation of CRM capabilities which contribute to top-line growth through the acquisition, development, and retention of their customers. He is a respected authority in many aspects of CRM, including CRM business architectures, customer contact centers, customer insight, enterprise technical architecture, and CRM data architecture. He is an active thought leader for Accenture's CRM practice and has developed the company's point of view around the integrated view of the customer, a key capability supporting a business's CRM processes across the enterprise. He has worked in a variety of industries, including marketing services, retail, media and entertainment, travel and transportation, automotive, health care, financial services, and high tech. He holds a BS in computer science.

Steven S. Ramsey is a partner in Accenture's customer relationship management practice. He leads the marketing and customer strategy global practice that houses the company's functional expertise in brand strategy, marketing effectiveness, customer strategy, and CRM transformational planning. In this role, he directs the creation of the company's market offerings and drives key client engagements. His primary areas of focus are related to helping companies with go-to-market issues and helping drive higher return on marketing and CRM investments. He has worked with clients in a variety of industries, including products, retail, and financial services. He holds an MBA in marketing and finance from the University of Chicago and a BS in mechanical engineering from Lehigh University.

Kenneth L. Reed is an associate partner in Accenture's customer relationship management practice and is an expert in the areas of data mining, data modeling, relational databases, and data warehousing technology. He pioneered the development of the customer analytic record and prospect analytic record (CAR/PAR) concepts and is currently leading a cross-industry team of data-mining experts dedicated to customer insight modeling. Prior to joining Accenture, he was chief scientist at Hyper-Parallel, a data-mining technology start-up, where he led a team of modelers and scientists. He received his BA and MS from the University of Washington and his PhD in forest ecology from Oregon State University.

Ron Ref is a senior manager in Accenture's customer relationship management practice and specializes in the strategic planning, process design, and implementation of partner relationship management initiatives. He has worked across many industries, including consumer packaged goods, specialty insurance, and electronics and high tech. Most recently, he has developed Accenture's PRM market offering for electronics and high tech, helping clients define their PRM capability investment road maps. His implementation experience includes working as principal functional architect on the Sharp Electronic Corporation's Communication and Information Systems Group's first partner relationship management platform in 1999, which was entered into the Smithsonian Institution's archives. He has contributed to several other PRM initiatives that have addressed the seamless integration of presales and commerce and direct and indirect channel integration. He holds a BS in management information systems from the University of Arizona School of Business.

Marianne Seiler is a senior manager in Accenture's marketing and customer strategy practice. She specializes in helping companies increase revenue and profitability through identifying and developing customer strategies, launching new products, expanding geographic and customer markets, valuing and retaining customers, creating segmentation strategies, creating and enhancing marketing databases, and restructuring marketing and sales organizations. She has spoken and published on numerous marketing topics, including customer retention, telemarketing, database marketing, and customer segmentation. She has a PhD in management from the Peter Drucker School at Claremont Graduate University and an MBA in marketing from the University of Texas at Austin.

Sean Shine is the lead partner for Accenture's customer relationship management practice within the company's government industry operating group. He is responsible for all projects and investments in the government CRM area and is a member of the Accenture Government Industry Program, which has responsibility for setting overall direction for the Accenture worldwide government practice. He has extensive worldwide government consultancy experience and specializes in advising revenue and customs authorities globally. He graduated from University College Cork with an Honours degree in civil engineering. He is a former president of the Republic of Ireland Council of the Chartered Institute of Management Accountants (CIMA), and a fellow of the institute.

Ruth E. Spencer is a senior manager in Accenture's customer relationship management practice and specializes in customer insight driven marketing. She focuses on helping companies create marketing strategies and plans that exploit customer insight, then develop the necessary supporting organization, processes, and technology. She has worked with a variety of companies across industries and specializes in the B2C market, with particular expertise in the financial services and retail industries.

Timothy Stephens is a senior manager in Accenture's customer relationship management practice and specializes in helping companies improve their CRM strategies by helping organizations become more customer-centric, understand their market opportunities, and develop and take to market new products. His current focus is on helping companies combine CRM and silent commerce. He has worked across many industries, including consumer and industrial products, communications, government, retail, and natural resources. He is also an active author and thought leader in the area of CRM. His articles have been published in *Beverage Marketing, Siebel Magazine,* and *Software Strategies.* In addition, he was a coauthor of the Accenture-sponsored report, "How Much Are CRM Capabilities Really Worth? What Every CEO Should Know." He obtained his BA from Amherst College and his MBA from the Amos Tuck School of Business.

Gregory J. Supron is the managing partner for the customer relationship management practice within the company's products operating group. He specializes in the areas of formulating business and CRM strategies and leading large-scale organizational change. He also has extensive experience in the areas of sales and marketing, post-merger integration, supply chain strategy, and shareholder value delivery. He has authored numerous articles on the topic of integrated business strategies and is a recent winner of Accenture's annual thought leadership award. He has worked across a variety of industries, including consumer goods and services, retail, apparel, and high tech. He obtained his MBA from the Amos Tuck School of Business Administration at Dartmouth College and his BS in mechanical engineering from Lehigh University.

Philip J. Tamminga is a partner in Accenture's customer relationship management practice and specializes in helping clients improve business performance in selling and customer service across all customer interaction channels, including direct, customer contact centers, and the Web. He leads Accenture's integrated channel solutions practice and is responsible for the company's CRM activities across North America. In addition, he is responsible for overseeing Accenture's globally sponsored CRM-related alliances. He has worked with clients in a variety of industries, including communications, high tech, energy, and manufacturing. He is also an author and thought leader in the area of CRM. He has published a number of articles on CRM, including "How Much Are Customer Relationship Management Capabilities Really Worth? What Every CEO Should Know" and "CRM, Implementing Customer-Centric Strategies." He received his BS and MBA from the University of Denver.

Dean J. Teglia is a partner in the Accenture industrial equipment industry and leads its North American practice. Based in the solutions engineering service line, he focuses on enterprise solutions implementation, IT strategy, and service management, where he works with clients including Komatsu, U.S. Filter, Vesuvius, Brunswick, and Flowserve. He sponsors the company's customer-centric service management and industrial telematics offerings. He has published numerous articles, including "Customer Centric Service Management, from 'Piece of Equipment' to 'Peace of Mind'" and "From Product Manufacturer to Solution Provider: The Future of Industrial Equipment Manufacturers." He received his bachelor's degree in industrial engineering from Bradley University, Peoria, Illinois. He was subsequently appointed to the university council and engineering advisory board.

Luis Vassal'lo is global managing partner for Accenture's industrial equipment practice. He specializes in organization and business administration in the industrial field. He has collaborated with numerous companies in the power generation and distribution, heavy equipment and automation, electronics, aerospace and defense, and automotive sectors. He has led numerous projects in areas such as business strategy, organizational restructuring, change management, and value creation programs, as well as collaborating with large global industrial organizations on major restructuring projects. He speaks at major industry conferences and has authored articles on production management, maintenance logistics, and strategy published in leading trade magazines. He holds a master's degree in industrial engineering from Universidad Politecnica de Madrid.

Dorothy V. VonDette is a partner in the Accenture human performance service line and leads the company's mission-critical workforce market offering. She has more than 20 years' experience leading organizational transformation projects. Based in Reston, Virginia, she is the location lead partner for the Washington, D.C., office.

Mitchell E. Wade is a researcher with the Accenture Institute for Strategic Change. He specializes in how information—with or without information technology—creates new opportunities for organizations large and small. He has conducted analyses and developed new approaches for very large enterprises (multinational corporations and major federal agencies), for tiny nonprofits, and for an Internet start-up. He earned his AB from Harvard University, magna cum laude, with a concentration in political theory.

Todd R. Wagner is a partner in Accenture's customer relationship management practice and leads the company's marketing automation practice. He specializes in helping companies integrate customer insight into marketing, sales, and service interactions. He has worked with clients in a variety of industries, including consumer products, telecommunications, automotive, and financial services. He has also authored a variety of articles, including "Multichannel Customer Interaction," published in *Defying the Limits,* Vol. 1, and "The Next Frontier" (*Journal of Business Strategy,* May/June 2001). He obtained his BS in electrical engineering from Stanford University.

Clive Whitehouse is a partner in Accenture's customer relationship management practice and specializes in helping organizations use their customer information more effectively in order to create more profitable interactions with customers. He is also responsible for Accenture's customer insight practice in the United Kingdom and coordinates the company's customer insight activities across Europe. He has worked with clients across a variety of industries, including retail and commercial financial services, high-street retailers, utilities, and telecommunications. He has extensive experience in CRM and has helped companies develop customer strategies and operating models, design and implement marketing automation systems, perform customer segmentation studies, and develop sales force automation systems.

Robert E. Wollan is a partner in Accenture's customer relationship management practice and leads the company's global customer contact transformation offering. He specializes in large-scale transformational sales and customer service initiatives and has worked extensively in a variety of industries, including telecommunications, financial services, direct marketing, consumer products, and transportation. He holds a BA in finance and economics from the University of St. Thomas, St. Paul, Minnesota.

Index

ABF Freight, and messaging technology, 177

Absolut Vodka, as strong brand, 32

Accenture, 148
analysis of product life-cycle costs, 184
research on customer knowledge, 95
research on customer segment management, 28
research on marketing, 191, 198–211, 235–236, 243–244, 246
study on CRM in government, 269, 270, 278
study on customization, 132
study on personalization and customization, 126, 127

Ace Hardware, and Web as channel, 51

Advanced planning system, and CCSM, 187

Advertising:
and brand building, 31–32
costs, and strong brands, 37
media, 6, 37

AEP (see American Electric Power)

AirlineHelper, and messaging technology, 177, 179

Airlines industry:
and m-commerce, 143
and messaging technology, 113–114, 177, 179–180

Alcatel eBusiness Group, and PRM, 155–156, 161

Algorithms:
and customer segment management, 27

Alignment:
and brand, 39, 42, 59
and CRM, 55, 56, 58, 61
of customer expenditure and revenue, 145–152
and customer segment management, 23–25
and customization, 122
of marketing organization, 194, 252–253
and PRM, 160
of Web sites with consumer behaviors, 225
(See also Workforce)

Allegheny Energy, 294

Amazon.com:
and cross-selling, 95
and e-marketing, 226
and m-commerce, 143
and personalization and customization, collaboration of, 133
and wireless Web, 135–136, 140

Amerada Hess, and customer segments, 297–298

American Electric Power, 294

Ameritech, and e-CRM, 258

Ameritrade, and m-commerce, 143

Anatel, 263, 264, 267

Anticounterfeiting, and silent commerce, 88, 92

AOL Instant Messenger, 113, 177
and virtual agent architecture, 179

Application service providers,
    275
APS (*see* Advanced planning system)
ASPs (*see* Application service
    providers)
AT&T, 148
    and CRM, 259, 268
    and Web-Based Interactive Advantage
    CRM, 258
Australia, e-government initiatives in,
    272–273
Autonomous purchasing object, and silent
    commerce, 90

Banner ads, effectiveness of, 221,
    222
Bar code, 86, 93
Barnes & Noble:
    and m-commerce, 143
    and wireless Web design, 139
B2B relationships (*see* Business-to-
    business relationships)
B2C relationships (*see* Business-to-
    customer relationships)
Behavior (*see* Customer behavior)
BellSouth:
    and CRM integration, 260
    and e-learning, 172–173
    and turnkey solutions, 267
BEST (*see* Business Excellence through
    Simulations Training)
Best Buy, 311
    and in-store optimization, 308
    and m-commerce, 143
    and precision pricing, 310
    and promotion effectiveness, 311
    and wireless Web design, 138
Binkley-Seyer, Kim, 273
Biztravel, and m-commerce, 143
BMW Group, as strong brand, 6
Borders bookstores, use of kiosks in,
    304
Bouygues Telecom, and CRM integration,
    260–262, 267

Brand:
    advertising, 32–33, 37, 43
    and B2B relationships, 30, 37–39
    and B2C relationships, 33–34, 39
    building, 16–17, 31, 32, 43, 194, 235,
        295–296
    and call centers, 16, 30, 34
    and channel, 15, 31, 49–50
    and cobranding, 36, 38
    and customer conversation, 123, 125
    defined, 16–17, 30–32
    loyalty, 5–7, 30–32, 36–37, 191, 211,
        231, 238
    management, 30, 39, 42, 234–235
    manners, 39, 42
    and marketing funnel, 38
    measurement and analysis, 37–38
    memory, 236
    misconceptions, 31–34
    and mission-critical workforce, 166
    and silent commerce, 87
    strategy, 7, 8, 13, 14, 17, 30–43
    strength, 7, 16, 37, 38, 43
    strong, 31, 34–43
    top-of-mind awareness of, 31–33
    value, 7, 14, 16, 34, 38–39, 43
    Visa, as case study of, 40–42
Branding (*see* Brand, building)
Brazil, telecommunications industry in,
    262–267
    and Region II, 263, 264
Brazil Telecom, 264, 266, 267
Bricks-and-mortar stores, 136, 288
    and online returns, 234
British Airways, and customer insight,
    95
British Gas, 295–297, 301
British Telecom, 241
    and e-CRM, 268
BrT (*see* Brazil Telecom)
Burns, Lawrence D., 120
Bush, Jeb, 273, 278
Business Excellence through Simulation
    Training, 172–173

Business-to-business relationships:
  and brand choice, 30
  and brand value, 33–34, 39
  and Citibank, 39
  in manufacturing industry, 282
  and McDonald's, 39
  and m-commerce, 140–141
  and messaging technology, 178
  in resources industry, 293, 294
Business-to-commerce relationships, and
    m-commerce, 142–143
Business-to-consumer relationships (*see*
    Business-to-customer relationships)
Business-to-customer relationships, 116
  and brand value, 33–34, 39
  and m-commerce, 140
  and messaging technology, 178
Buyer behavior (*see* Customer behavior)
BuyPower (General Motors), 287–288

Cable television, 6
  brand value of, 34
  call centers in, 34
Cadillac, as brand, 233
California:
  e-government initiatives in, 271
  energy companies in, 301
Call centers, 164, 176
  and brand building, 16
  and brand management, 30
  and brand manners, 39, 42
  and brand value, 30, 34
  in cable television service providers, 34
  and cost, 147–148, 151–152
  and CRM, 13, 56, 59, 60, 62, 103,
    283–287, 299–300
  and customer data, 70, 99, 108
  and e-government initiatives, 270,
    275–278
  and improving mission-critical work-
    force, 171–173
  in manufacturing industry, 283–287
  during 1990s, 4, 111–112
  outsourcing of, 151–152

Call centers (*Cont.*):
  in resources industry, 299–300
  as single-service channel, 4
  in telecommunications industry,
    258–260, 262, 264, 266
  and Web, 103, 270, 278, 286–290
Capital One, and customer conversation,
    124
CCSM (*see* Customer-centric service
    management)
Centrelink, 272–273
Channel conflict strategy matrix (*see*
    Channel strategy, and conflict strat-
    egy matrix)
Channels:
  added value, 48–51
  and brand, 15, 31, 49–50
  and call centers, 4, 103, 104
  conflict of, 15, 44–46, 48–53
  and CRM strategy, 8, 58
  fragmentation of, 51
  and IVoC, 103–108
  management of, 21, 25, 30, 154, 155
  new, 15, 44–46
  and PRM, 116, 153–164
  self-service, 150–152, 154, 163, 258
  service and sales of, 4
  (*See also* Channel strategy)
Channel strategy, 7, 13, 17, 44–53
  and conflict strategy matrix, 15–16, 46,
    48–53, 50
  core strategies of, 50–53
  defined, 8, 14
  maps of, 15–16, 46–48, 53
Charles Schwab & Company, 151
  and integrated marketing, 229
Chevron, 293
CIM (*see* Customer interaction manage-
    ment)
Cingular, and brand awareness, 32
Cisco Systems, and Web as channel, 51
Closed-loop processes:
  and channel integration, 228
  and PRM, 158–159, 161

CNW Marketing Research, 231
Cobranding, 36, 38
Coca-Cola, 251
    and competition with Sainsbury
        (private label), 50
    ineffective marketing by, 234
    and McDonald's, 33, 36
    and PepsiCo, 33–36, 49–50, 234
    as strong brand, 33–36, 49–50
Colonial Braided Rug, and channel inte-
    gration, 228
Comarketing, 218–219
Commerzbank, and customer differentia-
    tion, 217
Communications, and CRM, 9
Compaq, 75
    and customer service meritocracy,
        149
Competitive intelligence:
    and customer insight, 183
    and marketing teams, 249
Complex buying, 223, 224
Conran, as strong brand, 36
Consumer behavior (*see* Customer
    behavior)
*Consumer Behavior and Marketing
    Action* (Henry Assael), 223, 224
Conversational marketing, 118–125, 196
    (*See also* Customer conversation)
Cookies, 89, 140
Country stores concept (Gateway), 51
Coupons, 232
    effectiveness of, 235
    instant-purchase, 239
    (*See also* E-coupons)
CRM (*see* Customer relationship manage-
    ment)
Cross-selling:
    and Amazon.com, 95
    by British Gas, 296
    and CRM, 103, 305
    and customer service meritocracy, 149
    by telecommunications companies,
        268

Customer behavior, 221–230
    and "bricks-and-clicks" movement,
        228
    and focus groups, 227
    types of, 223, 224
Customer care centers (*see* Call centers)
Customer-centric continuum, 15,
    20–29
Customer centricity, 78
    and customer behavior segmentation,
        82–84
    and customer buyer values, 80–82,
        84
    and customer profitability, 78–80
    in manufacturing industry, 280–291
Customer-centric service management,
    116–117, 181–188
    and data warehousing, 186
    and m-commerce, 187
    and predictive maintenance program,
        183, 185–186
Customer conversation:
    and courtesy, 121
    influence on sales, 120
    and marketing, 118–125, 196, 218
    and polylogues, 124, 125
    styles of, 122–125
    (*See also* Conversational marketing)
Customer delight experience, 31
Customer insight:
    and alignment of cost and revenue,
        150
    and CCSM, 183–184
    and companies, 95–101
    and competitive intelligence, 183
    and conversational marketing,
        118–125
    and marketing, 194–196
    in resources industry, 298, 299
    in retail industry, 306–312
    from silent commerce, 69, 86, 88, 90
    (*See also* Customer knowledge)
Customer interaction management,
    299–300

Customer knowledge, 95–101
  and conversational marketing,
    118–125
  and CRM, 111–112
  and customer equity, 95
  (*See also* Customer insight)
Customer long-term value analysis, 79
Customer relationship management:
  and brand building, 43
  and brand manners, 39, 42
  and CCSM, 116–117
  as competitive differentiator, 269
  focus of, 4–5, 7
  in government, 269–279
  investment models of, 146–147,
    151
  and IVoC, 102–103
  leadership of, 13–14
  during 1990s, 54, 111–112, 145, 153
  in manufacturing industry, 280–291
  pitfalls of, 3–4, 54–57
  and PRM, 116–117, 155
  reasons for, 3, 9
  in resources industry, 292–302
  in retail industry, 303–312
  and ROI, 57, 58, 62, 281–282
  and "sexy technology" trap, 56
  Strategy and Road Map project of,
    57–61
  strategy of, 8, 13, 14, 17, 54–64
  successful, 8–9
  in telecommunications industry,
    258–268
  war room technique of, 58–59
Customer segment management:
  benefits of, 15, 18, 28–29
  and customer-centric continuum, 15,
    20–29
  defined, 15, 18–19
  and marketing, 19, 21, 25–26
  in retail financial services industry,
    19–29
  successful, factors in, 26–29
  and teams, alignment into, 23–25

Customer segments:
  attitudinal, 83
  behavioral, 82–83, 227
  and channel targeting, 45–46, 48
  and CRM strategy, 63
  differentiation of, 217, 219
  dynamic, 196, 221
  and insight, 96
  and loyalty programs, 149
  in resources industry, 297–299
  in telecommunications industry, 259,
    261–262
Customer service meritocracy, 149, 152
Customer strategy, 7, 13, 17, 194, 200,
    210
  and capital, 151
  and customer segment management,
    18–29
  defined, 8, 14
  and IVoC, 102–103
Customization, 122
  collaboration with personalization, 114,
    126–134

DaimlerChrysler:
  and call centers, 284–285
  and customer knowledge, 99, 100
  and ServiceAnalyzer, 288–290
Data:
  and fragmented marketing processes,
    235
  from human-based knowledge, 96,
    99–101
  incentives to customer for providing,
    75
  and IVoC, 103–108
  perishable nature of, 209–210
  and privacy laws, 69–70, 76, 105
  and silent commerce, 69
  third-party, 69–70, 73–76
  transaction-driven, 96, 98, 99–101, 108
  transformation of, 105, 107
  warehousing of, 76–77, 103, 104, 186,
    218–219

Data (*Cont.*):
  (*See also* Customization; Personalization)
DBPR (*see* Department of Business and Professional Regulation)
Dell Computer Corp., 127, 288
Demographic overlays, 69–70, 75–76
Department of Business and Professional Regulation (Florida), 273–278
  and IVR technology, 276
Design Your Own (FranklinCovey), 45
Deutsche Telekom, 258–259
Diageo PLC, 251
Differentiation:
  of companies, 258, 296, 303
  of customer segments, 217, 219
  of products, 223
Digital asset management, and MRM, 248–250, 253–254
Direct mail, and brand loyalty, 6, 37
Disney, and brand manners, 42
Dissonance reduction, 223, 224
DLJ Direct, and m-commerce, 143
Dot-com companies:
  and customer conversation, 123
  and brand awareness, 31
Drexler, Mickey, 234
Driver's Privacy Protection Act (*see* Shelby Act)
Drugstore.com, and integrated marketing, 228–229
Duke Energy, 293
DuPont, as strong brand, 35

EAI (*see* Enterprise application interface)
E-Business Center, 271
eCards (Barnes & Noble), and m-commerce, 143
E-commerce, 137
  compared with m-commerce, 113, 135–136
  and messaging technology, 176
  and TotalFina, 294
Econometric analysis, 194, 235, 237

E-CRM, 153
  (*See also* Partner relationship management; Telecommunications industry; Web)
Efficient Consumer Response, study in grocery industry marketing, 235
E-government (*see* Government, and CRM implementation)
E-ink, and silent commerce, 86, 87
E-learning:
  and mission-critical workforce performance, 115, 151, 172
  and reducing employee training costs, 151
E-marketing, 196, 221–230
  and banner ads, 221, 222
  and coupons, 221
Embratel, 263
EMC Corporation, 291
  and customer service, 280–281
Emerson, and e-CRM, 288
Employees:
  and brand manners, 42
  of companies with strong brands, 36, 42
  and customer conversation, 124–125
  and customer knowledge, 99
  KPIs for, 239
  turnover of, and marketing effectiveness, 236, 237, 244
  (*See also* Workforce)
Enabling technology tools, and MRM, 248–249, 251
Energy providers (*see* Resources industry, and CRM)
Entergy, 299–300
Enterprise application interface software, and CCSM, 187
Enterprise resource management (*see* Marketing resource management)
Enterprise resource planning, 193, 263
  and CCSM, 187
  and PRM, 155–157, 162, 164
  and silent commerce, 87, 193

Equipment, industrial, and CCSM, 181–188
ERP (*see* Enterprise resource planning)
e-Services (*see* Centrelink)
e-Sixt, and WAP, 142
eToys, and brand awareness, 32
E*Trade:
    and incentives for providing customer data, 75
    marketing campaigns of, 219
    and m-commerce, 143

FAO Schwarz, and messaging technology, 177
FedEx:
    and customer insight, 96
    and messaging technology, 178
    as strong brand, 6, 55
Fidelity Investments:
    and customer knowledge, 99
    and m-commerce, 143
Financial Modernization Act (*see* Gramm Leach Bliley, and NPPI)
First Union, and customer data, 75–76
Florida, e-government initiatives in, 273–278
Focus groups, 236
    and buyer behavior, 227
Ford, marketing by, 233
Forman, Mark, 270
Forrester Research:
    study on channel conflict, 45
    survey of U.S. utilities using CRM, 301
France:
    resources industry in, 294–295
    telecommunications industry in, 260–262, 267
FranklinCovey, and channel targeting, 45
Frito-Lay, and customer insight, 95
Frost and Sullivan, and research on silent commerce, 88

FTD.com:
    and e-marketing, 227
    and wired Web, 143
    and wireless Web design, 139
Future maps (*see* Channel strategy)

Gap Inc., 233
    pricing strategies of, 246
Gartner:
    and CRM effectiveness surveys, 3, 55
    research on government CRM spending, 269
Gas producers (*see* Resources industry, and CRM)
Gateway, and country stores concept, 51
General Electric, and customer knowledge, 99
General Motors:
    and competition with Toyota, 35
    and customer conversation, 120
    and e-CRM, 287–288
    and marketing limitations, 233
Generation X, marketing for, 233
Generation Y, marketing for, 233
Geographic information system, 263, 266
Getpowercareers.com, and focus groups, 227
GIS (*see* Geographic information system)
Global 1000, and marketing costs, 194, 231, 242, 245
Global Positioning System:
    and silent commerce, 86, 87
    and telematics, 186
Global Village Telecom, and CRM integration, 262–267
GM (*see* General Motors)
GMBuyPower.com, and channel integration, 228
Government, and CRM implementation, 9, 269–279
    reasons for, 269–270
GPS (*see* Global Positioning System)
Gramm Leach Bliley, and NPPI, 76

GVT (*see* Global Village Telecom, and CRM integration)

Habitual buying, 223, 224
Hackett Benchmarking & Research, and study on customer contact agents, 151
Harley-Davidson, and customer insight, 97–99, 100
Harrah's Resorts, 149
  and customer insight, 95
Hewlett-Packard, and customer insight, 95, 97, 98
Home Depot:
  and brand loyalty, 232
  and cobranding, 36
  and customer conversation, 120, 227
  and e-marketing, 227
  and wireless technology, 304
Honda, marketing by, 233
Honeywell Aerospace, 282
HTML (*see* HyperText Transfer Protocol)
HugeClick, and Web design standardization, 136
HyperText Transfer Protocol, 136

IBM, as strong brand, 36
Industry segments (*see* Portfolios)
Information technology:
  as business enabler at GVT, 265–266
  and CRM, 13–14, 56, 62, 273
  and customer segment management, 19–20, 24–26
  and IVoC, 105
  (*See also* Messaging technology; Web; Wireless technology)
Ingersoll-Rand, and e-CRM, 288
Instant messaging (*see* Messaging technology; Wireless technology)
Integrated view of customer, 102–108
  and data warehousing, 104
  and privacy laws, 105
Interactive voice response technology, and DBPR, 276

Inter-Continental Hotels and Resorts, and conversational marketing, 119
Internet, broadband, 257
  (*See also* Messaging technology; Web; Wireless technology)
Inventory management, and silent commerce, 87, 88
IS 300 sports sedan (Lexus), and customer conversation, 124
IVoC (*see* Integrated view of customer)

Japan, post–World War II just-in-time manufacturing, 195
  as model for U.S. manufacturing, 212
Java:
  and cost value, 141
  and Web design standardization, 136
J.C. Penney, 233
JIT manufacturing (*see* Just-in-time manufacturing)
JIT marketing (*see* Just-in-time marketing)
Jupiter Research, and study on Web site dissatisfaction, 222
Just-in-time manufacturing:
  as model for marketing, 195, 212–215, 217–219
  and workforce behaviors, 166, 171
Just-in-time marketing, 193, 195–196, 212–220

Key performance indicators, 239
Kmart, marketing by, 233
KPIs (*see* Key performance indicators)
Kraft Food, and customer data, 74

L. L. Bean, and brand loyalty, 232
Lands' End, and channel integration, 228
Laser Jet V (Hewlett-Packard), and customer insight, 95
Laury, Oliver, 262
Levi Strauss & Company:
  marketing limitations of, 233
  and Web as channel option, 44–45

Lexus, and customer conversation, 124
Liberty Mutual Insurance, and customer conversation, 124
Life-cycle revenue, and CCSM, 116–117, 181–188
The Limited, 305
Listening Wall (Barnes & Noble), and wireless Web design, 139

Manufacturing industry:
   cells, 214–215, 217, 218
   and CRM, 280–291
   data integration in, 282–283
   JIT, 166, 171, 195, 212–215, 217–219
   product-centricity in, 280–281
   push and pull scheduling of, 195–196, 218
   and ROI, 281–282
Manufacturing resource planning, 193, 213
Manulife Financial, and self-service channels, 150–151
Marketing:
   and B2B relationships, 33
   and brand building, 16, 31, 194, 235
   and brand loyalty, 191, 194, 211, 225, 231, 232, 242
   and brand value, 34
   challenges in creating and executing, 191–193, 198–205
   channels, 153, 160, 219
   conversational, 118–125, 196, 213–215, 218
   copromotional, 218–220
   costs of, 36–37, 192–194, 231, 242, 244–246, 281
   and CRM, 7, 8–9, 54, 60, 62, 198
   and customer insight, 194, 196, 219
   and customer segment management, 19, 21, 25–26
   and customization, 122
   direct, 56, 59, 60, 62, 119, 218, 244
   and econometric analysis, 194

Marketing (*Cont.*):
   effectiveness and efficiency of, 191–199, 205–211, 231–241, 243–246
   integrated, 193, 196, 221–230, 243, 250, 285
   JIT, 193, 195–196
   length of time to complete, 191, 199, 208–210, 215–216
   management, 38–39, 42–43, 99
   mass, 218, 235, 261
   messages of, pulling and pushing, 196, 218
   "one segment, one channel" model of, 196, 221
   performance of, measuring, 191, 199, 206–208, 210, 235
   portfolios of, 193–195
   real-time, 261
   and ROI measurements, 191, 194–195, 199, 201–205, 215, 231–241
   targeted, 119, 192, 218, 219, 246
   time-series analysis for, 238
   and wireless Web, 143
   workbench concept of, 193, 194, 219–220, 247–251, 254
Marketing funnel, 38
Marketing process management (*see* Marketing resource management)
Marketing process workspace, 247–249
Marketing program execution, and CRM strategy, 59, 60
Marketing resource management, 193–195
   benefits of, 243, 245–246
   and digital asset management, 248–250, 253–254
   elements of, for effectiveness, 247–253
   technology solutions of, 244–254
Marketing Science Institute study, and brand value, 34
Marketplace noise and clutter, 199, 201–203
   and JIT marketing, 217

Marriott, and customer data, 76
Marshall School of Business, and study
    on banner ads, 222
Maytag, and direct selling, 45
McDonald's:
    cobranding with Coca-Cola, 33, 36
    and PepsiCo, 33, 36
M-commerce:
    and B2B relationships, 140–141
    and B2C relationships, 140
    and business-to-commerce relation-
        ships, 142–143
    and CCSM, 187
    compared with e-commerce, 113,
        135–136
    compared with u-commerce, 144
MEMS (see Microelectromechanical sys-
    tems, and silent commerce)
Messaging technology, 113–114, 174–180
    and airlines industry, 177, 179–180
    and e-commerce, 176
    and natural language processing, 176,
        177, 179
    and virtual agent architecture, 179
    (See also Information technology; Web;
        Wireless technology)
Microelectromechanical systems, and
    silent commerce, 87
Microsoft:
    and cobranding, 36
    and customer insight, 96
    and employee satisfaction, 36
Ministry of Labor and Social Affairs
    (Spain), and RED interchange sys-
    tem, 271–272
Ministry of Labor and Social Security
    (Spain), and social security smart
    card, 272
Mobile commerce (see m-commerce)
MobileOpinion, 142
MRM (see Marketing resource manage-
    ment)
MRP (see Manufacturing resource plan-
    ning)

MSN Messenger, 177
    and virtual agent architecture, 179
MyDell (Dell Computer Corp.), 288
    and customization, 127
My Yahoo!, and customization, 127

National Agency of Telecommunications
    (see Anatel)
National Australia Bank, 149
Natural language processing, 176, 177,
    179, 258
Net2Phone, and e-CRM, 258
Next Generation Network service, 264
NGN service (see Next Generation Net-
    work service)
Nike, 49
    and NIKE iD, 122, 288
1990s:
    business trends during, 145
    growth of CRM during, 4, 111–112,
        153
    growth of telecommunications industry
        during, 257–258
NLP (see Natural language processing)
Nokia, as strong brand, 30
Nonpublic personal information, 76
Nordic, and customer segmentation, 297
Nordstrom:
    and brand loyalty, 232
    "Personal Touch" program, 75, 99–100
NorthPoint Communications, 268
NPPI (see Nonpublic personal informa-
    tion)

Object Internet standard, 86
OEMs (see Original equipment manufac-
    turers)
Office Depot:
    and focus groups, 227
    and self-service channels, 150
Oil producers (see Resources industry,
    and CRM)
Old Navy, 246
Online marketing (see E-marketing)

Online medicine cabinet, and silent commerce, 89
Online wardrobe, and silent commerce, 89–90
OracleMobile, 143
Orbitz.com, 50
Original equipment manufacturers, 49
  and CCSM, 116–117, 181–188
  and channel maps, 47–48

Pacific Bell, and e-CRM, 258
Packaging, and silent commerce, 85, 86, 88–93
Palm devices, 136, 137
Partner relationship management, 116, 153–164
  benefits of, 160–161
  capabilities of, 162–164
  collaboration with channel partners, 158–159
  and e-CRM, 153
Pay-per-use object, and silent commerce, 90
PDAs (*see* Personal digital assistants)
PepsiCo:
  and Coca-Cola, 33–36, 49–50, 234
  and competition with Sainsbury, 33–36
  and McDonald's, 33, 36
Personal digital assistants, 228, 232
  and m-commerce, 113
  and messaging technology, 175, 176
  as part of CCSM, 181
  and silent commerce, 90
Personalization:
  of channel partners, 155
  collaboration with customization, 114, 126–134
  of customer data, 105, 107–108
  permissions-based, 133
  (*See also* Data)
Personal Touch (Nordstrom's), 75, 99–100
P&G (*see* Procter & Gamble)
Philips Electronics, 251
Pillsbury, as strong brand, 36–37

PMO concept (*see* Project management office concept)
Pocket Broker (Charles Schwab & Company), and marketing integration, 229–230
Polylogues, 124, 125
Pony Express, parallels with messaging technology, 174, 180
Portals, workspace, 172
Portfolios:
  and channel strategy, 52
  and customer-centric continuum, 22
  marketing, 193–195
Precision pricing, 310–311
Predictive maintenance program, 183, 185–186
  and telematics, 186
Pricing, and strong brands, 35
Prius (Toyota), 45–46
PRM (*see* Partner relationship management)
Procter & Gamble:
  and customer insight, 96–98
  and e-CRM, 288
  and MRM, 242, 251
  and principles of brand management, 234–235
Product-centric analysis (*see* Customer-centric continuum)
Project management office concept, 264–265

Radio frequency identification, and silent commerce, 86–91
Real-world showroom, and silent commerce, 90
Recency, frequency, and monetary value, 82
RED interchange system (*see* Remote electronic data interchange system)
Reed & Barton, and channel integration, 228
Reflect.com (Procter & Gamble), 288
Region II (Brazil), 263, 264

REI:
  and channel integration, 228
  and customer conversation, 120
Reinvention-of-the-wheel syndrome,
    192
  and MRM, 245
Remote electronic data interchange sys-
    tem, 271–272
Resources industry, and CRM, 9,
    292–302
  and customer segmentation,
    297–299
  effects from deregulation, 292–294,
    298, 301
  ROI in, 300–302
Retail industry, and CRM, 303–312
Return on investment, 213
  of e-government initiatives, 278
  of marketing campaigns, 191, 194–195,
    199, 201–205, 215, 231–241, 246,
    281–282
  in resources industry, 300–302
Revenue:
  and alignment with customer expendi-
    ture, 145–152
  and CCSM, 116–117, 181–188
  and CRM strategy, 58, 59–60, 259
  and customer profitability, 79–80, 112,
    145–152
  and customization, 114
  life-cycle, 116–117, 181–188
  from manufacturing CRM, 285, 286
  from marketing, 192, 193, 195, 246
  and mission-critical workforce, 166
  and PRM, 154
  from strong brands, 35–36
RFID (see Radio frequency identifica-
    tion, and silent commerce)
Ritz-Carlton Company, 42
Ross Controls, 282
Rubbermaid, and Web as channel option,
    45
Ryder System, and mission-critical work-
    force solution, 166, 168

Sainsbury (private label), and competition
    with Coca-Cola and PepsiCo, 50
Sales force, 13
  automation of, 4–5, 25, 60, 62, 67, 73,
    94–95, 259, 298
  and e-learning, 151
  improving effectiveness and efficiency
    of, 111–117, 250
  and PRM, 159–161
Samsung, as strong brand, 36
SBC Communications, 259, 267–268
Scotts, and e-CRM, 288
Segmentation (see Customer segments;
    Customer segment management)
ServiceAnalyzer (DaimlerChrysler),
    288–290
Severity index, of marketing campaign
    challenges, 202–205
"Sexy technology" trap, 56
Shareholder returns, and strong brands,
    34–36
Sharp Electronics Corporation, and PRM,
    156–158, 160
Shelby Act, 76
Shiozawa, Ruy, 262–266
Shipping industry, and messaging tech-
    nology, 178
Shop.org, study on online shopping, 222
Short-message service, 113
Siemens, as strong brand, 55
Silent commerce:
  and brand, 87
  costs of, 87, 88
  and customer insight, 69, 86, 88, 90
  defined, 85–86
  and ERP, 87, 193
  and inventory management, 87, 88
  perspectives of, 92–93
  profit potential of, 87–88, 92
  prototypes of, 89–91
  and supply chains, 86–88, 93
  technologies of, 86–93
  and Web, 89–91
  and wireless communication, 87, 90

SKUs (*see* Stock-keeping units)
Smart card, social security (Spain), 272
SmarterKids.com, and focus groups, 227
Smart packaging (*see* Packaging, and silent commerce)
Smart rooms, 91
Smart shelves (*see* Packaging, and silent commerce)
SMS (*see* Short-message service)
Sony, as strong brand, 35
Southern Company, and customer segmentation, 297
Southern Union Gas, 300–301
Southwestern Bell, 258
Spain, e-government initiatives in, 271–272
Speed-Trap, 224
Sprint, 267
    and CRM integration, 260
    and e-CRM, 258
Starbucks, as strong brand, 33
State Power Corporation (China), 293
Status quo maps (*see* Channel strategy)
Stock-keeping units, 308–309
SUG (*see* Southern Union Gas)
Supermarkets:
    self-service checkouts in, 304
    and Supermarket Scan, 237
Supply chains, and silent commerce, 86–88, 93
Syndication, and PRM, 159

Teams:
    CRM, 59
    customer segment management, 23–25
    at GVT, 265
    marketing, 193, 242, 244, 248–251
    PMO, 264–265
Telco (*see* Telecommunications industry)
Telebrás, 263

Telecommunications industry:
    call centers in, 258, 259, 260, 262, 264, 266
    and CRM integration, 258–268
    and customer loyalty, 258, 259
    3G mobile networks, 262
    growth of, 257–258
Telemarketing, 6
Telematics, 185–186
Third-generation mobile networks, 262
3G mobile networks (*see* Third-generation mobile networks)
TIAA-CREF, as strong brand, 33
Time-series analysis, 238
Timex, and channel targeting, 45
TotalFina, 294–295, 300
Totalgaz, 300
Toyota:
    and competition with General Motors, 35
    and new channel, 45–46
Travelocity:
    and customer insight, 95
    and m-commerce, 143

Ubiquitous supervision solution, and silent commerce, 91
U-commerce, 144
Uniform Resource Locator, 86
Unilever Philippines, and call centers, 283–284
United Kingdom:
    e-government initiatives by, 271
    marketing problems of as compared with United States, 191, 198–211
    and resources industry, 292–293, 295–297
United States, marketing problems of as compared with United Kingdom, 191, 198–211
Universal Product Code, and Object Internet Standard, 86, 93
UPC (*see* Universal Product Code, and Object Internet standard)

UPS, and messaging technology, 178
Upselling, 260
  by British Gas, 296
  and CRM, 103, 305
  and customer service meritocracy, 149
  by telecommunications companies, 268
URL (*see* Uniform Resource Locator)
U.S. Postal Service, and messaging technology, 178
Utility providers (*see* Resources industry, and CRM)

Variety seeking, as buying behavior, 223
VCRs, sales of, 232
Venture capital, and telecommunications industry, 257–258
Verizon, and CRM integration, 259
Victoria's Secret, 305
Virgin Atlantic, as strong brand, 6, 30, 36, 55
Virgin Wines, 305–306, 311
Virtual agent architecture, 179
Visa, as strong brand, 30, 40–42
VoiceNet USA, 268
Voice response units, 285
Volkswagen AG:
  marketing by, 233
  and Web as channel, 52
Volvo, 46
VRUs (*see* Voice response units)

Walgreens, 311
  BDM program of, 309–310
Wal-Mart:
  and Procter & Gamble, 96
  as strong brand, 6, 31, 36, 303
  and use of wireless technology, 55, 304
  and Whirlpool, 33

WAP (*see* Wireless Application Protocol)
Warehousing, data, 103
  and CCSM, 186
  at First Union, 76–77
  and IVoC, 104
  and marketing, 218–219
  stages of, 104
War room, 58–59
Wearable services platform, and silent commerce, 90
Web:
  and brand awareness, 30
  and brand loyalty, 6, 7
  and call centers, 103, 270, 278, 286–290
  for company differentiation, 258
  and cookies, 89, 140
  and CRM, 258–259, 268, 286–290, 293–302
  and customer segment management, 20
  and customization and personalization, collaboration of, 114, 126–134
  design, standardization of, 136–139
  and e-government initiatives, 270–278
  and marketing, 193, 196, 221–230, 238
  and silent commerce, 89–91
  wired, 136, 137
  wireless, 87, 90, 112–114, 135–144
  (*See also* Information technology; Messaging technology; Wireless technology)
Web-Based Interactive Advantage CRM (AT&T), 258
Whirlpool, and Wal-Mart, 33
WHSmith, and wireless technology, 304
Wine Wizard (Virgin Wines), 306
Wireless Application Protocol, 136, 137, 142, 143

Wireless technology:
  cost value of, 141
  and CRM, 259
  customer concerns of, 139–140
  and growth of telecommunications
    industry, 257
  and m-commerce, 113, 135–136,
    140–141, 187
  in resources industry, 300–301
  and silent commerce, 87, 90
  and telematics, 186
  and WAP, 136
  and Web, 87, 90, 112–114, 135–144,
    288
  (*See also* Information technology; Mes-
    saging technology; Web)
Workbench, marketing, 193, 194,
    219–220, 254
  components of, 247–251
Workforce:
  and cost savings, 151, 165, 169, 171,
    173

Workforce (*Cont.*):
  mission-critical, improving perform-
    ance of, 115–116, 165–173
  realignment of, 112, 115–116
  (*See also* Employees)
WorldCom, and e-CRM, 258
World Wide Web (*see* Web)

Xelector, and customer differentiation,
    217

Yahoo.com, and Web design standardiza-
    tion, 136
Yahoo! Messenger, 177
  and virtual agent architecture,
    179
Yellow Freight, and messaging
    technology, 177
Younology, and permissions-based
    personalization, 133

Zelikovsky, Alex, 288

About the Editor

John G. Freeland is the managing partner of Accenture's customer relationship management service line. In this role, he directs the worldwide growth and market leadership of Accenture's CRM business, with revenues in excess of $2.4 billion as of September 2001. He also serves on the Accenture Executive Committee, the firm's policymaking body.

Prior to assuming his current position, he held a variety of leadership positions within Accenture's financial services global market unit. Most recently, he was managing partner of financial services ventures, responsible for formulating and structuring new market-making opportunities across Accenture's insurance, banking, and health services industry groups. Before that, he led Accenture's insurance group globally from 1997 to 1999, and in North America from 1995 to 1997. He served on Accenture's Financial Services Executive Committee from 1996 to 2000 and on the Chairman's Advisory Council from 1996 to 1997.

As a respected thought leader in the area of CRM, he has lead the development of innovative CRM business strategies and new market-making opportunities across diverse industries. These have included innovative cosourcing arrangements focused on dramatically improving the quality and cost structure of customer sales and service operations for Accenture clients.

He joined Accenture in 1979 and became a partner in 1989. He is a graduate of Columbia College and holds an MBA from Columbia University's Graduate School of Business Administration. He currently resides in Warren, New Jersey, with his wife and three children.